THE BIG BOOK OF
Best-kept Secrets *of the*
WOMEN'S INSTITUTE

500 SEASONAL RECIPES

THE BIG BOOK OF
Best-kept Secrets *of the*
WOMEN'S INSTITUTE

500 SEASONAL RECIPES

The Big Book of Best-kept Secrets of the Women's Institute

First published in Great Britain by Simon & Schuster UK Ltd, 2006
A Viacom company

Simon & Schuster UK Ltd
Africa House, 64-78 Kingsway, London WC2B 6AH

1 3 5 7 9 10 8 6 4 2

Design: *Fiona Andreanelli*
Food photography: *Steve Baxter, Juliet Piddington*
Home Economist: *Joss Herd, Kim Morphew*
Stylists for food photography: *Liz Belton, Helen Trent*
Copy editor: *Judith Hann*
Proofreader: *Kim Yarwood*
Printed and bound in China

ISBN 0 7432 85778

Contents

KEY:

♥   healthy heart

v   vegetarian

★   quick recipe

▼   low calorie

Food should be a joy, a pleasure to be shared. The tasty, user-friendly recipes collected here, which have been written by women who know all about cooking for families from personal experience, are guaranteed to tempt you to sample the delights and flavours of home-made food.

Organised seasonally, the book features a wide variety of inspiring recipes that can be enjoyed whether you are a meat-eater or a vegetarian. It includes delicious soups made from the *simplest ingredients* which, with the addition of a few choice herbs and spices, can easily be made into tasty and nutritious meals, fast suppers that are ideal to enjoy during the week, simple weekend lunches for family and friends, hearty traditional fare for the cold winter months, as well as lighter dishes that take their inspiration from the Continent. All the recipes draw on the wealth of experience that is the **Women's Institute** and reflect the strengths for which the organisation is famous, not least in cake baking and the making of preserves. Many people claim not to eat puddings, yet very few when confronted with a mouth-watering dessert, can resist it! And few things conjure up the pleasures of home and hearth quite so vividly as a shelf of home-made jams.

Seasons vary and overlap throughout even a small island like ours, so you should not feel that you cannot make something in April because it doesn't appear as a 'Spring recipe'. Summer vegetables, for example, will be available in the south of England several weeks earlier than in Scotland. Indeed, although we spend a good deal of time in Britain complaining about the weather, it is our geographical situation and our variable island climate that we have to thank for the abundance and variety of produce we are able to enjoy year round. You should be wary, though of the imported fruits and vegetables on offer in the supermarkets: the air miles they travel can mean a decrease in flavour and a mark up on the price.

Each recipe here gives a freezing recommendation. It certainly saves time and effort if you make double the quantity and freeze half. You will then have a meal ready in the time it takes to defrost and reheat the dish – ideal for those days when the whole family arrive home late.

Vegetable Stock

MAKES about 1.1 litres (2 pints)
PREPARATION TIME: 15 minutes + 40 minutes cooking
FREEZING: recommended

You can use whatever vegetables you have to make stock, adding any herbs which you are fond of. Grace Mulligan particularly likes the addition of a lemon and she has been known to use some bottled lemon juice instead if she doesn't have a lemon.

1.1 litres (2 pints) cold water
1 small lemon, scrubbed and chopped roughly
1 thick stalk of celery, chopped
2 carrots, chopped
1 onion, chopped
5 ml (1 teaspoon) peppercorns
fresh herbs, e.g. parsley stalks, small bay leaf and sprig of thyme
(or ½ teaspoon dried thyme)
1 small garlic clove, sliced (optional)

1 Put everything into a large pan. Bring to the boil and then reduce the heat and leave to simmer for about 30–40 minutes. Any scum which rises should be skimmed off and discarded. A large spoon pulled at an angle across the surface will do it. Leave the lid of the pan at an angle. This prevents the stock from boiling over and also helps to reduce the volume and increase the flavour.
2 Strain the stock through a fine sieve and taste it. You may wish to reduce it further to strengthen the flavour. Simmer in an open pan until you are happy with the taste.
3 Use for soups or sauces or freeze for future use. Remember to label carefully stating type of stock and date. Season the stock when you use it.

Fish Stock

MAKES about 1.1 litres (2 pints)
PREPARATION TIME: 10 minutes + 25 minutes cooking
FREEZING: recommended

This is very quick to make and you can save white fish bones in the freezer or you can ask your fishmonger for some. It is best to order the bones in advance so that you get only white bones. Dry white wine gives the stock a lovely flavour.

900 g (2 lb) white fish bones, rinsed
2 glasses of dry white wine
1.7 litres (3 pints) water
115 g (4 oz) white closed-cup mushrooms, sliced
1 small onion, sliced
parsley stalks and tarragon leaves
5–6 peppercorns

1 Put everything into a large pan. Bring to the boil and then reduce the heat and leave to simmer gently for only 20 minutes.
2 Strain and taste. Carry on reducing the volume until you have a flavoursome liquid, if you wish.
3 Use or freeze for future use. Remember to label carefully, stating type of stock and date of making.
4 Season the stock when you use it.

Chicken Stock

MAKES about 1.1 litres (2 pints)
PREPARATION TIME: 10 minutes + 21/2 hours cooking
FREEZING: recommended

Chicken is probably the most useful of all stocks. It's a good idea to freeze chicken carcasses until you gather sufficient together to make a batch of stock. You can also include skin and jelly left behind after carving. Break the carcasses up a bit to fit into your pan.

The colour of this stock is quite light. To make a darker stock, first fry the broken carcasses in oil until they are brown. You can also sear the onion by cutting it in two and frying the cut sides until almost burnt. The resulting stock will be much darker after this treatment. The addition of a glass of dry white wine or even brandy gives another dimension to the flavour. Tarragon is one of the best herbs for adding to this stock.

2 large chicken carcasses or 3 smaller ones
1 large onion, sliced
2 celery sticks, chopped
1 large carrot, chopped
fresh herbs, e.g. parsley talks, sprig of thyme, bay leaf and
    sprig of tarragon
1 fat garlic clove, chopped (optional)
10 black peppercorns
1.1 litres (2 pints) cold water

1   Put all the ingredients in a large pan and bring to the boil; then reduce the heat and leave to simmer for about 2–21/2 hours. Whisk away any scum which rises to the surface and discard it. Refrain from boiling hard as this can make the stock cloudy.
2   Pour through a fine sieve. Taste the stock to check its strength. Reduce it in a clean pan with the lid off, if you wish.
3   Cool the stock overnight in the fridge and the following day you will be able to remove any fat from the surface. The stock is then ready to use or freeze for future use. Label carefully with type of stock and the date of making.
4   Season when about to use.

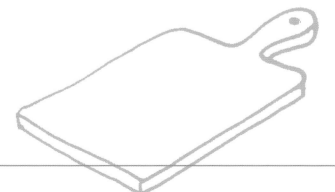

Beef Stock

MAKES about 1.1 litres (2 pints)
PREPARATION TIME: 15 minutes + 31/2 hours cooking
FREEZING: recommended

Meat stock needs to be dark in colour. It used to be made from marrow bones which can be bought raw from the butchers. If possible, have the bones cut up for you so that they would fit into the pan!

Grace Mulligun's preferred brown stock nowadays is made from the remains of the Sunday rib of beef. She collects them in the freezer and, when she has enough, roasts them again in the oven along with some vegetables. This intensifies the flavour and colour.

A fair substitute for home-made beef stock is a can of consommé, which you can dilute a bit to extend it.

1.3 kg (3 lb) beef bones from cooked joints
2 onions, topped and tailed and each cut into 4 (save the
    skin)
2–3 celery sticks, chopped
2 large carrots, chopped
10 whole black peppercorns
fresh herbs, e.g. parsley stalks, small bay leaf and sprig of
    thyme (or 2.5 ml / 1/2 teaspoon dried thyme)
1.7 litres (3 pints) cold water

1   First of all, turn the oven to its highest setting. Pack the bones into a large roasting tin. Push all the vegetables in with them and roast for about 45 minutes, by which time the bones should have darkened and the vegetables will have softened and scorched just a little.
2   Move all the contents of the tin into a big pan. Add the onion skins, peppercorns, herbs and water. Add some of the water (or a glass of red wine, if you have one, to the tin and stir vigorously to deglaze the tin and pick up all the flavour. Add the deglazed liquid to the pan.
3   Bring to the boil then reduce the heat and leave to simmer for about 21/2 hours. Remove quickly any scum which rises to the surface. Keep the lid on but at an angle.
4   Strain the liquid through a fine sieve, taste it and decide if you want to reduce the stock more.
5   Use or freeze for future use, removing any fat that rises to the surface during cooling before freezing. Label carefully with the type of stock and date of making. Season only when you are going to use it.

Basic Shortcrust Pastry

Shortcrust pastry is probably the most widely used pastry, and certainly the first to master if you are new to pastry-making. It is a soft, manageable dough, which can be filled for tarts and used also for pies. Bought shortcrust, fresh or frozen, is readily available. If substituting this for the quantities in a recipe, you will need double the quantity of bought to home made – so if a recipe uses 115 g (4 oz) plain flour you will need 225 g (8 oz) bought shortcrust.

115 g (4 oz) plain flour
25 g (1 oz) butter or block margarine
25 g (1 oz) lard or white vegetable fat
30 ml (2 tablespoons) cold water

1 Place the flour in a bowl.
2 Cut the fats into small pieces, and using just the tips of your fingers, and lifting the flour up as you work (so as to incorporate air into the pastry), rub them into the flour. The mixture should resemble fine breadcrumbs.
3 Sprinkle water over the surface and, using a round bladed knife, mix. The dough will look lumpy and should be soft but not sticky.
4 Turn out on to a lightly floured work surface and gently form into a soft, flattened ball, ready for rolling.

USING A FOOD PROCESSOR: Place all ingredients, except the water, in the bowl and pulse until the mixture resembles fine breadcrumbs. Turn the motor on again and add the water through the funnel. As soon as the dough comes together in a ball stop the machine. Turn the dough out on to a lightly floured surface and proceed from step 4.

This quantity is sufficient to line a shallow 23 cm (9-inch) or a deep 20 cm (8-inch) flan tin. Shortcrust pastry is usually cooked at Gas Mark 6/electric oven 200°C/fan oven 180°C.

Sweet Rich Shortcrust

This is my favourite pastry. It is very easy to make in a food processor, handles well and results in a lovely rich, short crumb. The following quantity is sufficient for a shallow 23 cm (9-inch) tart tin, or a deep 20 cm (8-inch) tin. Pastries flavoured with sugar are cooked at a lower temperature to prevent the sugar from burning. Bake at Gas Mark 5/electric oven 190°C/fan oven 170°C.

115 g (4 oz) plain flour
80 g (3 oz) unsalted butter
2 tablespoons icing sugar
1 egg yolk

1 Place the flour, butter and icing sugar in a processor. Turn on and blend until the mixture resembles fine breadcrumbs.
2 With the motor running add the egg yolk through the funnel, and process until the dough comes together.
3 Turn out on to a floured surface and gently bring together using your fingertips.

Pâte Sucrée

This is a traditional French, almost biscuit-like pastry – the one classically used for Continental tarts. It is rich and quite tricky to handle. This pastry is made on the worktop (marble slab if possible) and does need to be chilled for at least 1 hour before using. Nowadays I make it in a food processor, substituting 15 ml (1 tablespoon) of water for one of the egg yolks. Follow the same method as for ordinary shortcrust. This quantity is sufficient to line a shallow 23 cm (9-inch) or deep 20 cm (8 inch) flan tin, and is usually baked at Gas Mark 5/electric oven 190°C/fan oven 170°C.

115 g (4 oz) plain flour
a pinch of salt
50 g (2 oz) unsalted butter, softened
50 g (2 oz) caster sugar
2 egg yolks

1 Sift the flour and salt on to a work surface. Make a well in the centre.
2 Put butter, sugar and egg yolks into the middle of the flour.
3 Using one hand, work the butter, sugar and egg yolks together, until thoroughly mixed.
4 Then gradually incorporate the flour, bringing in a little at a time, until it is all worked in and you have

a very soft dough.

5 Wrap the pastry in clingfilm or a plastic bag and chill in the fridge for at least 1 hour.

Handling

It is important to try not to handle the pastry more than is necessary, and to treat it very gently. This is because if you overwork the dough you will be developing the gluten in it, and it is this that causes the pastry to toughen. You may notice this if the pastry springs back when you are rolling out. Use plain flour as this has a lower gluten content than strong bread flour.

ROLLING OUT: You will need to use a little flour to prevent the dough from sticking to the work surface and rolling pin, but you need to be careful not to use too much as this will change the consistency of the pastry. Therefore lightly sprinkle a little over the work surface and rolling pin, but not the pastry itself. Remembering that pastry-making requires a light touch, use gentle, even strokes, rolling in one direction only – away from your body. Avoid stretching the dough and rotate the pastry a quarter turn after each roll, to maintain an even circular shape. Stop your rolling pin at the edge of the pastry, do not roll it off the work surface; this way you will keep a uniform thickness. It helps if the pastry is at the correct temperature when rolling out: too warm and the fat becomes oily, resulting in a sticky dough; too cold and it tends to crack and be stiff to roll.

Pricking

Puncturing the base of the pastry with a fork releases any trapped air, thus preventing the pastry from rising up during cooking.

Chilling

The pastry needs to rest, in order for the gluten to 'shrink' back. This avoids the pastry collapsing down the sides of the tin during baking, leaving you with a shallow shell with spilt filling. There are two stages at which this can be done, and for rich pastries you may wish to do so at both opportunities. Firstly, after the dough has been made, it may be refrigerated for 30–60 minutes. It is important to wrap it in a plastic bag or clingfilm to prevent it drying out, otherwise it will crack when you come to roll it out. Alternatively, line your flan ring once you have made the dough, prick the base, and then refrigerate, for 30–60 minutes. The pastry will not need covering unless you plan to leave it overnight.

Baking Blind

This literally means baking the pastry shell without the filling inside. The shell can be either partially cooked, if a filling that requires baking is to be added, or completely cooked for a cold filling, such as for fruit and custard flans, or canapé savouries. By baking blind you prevent the pastry underneath from becoming soggy. To bake blind: lay a round of foil or greaseproof paper over the uncooked pastry, half fill the tin with baking beans, macaroni, dried beans or rice, to weigh it down. Bake in the centre of a preheated oven, on a metal baking tray, for 15 minutes. Remove beans and paper and bake for a further 5–15 minutes, depending on whether any further cooking is required.

Removing Scum

Some froth or scum may appear on the surface of the preserve as it cooks; this is simply the result of air bubbles forming in the preserve and the movement of ingredients. It is not harmful but doesn't look very nice in the finished preserve. The amount varies greatly; some recipes may not form any at all. Don't try to remove scum while the preserve is cooking, as this can be wasteful; wait until setting point has been reached but don't let the preserve cool. The simplest way to disperse small amounts of scum is to add a knob of butter to the finished preserve as soon as it is taken off the heat. Larger amounts can be removed by skimming the surface of the preserve with a spoon and then any traces dealt with by a knob of butter. Some recipes suggest rubbing the pan with a small knob of butter before cooking.

Sterilising Jars

This is an essential procedure as you need to eliminate all contamination, such as from the previous contents of the jar, which could cause the new batch of preserve to go off more quickly. Sterilising is especially important if you are using a jar that has contained a vinegar preserve, as you don't want the smell to linger and spoil the next batch of contents. The new preserve will look so much better in a nice clean and shiny jar. It is best to sterilise jars just before you are going to use them.

If you are re-using old jars, check for any chips or cracks and then wash the jars and remove any old labels. Thoroughly wash the jars in hot, soapy water. Just soaking in the hot water may remove labels cleanly or you may need to use something to remove any deposits of adhesive from the previous label. A very good product is called 'Sticky Stuff Remover', which has lots of other uses in addition to getting rid of the stickiness sometimes left after soaking a label off. (It's available from Lakeland, see Useful Addresses, page 80.)

Rinse the jars well in boiling water and turn upside-down to drain. Place on a cooling rack on a pad of kitchen paper and heat in the oven at 160°C/325°F/Gas Mark 3 for 10 minutes or until thoroughly dry. Leave to cool before filling.

Or place the jars in a deep pan and cover with boiling water. Bring to the boil and boil for 10 minutes. Carefully remove and allow to drain and dry as above.

It is possible to sterilise jars in the microwave; follow the manufacturer's instructions for your model. The general method is: half fill the jars with water and heat on full power until the water boils. Use oven gloves to remove the jars from the oven, swirl the water round inside them, and then throw away the water (or into your washing-up bowl) and stand them upside-down on kitchen paper to drain thoroughly before use.

Testing for a Set

There are three simple ways of testing whether a jam, jelly or marmalade has reached setting point. It is important to keep the preserve off the heat during the test or it may go beyond the point of setting. I usually use the flake and saucer tests together. The flake test is a good indicator and the saucer test will confirm.

FLAKE TEST

Dip a clean wooden spoon into the jam. Remove it and, holding it above the pan, twirl the spoon a few times to cool the jam. Let the jam fall off the spoon. If the drops run together and form flakes that 'hang' on the edge of the spoon, a setting point has been achieved.

COLD SAUCER TEST

Chill a plate in the refrigerator. Put a teaspoon of jam on to the plate and let it cool for 1 minute. Push the surface of the jam: if it wrinkles, the jam has reached setting point.

THERMOMETER TEST

Stir the jam. Dip the thermometer into hot water before dipping into the jam. If the temperature reaches 105°C/220°F, setting point should have been reached.

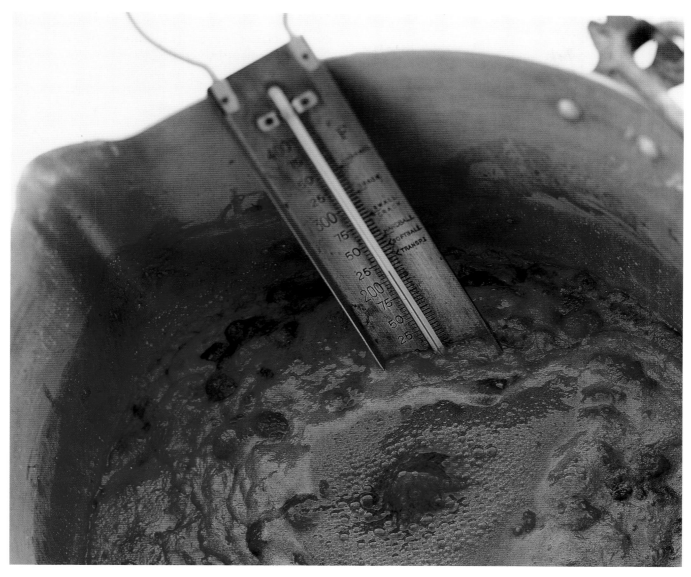

Covers

For general use, a supply of 63 mm twist tops and waxed discs and cellophane covers will be sufficient. DO NOT use both. It is a common mistake to put a waxed disc and a twist top – the waxed disc will prevent the twist top from forming a correct seal.

The cheapest way to cover jams, jellies and marmalades is to use a waxed disc and cellophane cover which is secured with a rubber band. These are available in different sizes from most supermarkets, stationers and kitchen shops, to fit 450 g (1 lb) and 900 g (2 lb) jars.

These are not suitable for chutneys and other vinegar preserves, however, as they are not vinegar-proof since they do not prevent evaporation. The twist-top type of lid is ideal instead, as it is usually lined with plastic, which prevents the vinegar from coming into contact

with the metal. They are widely available from kitchenware departments and shops. Scrupulously clean them before use: wash them in hot, soapy water and then rinse well. Then I pour boiling water over them and leave them in it for a few seconds before draining and drying thoroughly.

Applying Covers

Twist tops must be applied as soon as the preserve is ready and potted. Fill the jar to the brim. As the preserve cools it shrinks and forms a vacuum.

Waxed discs must also be applied immediately in order to melt the wax, which in turn forms a seal. Therefore it is essential that the disc fits the neck of the jar. The cellophane cover can be applied when the preserve is hot or cold and is simply a dust cover.

Guide to successful freezing

If your freezer is fitted with a fast freeze switch then better results will be obtained when placing food in the freezer, as smaller particles of ice are formed within the food and the food freezes faster in the colder temperatures. Turn the fast freeze switch on as recommended in your freezer instruction book. Always select containers suitable for the quantity of food, remember that liquids expand on freezing so allow a space above the food in a container, this will ensure that lids are not pushed off from the expanding liquids.

To avoid losing texture and flavour do not freeze any of the foods in this book for more than six weeks, it's easy to ensure this by clearly labelling everything. Pack food in suitable containers so they do not spoil on freezing. Suitable packaging materials include polythene bags which if using for soups can be placed in a rigid container so that when the contents are frozen the package can be stacked in the freezer. Foil dishes are ideal for stews, casseroles and pies; these can then be used in the oven for reheating. Foil containers are not recommended for the microwave.

Foods should be thawed slowly preferably overnight in the refrigerator and then reheated. Always ensure that the food is piping hot throughout before serving.

Freezing Desserts

I thought it might be helpful if I included some hints and tips in this introduction that are useful for many of the recipes.

Each recipe tells you if it can be frozen. As a general rule, the higher the fat content of a dessert, the more likely it will freeze well. It is best to 'open freeze' and wrap the pudding in suitable packaging when frozen. To thaw, the slower the thawing process, the better the end result. I try to take desserts out of the freezer several hours before I need them and allow them to thaw gradually in the fridge. It is better to decorate a frozen dessert when it has thawed rather than before it has been frozen.

Melting Chocolate

The most important thing to remember is that chocolate doesn't like to be overheated. Overheated chocolate won't set properly or blend well. Another rule is that chocolate should not be melted over direct heat, except when it is with other ingredients, and even then it should be placed over a very low heat.

When you are melting chocolate, you should never be in a rush. I know that this is often difficult when we all lead such busy lives. However, the best results will always be when chocolate has been allowed to melt very slowly – it will then have a glossy appearance and the flavour will be perfect.

The best way of melting chocolate is to use a double-boiler. Break the chocolate into pieces and place them in a bowl that fits tightly over a pan of hot water. The bowl should not touch the water and no steam or drops of water should come into contact with the chocolate. Once the chocolate begins to melt, stir it. Once it has nearly melted, remove it from the pan and stir gently just once or twice until it has melted completely (the bowl will retain some heat and this will help complete the melting process).

It is also possible to melt chocolate in the microwave. Place the chocolate pieces in a microwaveable bowl. The time taken to melt the chocolate will depend on the type and quality of chocolate as well as the power of your microwave. As a general guide, 115 g (4 oz) plain chocolate will take 2 minutes on full power and milk and white chocolate will take 2–3 minutes on medium power. Stir the chocolate and leave it to stand for a few minutes. If it hasn't melted completely, you will need to return it to the microwave for about 30 seconds.

Store cupboard ingredients

Stock up your cupboard, fridge and freezer with some basic foodstuffs and you will never be short of the ingredients for making a wholesome and delicious meal. Today, the home cook can draw upon a range of foods from all over the world, that have a long shelf life and are relatively inexpensive.

In the cupboard

Alongside your pepper and salt mill, it is wise to have a variety of dried herbs. Although fresh herbs are usually preferable, some, such as dried oregano, can be more flavourful. Try to have bay leaves, sage and thyme as well. Certain spices and flavourings will certainly stand you in good stead; these are saffron, cumin, coriander, cardamoms, turmeric, cinnamon, nutmeg and vanilla pods. Some good olive oil is an essential for your cupboard as well as sunflower oil. Wine or cider vinegar is invaluable for salad dressings and soy sauce will enhance any stir-fries or oriental-style dishes.

If you have cans of tuna and tomatoes, dried pulses, jars of sun-dried tomatoes, olives and capers alongside some dried pasta, rice (risotto as well as long-grain), couscous and polenta you have the makings of a delicious meal without having to step into a shop.

In the fridge

Why not have some Parmesan cheese or even some mozzarella to sit alongside the Cheddar in the fridge? Free-range eggs, some good bacon, yogurt and crème fraîche with some unsalted butter can form the makings of a delicious omelette, a Quiche Lorraine, macaroni cheese or pancakes.

After a long winter there's plenty to look forward to in spring. The **temperature is rising**, trees and hedgerows are becoming green and the early blossom appears. In April, there are Morel mushrooms – the only wild mushrooms that don't appear in autumn. April brings the first fruit of the season – outdoor rhubarb – and also the first potatoes, delicious **Jersey Royals**, the earliest of the 'earlies'. As for vegetables, there are fresh-tasting **spring greens**, rich in potassium, iron and vitamins A, C and E and available throughout April and May. Wild dandelions are a free treat – try adding the leaves to salads, French-style. Peppery rocket is in season, too.

But the greatest pleasure in May is English **asparagus**, esteemed since Roman times. With its delicate flavour and tender texture, it's arguably the finest. It has a short season – just six weeks – and doesn't keep well so must be eaten soon after picking. The first crop of tender peas and broad beans also arrive this month, as do beetroot and radishes.

In May, tasty, succulent spring lamb with its delicate flavour is starting to appear but is even better by early June. And, if you like fish, April to June is the season for wild salmon – in a different league to its farmed relative.

Spring

Salmon & Dill Soup

SERVES 4–5 ★
PREPARATION & COOKING TIME: 20 minutes
FREEZING: not recommended

This is a lovely soup for a special occasion, rich and creamy and one to impress your friends. Try to get hold of some wild salmon – spring is the time to take advantage of this delicious fish.

25 g (1 oz) butter
1 onion, chopped
50 g (2 oz) plain flour
850 ml (1½ pints) fish stock (page 8)
450 g (1 lb) fresh tomatoes, skinned and roughly chopped, or a 400 g can of tomatoes
425 g (15 oz) can of red salmon, drained, the skin and bones removed, flesh flaked
1 tablespoon chopped fresh dill
2 teaspoons lemon juice
150 ml carton of double cream
80 ml (3 fl oz) white wine
salt and freshly ground black pepper
fresh dill sprigs, to garnish

1 Melt the butter in a large saucepan, add the onion and sauté for 5 minutes, until just soft. Add the flour and cook, stirring, for a further minute.
2 Stir in the fish stock, making sure the flour is well blended. Then add the tomatoes and half the flaked salmon. Bring to the boil, cover and simmer for 10 minutes, stirring occasionally.
3 Allow to cool slightly and then purée until smooth.
4 Return the soup to the pan and add the remaining salmon, and the dill, lemon juice, cream and wine. Season to taste.
5 Reheat gently but do not allow to boil. Serve garnished with sprigs of dill.

Cullen Skink

SERVES 4
PREPARATION & COOKING TIME: 50 minutes
FREEZING: not recommended

The word 'skink' means stock or broth; Cullen is the name of a fishing village in Aberdeenshire. This is a traditional Scottish soup and is a meal in itself. The authentic recipe uses Finnan haddock (a particular type of smoked haddock) but, if you can't get this, choose a haddock that is smoked but not dyed. And remember that fish should not be cooked for too long, otherwise it becomes tough. Two pans are needed for this soup unless you cook the potatoes beforehand.

350 g (12 oz) Finnan haddock
1 onion, chopped
1 small carrot, chopped
4 whole cloves
850 ml (1½ pints) water or fish stock (page 8)
575 ml (1 pint) milk
450 g (1 lb) potatoes, chopped coarsely
25 g (1 oz) butter
salt and freshly ground black pepper
chopped fresh parsley, to garnish

1 Put the haddock, onion, carrot and cloves in a pan and pour on the water or stock. Bring gently to the boil and simmer for no more than 5 minutes.
2 Remove the fish and, when cool enough to handle, remove the skin and bones. Return the skin and bones to the pan, add the milk and continue cooking over a low heat. Flake the haddock flesh.
3 Meanwhile, cook the potatoes in boiling, salted water until tender. Drain, leaving a little water in the pan.
4 Mash the potatoes with the butter.
5 Strain the milky stock from the fish bones. Blend into the mashed potatoes until the mixture is smooth. Add the flaked haddock.
6 Reheat the soup without boiling, but be careful not to overcook it.
7 Adjust the seasoning and serve garnished with chopped parsley.

Scallop Chowder *(above)*

SERVES 4
PREPARATION & COOKING TIME: 50 minutes
FREEZING: not recommended

The name 'chowder' comes from the French chaudière, *a large cooking pan. Traditionally, chowder was made with belly pork but we have substituted bacon to reduce the cooking time. Although classed as a soup, chowder is more of a meal in itself. There are endless variations because you can use any combination of available fish and vegetables to suit your taste.*

115 g (4 oz) rindless streaky bacon, chopped
1 large onion, chopped
350 g (12 oz) potatoes, chopped
1 carrot, chopped
1 small parsnip, chopped
425 ml (¾ pint) fish stock (page 8)
8 scallops
juice of 1 lemon
25 g (1 oz) plain flour
575 ml (1 pint) milk
salt and freshly ground black pepper
1 tablespoon chopped fresh parsley, to garnish

1 Heat a large pan and fry the bacon over a low heat, without any added oil, until the fat is released.
2 Add the onion and soften until transparent.
3 Add the remaining vegetables and the stock. Bring to the boil and then reduce the heat and simmer for 15–20 minutes, or until the vegetables are cooked.
4 Meanwhile, clean the scallops by removing all the black parts. Set the corals aside. Roughly chop the white flesh and sprinkle with lemon juice.
5 Blend the flour with a little of the milk until smooth. Add the remainder of the milk and then pour the mixture into the vegetables. Stir until the soup has thickened.
6 Add the scallops and simmer for 5 minutes.
7 Add the corals and simmer for 2 minutes.
8 Adjust the seasoning and serve sprinkled with parsley.

Hot Tomato Soup

SERVES 4 ♥ V
PREPARATION & COOKING TIME: 40 minutes
FREEZING: recommended

This fresh soup is very quick to make and has a brilliant red colour – all natural! The little bit of chilli gives it a warming glow. Do take care to wash your hands thoroughly after handling chillies, though. If you wish, serve garnished with basil or chopped parsley and accompany with a cheesy bread.

1 tablespoon olive oil
1 onion, chopped
1 carrot, sliced
½ fat red chilli, de-seeded and chopped finely
400 g can of chopped tomatoes
about 575 ml (1 pint) good vegetable, ham or chicken stock (pages 8–9)
1 bay leaf
½ teaspoon brown sugar
sea salt and freshly ground black pepper

1 Heat the oil in a saucepan. Stir in the onion, carrot and chilli. Cover the pan and leave the vegetables to 'sweat', over a low heat, for 5 minutes, without browning. Shake the pan occasionally.
2 Add the tomatoes with their juice, the stock, bay leaf and sugar. Season to taste. Bring to the boil, reduce the heat, cover and simmer for 20 minutes, until the vegetables are cooked.
3 Allow the soup to cool slightly. Remove the bay leaf, pour into a blender and liquidise until smooth. Add a little more stock, if necessary, to achieve the required consistency.
4 Rinse out the pan. Return the soup to the hob and heat through gently, without boiling. Check the seasoning and serve.

Red Pepper & Goat's Cheese Soup *(above)*

SERVES 6 V
PREPARATION & COOKING TIME: 40 minutes
FREEZING: recommended after step 3

This creamy soup is a delicious blend of flavours enriched by the addition of goat's cheese. Everyone who's tried it agrees that it is moreish.

2 onions, chopped
1.7 litres (3 pints) vegetable stock (page 8)
60 ml (4 tablespoons) dry white wine
8 red peppers, chopped coarsely
1 large cooking apple, cored and chopped coarsely
1 teaspoon chopped fresh basil
salt and freshly ground black pepper
150 g (5 oz) goat's cheese, rind removed
6 fresh basil leaves, to garnish

1 In a large pan, boil the onions in a little of the stock until the stock has evaporated and the onions are beginning to caramelise.
2 Add the wine, remaining stock, peppers, apple and chopped basil. Cook over a low heat for 20 minutes.
3 Liquidise the soup. Return to the pan and reheat. Adjust the seasoning.
4 Add the cheese and whisk over a gentle heat until blended.
5 Serve each portion garnished with a basil leaf.

Italian Bean Soup

SERVES 6
PREPARATION & COOKING TIME: 1 hour
FREEZING: not recommended

There's a real flavour of the Mediterranean in this filling soup. Using canned beans makes the preparation so much speedier than with dried beans, which have to be soaked beforehand. However, do remember to rinse the canned beans thoroughly to wash off any excess saltiness from the brine. Serve this recipe as a 'main course' soup accompanied by ciabatta.

2 tablespoons olive oil
50 g (2 oz) cubetti di pancetta
1 onion, chopped
1 celery stick, trimmed and diced
1 carrot, diced
1 garlic clove, crushed
1/2 teaspoon dried sage
1 bay leaf
400 g can of chopped tomatoes
1 litre (1¾ pints) vegetable stock (page 8)
400 g can of borlotti beans, rinsed and drained
400 g can of cannellini beans, rinsed and drained
100 g (3½ oz) French beans, cut into 4 cm (1½ inch) lengths
75 g (2¾ oz) spaghetti, broken into short pieces
1 tablespoon chopped fresh flat leaf parsley
freshly ground black pepper

1 Heat the olive oil in a large saucepan. Add the pancetta and fry gently for 2–3 minutes. Stir in the onion, celery, carrot, garlic, sage and bay leaf. Cook gently for a further 4–5 minutes to soften the vegetables.
2 Stir in the chopped tomatoes and vegetable stock. Bring up to the boil then reduce the heat, cover the pan and simmer gently for 15 minutes. Add the borlotti and cannellini beans and simmer for a further 5 minutes. Remove the bay leaf.
3 Ladle half the soup into a liquidiser or food processor and blend until smooth. Return the purée to the pan with the French beans and spaghetti pieces. Cook for 7–8 minutes until the spaghetti is 'al dente' and the French beans just tender.
4 Remove from the heat and stir in the chopped parsley. Check the seasoning and add some freshly ground black pepper if required. Serve immediately in warmed bowls.

Tarragon Chicken Soup

SERVES 4–5
PREPARATION & COOKING TIME: 45 minutes
FREEZING: not recommended

25 g (1 oz) butter
1 large onion, sliced finely
2 tablespoons plain flour
850 ml (1½ pints) chicken stock (page 9)
finely grated zest and juice of 1/2 lemon
225 g (8 oz) cooked chicken, skinned and cubed
1 tablespoon chopped fresh tarragon
150 ml carton of double cream
salt and freshly ground white pepper
slices of lemon and fresh tarragon sprigs, to garnish

1 Heat the butter in a large saucepan and sauté the onion for 5 minutes, without browning, stirring occasionally.
2 Add the flour and cook for 1 minute, stirring all the time.
3 Gradually add the stock, making sure all the flour is well blended, and bring to the boil, stirring until thickened.
4 Add the lemon zest and juice, cover and simmer for 10 minutes.
5 Add the chicken and tarragon and simmer for a further 5 minutes.
6 Remove the soup from the heat and stir in the cream. Season to taste with salt and white pepper.
7 Reheat gently but do not allow to boil. Serve garnished with lemon slices and sprigs of fresh tarragon.

Creamy Spinach & Almond Soup

SERVES 4
PREPARATION & COOKING TIME: 35 minutes
FREEZING: not recommended

1 tablespoon oil
1 onion, chopped
1 potato, chopped
225 g (8 oz) frozen young leaf spinach
575 ml (1 pint) chicken stock (page 9)
a pinch of freshly grated nutmeg (optional)
salt and freshly ground black pepper
40 g (1½ oz) ground almonds
150 ml (5 fl oz) carton of single cream, to serve
1 tablespoon flaked almonds, toasted, to garnish

1 In a large saucepan, heat the oil. Add the onion and potato and sauté for 10 minutes, stirring occasionally. Do not allow to brown.
2 Add the spinach and sauté for a further 5 minutes.
3 Add the stock, nutmeg (if using) and seasoning; bring to the boil, cover and simmer for 15 minutes.
4 Liquidise half the soup until nearly smooth. Return to the pan and stir in the ground almonds and two-thirds of the cream. Reheat gently but do not allow to boil.
5 Ladle into individual bowls and serve with swirls of the remaining cream and a scattering of toasted flaked almonds.

Cream of Watercress Soup

SERVES 4
PREPARATION & COOKING TIME: 40 minutes
FREEZING: not recommended

25 g (1 oz) butter
1 onion, chopped
2 bunches of watercress, washed and chopped roughly
40 g (1½ oz) plain flour
850 ml (1½ pints) chicken stock (page 9)
150 ml carton of cream
salt and freshly ground black pepper
freshly grated nutmeg

1 In a large pan, melt the butter and soften the onion, without browning.
2 Add the watercress, reserving a few leaves to garnish. Cover with the lid and allow to sweat for 10 minutes.
3 Stir in the flour and cook for a minute; add the stock, stirring well to ensure the flour is well blended, and then bring to the boil.
4 Reduce to a simmer and cook for 5 minutes.
5 Allow the soup to cool slightly and then purée it.
6 Return the soup to a clean pan and stir in the cream. Season with salt, pepper and nutmeg to taste.
7 Reheat gently without boiling and serve garnished with the reserved watercress leaves.

Carrot & Coriander Soup

SERVES 4 ★
PREPARATION & COOKING TIME: 30 minutes
FREEZING: recommended before adding the yogurt

This soup could be cooked in the microwave.

25 g (1 oz) butter
1 onion, chopped
1 garlic clove, crushed
25 g (1 oz) plain flour
1 litre (1¼ pints) chicken stock (page 9)
450 g (1 lb) carrots, grated
2 teaspoons chopped fresh coriander
salt and freshly ground black pepper
60 ml (4 tablespoons) natural yogurt, to serve

1 Melt the butter in a pan and soften the onion and garlic.
2 Blend in the flour and then add the stock gradually, stirring all the time over a low heat.
3 Add the carrots and coriander. Bring the soup to the boil and then let it simmer for 15 minutes.
4 Remove the pan from the heat and adjust the seasoning.
5 Divide between four bowls and a swirl some yogurt into each.

Broad Bean Soup

SERVES 4 ★
PREPARATION & COOKING TIME: 30 minutes
FREEZING: recommended

Provided they're eaten young, broad beans have a delicate flavour. They freeze well and are delicious with ham or bacon, hence this soup.

25 g (1 oz) butter
1 onion, chopped
225 g (8 oz) podded and shelled fresh, or frozen, broad beans
175 g (6 oz) shelled fresh, or frozen, peas
425 ml (¾ pint) vegetable stock (page 8??)
115 g (4 oz) good-quality ham, cubed, or lean cooked bacon, chopped
425 ml (¾ pint) milk
salt and freshly ground black pepper

1 Heat the butter in a large pan and then sauté the onion until softened.
2 Add the beans and peas and the stock, with half the ham or bacon and bring to the boil. Reduce the heat and simmer for 15 minutes, or until the vegetables are tender.
3 Leave to cool slightly and then purée half the soup.
4 Return the soup to the pan, add the milk and mix well. Adjust the seasoning and reheat.
5 Serve garnished with the remaining ham or bacon.

Cheesy Cauliflower & Broccoli Soup

SERVES 4 V ★
PREPARATION & COOKING TIME: 25 minutes
FREEZING: recommended after step 5

The addition of walnuts gives this soup an interesting crunchy texture.

1 tablespoon sunflower oil
1 small onion, chopped
350 g (12 oz) cauliflower florets
350 g (12 oz) broccoli florets
1.1 litres (2 pints) vegetable stock (page 8)
25 g (1 oz) plain flour
2 tablespoons milk
25 g (1 oz) walnuts, chopped
½ teaspoon freshly grated nutmeg
200 g (7 oz) cream cheese
115 g (4 oz) mature Cheddar cheese, grated
salt and freshly ground black pepper
croûtons, to serve (see opposite)

1 Heat the oil in a large pan and soften the onion.
2 Add the cauliflower, broccoli and stock. Cook for 5–10 minutes; the cauliflower and broccoli should be tender but not soft.
3 Meanwhile, make the croûtons and keep them warm.
4 Blend together the vegetable stock, flour and milk and add to the cauliflower and broccoli mixture.
5 Add the walnuts and nutmeg.
6 Add the two cheeses and stir the soup over a gentle heat until the cheese is well blended and the soup has thickened.
7 Adjust the seasoning and serve each bowlful with a few croûtons.

sdnos

Sweet Potato & Onion Soup

SERVES 4 ♥
PREPARATION & COOKING TIME: 35 minutes
FREEZING: recommended

500 g (1 lb 2 oz) sweet potatoes, peeled and chopped roughly
1 large onion, sliced
575 ml (1 pint) good chicken (page 9) or vegetable stock (page 8)
freshly ground black pepper

1 Put the sweet potatoes in a saucepan. Add the onion but reserve a few slices.
2 Add half the stock to the vegetables. Bring to the boil, covered, and then simmer until tender.
3 In a small pan, cook the reserved onion slices in a little water.
4 Allow the soup to cool a little, then add the remaining stock. Liquidise the soup. Reheat and adjust the seasoning with pepper to taste.
5 Serve garnished with the separately cooked onion slices.

Leek & Fennel Soup

SERVES 4–5 V ★
PREPARATION & COOKING TIME: 10 minutes
  + 20 minutes cooking
FREEZING: recommended

This soup has a delicate flavour and will make a delicious starter to any meal – a great way to use the last of the winter leeks.

1 tablespoon oil
25 g (1 oz) butter
900 g (2 lb) leeks, white only, sliced
1 large fennel bulb, trimmed and sliced, leaves reserved to garnish
1 garlic clove, crushed
2 tablespoons plain flour
850 ml (1½ pints) vegetable (page 8) or chicken stock (page 9)
salt and freshly ground black pepper

1 Heat the oil and butter in a large saucepan, add the leeks, fennel and garlic and sauté for 5 minutes, stirring occasionally. Do not allow to brown.
2 Add the flour and stir well. Pour in the stock and make sure the flour is well blended. Then bring to the boil, cover and simmer for 20 minutes.
3 Leave to a cool for a short time. Purée until smooth.
4 Return to the pan and season to taste. Reheat gently.
5 Serve garnished with the chopped fennel leaves.

Curried Vegetable Soup with Coconut Milk

SERVES 6–8
PREPARATION & COOKING TIME: 1 hour
FREEZING: recommended

Do not be put off by the long list of ingredients in this soup – it is so unusual and delicious that it is worth making the effort!

50 g (2 oz) butter
seeds from 3 green cardamom pods (see Note)
1 teaspoon each ground coriander and ground cumin
a large pinch of ground turmeric
2 large carrots, chopped
2 leeks, chopped
225 g (8 oz) celeriac, chopped, or 4 thick celery sticks, chopped
3 thick stems of lemon grass, peeled and chopped
1 fat garlic clove, grated coarsely
a knob of fresh root ginger, grated
400 ml can of coconut milk
1.1 litres (2 pints) chicken stock (page 9)
salt and freshly ground black pepper

1 In a large pan, melt the butter and fry the cardamom pods, coriander, cumin and turmeric. Keep the heat low.
2 Add all the vegetables, including the lemon grass, garlic and ginger, and stir well. Put the lid on and sweat them for a few minutes, shaking often.
2 Stir in the remaining ingredients. Bring to the boil and then reduce the heat and leave to simmer until the vegetables are soft.
3 Reduce to a purée. Pour through a nylon sieve into a clean pan.
4 Reheat, adjust the seasoning to suit you and serve hot.

NOTE: To prepare the cardamom pods, roughly crush with the end of a rolling pin or with a pestle and mortar and extract the seeds.

Butternut Squash
& Apple Soup *(below)*

SERVES 4 **V**
PREPARATION & COOKING TIME: 45 minutes
FREEZING: recommended

*Butternut squash stores well and there should still be a good
supply during spring. You can also use up last autumn's apples
in this recipe.*

1 tablespoon oil
1 onion, sliced thinly
1 teaspoon curry powder
2 eating apples, peeled, cored and chopped
1 medium butternut squash, peeled, de-seeded and chopped
1 litre (1³/₄ pints) vegetable stock (page 8)
croûtons, to garnish (page 23)
salt and freshly ground black pepper

1 Heat the oil in a large pan, add the onion and cook for
4–5 minutes, until softened but not browned.
2 Stir in the curry powder and the apple and cook for 2
minutes.
3 Add the squash and stock. Bring to the boil and then
reduce the heat. Simmer for 15–20 minutes.
4 Meanwhile, make the croûtons and keep warm.
5 Remove the soup from the heat and leave to cool briefly.
Purée the soup. Adjust the seasoning and then reheat
gently. Thin the soup with a little more stock, if necessary.
Serve with crusty bread or a few croûtons sprinkled on
each bowl.

Chunky Spiced Houmous

SERVES 6 ♥ ∨ ★
PREPARATION & COOKING TIME: 25 minutes
FREEZING: not recommended

With its spices and added vegetables, this recipe gives houmous a bit more interest than the usual shop-bought variety. It is also wonderfully versatile – serve it as a starter on individual plates with a salad garnish and fingers of Melba toast (see page 28), or use it to fill warmed pitta breads along with sliced tomatoes and cucumber for a speedy snack, or it could even be part of a buffet selection with colourful crudités for dipping. It will keep happily in the fridge in a covered container for several days.

2 x 400 g cans of chick peas, rinsed and drained
4 tablespoons extra virgin olive oil
juice of 1 small lemon
1 red onion, chopped
1 garlic clove, chopped finely
1 teaspoon ground cumin
1/2 teaspoon ground coriander
1/4 teaspoon chilli powder
2 tomatoes, de-seeded and chopped finely
1 tablespoon chopped fresh coriander
salt and freshly ground black pepper

1 Put the chick peas in a food processor with 3 tablespoons of olive oil and the lemon juice. Blend to a rough purée. Transfer to a bowl.
2 Heat the remaining tablespoon of oil in a frying pan and gently cook the onion for 5–6 minutes. Add the chopped garlic and continue to cook for a further 4–5 minutes until softened. Remove from the heat and allow to cool.
3 Add the onion and garlic to the puréed chick peas together with the spices, tomatoes and chopped coriander. Carefully stir to combine all the ingredients, then season to taste with salt and black pepper. Serve as suggested above.

Pork Satay with Mango Salsa
(left)

SERVES 4
PREPARATION & COOKING TIME: 1 hour 35 minutes
FREEZING: not recommended

Pork is very tasty served this simple way, and the mango salsa really complements the dish. The recipe makes a good main course for two. It's very important for the mango to be really ripe, so it's worth buying one in advance and leaving it to ripen on a warm windowsill. The flavour is quite different once the fruit is soft and juicy. Satay sticks can be found at supermarkets in the barbecue section. If you are worried that the sticks may burn, wrap a little foil around the bare ends.

FOR THE SATAY:
2 x 175 g (6 oz) boneless pork steaks, trimmed of all fat and gristle
2 tablespoons dark soy sauce
a walnut-sized piece of fresh ginger, peeled and chopped finely
2 garlic cloves, crushed
a good squeeze of lime juice

FOR THE SALSA:
1 small very ripe mango, peeled and chopped finely
1 small fresh red chilli, de-seeded and chopped finely
1/4 red onion, chopped finely
juice of 1/2 lime
1 tablespoon fresh coriander, chopped finely
salt and freshly ground black pepper

1 Put the steaks between clingfilm and beat with a wooden rolling pin to a thickness of 5 mm (1/4 inch). Cut into bite size pieces and put into a bowl.
2 Pour over the soy sauce, ginger, garlic and lime juice. Stir to mix well, cover with clingfilm and leave to marinate for 1 hour.
3 Meanwhile, soak eight wooden satay sticks in cold water to prevent burning.
4 While the pork is marinating, prepare the salsa. Mix all the ingredients together, cover with clingfilm, and allow to stand at room temperature for at least 15 minutes.
5 Thread the pork on to the sticks, taking care not to push the pieces of meat too close together.
6 Cook under a hot grill (or on the barbecue) for 12–15 minutes, turning to brown all sides. Serve on the sticks with the salsa.

Chicken Filo Tartlets

MAKES 12
PREPARATION & COOKING TIME: 45 minutes
FREEZING: recommended

These tartlets make a delicious starter. They can also be cooked in mini muffin trays to make tasty appetisers to hand round with drinks. Don't be put off by the length of the instructions for preparing the tartlet cases; it really is quite straightforward! To prepare these in advance, you can bake the pastry cases and then cook the filling separately. Just prior to serving, fill the cases and pop them into the oven at Gas Mark 4/electric oven 180°C/fan oven 160°C for 15–20 minutes to warm through and crisp up.

FOR THE PASTRY:
2 sheets 48 cm x 26 cm (19 inches x 10½ inches) filo pastry
25 g (1 oz) butter, melted

FOR THE FILLING:
2 tablespoons olive oil
4 plum tomatoes, skinned and chopped roughly
1 garlic clove, peeled
¼ teaspoon salt
350 g (12 oz) chicken breasts, chopped small
6 sun dried tomatoes chopped finely
small amount of fresh chilli paste, to taste
150 ml (5 fl oz) double cream
freshly ground black pepper

1 Preheat the oven to Gas Mark 5/electric oven 190°C/fan oven 170°C. Lay one sheet of filo pastry on the work surface and place the other exactly on top, making sure the edges meet. Arrange the pastry so that the shortest edge is at the top.
2 Cut the pastry from top to bottom into three equal strips. Now cut the strips in half across the centre. You should have six pieces. Stack these pieces on top of each other and cut across twice to make three equal squares.
3 Take a 12-hole patty tin. You will need three squares of pastry for each hole. Take one square and brush it with melted butter and place it in the patty tin. Do the same with a second square, but lay it at an angle over the first. Repeat with a third square, so that you have a sort of star effect. Repeat with the remaining filo to make 12 tartlets
4 Bake in the centre of the oven for just 6–8 minutes, checking regularly to make sure that they end up golden, but not burnt!
5 Meanwhile, prepare the filling. Heat the oil and add the chopped tomatoes. Crush the garlic and salt together in a pestle and mortar, to a smooth purée and add it to the tomato mixture. Cook for about 5 minutes, until the tomatoes are soft.
6 Add the chopped chicken breasts, sun dried tomatoes and chilli paste. Cook for 2–3 minutes, until the chicken turns opaque.
7 Stir in the cream and cook briskly over a high heat, until the sauce has reduced and the chicken is tender. Season with black pepper.
8 Spoon the chicken mixture into the baked pastry cases and serve at once.

Tomato Tapenade Tartlets

SERVES 6
PREPARATION & COOKING TIME: 1 hour 15 minutes
FREEZING: not recommended

If you have not tried tapenade before this recipe will convert you. Its concentrated flavour means that a little goes a long way. Varieties based on red pepper and black or green olives are available in most major supermarkets. If you are not keen on feta you can use marinated artichoke hearts instead (also available in supermarkets). To make these tartlets into appetisers to hand round with drinks, cut each of them into six slices. Alternatively add some tuna chunks or Italian salami to make a more substantial lunch dish.

FOR THE PASTRY:
500 g packet puff pastry

FOR THE FILLING:
2 red peppers
2 tablespoons black olive tapenade
175 g (6 oz) feta cheese, diced
115 g (4 oz) cherry tomatoes, quartered
scant 25 g (1 oz) pine nut kernels
basil leaves
extra virgin olive oil, for brushing

1 Preheat the oven as high as it will go. Place the red peppers in a roasting dish and cook for 35–40 minutes until they are charred. Remove them from the oven immediately and place them in a polythene bag. Secure the bag and allow the peppers to cool – this helps the skins to peel off easily.
2 Reduce the oven temperature to Gas Mark 7/electric oven 220°C/fan oven 200°C.
3 On a lightly floured surface roll out the pastry and, using a plate as a guide, cut out six 13 cm (5-inch) rounds. Place the pastry on two baking sheets. Score a line on each round 1 cm (½ inch) in from the edge.
4 Spread 1 teaspoon of tapenade on top of each round and, using a palette knife, smooth it over the surface as far as the scored rim.
5 Dot feta cheese over the top of each tart and then add the tomatoes.
6 Remove the peppers from the bag, discard the skin and seeds, and slice them. Arrange the pepper slices over the tarts.
7 Sprinkle with pine nut kernels and scatter a few basil leaves over each – brush these with olive oil to prevent them from burning.
8 Bake the tartlets towards the top of the oven for 15–20 minutes, until the pastry is puffy and golden.

Roasted Peppers with Rosemary & Melba Toast
(*above*)

SERVES 4 ♥ V
PREPARATION & COOKING TIME: 1 hour
FREEZING: not recommended

Use an assortment of different coloured peppers, red, yellow, green or orange, for this recipe. Leaving the skins on adds to the texture and makes the cooking very simple. The peppers also make wonderful sandwiches, with no need for any spread on the bread. Make as much Melba toast at a time as you can manage – it is so moreish. Once cooled it can be stored in an airtight tin.

8 peppers, halved and de-seeded
4 tablespoons extra virgin olive oil
2 large sprigs of fresh rosemary, broken into 8
salt and freshly ground black pepper
8 slices of thin or medium sliced bread (white, wholemeal or granary)

1 Cut each of the pepper halves into three, and remove the white pith. Put the pieces of pepper into the bottom of the grill pan or on a shallow tray that will fit under the grill.
2 Pour over the oil and mix well so that all the peppers are coated. Tuck in the rosemary, season with salt and pepper, and put under a high grill.
3 Cook until the peppers are blackened and 'floppy', turning with tongs to cook both sides. This will take approximately 30–40 minutes. Remove the cooked peppers to a dish and leave to cool with all the cooking oils. Remove the rosemary stalks.
4 To make the Melba toast, have ready a sharp bread knife and a large chopping board. Using the grill, toast two slices of bread on both sides. Immediately cut off all the crusts, and then cut through the middle of the slices to make four slices (this is quite easy as the toast is hot). Put the four slices back under the grill, cut side up. Watch carefully – they will brown and curl up very quickly. Remove immediately and cool. Repeat with the remaining bread slices.
5 Serve the peppers either warm or cold in the cooking oil (add extra if you like), sliced into thin strips with the Melba toast. The peppers can be cooked the day before and stored in the fridge.

Warm Mushroom Salad with Lemon

SERVES 2 ♥ v ★
PREPARATION & COOKING TIME: 15 minutes
FREEZING: not recommended

Warm salads are tempting all year round. As well as being delicious served as a starter, this one complements poultry, beef and vegetarian options such as Quorn dishes.

250 g (9 oz) chestnut mushrooms, wiped
150 g (5 oz) button mushrooms, wiped
2 garlic cloves, chopped finely
grated zest of $^1/_2$ lemon
2 tablespoons lemon juice
1 tablespoon chopped fresh parsley
freshly ground black pepper

TO SERVE:
a few lettuce leaves, not bitter
2 tablespoons rocket leaves

1 Halve or quarter the chestnut mushrooms, depending on size. Leave the button mushrooms whole or halve if they are large.
2 Arrange the lettuce and rocket leaves on serving plates
3 Put the mushrooms, garlic, lemon zest and juice into a wok or large frying pan and 'stir-fry' for 3–4 minutes, until hot. Juice will start to run from the mushrooms so they will not burn. Add the parsley and stir-fry for 30 seconds. Season to taste with pepper.
4 Remove from the wok, using a slotted spoon, and spoon on to the lettuce and rocket leaves.
5 Reduce the remaining juices until there are only 1–2 teaspoons left and drizzle over the salad. Serve immediately.

Italian Style Beans on Toasted Ciabatta

SERVES 4 ♥
PREPARATION & COOKING TIME: 35 minutes
FREEZING: not recommended

A rather gourmet version of our traditional snack, beans on toast. Nonetheless, the beans provide lots of soluble fibre with its cholesterol-lowering properties. Serve with a rocket salad.

1 ciabatta loaf
2 tablespoons olive oil
130 g pack cubetti di pancetta
1 red onion, chopped finely
1 garlic clove, chopped finely
2 tablespoons tomato purée
400 g can of borlotti beans, rinsed and drained
400 g can of cannellini beans, rinsed and drained
2 large ripe tomatoes, de-seeded and chopped
2 tablespoons chopped fresh flat leaf parsley
freshly ground black pepper

1 Preheat the oven to Gas Mark 6/electric oven 200°C/fan oven 180°C.
2 Cut the ciabatta loaf in half lengthways, then cut each half into two equal pieces. Using 1 tablespoon of olive oil, brush the cut surfaces of the loaf. Place the four pieces of ciabatta on a baking sheet and bake in the oven for 5–10 minutes until lightly golden.
3 Heat the remaining tablespoon of oil in a large pan and cook the pancetta, red onion and garlic for 8–10 minutes until the onion is softened and the pancetta cooked. Stir in the tomato purée.
4 Add the beans and the chopped tomatoes. Simmer over a gentle heat for 5 minutes then stir in the chopped parsley and season well with freshly ground black pepper.
5 Arrange the slices of toasted ciabatta on warmed serving plates and spoon over the beans. Serve immediately.

Mexican Bean Salad

SERVES 4 ♥ ∨
PREPARATION & COOKING TIME: 1 hour 15 minutes
FREEZING: not recommended

This is not a palate-blowing concoction but more of a warming, satisfying one, with tangy flavours that mellow overnight once the beans have had a chance to absorb the spices in its dressing. This makes a good choice when entertaining, as it actually benefits from being prepared in advance. (Remember to wash your hands well after handling the chilli.)

Beans are an excellent source of protein and fibre, as well as being low in fat. They also depend on having some added salt to bring out their flavour.

FOR THE DRESSING:
$\frac{1}{2}$ teaspoon paprika
$\frac{1}{4}$ teaspoon ground cumin
$\frac{1}{8}$ teaspoon mild chilli powder
1 small garlic clove, peeled
juice of $\frac{1}{2}$ lime
$\frac{1}{4}$ teaspoon dried oregano
$1\frac{1}{2}$ tablespoons sunflower oil
$\frac{1}{4}$ teaspoon brown sugar
coarse sea salt

FOR THE SALAD:
420 g can of borlotti or mixed beans, rinsed and drained
$\frac{1}{2}$ orange, red or yellow pepper, de-seeded and diced
1 ripe tomato, skinned, de-seeded and chopped
$\frac{1}{2}$ bunch of spring onions, sliced
$\frac{1}{2}$ fat red chilli, de-seeded and chopped very finely (wear rubber gloves to protect your hands)
1 ripe avocado, halved, stone removed and flesh diced
1 rounded tablespoon chopped fresh coriander

1 Firstly make the dressing. Dry-fry the spices by placing the paprika, cumin and chilli powder in a small frying pan. Cook over a low heat for 1–2 minutes, just to release their flavour. Watch them like a hawk, as they tend to burn easily. (Your sense of smell will tell you when they are ready!)
2 Place the cooked spices in a small mixing bowl. Pound the garlic to a purée with a little sea salt and add, with the lime juice and oregano. Gradually whisk in the oil and sugar.
3 Combine all the salad ingredients in a serving dish, pour over the dressing and stir well to combine. Set aside for at least an hour, longer if possible, to allow the flavours to develop.

Warm Lentil Salad

SERVES 2 as a main course, 4 as a starter ♥ ∨
PREPARATION & COOKING TIME: 35 minutes
FREEZING: not recommended

Puy lentils are highly regarded and considered by some to be the best available. You will find them in the supermarket. They are a little more expensive than ordinary lentils but definitely worth paying for. This warm salad is also good when eaten cold.

125 g ($4\frac{1}{2}$ oz) Puy lentils
1 red onion, halved and sliced very thinly
1 tablespoon tarragon vinegar
juice of 1 lime
2 tablespoons olive oil
2 teaspoons ground cumin
1 garlic clove, crushed
salt
2 tablespoons chopped fresh coriander
natural yogurt, to serve

1 Put the lentils in a saucepan and cover with water. Simmer gently for about 20–25 minutes until just soft: they need to retain their shape but not be mushy.
2 Meanwhile, put the onion in a shallow bowl and pour over the vinegar. Cover with clingfilm and leave to marinate for 15 minutes.
3 Put the lime juice, olive oil, cumin, garlic and salt in a large bowl and stir to mix. When the lentils are cooked drain well, and add to the bowl while still hot.
4 Add the onions and vinegar, mix together gently and pile into a serving dish. Sprinkle over the coriander and serve warm with yogurt.

Prawn & Papaya Salad (left)

SERVES 2 ▼
PREPARATION & COOKING TIME: 50 minutes
FREEZING: not recommended

Papaya, also known as paw-paw, has a creamy but firm flesh, similar in texture to mango. However, it is much less sweet and complements the flavour of the prawns when tossed in this mildly spiced tomato dressing. The skins of the papaya can be used as shells in which to serve the salad.

150 g (5 oz) cooked king prawns
1 papaya, halved lengthways

FOR THE DRESSING:
4 tablespoons light Greek yogurt
1¹/₂ teaspoons tomato purée
1¹/₂ teaspoons lemon or lime juice
about 1 teaspoon sweet chilli sauce
freshly ground black pepper (optional)
watercress, trimmed of coarse stalks, to garnish

1 Soak the prawns in cold water for about 30 minutes to remove some of the salt. Drain and dry well.
2 Remove and discard the black papaya seeds. Remove the flesh from the skin using a melon baller or a teaspoon. If using a teaspoon cut the flesh into evenly sized pieces of about 1 cm (¹/₂ inch) square. Mix the papaya with the prawns.
3 Prepare the dressing: combine the yogurt, tomato purée, citrus juice and chilli sauce to taste. Taste and adjust the seasoning, adding pepper if required.
4 Just before serving, stir the prawns and papaya into the dressing and then spoon into the papaya shells. Use a little watercress to garnish.

VARIATION: If you prefer to serve the salad without the papaya shells, strew individual serving plates with mild-flavoured lettuce leaves, such as Little Gem, Oak Leaf and Apollo, and watercress. This could serve three, making a still lighter starter.

Low Cal Prawn Cocktail

SERVES 4 ★ ▼
PREPARATION TIME: 15 minutes
FREEZING: not recommended

Just because everyone makes jokes about prawn cocktail doesn't mean that you should not serve it. Made well, it is still a wonderful starter. The Tabasco and gin in this version really 'pep' it up. You can substitute vodka for the gin if you prefer.

3 tablespoons low calorie mayonnaise
1 tablespoon tomato purée
a few drops of Tabasco sauce
1 tablespoon gin
salt
300 g (1 oz) frozen prawns, defrosted naturally, and well drained
1 Little Gem or Cos lettuce, shredded
1 tablespoon chopped fresh parsley, to garnish
1 lemon, cut into 4 wedges, to serve

1 Mix together the mayonnaise and tomato purée with a small whisk and stir in the Tabasco, gin and salt. Taste to check the seasoning.
2 Add the prawns to the mayonnaise and mix well.
3 Divide the lettuce between four glasses or small bowls.
4 When you are ready to serve pile the prawns on to the lettuce, sprinkle over the parsley and place a lemon wedge on each bowl.

Rocket & Roasted Butternut Squash Risotto *(below)*

SERVES 4 V
PREPARATION & COOKING TIME: 50 minutes
FREEZING: not recommended

Risottos are currently enjoying a well deserved revival and can stand as a meal on their own. Some crisp pancetta, scattered on top with the butternut squash, makes a delicious addition. Alternatively, lightly cooked asparagus tips and smoked salmon strips with a squeeze of lemon juice make a lovely variation – omit the tomato purée and sherry and substitute dry white wine for 150 ml (¹/₄ pint) of the stock.

1 butternut squash, weighing about 1 kg (2¹/₄ lb), peeled,
    seeds removed and cut into bite-sized pieces
1 tablespoon olive oil
freshly ground black pepper

FOR THE RISOTTO:
50 g (2 oz) butter
1 tablespoon olive oil
350 g (12 oz) risotto rice
1 garlic clove, crushed
1 litre (1³/₄ pints) hot,
vegetable stock (page 8)
3 tablespoons sherry
1 teaspoon tomato purée
1 bay leaf
50 g (2 oz) grated Parmesan cheese
115 g (4 oz) rocket
1 tablespoon pine nut kernels, toasted

1 Preheat the oven to Gas Mark 7/electric oven 220°C/fan oven 200°C.
2 In a roasting tin, toss the squash with the olive oil and season with freshly ground black pepper. Bake for 30–35 minutes, turning the chunks of squash over halfway through.
3 Meanwhile, heat 25 g (1 oz) of the butter with the olive oil in a non-stick frying pan. Stir in the rice and garlic and cook for 2–3 minutes, until the rice is transparent.
4 Gradually add a little of the hot stock, plus the sherry, tomato purée and bay leaf. Allow the rice to absorb the liquid before pouring in some more stock, a ladleful at a time.
5 Simmer, uncovered, for 15–20 minutes, until the rice is tender and most of the stock has been used. Stir occasionally.
6 Remove the bay leaf. Stir in the remaining butter, most of the grated Parmesan and the rocket. Season.
7 Spoon the risotto on to serving plates. Scatter the roasted butternut squash on top and sprinkle with toasted pine nut kernels and the remaining Parmesan.

Oriental Braised Mushrooms

SERVES 4 ♥ v ★ ▼
PREPARATION & COOKING TIME: 30 minutes
FREEZING: not recommended

Mushrooms are a good source of protein and are extremely low in calories as long as they are not cooked in rich, creamy sauces. Oriental mushrooms, especially the shiitake, contain elements that are thought to help in lowering blood pressure and blood cholesterol levels and so are useful in maintaining a healthy cardiovascular system.

1 tablespoon vegetable oil
2 garlic cloves, chopped
125 g (4¹/₂ oz) shiitake mushrooms, thickly sliced
125 g (4¹/₂ oz) oyster mushrooms, thickly sliced
200 g (7 oz) chestnut mushrooms, quartered
1 tablespoon reduced-salt soy sauce
1 tablespoon dry sherry
3 tablespoons oyster sauce
1 teaspoon soft light brown sugar
100 ml (3¹/₂ fl oz) hot vegetable stock
1 bunch of spring onions, trimmed and chopped
200 g (7 oz) bean sprouts
300 g (1 oz) 'straight to wok' noodles

1 Heat the vegetable oil in a wok or large frying pan and stir-fry the chopped garlic for 30 seconds; do not allow it to brown. Add all the mushrooms and stir-fry for 1 minute, tossing and mixing well.
2 Add the soy sauce, sherry, oyster sauce, sugar and hot vegetable stock. Reduce the heat slightly and simmer for 4–5 minutes until the mushrooms are just tender.
3 Stir in the spring onions, bean sprouts and noodles. Continue cooking for 2 minutes to warm through the noodles thoroughly. Serve immediately in warm bowls.

Extra-Special Fried Rice

SERVES 4 ★
PREPARATION & COOKING TIME: 25 minutes
FREEZING: not recommended

This Chinese-style dish is a meal in itself, packed with meat, fish, eggs and vegetables. Here ham is used in place of pork but you could always add some pork tenderloin, cooked in the pan before adding the mushrooms and onion. Serve piled high in bowls.

2 tablespoons sunflower or vegetable oil
1 bunch of spring onions
115 g (4 oz) button mushrooms, wiped and sliced
450 g (1 lb) cooked basmati or fragrant rice, approximately 200 g
  (7 oz) uncooked weight, cooled and refrigerated
80 g (3 oz) frozen prawns, defrosted
1 small cooked chicken breast, weighing about 80 g (3 oz), cubed
80 g (3 oz) dry-cured ham, cubed
80 g (3 oz) frozen peas, cooked
175 g (6 oz) bean sprouts, rinsed and patted dry
1 tablespoon reduced-salt soy sauce
1 teaspoon sesame oil

TO GARNISH:
1 teaspoon butter or margarine
2 eggs, lightly beaten
25 g (1 oz) shelled peanuts, chopped roughly

1 Heat 1 tablespoon of oil in a non-stick wok or large frying pan. Reserve 2 spring onions, finely chop the remainder and add to the pan, with the mushrooms. Stir-fry for 2 minutes.
2 Add the remaining oil. Using a fork, break up the rice if lumpy. Add to pan with the prawns, chicken and ham. Cook gently for 5 minutes to heat through. Stir occasionally. Cover while you cook the garnish.
3 Heat half a teaspoon of the butter or margarine in an omelette pan. Pour in the eggs and cook for a couple of minutes until just set, and lightly browned underneath. Shred on a chopping board.
4 Add the remaining butter to the pan and brown the peanuts. Drain on kitchen paper.
5 Stir the peas, bean sprouts, soy sauce and sesame oil into the rice mixture and heat through.
6 Finely shred the reserved spring onions. Pile the rice mixture into individual serving bowls. Top with strips of egg and spring onion. Finish with a sprinkling of peanuts.

Mediterranean Roasted Vegetable Strudel *(below)*

SERVES 4 ♥ ∨

PREPARATION & COOKING TIME: 1 hour
FREEZING: not recommended

This strudel is bursting with Mediterranean flavours, and using filo pastry keeps the fat content low. Serve in thick slices with the season's new potatoes and a crisp green salad.

1 red pepper, de-seeded and diced
1 orange pepper, de-seeded and diced
1 aubergine, cubed
2 small red onions, quartered
2 courgettes, trimmed and thickly sliced
4 garlic cloves
3 tablespoons olive oil
1 teaspoon dried thyme
freshly ground black pepper
100 g (3¹/₂ oz) Feta cheese, cubed
1 tablespoon balsamic vinegar

FOR THE PASTRY:
5 large sheets of filo pastry
1 tablespoon olive oil

3 sprigs of fresh thyme, to garnish

1 Preheat the oven to Gas Mark 7/electric oven 220°C/fan oven 200°C.
2 Place the prepared peppers, aubergine, onions, courgettes and garlic cloves in a large roasting tin. Drizzle over the olive oil and stir well to ensure the vegetables are thoroughly coated. Sprinkle over the thyme and season with black pepper.
3 Roast in the oven for 20–25 minutes until the vegetables are tender and the edges just beginning to char. Remove from the oven and leave aside to cool for about 10 minutes. When cool, carefully stir in the Feta cheese and balsamic vinegar.
4 Reduce the oven temperature to Gas Mark 5/electric oven 190°C/fan oven 170°C. Place a sheet of non-stick baking parchment on a baking sheet measuring 33 x 23 cm (13 x 9 inches).
5 Lay one sheet of filo pastry on a clean work surface and lightly brush with a little of the olive oil. Lay the second sheet on top of the first and lightly brush with oil. Repeat the process with the remaining sheets.
6 Carefully spread the roasted vegetable mixture over the pastry, leaving a border of 2.5 cm (1 inch) around the edges. Fold over each short end and then roll up the pastry lengthways like a Swiss roll. Ensure the short ends remain tucked in. Transfer carefully to the baking sheet, making sure that the seam is underneath. Lightly brush the top surface of the pastry with any remaining oil. Using a sharp knife make light diagonal slashes across the top of the pastry.
7 Place in the oven and bake for 20–25 minutes until the pastry is crisp and golden. Remove from the oven and cut into thick slices to serve.

Leek, Chorizo & Gruyère Tart

SERVES 6
PREPARATION & COOKING TIME: 2 hours
FREEZING: recommended

Chorizo is a spicy Spanish sausage seasoned with paprika and garlic, its intense flavour gives a real kick to this tart. If you prefer a less distinctive taste, pancetta makes a good substitute – you can cook it in the same way. This tart is a good way to use the last of the winter leeks. Serve warm.

FOR THE PASTRY:
shortcrust pastry made using 115 g (4 oz) plain flour (page ??)

FOR THE FILLING:
175 g (6 oz) leeks, washed
1 teaspoon olive oil
115 g (4 oz) chorizo sausage, diced into 1 cm (¹/₂ inch) cubes
115 g (4 oz) Gruyère cheese, grated
300 ml (¹/₂ pint) milk
2 large eggs + 1 large yolk, beaten
salt and freshly ground black pepper

1 Line a shallow 23-cm (9-inch) flan ring with the shortcrust pastry and chill for 30 minutes.
2 Preheat the oven to Gas Mark 5/electric oven 190°C/fan oven 170°C. Place a baking sheet on the centre shelf.
3 Trim all but 2.5 cm (1 inch) of green from the ends of the leeks. Heat the oil in a frying pan. Fry the leeks with the chorizo for 3–4 minutes, turning, until the sausage is crisp and golden. Drain on kitchen paper.
4 On the heated baking sheet, bake the pastry case blind (see page 11) for 15 minutes. Remove the foil or paper and beans and cook for a further 5 minutes.
5 Scatter the chorizo over the pastry base. Sprinkle the cheese over the top, and arrange the leeks in a pinwheel shape, whites inwards. Whisk together the milk, eggs and seasoning. Pour this into the pastry case and bake for 30–35 minutes, until puffy and set.

Quiche Lorraine

SERVES 4
PREPARATION & COOKING TIME: 1¹/₂ hours
FREEZING: recommended

Ask anyone to name a quiche and this rich bacon and egg tart will immediately spring to mind. As with many classic recipes it is open to variations – for instance grated cheese is often included. Here a cheese pastry has been used instead of the traditional shortcrust. The cheese subtly flavours the tart and gives it a lovely golden colour. Great for spring picnics.

FOR THE CHEESE PASTRY:
115 g (4 oz) plain flour
¹/₂ teaspoon dry mustard
25 g (1 oz) butter
25 g (1 oz) lard
50 g (2 oz) Cheddar cheese, grated finely

FOR THE FILLING:
115 g (4 oz) smoked streaky bacon
2 large eggs + 1 large yolk, beaten
300 ml (¹/₂ pint) double cream
salt and freshly ground black pepper

1 For the pastry: sift together the flour and mustard. Rub in the butter and lard. Stir in the cheese, and mix to a soft, stiff dough with 2 tablespoons of cold water.
2 Roll out the dough on a lightly floured surface and use it to line a deep 20-cm (8-inch) flan tin. Prick the base with a fork and chill for 30 minutes.
3 Preheat the oven to Gas Mark 6/electric oven 200°C/fan oven 180°C. Place a baking sheet on the centre shelf.
4 On the warmed baking sheet, bake the pastry case blind (see page 11) for 15 minutes. Remove the foil or paper and baking beans, and cook for a further 5 minutes. Remove from the oven and reduce the oven temperature to Gas Mark 5/electric oven 190°C/fan oven 170°C.
5 Meanwhile make the filling. Cook the bacon in a frying-pan for 3–4 minutes until cooked, but not crisp. Using scissors, cut it into bite-sized pieces.
6 Whisk the beaten eggs and yolk with the cream, and season with salt and pepper (depending how salty the bacon is).
7 Scatter the bacon over the base of the pastry case. Return it to the oven and, with the shelf half way out of the oven, carefully pour in the cream mixture. Slowly slide the shelf back into the oven, and bake for 25–30 minutes, until the filling is just set.

Pizza Margherita *(below)*

SERVES 4 ♥ ▼
PREPARATION & COOKING TIME: 25 minutes + proving and
   resting + 25 minutes cooking
FREEZING: recommended

*Pizza Margherita is one of the original pizzas and would
usually be high in fat. This low fat version is as delicious as the
original. Add a few olives if you like, but remember, they raise
the fat content.*

FOR THE DOUGH:
175 g (6 oz) strong flour
$\frac{1}{4}$ teaspoon salt
$\frac{1}{2}$ sachet dried yeast
$\frac{1}{2}$ tablespoon olive oil
80 ml (3 fl oz) warm water

FOR THE SAUCE:
400 g can of chopped tomatoes
1 shallot or very small onion, chopped finely
1 garlic clove, crushed
1 tablespoon tomato purée
1 teaspoon dried oregano
freshly ground black pepper

FOR THE TOPPING:
1 onion, sliced into rings
125 g (4$\frac{1}{2}$ oz) light mozzarella cheese
$\frac{1}{2}$ tablespoon olive oil

1 Make the dough. Sieve the flour and salt. Stir in the yeast.
  Mix in the oil and then sufficient water to make a soft
  dough.
2 Knead the dough until it feels smooth and silky. Leave to
  prove, covered, in a warm place, for about 40 minutes, or
  until it has doubled in size.
3 Make the sauce. Drain the tomatoes well and reserve both
  the tomatoes and liquid. Cook the onion and garlic with
  the reserved tomato juice in a covered saucepan until
  softened. Add the remaining ingredients and simmer until a
  thick sauce is formed.
4 Cook the onion for the topping in sufficient water to cover
  it until it has softened. If there is still some liquid left, boil
  it hard to evaporate it. Slice the cheese about 5 mm ($\frac{1}{4}$
  inch) thick.
5 When the dough has proved, turn it on to a lightly floured
  surface. Knead for a minute and then roll into a circle
  about 23 cm (9 inches) across. Place the dough on a non-
  stick baking sheet or pizza dish and leave it to rest for 15
  minutes. Meanwhile, preheat the oven to Gas Mark 6
  electric oven 200°C/fan oven 180°C.
6 Brush the dough with the oil.
7 Spread the sauce over the oiled dough, place the onion
  rings over this and lastly add the slices of cheese.
8 Bake for 15–20 minutes, until the top is golden and the
  base cooked.

Scottish Salmon Flan

SERVES 4–6
PREPARATION & COOKING TIME: 1½ hours
FREEZING: not recommended

Although not strictly an authentic Scottish tart, this recipe does make use of two of its greatest products – smoked salmon and oatmeal. A peppery rocket salad would complement this flan's rich flavour perfectly.

FOR THE OATMEAL PASTRY:
50 g (2 oz) medium oatmeal
50 g (2 oz) plain flour
a good pinch of salt
25 g (1 oz) butter
25 g (1 oz) lard

FOR THE FILLING:
175 g (6 oz) smoked salmon pieces
2 large eggs, beaten
500 g carton of plain fromage frais
2 tablespoons snipped chives
salt and freshly ground black pepper

1 To make the pastry, mix together the oatmeal, flour and salt. Rub in the butter and lard, and then add 2 tablespoons cold water and mix to a soft dough.
2 Roll out the pastry and use it to line a 20-cm (8-inch) deep, loose-bottomed flan tin. Prick the base with a fork. Chill for at least 30 minutes.
3 Preheat the oven to Gas Mark 6/electric oven 200°C/fan oven 180°C. Place a baking sheet on the middle shelf.
4 On the warmed baking sheet, bake the pastry case blind for 15 minutes. Remove the foil or paper and beans, and return it to the oven for a further 5 minutes.
5 Scatter smoked salmon over the base of tart. Whisk together beaten eggs, fromage frais and chives. Season the mixture and pour this over the salmon. Return the flan to the oven for a further 30 minutes, until the filling is just set.

Baked Trout with Lemon & Parsley Stuffing

SERVES 4 ♥
PREPARATION & COOKING TIME: 45 minutes
FREEZING: not recommended

Trout, being an oily fish, should be one of those eaten at least once a week for its omega-3 fatty acids. This is a straight-forward but delicious way of cooking the trout. It only needs a simple accompaniment of new potatoes and perhaps some lightly steamed spring greens.

4 medium trout, cleaned
2 tablespoons olive oil, plus extra for greasing
1 tablespoon lemon juice
freshly ground black pepper

FOR THE STUFFING:
125 g (4½ oz) fresh white breadcrumbs
2 tablespoons chopped fresh parsley
2 garlic cloves, chopped finely
grated zest of 1 lemon, plus 1 tablespoon juice
4 tablespoons olive oil

1 Preheat the oven to Gas Mark 5/electric oven 190°C/fan oven 170°C.
2 Lightly grease a roasting tin large enough to hold the four trout.
3 To prepare the stuffing, place the breadcrumbs, parsley, garlic and grated lemon zest in a bowl. Stir in the olive oil and 1 tablespoon of lemon juice. Season with black pepper and mix well to combine the ingredients.
4 Divide the stuffing evenly between the cavities of the four trout. Place the trout side by side in the roasting tin.
5 In a small bowl, whisk together 2 tablespoons of olive oil and a further tablespoon of lemon juice. Season lightly with black pepper and drizzle the dressing over the trout.
6 Bake in the oven for 20–25 minutes or until the fish is cooked. Serve immediately, spooning any pan juices over the trout.

Fish Pie *(right)*

SERVES 4 ♥
PREPARATION & COOKING TIME: 1 hour 15 minutes
FREEZING: not recommended

Cod or haddock both work well with this recipe. Including some cooked spinach in the base could make a dinner party variation of this pie. Use a mixture of white wine and stock instead of milk for the sauce and slices of cooked potato for the topping. Serve traditionally, with peas.

FOR THE POTATO TOPPING:
675 g (1½ lb) potatoes, peeled and quartered
3 tablespoons semi-skimmed milk
25 g (1 oz) butter or margarine
sea salt and freshly ground black pepper

FOR THE PARSLEY SAUCE:
40 g (1½ oz) butter or margarine
40 g (1½ oz) plain flour
425 ml (¾ pint) semi-skimmed milk, warmed
a squeeze of lemon juice
1 tablespoon chopped fresh parsley
freshly ground black pepper

FOR THE FILLING:
450 g (1 lb) white fish fillets, skinned and cut into 2.5 cm (1-inch) cubes
115 g (4 oz) cooked prawns
2 hard-boiled eggs, quartered

1 Preheat the oven to Gas Mark 6/electric oven 200°C/fan oven 180°C. Place a baking sheet on a high shelf. Butter a 2-litre (3¼-pint) shallow ovenproof dish.
2 Place the potatoes in a large pan with cold water, bring to the boil, cover, and simmer for about 15–20 minutes, or until cooked.
3 Meanwhile, make the parsley sauce. Melt the butter, stir in the flour and cook for 1 minute. Gradually blend in the milk, bring to the boil and simmer for a couple of minutes. Stir in the lemon juice and chopped parsley and season to taste with freshly ground black pepper.
4 Arrange the white fish cubes, in a single layer, over the base of the prepared dish. Scatter on the prawns and place the hard-boiled eggs on top. Pour over the parsley sauce, covering the fish completely.
5 Drain the potatoes and return to the heat to dry off any excess moisture. Mash the potatoes until lump free. Beat in the milk and butter and season to taste. Spoon equally over the fish and sauce. Smooth the top and then fork through a pattern. Bake for 45 minutes, until the fish is cooked and the potato golden.

Poached White Fish with Green Salsa

SERVES 4 ♥ ★ ▼
PREPARATION & COOKING TIME: 25 minutes
FREEZING: not recommended

This is a very simple and delicious recipe which could be used for any white fish. The green chilli adds only a little heat, but you can use half a chilli or leave it out completely if preferred. Serve the fish with new potatoes and spring greens.

FOR THE FISH:
4 x 175 g (6 oz) portions of white fish (turbot, brill, halibut, skate wing), skinned
1/2 small onion, sliced
2 tablespoons white wine vinegar
salt and freshly ground black pepper

FOR THE SALSA:
3 tablespoons olive oil
grated zest and juice of 1 lime
1 fresh green chilli, de-seeded and finely chopped
2 tablespoons chopped fresh coriander

1 Put the fish into a shallow pan, just cover with water and add the onion, vinegar, salt and pepper. Bring to the boil and simmer for 3 minutes.
2 Turn off the heat, and leave to stand for 10 minutes. Remove the fish with a fish slice and drain on kitchen paper. Put on a plate and keep warm.
3 For the salsa, heat the oil gently in a small saucepan. Add the lime zest and juice, the chilli and coriander. Allow to bubble up, then pour over the fish.
4 Serve immediately.

Monkfish Kebabs with Couscous

SERVES 4 ♥ ▼
PREPARATION & COOKING TIME: 2 hours marinating
  + 45 minutes
FREEZING: not recommended

The firmness of monkfish flesh makes it ideal for kebabs. They can, of course, be barbecued instead of grilled if there are some fine spring days. Choose herbs which complement each other as well as the fish. A side salad makes a good accompaniment.

3 tablespoons reduced-salt soy sauce
3 tablespoons lemon juice
2 garlic cloves, crushed
225 g (8 oz) couscous
300 ml (1/2 pint) boiling vegetable stock (page 8)
2 tablespoons mixed chopped fresh herbs, e.g. thyme, lemon balm, chives, parsley and/or oregano
freshly ground black pepper

FOR THE KEBABS:
400 g (14 oz) monkfish, cut into 4-cm (1 1/2-inch) pieces
2 courgettes, cut into 1-cm (1/2-inch) pieces
4 shallots, halved
4 cherry tomatoes

1 Mix together the soy sauce, lemon juice and garlic. Season with pepper.
2 Place the fish pieces in a shallow dish and pour the marinade over them. Cover and leave for 2 hours in a refrigerator.
3 Thread the monkfish and vegetables on to skewers, alternating the ingredients.
4 Place the kebabs on a baking sheet and grill them under a medium heat for 15 minutes, or until they are cooked.
5 Spoon the couscous into a basin and pour the boiling stock over. Cover and leave to stand for 5 minutes. Stir in the herbs and season with pepper.
6 Fork the couscous to make it fluffy, spoon it on to serving plates and place the kebabs on top.

Baked Cod In A Herb & Lemon Crust

SERVES 4 ♥ ★ ▼
PREPARATION & COOKING TIME: 25 minutes
FREEZING: not recommended

A crisp coating adds texture and flavour to cod. Wholemeal breadcrumbs give a better flavour but white can be used. Use whichever herbs you have available: a mix of two or three is best. If you have to use dried herbs, reduce the quantity to 3 teaspoons. Serve with steamed new potatoes and broad beans.

4 x 125 g (4½ oz) pieces of thick cod fillet
50 g (2 oz) fresh wholemeal breadcrumbs
3 tablespoons chopped fresh herbs, e.g. parsley,
   thyme or lemon balm
1 small garlic clove, chopped finely
grated zest of 1 lemon
1 teaspoon lemon juice
1 tablespoon olive oil
freshly ground black pepper

1 Preheat the oven to Gas Mark 6/electric oven 200°C/fan oven 180°C.
2 Remove any bones from the cod and place the pieces on a baking sheet lined with non-stick baking paper. Season with black pepper.
3 Put the breadcrumbs, chopped herbs, garlic and lemon zest into a basin and mix well. Stir in the lemon juice and oil. Season with pepper.
4 Carefully spoon the breadcrumb mixture on top of the cod fillets, pressing it down well so that it stays in place.
5 Bake for about 12 minutes, until the top is golden and the fish cooked. Serve immediately.

Prawns with Tomato & Caraway

SERVES 4 ♥ ▼
PREPARATION & COOKING TIME: 45 minutes
FREEZING: not recommended

This may seem to be a very unusual combination of flavours, but it really works and tastes wonderful. Serve with a green salad and some crusty bread to mop up the juices.

2 tablespoons olive oil
2 garlic cloves, sliced finely
1 teaspoon caraway seeds
1 or 2 dried red chillies, crumbled
1 green pepper, de-seeded and chopped finely
400 g can of chopped tomatoes
salt and freshly ground black pepper
a pinch of sugar
350 g (12 oz) prawns, defrosted naturally (if frozen) and well
   drained
1 tablespoon chopped fresh coriander

1 Heat the oil in a medium saucepan and fry the sliced garlic until just golden. Add the caraway seeds, chillies and green pepper, and stir well.
2 Add the tomatoes, salt and pepper and sugar. Simmer for 20 minutes until the pepper is soft and the sauce thickened.
3 Add the prawns and reheat for 3 minutes. Serve immediately, sprinkled with chopped coriander.

Gingered Orange Chicken (left)

SERVES 4
PREPARATION & COOKING TIME: 1 hour
FREEZING: recommended

Papaya, orange, ginger and caramelised onions make a wonderful combination of ingredients for stuffing chicken breasts. The breasts are wrapped in bacon and foil to seal in all the delicious flavours during cooking. Serve with wild and long grain rice and tender peas or broad beans.

1 onion, diced finely
2 tablespoons sunflower oil
1 teaspoon brown sugar
5-cm (2-inch) piece of fresh root ginger, peeled and diced finely
100 g (3¹/₂ oz) dried papaya, chopped
1 orange
150 ml (¹/₄ pint) white wine
4 boneless, skinless chicken breasts
12 rashers smoked streaky bacon
salt and freshly ground black pepper

1 Place the onion and oil in a medium saucepan and cook over a gentle heat for 10 minutes, until the onion is soft. Sprinkle in the sugar, increase the heat to high and cook for 2–3 minutes until caramelised.
2 Add the ginger and papaya to the onions. Grate the zest from the orange and add to the pan. Peel the orange, chop up the flesh and add to the pan with the white wine and heat the mixture until boiling. Add seasoning.
3 Place 2 tablespoons of mixture into the pocket in each chicken breast. Reserve the remaining mixture.
4 Wrap three rashers of bacon tightly around each chicken breast to enclose the filling and wrap each breast securely in foil.
5 Place in a baking dish and cook at Gas Mark 5/electric oven 190°C/fan oven 170°C for 30–40 minutes or until the chicken is cooked through completely.
6 Purée the remaining onion and orange mixture and heat through and serve with the chicken.

Grilled Chicken Thighs with Lemon, Mustard & Thyme

SERVES 4 ▼
PREPARATION & COOKING TIME: 2 hours marinating
  + 30 minutes
FREEZING: not recommended

Served with a green salad, this makes a great supper or lunch. The chicken is also good served cold. The pieces of lemon can be eaten as well, the juices will 'leak' into the potatoes – it's delicious.

8 chicken thighs, all skin and fat removed
2 tablespoons olive oil
1 tablespoon Dijon mustard
1 lemon, cut into 4
a large sprig of thyme, broken into 4
2 garlic cloves, crushed
salt and freshly ground black pepper
700 g (1 lb 9 oz) new potatoes, unpeeled

1 Put the chicken and all the other ingredients except the potatoes, into a large bowl. Mix well so that all the chicken thighs are coated. Cover and leave to marinate in the fridge for at least 2 hours or overnight.
2 Preheat the grill and the oven to Gas Mark 6/electric oven 200°C/fan oven 180°C.
3 Put the chicken and all the marinade ingredients into a shallow dish or tray. Grill for 10 minutes on each side until golden and crispy.
4 Put into the oven for 20 minutes to finish cooking all the way through. Meanwhile, cook the potatoes in boiling water, drain well and crush lightly.
5 Put the potatoes on a serving dish, pile the chicken and the marinade on top and serve.

Thai Chicken Curry

SERVES 4 ★ ▼
PREPARATION & COOKING TIME: 25 minutes
FREEZING: not recommended

This is a wonderfully fragrant dish. The ingredients used are available from large supermarkets. If you can, use galangal in place of ginger, and kaffir lime leaves rather than lime zest, for a truly authentic curry. A reduced-fat coconut milk is now available (containing 45 per cent less fat), and reduced-salt soy sauce makes for a far healthier dish than any ready-made Thai chicken curry. Just be sure to prepare everything in advance, before you commence cooking. Serve the curry in bowls, on a bed of steamed jasmine rice.

1 lemon grass stalk
450 g (1 lb) skinless, boneless chicken breasts
1 tablespoon sunflower or vegetable oil
1 red chilli, de-seeded and chopped finely
1 teaspoon grated fresh ginger or galangal paste
1 garlic clove, crushed
225 g (8 oz) chestnut, oyster or shiitake mushrooms, (stalks removed), wiped and halved
1 bunch of spring onions, sliced thinly, 1 reserved for garnish
300 ml (½ pint) reduced-fat coconut milk
150 ml (¼ pint) chicken stock
zest of ½ lime, pared in thick strips, white pith removed, or 2 kaffir lime leaves
1 rounded tablespoon chopped fresh coriander
1 tablespoon reduced-salt soy sauce

1 Remove any tough outer leaves from the lemon grass. Cut the stalk into three and bruise the pieces. Cut the chicken breasts into bite-sized pieces, about eight each.
2 Heat the oil in a wok. Add the lemon grass, chicken, chilli, ginger or galangal and garlic. Stir-fry for 2 minutes, to seal the meat.
3 Stir in the mushrooms and cook for a further minute.
4 Add the spring onions, coconut milk, stock, lime zest or lime leaves, coriander and soy sauce to the wok. Bring to the boil, reduce the heat and simmer gently for 8 minutes or until the chicken pieces are cooked.
5 Remove the lemon grass and the lime zest or leaves. Shred the remaining spring onion and scatter it over to garnish.

Pork Spare Ribs with Barbecue Sauce & Couscous

SERVES 4
PREPARATION & COOKING TIME: 2 hours
FREEZING: recommended

Spare ribs make a great supper dish. You need to use your fingers to eat them, so make sure you have lots of paper napkins. Do try the couscous. It makes a change from rice, and is much easier and quicker to prepare. It's really important to use a fork to 'fluff up' the couscous before serving. It can be reheated the next day in the microwave.

16 pork spare ribs
1 tablespoon sunflower oil
1 onion, chopped finely
1 red pepper, de-seeded and chopped finely
2 garlic cloves, crushed
5 cm (2 inches) fresh ginger, peeled and chopped finely
2 tablespoons tomato purée
1 tablespoon clear honey
1 tablespoon cider vinegar
a good shake of Tabasco sauce
1 wine glass white wine
salt and freshly ground black pepper

FOR THE COUSCOUS:
175 g (6 oz) couscous
350 ml (12 fl oz) boiling water
25 g (1 oz) low fat spread
1 teaspoon ground cumin
pinch of chilli powder

1 Preheat the oven to Gas Mark 6/electric oven 200°C/fan oven 180°C.
2 Put the ribs into a large saucepan, completely cover with water and simmer for 20 minutes. Pour into a colander and leave to drain.
3 Meanwhile, heat the oil and gently fry the onion. Add the pepper and garlic and continue to cook for 2 minutes.
4 Add all the other ingredients and bring to the boil, stirring well. Taste to check the seasoning. It should be sweet, sour and spicy – adjust as necessary.
5 Put the ribs into a shallow roasting tin and pour over the sauce. Cook in the oven for 1¼ hours until tender, browned and crunchy looking.
6 Once the ribs are ready, put the couscous in a large bowl (it will increase in bulk) and pour over the boiling water. Stir well, cover with clingfilm and leave to stand for 3 minutes.
7 Pierce the clingfilm and put into the microwave on High for 2 minutes. Remove the clingfilm, and with a fork 'fluff up' the grains. Stir in the spread, cumin and chilli powder. Pile into a warm dish to serve.

Madeira Pork

SERVES 4
PREPARATION & COOKING TIME: 45 minutes
FREEZING: recommended

A creamy sauce flavoured with Madeira and mushrooms – a simple but delicious dish. Ruby port can be used in place of the Madeira if you prefer. Serve with buttered noodles and steamed spring greens.

2–3 tablespoons sunflower oil
1 onion, chopped
1 large yellow pepper, de-seeded and diced
675 g (1½ lb) pork fillet, trimmed and cut into 1-cm (½-inch) slices
1 tablespoon paprika
1 tablespoon plain flour
300 ml (½ pint) stock
150 ml (¼ pint) Madeira
175 g (6 oz) button mushrooms
1 tablespoon tomato purée
salt and freshly ground black pepper
150 ml (¼ pint) single cream

1 Heat the oil in a large frying-pan. Add the onion and pepper to the pan and cook for 3–4 minutes.
2 Add the pork slices to the pan and brown on all sides. Stir in the paprika and flour and cook for 1 minute.
3 Blend in the stock and Madeira, bring to the boil, and reduce the heat to simmer, stir in the mushrooms, tomato purée and seasoning.
4 Cover the pan and simmer gently for 20 minutes or until the pork is tender and cooked through.
5 Stir in the cream, heat gently and serve straight away.

Lamb Noisettes with Apricots & Tomatoes

SERVES 4
PREPARATION TIME: 15 minutes + 1 hour to marinate
COOKING TIME: 30–40 minutes
FREEZING: recommended

Spring is, of course, the best time for lamb and these boned lamb chops topped with apricots and baked in the oven in a tangy sauce are delicious. Serve with new season broad beans and boiled brown rice to soak up all the delicious sauce.

4 lamb loin chops
4 ready-to-eat apricots

FOR THE MARINADE:
2 tablespoons soft dark brown sugar
6 tablespoons tomato ketchup
2 tablespoons soy sauce
2 tablespoons sweet sherry
1 teaspoon ground ginger
2 tomatoes, halved

1 Trim any excess fat off the lamb chops. With a sharp knife remove the T-bone from each chop.
2 Place an apricot in the centre of each chop, curl the meat around and secure in place with wooden cocktail sticks.
3 In a small jug mix together the marinade ingredients.
4 Place the chops in a shallow ovenproof dish and pour over the marinade. Cover and leave for an hour to marinate.
5 Uncover and bake at Gas Mark 6/electric oven 200°C/fan oven 180°C for 20–30 minutes.
6 Add the tomatoes to the dish and cook for a further 10 minutes.

Lamb & Apple Burgers *(above)*

MAKES 6–8
PREPARATION & COOKING TIME: 25 minutes
FREEZING: recommended

Lamb and apple plus classic Middle Eastern flavours of chilli and cumin combine to make these really special burgers. In the summer, cook them on the barbecue and serve in buns with salad leaves and tomato slices to garnish. Or grill them and serve with potato wedges and a spicy tomato relish.

450 g (1 lb) lean lamb mince
1 small onion, grated
1 small eating apple, grated
1 teaspoon ground cumin
1 chilli, de-seeded and chopped finely
1 egg, beaten
50 g (2 oz) fresh wholemeal breadcrumbs
1 tablespoon sunflower oil
salt and freshly ground black pepper

1 Place the lamb in a mixing bowl and add the onion, apple, cumin, chilli, egg, breadcrumbs and seasoning. Mix thoroughly.
2 Shape the mixture into 6–8 even-sized burgers.
3 Brush both sides of the burgers with the oil and cook on a preheated grill or barbecue for 5–7 minutes, on each side, until cooked right through.

45

Stir-fry Lamb Fillet on a Bed of Aubergine

SERVES 3 ★ ▼
PREPARATION & COOKING TIME: 30 minutes
FREEZING: not recommended

Cooked quickly, the lamb retains its full sweet flavour. The aubergine slices can be grilled if you prefer a firmer texture; place on a grill pan lined with foil, cut side up, and spray with oil. Place under the grill and cook for 3–5 minutes, until golden. Serve with a green salad and crusty bread.

1 aubergine, cut into 5-mm ($^1/_4$-inch) slices
lemon juice
200 g lean lamb fillet, sliced into thin strips about 9 cm (3$^1/_2$ inches) long, excess fat removed
8 spring onions, cut into 5-mm ($^1/_4$-inch) pieces
2–3 garlic cloves, chopped finely
16 cherry tomatoes, halved
2 tablespoons chopped fresh herbs, e.g. rosemary, thyme and/or parsley
freshly ground black pepper

1 Brush the aubergine slices with lemon juice to prevent discoloration. Prepare a steamer for the aubergine slices. Bring the water to the boil.
2 Meanwhile, spoon 2 tablespoons of water into the base of a wok or large frying pan. Bring to the boil and add the lamb, spring onions and garlic. 'Stir-fry' for 2 minutes.
3 When the steamer is ready, place the aubergine slices in it and cook until tender, about 3 minutes.
4 Add the tomatoes and herbs to the lamb and 'stir-fry' for 1–2 minutes or until the lamb is cooked and the vegetables hot. Season with pepper to taste.
5 Arrange the aubergine slices on individual serving plates and spoon the stir-fry on top. Serve immediately.

Peppered Steak Tortilla with Charred Vegetables *(right)*

SERVES 4 ★
PREPARATION & COOKING TIME: 30 minutes
FREEZING: not recommended

FOR THE STEAK:
2 teaspoons whole black peppercorns
350 g (12 oz) rump or sirloin steak, trimmed of any excess fat
1 garlic clove, crushed
1$^1/_2$ tablespoons olive oil

FOR THE VEGETABLES:
1 red pepper, de-seeded and sliced into 1-cm ($^1/_2$-inch) wide strips
1 orange pepper, de-seeded and sliced into 1-cm ($^1/_2$-inch) wide strips
1 red onion, sliced into thin wedges
1 tablespoon olive oil

FOR THE DRESSING:
200 ml tub of half-fat crème fraîche
2 teaspoons finely chopped fresh chives

TO SERVE:
$^1/_2$ cos or romaine lettuce, shredded finely
4 wheat flour tortillas, 25 cm (10 inches) in diameter

1 Coarsely grind the peppercorns in a pestle and mortar. Press firmly into both sides of the steak.
2 Mix together the garlic and oil. Turn the steak in the mixture until thoroughly coated. Set to one side.
3 Combine the peppers and onion in a bowl. Drizzle with the oil and toss well.
4 Heat a griddle pan over a medium/high heat. Add the steak and cook for 2–3 minutes on each side. Remove from the pan and leave to stand while you prepare the rest of the ingredients. (This gives the juices a chance to be reabsorbed into the meat.)
5 Add the vegetables to the pan and cook for 5 minutes, until they have softened and are charred. Turn frequently.
6 Mix together the crème fraîche and chives.
7 Warm the tortillas as directed on the packet. Scatter the lettuce over the surfaces of each.
8 Thinly slice the steak and divide it between the tortillas. Distribute the vegetables and spoon the crème fraîche and chive sauce over each. Fold the bottom quarter of tortilla up, then each side in to enclose the filling. Serve at once.

Pink Rhubarb Fool

SERVES 4 ♥ ▼
PREPARATION & COOKING TIME: 50 minutes
FREEZING: not recommended

Forced or Champagne rhubarb, the beautiful pink spears that are in the shops in early spring, is best for this recipe. You can use other types of rhubarb available throughout the year. Just add a little more honey, and you might need to remove the tough outer skin as well. Serve with Oat & Cinnamon Biscuits.

450 g (1 lb) forced rhubarb, leaves removed and stalks trimmed
1 tablespoon clear honey
juice of 1 orange
250 g tub of virtually fat free Quark

1 Preheat the oven to Gas Mark 5/electric oven 190°C/fan oven 170°C.
2 Chop the rhubarb into chunks and put in an ovenproof dish with the honey and orange juice.
3 Cook in the oven for 15–20 minutes until the rhubarb is soft. It will make its own juice. Leave to cool.
4 Put the cooled rhubarb and all the juices in a food processor. Add the Quark and pulse gently to mix. Pile into a serving dish and serve with oat & cinnamon biscuits.

Oat & Cinnamon Biscuits

MAKES 12
PREPARATION & COOKING TIME: 30 minutes
FREEZING: not recommended

50 g (1¼ oz) self raising flour
50 g (1¼ oz) ground rice
50 g (1¼ oz) porridge oats
25 g (1 oz) soft brown sugar
1 teaspoon ground cinnamon
grated zest of 1 orange
65 g (2¼ oz) low fat spread, plus extra for greasing

1 Preheat the oven to Gas Mark 6/electric oven 200°C/fan oven 180°C.
2 Mix all the dry ingredients and orange rind together in a large bowl.
3 Melt the low fat spread, cool, then pour on to the flour mixture. With a wooden spoon bring together to form a ball.
4 Divide the dough into 12, and roll into small balls. Put on a greased baking sheet and press down on each one with the back of a fork.
5 Cook in the oven for 12–15 minutes until golden. Cool on a wire rack. The biscuits can be stored 3–4 days in an airtight tin.

Rhubarb Streusel Tart (right)

SERVES 6–8
PREPARATION & COOKING TIME: 30 minutes + 30 minutes chilling + 25 minutes cooking
FREEZING: recommended

This crisp tart, topped with tender pieces of rhubarb and a crunchy almond streusel, served with real vanilla ice cream or thick cream, is an absolute winner.

FOR THE PASTRY:
115 g (4 oz) butter, diced
225 g (8 oz) plain flour
80 g (3 oz) icing sugar
a pinch of salt
1 large egg
a few drops of vanilla extract

FOR THE FILLING:
675 g (1½ lb) tender rhubarb, trimmed and cut into 2.5-cm (1-inch) pieces
25 g (1 oz) stem ginger in syrup, diced (optional)
50 g (2 oz) soft brown sugar

FOR THE STREUSEL:
50 g (2 oz) butter, diced
50 g (2 oz) ground almonds
3 tablespoons wholemeal flour
50 g (2 oz) demerara sugar

1 First, make the pastry by rubbing the butter into the flour, icing sugar and salt until the mixture resembles breadcrumbs. Make a well in the middle and add the egg and vanilla extract. Gradually work the mixture in from the edges and mix to a smooth dough. Wrap in clingfilm and rest in the fridge for 30 minutes.
2 Preheat the oven to Gas Mark 5/electric oven 190°C/fan oven 170°C.
3 Roll out the pastry to fit a greased 25-cm (10-inch), loose-bottomed flan tin and prick the base with a fork. Scatter the rhubarb pieces over the pastry, followed by the ginger and sugar.
4 To make the streusel topping, simply rub the butter into the ground almonds, wholemeal flour and sugar and sprinkle this over the rhubarb.
5 Bake in the oven for about 25 minutes, until both the pastry and streusel are crisp and golden brown.

Rhubarb & White Chocolate Flan

SERVES 8
PREPARATION & COOKING TIME: 25 minutes + 30 minutes
   chilling + 40 minutes cooking
FREEZING: not recommended

This is a complete pudding in itself, without the need for any accompaniments! A thick covering of white chocolate shavings gives a feathery effect to the dessert. You will need to assemble this flan just a couple of hours before serving, as the rhubarb does tend to make the pastry shell go soggy.

FOR THE RHUBARB FILLING:
450 g (1 lb) trimmed rhubarb, cut into 2.5-cm (1-inch) batons
50 g (2 oz) golden caster sugar

FOR THE PASTRY:
sweet rich shortcrust pastry made with 115 g (4 oz) flour (page 10)

FOR THE CRÈME PÂTISSIÈRE:
2 large eggs
50 g (2 oz) caster sugar
1 rounded tablespoon plain flour
1 rounded tablespoon cornflour
300 ml ($^1/_2$ pint) milk
$^1/_4$ teaspoon vanilla extract
150 g (5 oz) white chocolate

1 Line a 20-cm (8-inch) loose-bottomed, deep flan tin with the pastry. Chill for 30 minutes.
2 Preheat the oven to Gas Mark 5/electric oven 190°C/fan oven 170°C. Place a baking sheet on the middle shelf of the oven.
3 Place the rhubarb in a shallow baking dish and sprinkle with the sugar. Bake in the oven for 30–40 minutes, stirring a couple of times during cooking. Remove from the oven and cool.
4 For the crème pâtissière, whisk together the eggs and sugar, until thick and creamy. Sift together the flour and cornflour and add this to the egg mixture. Heat the milk in a medium saucepan to just below boiling point and pour this on to the egg mixture, stirring continuously. Return it all to the pan and bring slowly to a simmer. Simmer for 1 minute, stirring all the time. Stir in the vanilla.
5 Melt 80 g (3 oz) of the white chocolate in a bowl over a pan of hot (not boiling) water. Beat the chocolate into the crème pâtissière. Pour it into a bowl to cool and press some dampened clingfilm on to the surface to prevent a skin from forming.
6 On the warmed baking sheet, bake the pastry shell blind for 15 minutes. Remove the foil and beans and return it to the oven for a further 5 minutes until the pastry is crisp and golden. Allow to cool.
7 When you are ready to assemble the flan, carefully ease the pastry case from the tin. Strain any juices off the rhubarb and scatter the fruit over the base of the flan. Smooth the white chocolate crème pâtissière over the top. Grate the remaining chocolate and sprinkle it all over the flan.

Apricot, Prune & Orange Macaroon Tart

SERVES 8
PREPARATION & COOKING TIME: 45 minutes
FREEZING: recommended

Apricots start to appear in the shops in late spring. Use them in this delicious fruit tart recipe – a combination of light puff pastry, soft almond cake and moist, concentrated fruits.

FOR THE PASTRY:
350 g (12 oz) ready-made puff pastry

FOR THE FILLING:
150 g (5 oz) mixture of ready-soaked dried apricots and stoned prunes
grated zest and juice of $^1/_2$ large orange
50 g (2 oz) unsalted butter, softened
50 g (2 oz) caster sugar
50 g (2 oz) ground almonds
1 large egg, beaten
50 g (2 oz) self-raising flour
$^1/_4$ teaspoon baking powder
4–5 tablespoons no-added-sugar apricot spread or conserve
15 g ($^1/_2$ oz) flaked almonds
1 egg, beaten, to glaze
icing sugar, for dusting

1 Preheat the oven to Gas Mark 7/electric oven 220°C/fan oven 200°C.
2 Place the dried apricots and prunes in a small saucepan with the orange juice. Cover and simmer for about 20 minutes, or until all the liquid has evaporated.
3 To make the macaroon topping, cream the butter and sugar with the orange zest. Gradually beat in the ground almonds with the egg. Sift together the flour and baking powder and incorporate it into the macaroon mixture.
4 On a lightly floured surface roll out the pastry thinly. Find a large plate or round tray, 30 cm (12 inches) in diameter. Place it on the pastry and cut round it to make a circle. Place the circle on a baking sheet. Using a sharp knife, lightly score an inner circle, 4 cm (1½ inches) from the edge. Prick the pastry all over with a fork.
5 Spread a thin layer of apricot spread or conserve over the circle, as far as the marked line. Dot teaspoonfuls of macaroon mixture over the surface and lightly press the dried fruit into the pastry so that it fills the gaps.
6 Carefully turn the edges of the pastry in, as far as the scored line, to make a rim for the tart. Do this fairly tightly, folding over a couple of times, to make a tart approximately 23 cm (9 inches) in diameter. Scatter flaked almonds over the top and brush the pastry rim with beaten egg.
7 Bake in the centre of the oven for 20–25 minutes until the tart is risen and golden. Dust with sifted icing sugar and serve warm.

Classic Apricot Tart

SERVES 6–8

PREPARATION & COOKING TIME: 35 minutes + 1 hour chilling + 20–25 minutes cooking

FREEZING: not recommended

This is a beautifully textured and flavoured French-style tart that looks stunning. If you are short of time, buy a ready-made sweet pastry case and, in place of the crème pâtissière, combine a 250 g tub of mascarpone with 200 ml (7 fl oz) ready-made fresh custard. This tart is served cold and can be made the day before you plan to serve it.

FOR THE PASTRY:

pâte sucrée made with 115 g (4 oz) plain flour (page 10)

FOR THE FILLING:

3 large eggs

80 g (3 oz) caster sugar

3 tablespoons plain flour

3 tablespoons cornflour

425 ml (¾ pint) milk

a few drops of vanilla extract

411 g can of apricot halves

2 tablespoons apricot jam, sieved

1 Line a 20-cm (8-inch) loose-bottomed, deep flan tin with the pâte sucrée. Chill for 1 hour.

2 Preheat the oven to Gas Mark 5/electric oven 190°C/fan oven 170°C. Put a baking sheet on the middle shelf.

3 To make the crème pâtissière, whisk together the eggs and sugar in a bowl. Sift together the flour and cornflour, and fold this in to the eggs and sugar. Heat the milk in a medium saucepan to just below boiling. Pour this on to the flour mixture, whisking all the time. Return the sauce to the pan and cook over a low heat, whisking continuously, until it comes to the boil and thickens. (Don't worry if it appears slightly lumpy, keep whisking, and the lumps should disappear.) Stir in the vanilla extract and pour the sauce into a jug. Press a piece of wetted clingfilm on to the surface to prevent a skin from forming, and leave to cool.

4 On the warmed baking sheet, bake the pastry case blind for 15 minutes. Remove the foil or paper and the baking beans and cook for a further 5–10 minutes, until the pastry is lightly browned. Allow to cool.

5 To assemble the tart, carefully remove the pastry case from the tin and place it on a serving plate. Spoon in the crème pâtissière, and smooth it evenly over the pastry base. Drain the canned apricots, pat dry and arrange them over the custard base. Warm the jam and brush it over the apricots to give a lovely glossy finish.

Bakewell Tart

SERVES 8

PREPARATION & COOKING TIME: 40 minutes

FREEZING: recommended

It is no wonder that this tart has stood the test of time. It doubles up as a pudding or teatime treat, and is simplicity itself to make. Puff pastry is used here, but shortcrust can also be used.

FOR THE PASTRY:

225 g (8 oz) ready-made puff pastry

FOR THE FILLING:

3 slightly rounded tablespoons raspberry jam

2 large eggs, plus 2 large yolks

115 g (4 oz) unsalted butter, melted

115 g (4 oz) caster sugar

115 g (4 oz) ground almonds

a few drops of almond essence

flaked almonds, to decorate

1 Preheat the oven to Gas Mark 6/electric oven 200°C/fan oven 180°C. Place a baking sheet on the middle shelf.

2 On a lightly floured surface roll out the pastry and use it to line a 20-cm (8-inch) loose-bottomed, deep flan tin. Prick well with a fork.

3 Spread jam over the base of the pastry case.

4 Place the eggs and yolks in a bowl. Beat gently to just combine them. Trickle in the slightly cooled melted butter, stirring constantly. Add the sugar and almonds and just a few drops of almond essence for flavour.

5 Pour the mixture into the pastry case and scatter flaked almonds over the surface. Bake (on the heated baking sheet) for about 30 minutes, or until the centre is just firm to the touch. Allow to cool for at least half an hour before serving warm

Mocha Tart

SERVES 6

PREPARATION & COOKING TIME: 35 minutes + 50 minutes
  chilling + 25 minutes cooking

FREEZING: recommended

*Coffee combined with chocolate is a classic combination. The
mocha filling is a mousse that makes this dessert lighter than
you would expect. You will need a few mixing bowls – but you
won't mind the extra washing up once you have tasted this.*

FOR THE PASTRY:
175 g (6 oz) plain flour
80 g (3 oz) butter, diced
80 g (3 oz) icing sugar
3 egg yolks

FOR THE FILLING:
2 teaspoons gelatine
100 g (3½ oz) plain chocolate
1 teaspoon instant coffee granules
2 eggs, separated
50 g (2 oz) caster sugar
150 ml (5 fl oz) double cream, whipped to soft peaks

TO DECORATE:
150 ml (5 fl oz) double cream, whipped
chocolate-covered coffee beans

1 To make the pastry, place the flour, butter and icing sugar
  in a food processor and pulse until the mixture resembles
  breadcrumbs. Add the yolks and continue to process until
  a dough is formed. If you don't have a food processor,
  simply rub the butter into the flour and sugar and when
  the mixture resembles breadcrumbs, add the egg yolks and
  bring it all together to form a dough. Wrap the dough in
  clingfilm and chill for 30 minutes.
2 On a floured surface, roll out the pastry to fit a 20-cm
  (8-inch) loose-bottomed flan tin. Line the pastry case with
  baking parchment or foil and fill with baking beans. Chill
  for a further 20 minutes. Preheat the oven to Gas Mark
  4/electric oven 180°C/fan oven 160°C. Bake the pastry
  case in the oven for 10 minutes, remove the parchment or
  foil and beans and bake for a further 10–15 minutes until
  the pastry is cooked and golden brown. Allow to cool on a
  wire rack.
3 In a small dish, sprinkle the gelatine over 2 tablespoons
  water and leave it to go spongy for 1 minute. Dissolve the
  gelatine by placing the dish in a larger one filled with hot
  water or by placing the dish in the microwave for 20
  seconds. Stir the mixture to dissolve the gelatine
  completely and allow to cool.
4 Place the chocolate, coffee and 2 tablespoons water in a
  bowl and set it over a pan of barely simmering water,
  stirring from time to time until the chocolate melts.
  Remove the bowl from the heat and allow to cool. Stir in
  the egg yolks and sugar and mix thoroughly. Add the
  gelatine in a steady stream while mixing. Fold in the
  whipped cream.

5 Whisk the egg whites until they are stiff and fold in 1
  tablespoon to loosen the chocolate mixture. Now add the
  remaining whites and fold them in using a figure-of-eight
  action until there are no whites visible. Pour the mixture
  into the pastry case, level the surface and chill until the
  mousse has set.
6 Place the whipped cream into a piping bag fitted with
  a star nozzle and pipe cream rosettes around the edge.
  Place a chocolate-covered coffee bean on each rosette.

NOTE: If you are vegetarian you can replace the gelatine with
Vegegel.

Crêpes Gâteau with Banoffee
Cream & Bananas *(right)*

SERVES 6–8 ★

PREPARATION TIME: 15 minutes

FREEZING: not recommended

*This is very rich, but extremely easy to prepare, and both
adults and children will love it. Most supermarkets stock
ready-made pancakes/crêpes in their bakery departments.*

450 g jar of banoffee toffee sauce (I used Merchant Gourmand's)
300 ml (½ pint) double cream, whipped to soft peaks
4 ready-made crêpes
3 firm bananas, sliced
grated chocolate, to decorate

1 Empty the banoffee toffee sauce into a bowl and fold in
  just over half the cream.
2 Place a crêpe on a serving plate, spread a third of the
  banoffee cream over it, evenly but not right to the edge,
  arrange a third of the banana slices on top, place another
  crêpe on top and repeat with the remaining cream and
  crêpes.
3 Spread the remaining whipped cream on to the fourth
  pancake before you place it on the gâteau. Sprinkle the
  grated chocolate on top of the cream and serve as soon as
  possible.

Desserts

Silken Tofu Coffee Cheesecake

SERVES 6 ▼
PREPARATION & COOKING TIME: 30 minutes + 2 hours
  setting
FREEZING: not recommended

*Silken tofu, available from health food shops, makes an
excellent smooth cheesecake. It's a good alternative to calorie-
rich cream cheese. Don't be nervous of gelatine: as long as it
is not overheated or added to a very cold mixture, it is easy to
use. Low fat crème fraîche would be a good accompaniment.*

12 ginger nut biscuits
25 g (1 oz) low fat spread
3 teaspoons good quality instant coffee granules
1 sachet powdered gelatine
300 g (1 oz) silken tofu
1 tablespoon clear honey
a small bunch of black grapes, halved and de-seeded, to decorate

1 Crush the biscuits in a food processor. Melt the spread
  in a saucepan over a low heat. Add the crushed biscuits
  and mix well. Press into the bottom of a 20-cm (8-inch)
  shallow dish (or foil tray) and leave to set.
2 Meanwhile, put 150 ml (^{1}/4 pint) cold water and the coffee
  in a small saucepan, and sprinkle over the gelatine. Set
  over a low heat and stir with a wooden spoon until the
  gelatine has dissolved and the liquid is clear. Be careful not
  to overheat. Leave to cool for 5 minutes.
3 Rinse out the processor, add the tofu and honey, and pulse
  to mix. With the motor running, pour in the cooled coffee
  and gelatine until mixed well.
4 Quickly pour the tofu mixture over the biscuit base. Put in
  the fridge to set for about 2 hours. Decorate with the
  grapes to serve.

NOTE: If you are vegetarian replace the gelatine with Vegegel.

Chocolate & Amaretti Crunch Cheesecake

SERVES 8
PREPARATION TIME: 40 minutes + 2 hours chilling
FREEZING: recommended

*The pieces of chocolate and amaretti biscuits provide an
interesting contrast to the creaminess of the rest of the filling.
The ricotta cheese is used to create a lighter taste but you
could use a cream or curd cheese instead.*

175 g (6 oz) digestive biscuits, crushed
50 g (2 oz) butter, melted

FOR THE FILLING:
11.7 g sachet of gelatine
2 x 250 g tubs of ricotta cheese
115 g (4 oz) caster sugar
100 g (3^1/2 oz) plain chocolate, cut into small pieces
100 g (3^1/2 oz) amaretti biscuits, crushed roughly
350 ml (12 fl oz) double cream, whipped to soft peaks
cocoa powder, to decorate

1 Lightly oil a 20-cm (8-inch) cheesecake or springform tin.
  Combine the digestive biscuits and butter, spoon into the
  tin and press down with a potato masher. Chill while you
  make the filling.
2 Measure 3 tablespoons of water into a small bowl,
  sprinkle over the gelatine and leave to go 'spongy' for a
  minute or two. Dissolve by placing the bowl in a larger
  bowl of hot water and stirring. Alternatively, you could
  microwave it on high for 30 seconds. Allow to cool.
3 Combine the ricotta and sugar in a large bowl and mix
  well. Beat in the cooled gelatine and then fold in the
  chocolate and amaretti biscuits, followed by the cream.
  Spoon on to the biscuit base and chill for a couple of
  hours, or until set.
4 Run a knife around the sides of the cheesecake and remove
  the sides of the tin. Sift cocoa powder on top to decorate
  and serve.

Boozy Chocolate Custards

SERVES 6
PREPARATION & COOKING TIME: 15 minutes + 25 minutes
   cooking + 2 hours chilling
FREEZING: not recommended

These baked versions of chocolate mousse are a little bit like a baked chocolate cheesecake without the base. They are heavenly and are even better eaten a day or two after they have been made.

300 ml (^{1}/$_2$ pint) double cream
150 ml (^{1}/$_4$ pint) milk
115 g (4 oz) plain chocolate (at least 70% cocoa solids),
   broken into pieces
3 medium egg yolks
2 medium eggs
2 tablespoons demerara sugar
3 tablespoons dark rum or brandy

TO DECORATE:
whipped cream (see Note)
grated chocolate or chocolate curls, to decorate

1 Preheat the oven to Gas Mark 4/electric oven 180°C/fan oven 160°C.
2 Place the cream and milk in a saucepan and bring to the boil over a moderate heat. Remove from the heat, add the chocolate pieces and stir until the chocolate has melted.
3 Meanwhile, combine the egg yolks, eggs, demerara sugar and rum or brandy in a bowl and whisk gently to combine.
4 Pour the chocolate cream over the egg mixture, whisk to combine and then pass through a sieve. Lightly oil six ramekin dishes and pour the chocolate custard into the dishes.
5 Place the ramekin dishes in a roasting dish and pour boiling water into the roasting dish so that it is halfway up the sides of the ramekin dishes. Bake in the bottom of the oven, for 20–25 minutes until the custard is set and firm to a gentle touch.
6 Chill the custards for 2 hours.
7 Put the whipped cream in a piping bag with a star nozzle. Decorate the mousses with cream rosettes and grated chocolate or chocolate curls.

NOTE: Whenever I have more cream than I need, I often pipe rosettes on to a tray, open-freeze them and then pop them into a bag. They are useful for instant decorations for desserts like this one.

Light Lemon Cheesecake

SERVES 10 ▼
PREPARATION TIME: 30 minutes + 3–4 hours chilling
FREEZING: recommended

Cheesecakes are notoriously fattening, but this one, using low-fat dairy products, is an exception. Ginger biscuits would make a nice variation in place of digestives in the base.

FOR THE BASE:
50 g (2 oz) butter or block margarine
115 g (4 oz) digestive biscuits, crushed

FOR THE TOPPING:
1 sachet of powdered gelatine
juice and grated zest of 2 lemons
200 g tub of light cream cheese
250 g tub of ricotta cheese
200 ml tub of half-fat crème fraîche
115 g (4 oz) caster sugar
150 ml (^{1}/$_4$ pint) double cream
1 rounded tablespoon home-made or good-quality lemon curd

1 Lightly grease a 20-cm (8-inch) springform tin and base-line with greaseproof paper.
2 To make the base, melt the butter. Stir in the crushed digestive biscuits. Using the back of a spoon, press them evenly over the base of the prepared tin. Chill in the fridge while you make the topping.
3 In a small bowl, sprinkle the gelatine over the juice of 1 lemon. Stand over a pan of hot (not boiling) water and stir until dissolved. Remove from the heat and leave to cool a little.
4 Using a wooden spoon, mix together the cream cheese, ricotta, crème fraîche, caster sugar and lemon zest until smooth. Slowly beat in the remaining lemon juice.
5 Gradually whisk in the gelatine in a thin stream, stirring all the time.
6 Lightly whisk the cream until slightly thickened but still of a pouring consistency. Carefully fold into the cheese mixture and pour over the biscuit base. Gently shake the tin to level the surface.
7 Spoon the lemon curd in a rough spiral over the top of the cheesecake. Using a skewer, swirl through randomly to give a decorative effect. Chill until set, about 3–4 hours.
8 When ready to serve, loosen gently around the edge and open out the tin. Slide a palette knife between the biscuit base and greaseproof paper and ease the cheesecake on to a serving plate.

NOTE: Replace the gelatine with Vegegel if you are vegetarian.

Lemon Curd Ice Cream (*right*)

SERVES 6
PREPARATION TIME: 15 minutes + 4–6 hours freezing
FREEZING: essential

450 g (1 lb) jar of lemon curd
grated zest and juice of 1 lemon
300 ml ('/₂ pint) whipping cream
450 g (1 lb) Greek-style yogurt

1 Use a long loaf tin, lined with clingfilm, or a plastic container.
2 Beat the zest and juice into the curd.
3 Add the cream and yogurt and stir until smooth.
4 Pour the mixture into the tin and freeze for 4–6 hours or until firm.
5 Remove from the freezer to refrigerator about 1 hour before serving. Remove from tin and cut into slices.

NOTE: The ice cream can be kept for up to 3 months.

Speedy Lemon Meringue Tarts

SERVES 6
PREPARATION & COOKING TIME: 15 minutes + 35–40 minutes cooking
FREEZING: not recommended

Lemon meringue pie is quite time-consuming to make but the ready-made versions are usually disappointing. This version takes advantage of convenience foods but tastes totally home-made. A delicious, light, spring dessert.

6 ready-made sweet pastry cases
6 tablespoons good-quality lemon curd
grated zest of 2 lemons and juice of 1 lemon
2 large egg yolks
3 large egg whites
125 g (4'/₂ oz) caster sugar

1 Preheat the oven to Gas Mark 2/electric oven 150°C/fan oven 130°C. Place the lemon curd, lemon zest, lemon juice and egg yolks in a mixing bowl and mix until all the ingredients are combined. Divide the mixture between the pastry cases, which have been placed on a baking sheet.
2 Whisk the egg whites until they are stiff and then add the sugar, a teaspoon at a time, while continuing to whisk. Spoon the mixture into a large piping bag fitted with a large star nozzle.
3 Pipe the meringue on to the lemon filling, starting with the edges and fininshing with a peak in the centre (or you could simply spoon the meringue on top and 'fluff' into a peak with a palette knife).
4 Bake in the oven for 35–40 minutes, until the meringue is crisp and golden brown. Serve warm or cold.

Lemon Lush

SERVES 6
PREPARATION TIME: 15 minutes + 30 minutes chilling
FREEZING: not recommended

This looks pretty in individual glass dessert dishes but it could be served in a trifle bowl. It would be perfect at the end of a rich or heavy meal.

12 sponge fingers, broken into pieces
180 ml (12 tablespoons) fresh orange juice
300 ml ('/₂ pint) double cream
grated juice and zest of 1 lemon
150 g Greek-style yogurt
3 tablespoons good-quality lemon curd
toasted flaked almonds or grated chocolate, to decorate

1 Divide the sponge finger pieces between the glass dishes and sprinkle 2 tablespoons fresh orange juice over the sponges in each dish.
2 Pour the cream into a large bowl, add the lemon zest and juice and whisk until soft peaks form. Combine the yogurt and lemon curd in a bowl and fold into the lemon cream. Spoon over the soaked sponges and chill until ready to serve. Just before serving, decorate with either the almonds or chocolate.

Tarte au Citron

SERVES 10–12
PREPARATION & COOKING TIME: 20 minutes + 1 hour chilling + 50 minutes cooking
FREEZING: not recommended

The freshness of this lemon tart gives a real zing to the tastebuds. It is best served without a dusting of icing sugar, to show off its pure yellow colour. Slightly undercook this tart, if anything, and make it the day before to allow plenty of time for cooling, and chilling overnight. Delicious served with crème fraîche.

sweet rich shortcrust pastry made with 115 g (4 oz) plain flour (page 10)

FOR THE FILLING:
5 large eggs, beaten
150 g (5 oz) caster sugar
grated zest and juice of 5 unwaxed lemons
300 ml (½ pint) double cream

1 Line a 23-cm (9-inch) loose-bottomed, deep flan tin with the sweet rich shortcrust pastry. Chill for 1 hour.
2 Preheat the oven to Gas Mark 5/electric oven 190°C/fan oven 170°C. Place a baking sheet in the centre of the oven for the tart.
3 On the warmed baking sheet, bake the pastry case blind for 15 minutes. Remove the foil or paper and beans and cook for a further 5 minutes.
4 Meanwhile, mix the eggs and sugar in a bowl to just combine them.
5 Stir the lemon zest and juice into the bowl followed by the double cream.
6 Reduce the oven temperature to Gas Mark 2/electric oven 150°C/fan oven 130°C. Slide the oven shelf half out for the tart and pour the lemon mixture into the pastry case. Very carefully slide back the shelf and cook for 30 minutes. The tart should have a slight tremor in the centre, but will continue cooking when the oven is switched off. Leave the oven door ajar and leave the tart inside to cool. Chill thoroughly before serving.

Lemon & Lime Ginger Crunch Pie

SERVES 8
PREPARATION & COOKING TIME: 15 minutes + 30 minutes chilling
FREEZING: not recommended

This recipe is based on one of those classic dishes of the 70s. Its ease of preparation and few, mainly store cupboard, ingredients still make it an attractive dessert today. It requires virtually no cooking and is best left to chill overnight, but will set within an hour if need be.

FOR THE BISCUIT BASE:
80 g (3 oz) unsalted butter
175 g (6 oz) ginger nut biscuits

FOR THE FILLING:
grated zest and juice of 2 limes
grated zest and juice of 2 lemons
397 g can of sweetened condensed milk
300 ml (½ pint) double cream
grated chocolate, to decorate

1 Melt the butter in a medium saucepan over a low heat. Meanwhile put the ginger nuts in a polythene bag and crush them with a rolling pin to a sand-like consistency.
2 Stir the crumbs into the butter. Press the crumb mixture into the base and up the sides of a 20-cm (8-inch) ceramic flan dish. Chill for at least 30 minutes.
3 Put all the filling ingredients into a mixing bowl. Whisk for about 2 minutes until the mixture is thick and creamy. Pour this into the crumb case and chill overnight until set. Decorate with a sprinkling of grated chocolate.

Lime Bread & Butter Pudding

SERVES 6
PREPARATION & COOKING TIME: 1 hour 15 minutes
FREEZING: not recommended

This popular pudding is given a 'makeover' both in its contents and preparation. If you prefer, you can make it in a large dish rather than in individual ones.

6 slices of fruit bread
50 g (2 oz) butter, softened
lime marmalade
grated zest of 1 lime
300 ml (½ pint) single cream
300 ml (½ pint) milk
2 large eggs
2 large egg yolks
25 g (1 oz) granulated sugar

1 Butter the fruit bread slices and then spread with lime marmalade. Cut the slices into about six pieces. Butter and base-line six ramekin dishes. Layer the bread in the ramekin dishes.
2 Whisk together the lime zest, cream, milk, eggs, egg yolks and sugar and strain through a sieve into a jug. Pour the custard over the bread and leave to soak for 30 minutes.
3 Preheat the oven to Gas Mark 4/electric oven 180°C/fan oven 160°C. Bake for about 30 minutes, until the custard has set. Allow to cool a little.
4 Meanwhile, heat 1–2 tablespoons of the marmalade and sieve to remove any peel.
5 Run a knife around the edges of the puddings to loosen, invert into the palm of your hand and place in the centre of serving plates. Brush the tops with the marmalade glaze. Serve surrounded with some single cream.

Pink Grapefruit & Vodka Sorbet (*above*)

SERVES 4 ▼
PREPARATION TIME: 10 minutes + 2 hours freezing
FREEZING: essential

This sorbet looks very pretty and has a wonderful palate-cleansing taste. It can be made by hand, but an ice cream machine is an excellent investment.

425 ml (¾ pint) pink grapefruit juice
75 g (2¾ oz) caster sugar
3 tablespoons vodka or gin

1 Heat a little of the grapefruit juice with the sugar in a small saucepan until the sugar has dissolved. Remove from the heat and stir in the remaining grapefruit juice together with the vodka or gin.
2 If using an ice cream machine follow the manufacturer's instructions. Otherwise, pour into a suitable plastic container and freeze until ice crystals form around the edges. Beat well and return to the freezer.
3 Repeat this two or three times until the sorbet is thick, smooth and well frozen. It should not contain any large lumps of ice.
4 Allow to 'soften' in the fridge for about 15 minutes before serving.

Chocolate Ganache Tart

SERVES 6
PREPARATION & COOKING TIME: 30 minutes + 30 minutes
  chilling + 25 minutes cooking
FREEZING: recommended

*Crisp buttery pastry, filled with a dark chocolate cream makes
eating this tart a heavenly experience! It is delicious served by
itself, or you could accompany it with some raspberries and
cream.*

FOR THE PASTRY:
175 g (6 oz) plain flour
80 g (3 oz) butter, diced
80 g (3 oz) caster sugar
3 egg yolks

FOR THE FILLING:
300 ml (½ pint) double cream
225 g (8 oz) plain chocolate, broken into pieces
40 g (1½ oz) butter
1 tablespoon brandy (optional)
icing sugar, to decorate

1 To make the pastry, place the flour, butter and sugar in a
   food processor and pulse until the mixture resembles
   breadcrumbs. Add the egg yolks and process briefly until
   the mixture starts to come together. Wrap the dough in
   clingfilm and place it in the fridge for 30 minutes. If you
   don't have a food processor, rub the butter into the flour in
   a bowl, stir in the sugar and then add the yolks and mix
   until the dough is formed.
2 Preheat the oven to Gas Mark 4/electric oven 180°C/fan
   oven 160°C. Roll out the pastry on a floured work surface
   and use it to line a 20-cm (8-inch) loose-bottomed tart tin.
   Prick the base with a fork. Line the pastry with baking
   parchment or foil and fill with baking beans.
3 Bake the pastry case for 10 minutes. Remove the
   parchment or foil and beans, and continue to bake for a
   further 10–15 minutes until the pastry is golden and
   cooked. Allow to cool in the tin on a wire rack.
4 To make the filling, place the cream in a medium saucepan
   and bring it to the boil over a moderate heat. Remove the
   pan from the heat and add the chocolate pieces. Stir until
   the chocolate is melted and then add the butter, stirring
   until the butter has melted. Add the brandy, if using, and
   mix it in. Pour the filling into the cooled pastry shell and
   smooth it so that the surface is level. Allow to cool and
   then chill in the fridge until ready to serve.
5 Remove from the fridge 30 minutes before serving, so that
   it is at room temperature. Dust the surface with sifted icing
   sugar.

Pineapple Pastries

MAKES 6 ★
PREPARATION & COOKING TIME: 30 minutes
FREEZING: recommended

*Pineapple topped with sugary spice makes a perfect partner
for pastry because of its intense flavour. Make sure that your
pineapple is ripe and juicy, otherwise use the canned variety –
you can also buy very good ready-prepared fresh pineapple in
most supermarkets. It is so quick to make you will not believe
how such a simple recipe can taste so good. Serve warm with
pouring cream.*

FOR THE PASTRY:
350 g (12 oz) ready-made puff pastry
1 egg, beaten
1 tablespoon icing sugar

FOR THE FILLING:
½ small fresh pineapple, approximately 350 g (12 oz) unprepared
  weight
25 g (1 oz) unsalted butter, melted
2 tablespoons demerara sugar
1 teaspoon mixed spice

1 Preheat the oven to Gas Mark 7/electric oven 220°C/fan
   oven 200°C.
2 On a lightly floured surface roll out the pastry thinly. Use a
   10-cm (4-inch) diameter round guide to cut out six circles.
   Place the circles on a baking sheet. Using a sharp knife,
   Score a line 1 cm (½ inch) in from the edge of each circle.
   Prick the pastry well with a fork.
3 Brush the pastry all over with the beaten egg and dredge
   with icing sugar.
4 Remove the skin and core from the pineapple. Slice it
   fairly thinly and cut into triangles. Divide these triangles
   between the pastries, taking care to keep the fruit within
   the inner circle.
5 Brush the pineapple with melted butter. Mix together the
   sugar and mixed spice and sprinkle this liberally all over
   the pastries.
6 Bake towards the top of the oven for 15–20 minutes, until
   the pastries are crisp and golden and the pineapple is
   beginning to caramelise.

Creamy Mousses with Passion Fruit & Papaya Coulis

SERVES 6 ▼
PREPARATION TIME: 25 minutes + 1–2 hours chilling
FREEZING: not recommended

This dessert tastes as if it is laden with calories but it has surprisingly few (only 162 per dessert), because it uses low-fat ricotta instead of cream cheese. It is very refreshing and light and therefore ideal to serve after a rich or heavy meal.

115 ml (4 fl oz) fresh orange juice
2¹/₂ tablespoons fresh lemon juice
11.7 g sachet of gelatine
450 g (1 lb) ricotta cheese
grated zest from 1 orange and 1 lemon
3 large egg whites, whisked stiffly

FOR THE COULIS:
4 passion fruit
1¹/₂ ripe papayas (pawpaws)
175 ml (6 fl oz) fresh orange juice
6 physalis, to decorate

1 Pour the orange and lemon juices into a cup or small bowl, sprinkle the gelatine on top and leave until it becomes sponge-like. Dissolve by placing the cup/bowl in a pan of hot water and stirring or microwave on high for 30–40 seconds. Allow to cool.
2 Meanwhile, place the ricotta cheese and citrus zests in a bowl and beat to mix thoroughly. Stir in the cooled citrus juices. Fold in a tablespoon of the egg whites to loosen the mixture and then fold in the remaining egg whites gently, until they have been thoroughly incorporated. Spoon into six base-lined ramekins and chill for 1–2 hours, until set.
3 Cut the passion fruit in half and scoop the flesh with a teaspoon into a sieve placed over a bowl. Press the flesh to extract as much juice as possible. Place the juice, with the flesh from the papaya and the orange juice, in a liquidiser or blender and blend until smooth.
4 Unmould a mousse on to the centre of each serving plate and surround with the coulis. Unwrap the papery skin from each physalis, twist and place one in the centre of each mousse.

NOTE: Use Vegegel instead of gelatine if you are vegetarian.

Pashka Iced Bombe

SERVES 6
PREPARATION TIME: 40 minutes + 3 hours freezing
FREEZING: essential

Pashka is a Russian dessert traditionally served at Easter. This iced version has some of the ingredients usually included in the dessert but I have added marzipan, which is in simnel cake, and amaretto liqueur to complement the almond in the marzipan. The chocolate marzipan balls represent the disciples, again as on a simnel cake.

50 g (2 oz) sultanas
25 g (1 oz) dried apricots, chopped into small pieces
3 tablespoons amaretto liqueur
125 g (4¹/₂ oz) marzipan, cut into small pieces
500 g tub of custard
200 g tub of cream cheese
150 ml (¹/₄ pint) double cream, whipped

FOR THE CHOCOLATE BALLS:
125 g (4¹/₂ oz) marzipan
80 g (3 oz) plain chocolate, melted

1 Soak the sultanas and the apricots in the amaretto for 20–30 minutes.
2 In the meantime, place the marzipan and custard in a saucepan and heat over a moderate heat, stirring, until the marzipan melts. Allow to cool a little.
3 Whisk the cream cheese into the custard mixture and fold in the soaked dried fruit, with its soaking liquid, followed by the cream.
4 Lightly oil a 1-litre (1³/₄-pint) pudding basin and line with clingfilm. Spoon the pashka into the basin and freeze until solid, about 3 hours.
5 To make the chocolate marzipan balls, divide the marzipan into 12 or 13 pieces and roll into balls. Using two teaspoons, dip the balls into the melted chocolate and place on a piece of baking parchment to set.
6 To serve, invert the bombe on to the serving dish, peel off the clingfilm and surround with the chocolate balls.

Rocky Road Ice Cream Pie

SERVES 8
PREPARATION & COOKING TIME: 45 minutes
FREEZING: essential

This 'pile it high' ice cream pie would make a great special occasion pudding for kids. The Maltesers in the base give it a lovely surprise crunch.

80 g (3 oz) unsalted butter
200 g (7 oz) chocolate digestive biscuits
500 ml tub of good quality toffee ice cream, softened slightly
58 g (giant size!) bag of Maltesers – halved if you can!
2 large egg whites
115 g (4 oz) caster sugar
50 g (2 oz) coloured mini marshmallows

1 Preheat the oven to Gas Mark 8/electric oven 230°C/fan oven 210°C.
2 Melt the butter in a medium saucepan. Crush the digestive biscuits and stir them into the butter. Press the crumb mixture into the base and sides of a buttered 20-cm (8-inch) loose-bottomed, deep flan tin. Chill for 30 minutes.
3 Scoop half the ice cream out and pack it carefully into the biscuit case. Press half the Maltesers randomly on top. Repeat this with the remaining ice cream and Maltesers.
4 Whisk the egg whites until stiff. Gradually beat in half the sugar. Fold in the rest, reserving 1 teaspoon and then add the marshmallows. Spread this meringue mixture completely over the ice cream and Maltesers, leaving nothing visible underneath. Make dramatic swirls with the meringue and sprinkle with the reserved sugar.
5 Bake as near the top of the oven as possible for 3–5 minutes, watching carefully, until the meringue is just crisp and browned. Serve at once.

Cappuccino Cups

SERVES 6–8
PREPARATION TIME: 50 minutes
FREEZING: not recommended

This is a light and elegant dessert to serve at the end of a spring dinner party. Ricotta cheese has a lovely creamy taste but contains about the same calories as cottage cheese.

2 medium eggs, separated
115 g (4 oz) caster sugar
2 x 250 g tubs of ricotta cheese
3 tablespoons very strong black coffee, cooled
2 tablespoons coffee liqueur, such as Tia Maria or Kahlua
chocolate-covered coffee beans
150 ml (¼ pint) whipping cream or 150 g Greek-style yogurt
grated chocolate, to decorate

1 Place the egg yolks and sugar in a bowl and whisk until pale and creamy. Add the ricotta, coffee and half the liqueur and beat well.
2 Whisk the egg whites until they are stiff. Add a tablespoon to the ricotta mixture and beat in to loosen the mixture. Fold in the remaining whites until completely incorporated.
3 Place a few chocolate-coated coffee beans in the bottom of 6–8 (the number will depend on the size of the cups) small coffee cups. Spoon over the 'cappuccino' mixture. Whip the cream and remaining liqueur lightly or fold the liqueur into the yogurt, if using. Spoon over the ricotta mixture to look like frothy milk. Sprinkle the grated chocolate over the 'froth'. Chill for at least 30 minutes or until ready to serve.

Simnel Cake *(right)*

MAKES 12–16 slices
PREPARATION TIME: 40–45 minutes + 60 minutes for fruit
  to stand + 15 minutes to complete
COOKING TIME: 2–2½ HOURS

This spiced fruit cake has a layer of marzipan in the centre, and another on the top. Originally, the cake was baked by girls in service to take home with them on Mothering Sunday. It is now more usual to have simnel cake at Easter time, with eleven almond-paste eggs on the top, representing the Apostles but omitting Judas. This is a modern variation and is extremely tasty.

FOR THE MARZIPAN:
225 g (8 oz) ground almonds
225 g (8 oz) caster sugar
115 g (4 oz) icing sugar, sieved
1 egg, separated
juice of ½ lemon

FOR THE CAKE:
175 g (6 oz) raisins
175 g (6 oz) sultanas
80 g (3 oz) glacé cherries, chopped
80 g (3 oz) walnut pieces, chopped
115 ml (4 fl oz) stout
175 g (6 oz) butter, softened
175 g (6 oz) soft dark brown sugar
3 eggs
sieve together: 225 g (8 oz) plain flour and ½ teaspoon baking
  powder and 1 teaspoon ground mixed spice

TO FINISH:
3 tablespoons apricot jam, sieved

1 First make the marzipan. Mix the ground almonds and sugars. Add the egg yolk, lemon juice and enough egg white to mix to a stiffish paste. Retain the rest of the egg white.
2 Wrap the marzipan in clingfilm and put in the refrigerator.
3 Place the raisins, sultanas, glacé cherries, walnut pieces and stout in a saucepan and heat until steaming. Remove from the heat; allow to stand for 60 minutes.
4 Cream the butter and sugar until light in colour and fluffy; then gradually beat in the eggs.
5 Fold in the flour, baking powder and spice. Carefully stir in the soaked fruit with its liquid.
6 Grease and line an 18-cm (7-inch) round cake tin, place half the mixture in the tin and smooth the top.
7 Roll out one-third of the marzipan into a 18-cm (7-inch) circle, and place it on the top of the mixture in the tin. Add the remaining cake mixture and smooth the top.
8 Cook at Gas Mark 3/electric oven 160°C/fan oven 140°C for 2–2½ hours until pale golden, and a skewer inserted into the centre of the cake comes out clean.
9 Leave the cake to stand in the tin for 15 minutes before turning it out on to a wire rack to cool completely.
10 When cold, remove the lining paper and brush the top of the cake with apricot jam.

11 Roll out half the remaining marzipan to fit top of the cake and press in position.
12 Score the surface of the marzipan to make a diamond pattern and brush with the remaining egg white.
13 Roll the remaining marzipan into eleven even-sized balls and press around the rim of the top of the cake; brush with egg white.
14 Place the cake under a preheated grill and toast gently until the marzipan is golden brown.

Apricot & Orange Cake

MAKES 12–16 slices
PREPARATION TIME: 45 minutes
COOKING TIME: 1–1¼ HOURS

The soaking of the fruit gives this light-textured cake a delicious orange flavour.

115 ml (4 fl oz) Cointreau
115 ml (4 fl oz) freshly squeezed orange juice
225 g (8 oz) ready-to-eat dried apricots, finely chopped
115 g (4 oz) sultanas
175 g (6 oz) butter, softened
3 tablespoons clover honey
4 eggs, separated
sieve together: 175 g (6 oz) self-raising flour and 2 teaspoons baking
  powder

1 Place the orange liqueur, orange juice, apricots and sultanas in a saucepan and bring to the boil. Remove from the heat and leave to cool.
2 Cream together the butter and the honey until well blended.
3 Beat in the egg yolks. Fold in the flour and baking powder, and then gradually mix in the fruit.
4 In a clean, grease-free bowl whisk the egg whites until stiff; fold into the cake mixture.
5 Spoon the mixture into a greased and lined 20-cm (8-inch) round cake tin; smooth the top.
6 Bake at Gas Mark 4/electric oven 180°C/fan oven 160°C for 1–1¼ hours until it is pale golden in colour and springy to the touch.
7 Leave to cool completely in the tin.

Apricot Sunshine Bars

MAKES 18 ♥
PREPARATION & COOKING TIME: 35 minutes
FREEZING: recommended

This variation on a flapjack is more crumbly in texture than chewy and 100 per cent more flavour-filled than the traditional flapjack. The 'heart friendly' fats from the sunflower margarine and the seeds, along with the soluble fibre from the oats, make this a good choice to accompany an afternoon cup of tea or to pop in a lunchbox.

150 g (5½ oz) sunflower margarine plus extra for greasing
100 g (3½ oz) golden syrup
50 g (2 oz) soft light brown sugar
225 g (8 oz) rolled oats
50 g (2 oz) sunflower seeds
50 g (2 oz) sesame seeds
100 g (3½ oz) ready to eat dried apricots, chopped

1 Preheat the oven to Gas Mark 4/electric oven 180°C/fan oven 160°C. Lightly grease a 28 x 19 cm (11 x 7½ inch) baking tin with a little sunflower margarine.
2 In a large saucepan, melt together the margarine, golden syrup and brown sugar – do not allow to boil.
3 Stir in the oats, sunflower and sesame seeds and dried apricots. Mix well and then transfer to the baking tin. Spread the mixture evenly in the tin and press down lightly.
4 Bake in the oven for 20–25 minutes until lightly golden. Remove from the oven and leave to cool for 5 minutes, then mark into 18 squares with a knife.
5 When completely cold, cut through the squares, lift them out of the tin and store in an airtight container.

Apricot, Cherry & Walnut Buns (right)

MAKES 9 buns
PREPARATION TIME: 25–30 minutes + rising
COOKING TIME: 25–30 minutes
FREEZING: recommended

These are made in a similar way to Chelsea Buns, and have a fresh, crunchy taste and texture.

225 g (8 oz) strong white flour
½ teaspoon salt
25 g (1 oz) caster sugar
25 g (1 oz) margarine
½ sachet easy-blend yeast
1 egg, beaten
5 tablespoons hand-hot milk

FOR THE FILLING:
25 g (1 oz) butter
50 g (2 oz) dark brown sugar
50 g (2 oz) walnuts
25 g (1 oz) dried apricots, chopped
25 g (1 oz) glacé cherries, chopped

1 In a large bowl, sift together the flour and salt and mix in the sugar. Rub in the margarine and add the yeast. Stir in the egg and milk to give a soft dough.
2 Turn on to a floured surface and knead for 8–10 minutes, until the dough is smooth, elastic and no longer sticky. Place the dough in a clean, greased bowl, cover and leave to rise until doubled in size.
3 Transfer the risen dough to a lightly floured surface. Knock back and knead. Roll the dough into a rectangle 30 x 23 cm (12 x 9 inches).
4 In a small bowl, soften the butter, creaming it with the brown sugar. Spread this over the dough. Sprinkle with the walnuts, apricots and cherries.
5 Roll up the dough like a swiss roll, starting at the longest side.
6 Cut into nine equal pieces and place on a greased baking sheet, cut-side down, to form a square, about 1 cm (½ inch) apart. Cover and leave to prove for about 30 minutes, until well risen.
7 Preheat the oven to Gas Mark 6/electric oven 210°C/fan oven 190°C.
8 Bake for 25–30 minutes, until golden brown. Place on a wire rack to cool.

Cardamom & Lemon Cake

MAKES 12–16 slices
PREPARATION & COOKING TIME: 1 hour 20 minutes

Cardamom is a member of the ginger family. It has small husks that contain tiny seeds, which have a strong bitter-sweet and slightly lemony flavour. The seeds can be crushed or ground in a spice or coffee grinder or in a pestle and mortar.

225 g (8 oz) butter, softened
225 g (8 oz) caster sugar
4 eggs
sieve together: 350 g (12 oz) plain flour and 2 teaspoons baking powder
10 cardamom pods, seeds removed and ground coarsely
grated zest and juice of 2 unwaxed lemons
50 g (2 oz) ground almonds

1 Cream the butter and sugar until light and fluffy.
2 Beat in the eggs; fold in the flour and baking powder.
3 Stir in the cardamom, zest and juice of the lemons and the ground almonds.
4 Spoon the mixture into a greased and lined 20-cm (8-inch) round cake tin; smooth the top.
5 Bake at Gas Mark 4/electric oven 180°C/fan oven 160°C for 45–60 minutes until golden in colour and springy to the touch.
6 Leave the cake in the tin for 10 minutes; then remove from the tin and leave it on a wire rack until completely cool.

Citrus Poppy Seed Cake

MAKES 12–16 slices
PREPARATION & COOKING TIME: 1 hour 15 minutes

This Madeira-type cake contains poppy seeds, which give it a nutty flavour, while the addition of lime and lemon juice gives it a fresh taste. Poppy seeds are available from supermarkets or health food shops.

250 g (9 oz) butter, softened
200 g (7 oz) caster sugar
grated zest and juice of 2 unwaxed limes
grated zest and juice of 1 unwaxed lemon
4 eggs
300 g (11 oz) self-raising flour, sieved
2 tablespoons poppy seeds

1 Cream the butter and sugar in a large bowl until light in colour and fluffy. Beat in the zest of the limes and the lemon.
2 Beat in the eggs, then fold in the flour followed by the lime and lemon juice and the poppy seeds.
3 Spoon into a greased and lined 20-cm (8-inch) round cake tin, and smooth the top.
4 Bake at Gas Mark 3/electric oven 160°C/fan oven 140° for 50–60 minutes.
5 When cooked, leave the cake in the tin for 15–20 minutes before placing it on a wire rack to cool completely.

Chocolate & Date Squares

MAKES 24
PREPARATION & COOKING TIME: 55 minutes
FREEZING: recommended

Including dates in these little cakes makes them incredibly moist and seems to accentuate their chocolate flavour. You could mix in some chopped walnuts or pecan nuts to add some crunch. If you pop them in the fridge in a sealed container for a while before serving, the topping will be nice and crunchy.

250 g (9 oz) stoned dates
150 ml (5 fl oz) apple juice
175 g (6 oz) plain chocolate, broken into pieces
115 g (4 oz) soft margarine
115 g (4 oz) dark muscovado sugar
2 eggs, beaten lightly
175 g (6 oz) self-raising flour

FOR THE TOPPING:
175 g (6 oz) white chocolate, broken into pieces
80 g (3 oz) unsalted butter
115 g (4 oz) icing sugar, sifted

1 Preheat the oven to Gas Mark 5/electric oven 190°C/fan oven 170°C. Grease a swiss roll tin and line it with greaseproof paper.
2 Place the dates, apple juice and 80 ml (3 fl oz) water in a saucepan, bring to the boil and simmer for 5 minutes. Add the chocolate and stir until melted.
3 Cream the margarine and sugar together until the mixture is fluffy and then beat in the eggs, a little at a time. Fold in the flour and then the date and chocolate mixture until all the ingredients have been incorporated.
4 Spoon the mixture into the prepared tin and spread evenly into the corners. Bake for 20–25 minutes until the cake is risen and firm to the touch, and is coming away from the sides of the tin. Allow to cool in the tin.
5 Meanwhile, make the topping. Place the chocolate and butter in a bowl and place over a pan of barely simmering water and melt, stirring from time to time. Whisk in the icing sugar, a little at a time. Spread over the surface of the cake and leave to set before cutting into squares

Lemon Drizzle Cake

MAKES 10–12 slices
PREPARATION & COOKING TIME: 1 hour 15 minutes

The lemon juice and sugar poured over the cooked cake produces a crunchy glaze and gives it a tangy flavour.

175 g (6 oz) butter, softened
175 g (6 oz) caster sugar
2 eggs
4 tablespoons milk
175 g (6 oz) self-raising flour, sieved
grated zest and juice of 1 unwaxed lemon
1 tablespoon icing sugar

1 Cream the butter and sugar together until light in colour and fluffy. Gradually beat in the eggs and milk.
2 Fold the flour into the mixture with the grated lemon zest.
3 Spoon the mixture into a greased and lined 900 g (2 lb) loaf tin.
4 Bake at Gas Mark 4/electric oven 180°C/fan oven 160°C for 50–65 minutes until the cake is golden-brown and firm to the touch.
5 Mix the lemon juice and icing sugar together and pour over the cake as soon as it is removed from the oven. Allow the glaze to set before removing the cake from the tin. Set on a wire rack to cool completely.

Easter Biscuits

MAKES 24 ★
PREPARATION & COOKING TIME: 30 minutes

These are small, soft fruit biscuits.

115 g (4 oz) butter, softened
80 g (3 oz) caster sugar
1 egg, separated
sieve together: 200 g (7 oz) plain flour and a pinch of salt and 1/2 teaspoon ground mixed spice and 1/2 teaspoon ground cinnamon
50 g (2 oz) currants
25 g (1oz) mixed peel, chopped
1–2 tablespoons milk
a little caster sugar

1 In a bowl, cream together the butter and sugar until light and fluffy. Beat in the egg yolk.
2 Fold the flour, salt and spices into the mixture, with the currants and peel. Add enough milk to give a soft dough.
3 Lightly knead the dough on a floured surface and roll out to 5-mm (1/4 inch) thick. Cut out, using a 6-cm (2 1/2-inch) fluted cutter. Place the biscuits on greased baking sheets.
4 Bake at Gas Mark 6/electric oven 200°C/fan oven 180°C for 8–10 minutes, then brush with egg white and sprinkle with caster sugar. Return to the oven for a further 8–10 minutes.
5 Allow the biscuits to cool for a few minutes before placing them on wire racks to cool completely.

Banana & Carrot Cake

MAKES 10–12 slices ♥
PREPARATION & COOKING TIME: 1 hour 20 minutes
FREEZING: recommended

If you like bananas you will enjoy this lovely moist cake.

225 g (8 oz) self-raising flour
2 teaspoons baking powder
80 g (3 oz) light soft brown sugar
110 g (4 oz) carrots, grated finely
55 g (2 oz) sultanas or chopped dates (optional)
2 eggs, beaten
110 g (4 oz) sunflower or olive oil spread, melted
2 ripe bananas, mashed

1 Preheat the oven to Gas Mark 5/190°C/375°F and grease and line a 900 g (2 lb) loaf tin.
2 Sift the flour and baking powder into a mixing bowl. Add the sugar, carrots and sultanas or dates (if used). Mix well.
3 Stir in the eggs, margarine and bananas to make a soft dropping consistency.
4 Spoon into the prepared tin and bake for 1 hour, or until a skewer inserted into the centre comes out clean.
5 Cool in the tin for 5 minutes; then turn out to cool on a wire rack.

Chocolate Banana Cookies

MAKES 36 ★
PREPARATION & COOKING TIME: 30 minutes

These cookies have a crisp texture.

250 g (9 oz) butter, softened
150 g (5 oz) soft dark brown sugar
100 g (3 1/2 oz) granulated sugar
2 eggs
1 teaspoon vanilla essence
1 large banana, peeled and mashed
sieve together: 350 g (12 oz) plain flour and 1 teaspoon bicarbonate of soda
115 g (4 oz) chocolate chips
80 g (3 oz) banana chips, coarsely chopped

1 Cream the butter and sugars together until light in colour and fluffy.
2 Beat in the eggs and essence. Stir in the mashed banana. Fold in the flour and bicarbonate of soda, mixing thoroughly.
3 Stir in the chocolate and banana chips.
4 Drop large teaspoonfuls of the mixture on to greased baking sheets, making sure you leave space for the mixture to spread out.
5 Bake at Gas Mark 5/electric oven 190°C/fan oven 170°C for 15–20 minutes until golden-brown.
6 Remove the cookies from the oven, leaving them on the baking sheets for a few minutes before placing them on a wire rack to cool completely. Store in airtight container.

Coconut & Lime Loaf *(below)*

MAKES a 450 g (1 lb) loaf
PREPARATION & COOKING TIME: 40–50 minutes + 1 hour
  rising
FREEZING: recommended

The exotic combination of flavours makes this ideal for breakfast or a springtime picnic tea.

225 g (8 oz) strong white flour
1 teaspoon easy-blend yeast
1/2 teaspoon salt
25 g (1 oz) margarine
grated zest of 1 lime
25 g (1 oz) caster sugar
1 egg, beaten
125 ml (4 1/2 fl oz) coconut milk

1 In a large bowl, sift together the flour, yeast and salt. Rub in the margarine until the mixture resembles fine breadcrumbs. Stir in the lime zest and sugar. Stir in the egg and coconut milk, mixing to give a soft dough.
2 Turn on to a floured surface and knead for 8–10 minutes, until the dough is smooth, elastic and no longer sticky.
3 Oil or grease a 450 g (1 lb) loaf tin. Press the dough out and shape to fit the tin. Cover the tin with an oiled polythene bag and leave to rise in a warm place for about 1 hour, until doubled in size.
4 Preheat the oven to Gas Mark 6/electric oven 210°C/fan oven 190°C.
5 Bake for 25–30 minutes, until the loaf is golden and the base sounds hollow when tapped.
6 Transfer to a wire rack to cool.

Fruit Loaf

MAKES a 900 g (2 lb) loaf
PREPARATION & COOKING TIME: About 1 hour + 1 1/2 hours
  rising
FREEZING: recommended

A traditional fruit bread that tastes equally good toasted, with lots of butter.

150 ml (1/4 pint) hand-hot water
150 ml (1/4 pint) hand-hot milk
1 teaspoon + 25 g (1 oz) caster sugar
15 g (1/2 oz) dried yeast
450 g (1 lb) strong white flour
1 teaspoon salt
25 g (1 oz) margarine
175 g (6 oz) mixed dried fruit

1 Mix together the water and milk and dissolve the teaspoon of sugar in the liquid. Sprinkle in the yeast and stir to mix. Leave in a warm place for 10–15 minutes, until frothy.
2 Sift the flour and salt into a bowl, rub in the margarine and add the 25 g (1 oz) of caster sugar. Stir in the dried fruit. Add the yeast mixture and mix to form a soft dough.
3 Knead the dough on a floured surface until smooth and elastic. Place in a clean, greased bowl, cover and leave to rise until doubled in size.
4 Turn the dough on to a floured surface, knock back and knead.
5 Shape to fit a 900 g (2 lb) greased loaf tin. Cover and leave to prove for 30 minutes.
6 Preheat the oven to Gas Mark 6/electric oven 200°C/fan oven 180°C.
7 Bake the loaf for 25–35 minutes, until golden and hollow-sounding when tapped on the base. Transfer to a wire rack to cool.

Hot Cross Buns

MAKES 12 buns
PREPARATION & COOKING TIME: 1– 1 1/4 hours +
  1 1/2 –2 hours rising
FREEZING: recommended

Hot cross buns are traditionally eaten on Good Friday, the cross on the top symbolising, for Christians, the death of Jesus Christ.

450 g (1 lb) strong white flour
50 g (2 oz) caster sugar
25 g (1 oz) fresh yeast
150 ml (5 fl oz) hand-hot milk
4 tablespoons hand-hot water
1 teaspoon salt
1 teaspoon ground mixed spice
1/2 teaspoon ground cinnamon
100 g (3 1/2 oz) currants
50 g (2 oz) chopped mixed candied peel
1 egg, beaten
50 g (2 oz) butter, melted

FOR THE GLAZE:
50 g (2 oz) granulated sugar
3 tablespoons milk

1 Sift 115 g (4 oz) of the flour into a bowl and add 1 teaspoon of the caster sugar.
2 Blend the yeast with the milk and water. Leave to stand for 10 minutes in a warm place, until frothy.
3 Add the yeast mix to the sifted flour and sugar. Leave to stand again for 20 minutes, or until frothy.
4 Sift the remaining flour, salt and spices into a large bowl. Add the remaining caster sugar, currants and mixed peel. Mix lightly. Add the yeast mixture, with the egg and melted butter, and mix to form a soft dough.
5 Turn on to a floured surface and knead until smooth and no longer sticky. Place in a clean, greased bowl and leave to rise for about 40 minutes or until doubled in size.
6 Turn out on to a floured surface and knock back.
7 Divide into 12 equal pieces and shape each into a round bun. Place, well apart, on a greased baking tray and leave to prove until doubled in size.
8 Preheat the oven to Gas Mark 7/electric oven 220°C/fan oven 200°C.
9 Cut a cross on the top of each bun using a sharp knife. Bake for 25–30 minutes, until golden brown.
10 Make the glaze by dissolving the granulated sugar in the milk over a low heat and then boiling for 2 minutes.
11 Transfer the cooked buns to a wire rack and brush twice with the glaze while still warm.

Gluten-free Bread

MAKES 1 loaf
PREPARATION & COOKING TIME: 35–45 minutes + 30 minutes rising
FREEZING: recommended

Perfect when entertaining friends on gluten-free diets, it's often happily eaten by others as well.

300 g (11 oz) gluten-free flour
80 g (3 oz) ground almonds
1 teaspoon salt
1¹/₂ teaspoons sugar
2 teaspoons easy-blend yeast
150 ml (¹/₄ pint) hand-hot milk
175 ml (6 fl oz) hand-hot water
beaten egg, to glaze (optional)

1 Mix together the flour, almonds, salt, sugar and yeast in a mixing bowl.
2 Beat in the milk and water to form a batter.
3 Pour into a 900 g (2 lb) greased loaf tin and leave to rise for 30 minutes.
4 Preheat the oven to Gas Mark 7/electric oven 220°C/fan oven 200°C.
5 Bake for 25–30 minutes. If you like, brush the loaf with beaten egg after 20 minutes for a more golden appearance. Transfer to a wire rack to cool.

Cheese Scone Ring

MAKES 10–12 slices
PREPARATION & COOKING TIME: 45 minutes
FREEZING: recommended

This is delicious cut into slices and served lightly buttered. Savoury scones are traditionally cut with a plain or straight-sided cutter rather than a fluted one.

115 g (4 oz) butter
1 onion, chopped
450 g (1 lb) self-raising flour
1 tablespoon baking powder
80 g (3 oz) butter
2 tablespoons wholegrain mustard
2 eggs
150 ml (¹/₄ pint) milk
50 g (2 oz) Cheddar cheese, grated

1 Preheat the oven to Gas Mark 6/electric oven 200°C/fan oven 180°C.
2 Heat 25 g (1 oz) of the butter in a frying-pan and fry the onion until soft and golden brown .
3 Sift the flour and baking powder into a mixing bowl and rub in the remaining butter until the mixture resembles fine breadcrumbs.
4 Stir in the cooked onion.
5 Beat together the mustard, eggs and milk. Make a well in the centre of the flour mixture and add enough egg mixture to make a soft dough.
6 Turn on to a floured surface and knead lightly. Form into a long sausage and shape into a ring.
7 Lift on to a greased baking tray, score the top several times with a sharp knife and sprinkle with grated cheese.
8 Bake for 25–30 minutes, until well risen and golden. Transfer to a wire rack to cool.

Lemon Curd *(right)*

MAKES about 1.3 kg (3 lb) ★
PREPARATION & COOKING TIME: 25 minutes

*The beauty of this classic recipe for lemon curd is that the eggs
and the lemon juice are measured and therefore you get a
consistent result whatever the size of eggs or juice content of
the lemons. It is wonderful on toast or as a filling for a
pudding or in a deliciously simple ice cream (see page 56).*

*It can also be cooked in the microwave, which only takes
about 10 minutes, compared with about 40 minutes in a
double-boiler or in a bowl over a pan of hot water.*

200 g (7 oz) butter, preferably unsalted
700 g (1 lb 9 oz) granulated or caster sugar
grated zest of 4–5 lemons
300 ml (^{1}/$_2$ pint) lemon juice (about 4–5 lemons)
300 ml (^{1}/$_2$ pint) beaten eggs (about 4–5 eggs)

1 Place the butter, sugar, lemon zest and juice in a large bowl
  and microwave on full power for about 2 minutes or until
  the butter has melted and the sugar has dissolved. (Or use
  the top of a double-boiler or a bowl over a pan of hot
  water.)
2 Add the beaten eggs and continue cooking in 1-minute
  bursts and stirring each time, reducing to 30 seconds for
  each burst as the mixture thickens, until the mixture is
  thick enough to coat the back of the spoon.
3 Strain through a sieve into a wide-necked jug, to remove
  the lemon zest and any cooked egg bits. Put into cooled,
  sterilised jars and cover with a waxed disc and cellophane.
  Label and store in the refrigerator.

PASSION FRUIT CURD: Add the seeds and pulp of four ripe
passion fruit just before potting.

ELDERFLOWER CURD: Carefully strip the tiny flowers from
the stems of 2–3 handfuls of elderflowers and add to the
curd when cooking.

SERVING IDEAS: Use to fill a meringue pavlova or roulade,
with whipped cream or half and half cream and Greek-style
yogurt.
Serve folded through Greek-style yogurt or a thick natural
yogurt.
Use to fill a freshly baked sandwich cake or Swiss roll.

Orange & Lemon Marmalade

MAKES about 450 g (1 lb)
PREPARATION & COOKING TIME: 1 hour

*This recipe does not contain added sugar. A good way of
cleaning the skins of oranges and lemons is to scrub well
in a solution of 1 tablespoon of cider vinegar to 575 ml
(1 pint) of water. Rinse well and use as required.*

peel of 1 orange, sliced finely
peel of 1 lemon, sliced finely
425 ml (15 fl oz) freshly squeezed orange juice (commercial heat-
   treated orange juice is not suitable)
300 ml (^{1}/$_2$ pint) apple juice concentrate (from healthfood shops)

1 Place the orange and lemon peels in a saucepan with the
  orange juice and simmer gently until the rind is soft –
  about 30 minutes.
2 Add the apple juice and continue to boil for 10 minutes.
  Test for a set. Remove any scum.
3 When setting point is reached (see page 12), pour into
  cooled, sterilised jars and cover. Label and store in the
  refrigerator.

Orchard Jam

MAKES about 2.2 kg (5 lb)
PREPARATION & COOKING TIME: about 2½ hours

Early spring is when you can find good oranges in greengrocers. This is a sort of cross between jam and marmalade in texture and flavour and, like all home-made jam, makes a delicious topping for a steamed sponge pudding. The combined weight of the fruits needs to be around 1.3 kg (3 lb) but don't worry if the proportion of each fruit varies slightly.

225 g (8 oz) oranges, juice squeezed, pips and peel reserved
225 g (8 oz) grapefruits, juice squeezed, pips and peel reserved
225 g (8 oz) lemons, juice squeezed, pips and peel reserved
350 g (12 oz) large cooking apples, peeled, cored and quartered, core reserved
350 g (12 oz) large pears, peeled, cored and quartered, core reserved
1.7 litres (3 pints) water
1.3 kg (3 lb) granulated sugar

1 Cut the citrus peel into thin strips. Tie the apple and pear cores and the citrus pips in a piece of muslin.
2 Put the fruit, juice, peel and muslin bag into a large saucepan, with the water.
3 Simmer gently for 2 hours or until the fruit is very soft and the mixture is reduced by almost half.
4 Press the contents of the bag through a sieve and return the resulting thick purée to the pan. Add the sugar and stir until dissolved.
5 Bring to the boil and boil vigorously for 15 minutes or until setting point is reached (see page 12). Remove any scum.
6 Pour into cooled, sterilised jars, seal and label.

Tangier Jam

MAKES about 2.2 kg (5 lb)
PREPARATION TIME: 15 minutes + overnight soaking
COOKING TIME: 30 minutes

This recipe is a useful standby for when the fruit is finished and the store is empty. It makes a great filling for pancakes and also a topping for ice cream.

225 g (8 oz) dried apricots, chopped
450 g (1 lb) raisins
450 g (1 lb) dates, chopped
450 g (1 lb) peeled weight bananas, chopped
1.8 kg (4 lb) light soft brown sugar

1 Cover the apricots and raisins with water and leave to soak overnight.
2 Drain away the water and place all the fruit in a large preserving pan. Simmer for 15 minutes.
3 Add the sugar and stir until dissolved.
4 Bring to the boil and boil rapidly for about 10 minutes or until setting point is reached (see page 12). Remove any scum.
5 Pot into cooled, sterilised jars, seal and label.

Medicinal Jam

MAKES about 1.3 kg (3 lb)
PREPARATION TIME: overnight soaking + about 20 minutes
COOKING TIME: 30 minutes

This title may sound off-putting but it really is a delicious jam and you do feel that it is doing you some good as you eat it. It is sometimes known as 'All the Year Round Jam' as it is made from dried fruits and nuts which, of course, are always available – good in the spring when your stock of last year's fruit has ended.

115 g (4 oz) whole almonds, blanched and chopped
450 g (1 lb) prunes (preferably ready-stoned prunes)
450 g (1 lb) raisins
450 g (1 lb) demerara sugar

1 Put the nuts and fruit in a bowl and pour on 575 ml (1 pint) of water. Leave to soak overnight.
2 Next day, strain off the water and keep to one side. Chop the prunes and raisins and then place everything, including the reserved water, in a large preserving pan.
3 Heat gently, stirring continuously until all the sugar is dissolved.
4 Bring to the boil and cook rapidly until setting point is reached – about 20 minutes (see page 12). Remove any scum.
5 Pour into cooled, sterilised jars, seal and label.

Rhubarb & Orange Jam

(pictured opposite, left)

MAKES about 2.2 kg (5 lb)
PREPARATION & COOKING TIME: overnight standing
  + 1 hour 40 minutes

*This is just about the easiest and a most delicious jam to make.
It looks great, too.*

1.3 kg (3 lb) rhubarb, cut into 2.5-cm (1-inch) lengths
1.3 kg (3 lb) granulated sugar
grated zest and juice of 1 lemon
2 thin-skinned oranges

1 Put alternate layers of rhubarb and sugar into a non-
   metallic bowl. Add the lemon zest and juice. Cover and
   leave for 24 hours.
2 Next day, boil the oranges in 575 ml (1 pint) of water for
   about 1 hour or until translucent.
3 Cut five thin slices from the oranges and then chop the
   remaining orange, discarding any pips.
4 Place the rhubarb and sugar mixture with the chopped
   oranges into a large preserving pan and bring slowly to the
   boil, stirring until the sugar has dissolved.
5 Boil rapidly until setting point is reached, stirring only
   occasionally. Cool slightly and remove any scum (see page
   12). Stir again.
6 Fill each sterilised jar a quarter full and then slide an
   orange slice down the side of each jar. Fill to the brim
   carefully, without disturbing the orange slice. Cover and
   label on the side opposite the orange slice.

RHUBARB, ORANGE & GINGER JAM: Add 50–80 g (2–3 oz)
finely chopped stem ginger preserved in syrup or crystallised
ginger.

Rhubarb & Fig Jam

(pictured opposite, right)

MAKES about 2.2 kg (5 lb)
PREPARATION & COOKING TIME: overnight standing
  + 55 minutes

1.3 kg (3 lb) rhubarb, cut into 2.5-cm (1-inch) pieces
1.3 kg (3 lb) granulated sugar
225 g (8 oz) dried figs, chopped
juice of 3 lemons

1 Place the rhubarb in a large bowl (not metal) and cover
   with the sugar. Leave overnight.
2 Next day, place the rhubarb, sugar, figs and lemon juice in
   a large preserving pan. Heat gently until the sugar has
   dissolved.
3 Bring to the boil and boil until setting point is reached –
   about 30 minutes. Remove any scum (see page 12).
4 Ladle into cooled, sterilised jars and seal.

Spillikins

MAKES 225–350 g (8–12 oz)
PREPARATION & COOKING TIME: about 30 minutes

Another useful recipe for using up orange peel that would otherwise be discarded. Use as a garnish or decoration for dishes containing oranges.

115 g (4 oz) sugar
thinly pared zest of 2 oranges

1 Dissolve the sugar in 300 ml (¹/₂ pint) of water and then bring to the boil and boil for 3 minutes.
2 Cut the peeled zest into strips – matchstick thickness. Place in a pan with cold water to cover and bring to the boil. Strain.
3 Reboil in fresh water, strain and add to the sugar syrup. Bring to the boil and simmer for 5 minutes.
4 Pour into a cooled, sterilised jar and cover with a twist-top. Label and store in a cool, dry place, for up to 6 months. Once open, use within 2–3 weeks.

Rhubarb & Date Chutney

MAKES about three 450 g (1 lb) jars
PREPARATION TIME: about 20 minutes
COOKING TIME: 1–2 hours

This is a good recipe to make earlier in the year rather than during the usual chutney season in the autumn. It is particularly delicious in a strong-flavoured cheese sandwich or with cold meats.

900 g (2 lb) rhubarb, trimmed and cut into 5-cm (2-inch) chunks
450 g (1 lb) onions, chopped roughly
115 g (4 oz) dates, chopped
300 ml (¹/₂ pint) each of malt vinegar and water
450 g (1 lb) granulated or demerara sugar
1 level tablespoon salt
1 level tablespoon ground ginger
¹/₂ teaspoon cayenne pepper

1 Place all the ingredients in a large saucepan and bring to the boil. Reduce the heat and simmer gently until the chutney has a jam-like consistency and there is no excess liquid on the surface. Stir from time to time to prevent sticking.
2 Allow to cool slightly.
3 Spoon into cooled, sterilised jars and seal with vinegar-proof tops. Label and store for 6–8 weeks before use.

RHUBARB & GARLIC CHUTNEY: Add 2 crushed cloves of garlic and the zest of 1 orange and 1 lemon.

RHUBARB & GINGER CHUTNEY: Omit the dates and add 50 g (2 oz) of finely chopped stem ginger preserved in syrup or crystallised ginger.

RHUBARB & APRICOT, RAISIN OR SULTANA CHUTNEY: Replace the dates with chopped dried apricots or with raisins or sultanas.

Eastern Chutney

MAKES about 1.8 kg (4 lb)
PREPARATION & COOKING TIME: about 1 hour

450 g (1 lb) oranges (3–4 medium-size)
450 g (1 lb) onions, chopped
450 g (1 lb) stoned dates
225 g (8 oz) sultanas
675 g (1¹/₂ lb) demerara sugar
2 teaspoons salt
¹/₂ teaspoon cayenne pepper
575 ml (1 pint) malt vinegar

1 Remove the zest of 1 orange using a potato peeler and leave to one side.
2 Peel all the oranges, removing as much pith as possible. Chop the fruit roughly and discard the pips and the peel (or pop it in a bag in the freezer to make marmalade later).
3 Coarsely mince (or use a food processor to shred) the onions, dates, orange flesh and reserved orange zest and put on a plate.
4 Put the sultanas, sugar, salt, cayenne pepper and vinegar into a preserving pan. Bring the mixture to the boil and add the minced/shredded mixture.
5 Return to the boil and then reduce the heat and simmer until the chutney is thick and free of liquid – about 30 minutes.
6 Spoon the chutney into cooled, sterilised jars and cover with vinegar-proof lids. Label and store for 6–8 weeks before use.

South Seas Chutney

MAKES about 1.5 kg (3 lb 5 oz)
PREPARATION & COOKING TIME: 2½ hours

This was Sue Prickett's entry in the WI Country Markets Millennium Preserve Competition and it came top in Cumbria Westmorland. Sue reckons ripe mangoes are the best choice as they break down more easily. The raspberry vinegar and the lime juice add that indefinable something which is the key to the different and exotic taste.

450 g (1 lb) onions, chopped
300 ml (½ pint) raspberry vinegar
300 ml (½ pint) white wine vinegar
3 mangoes, peeled and chopped
432 g can of crushed pineapple in juice
1 tablespoon grated fresh root ginger
3 teaspoons ground ginger
2 teaspoons ground coriander
1 teaspoons ground cumin
½ teaspoon ground cloves
½ teaspoon ground allspice
2 teaspoons lime juice
50 g (2 oz) sultanas
450 g (1 lb) golden granulated sugar
25 g (1 oz) flaked almonds

1 Gently cook the onion in the vinegars for 5 minutes. Add the mangoes, pineapple with juice, ginger, spices and lime juice and cook until soft – about 40 minutes to 1 hour.
2 Add the sultanas and salt and cook for a further 15 minutes.
3 Add the sugar and cook until reduced and there is no free vinegar. Add the almonds.
4 Spoon into cooled, sterilised jars, seal and label (see pages 16 and 22). Store for 6–8 weeks before using.

Jane's Mango Chutney

MAKES about 1.3 kg (3 lb)
PREPARATION & COOKING TIME: 50 minutes

This recipe comes from Jane Stennett in America. Serve with any curry, or tandoori dishes or cold cuts. It can be used immediately but will develop even more flavour on keeping.

1 tablespoon raisins
6 dried chillies, ground or crumbled
2.5-cm (1-inch) piece of fresh root ginger, shredded
1 teaspoon chilli powder
1 teaspoon black peppercorns, lightly crushed
115 ml (4 fl oz) vinegar
225 g (8 oz) sugar
3 teaspoons salt
2 garlic cloves, crushed
6 green mangoes, peeled and sliced, stones discarded

1 Soak the raisins in just enough water to cover them for 10–15 minutes.
2 Mix together the chillies, ginger, chilli powder and peppercorns.
3 Boil together the vinegar, sugar and salt. Add the chilli-paste mixture, with the garlic and 115 ml (4 fl oz) of water. Cook for 2 minutes.
4 Add the prepared mangoes and simmer for 10–12 minutes. Add the drained raisins .
5 Spoon into cooled, sterilised jars, seal and label (see pages 16 and 22).

Mango Pickle

MAKES six 450 g (1 lb) jars
PREPARATION & COOKING TIME: 1 hour

This pickle is rather a change from the usual mango chutney. It was sent in by Margaret Hanford, of Quorn, in Leicestershire, who has written many books herself. Margaret says it is an excellent way to preserve mangoes; look out for boxes of mangoes which can be bought on markets up and down the country.

3.6 kg (8 lb) ripe mangoes, peeled
pared zest of ½ lemon
15 g (½ oz) whole cloves
15 g (½ oz) whole allspice berries
7 g (¼ oz) fresh root ginger
7 g (¼ oz) cinnamon sticks
1.1 litres (2 pints) distilled or malt vinegar
1.8 kg (4 lb) sugar

1 Cut slices of flesh from the mangoes down to the stone, so that each mango provides 10–12 slices.
2 Place the lemon zest and spices in a muslin bag and secure. Place the vinegar and sugar in a large pan and heat slowly, stirring continuously, until the sugar is dissolved.
3 Add the fruit and the bag of spices and simmer until the fruit is tender but not too soft.
4 Remove the bag of spices and drain the fruit. Pack into cooled, sterilised jars (see page 12–13). Pour the syrup back into the pan and bring to the boil.
5 Boil the syrup until it starts to thicken and then pour over the fruit. Seal with vinegar-proof top (see page 13). Keep any leftover vinegar syrup and use to top up the jars if necessary, as the fruit absorbs the liquid on standing. Allow to mature for at least a month before use.

June brings fresh garlic, renowned for its health benefits. On the Isle of Wight, there's even an annual festival to celebrate it. Fresh beetroot is in season now and goes well with other seasonal produce such as fresh greens and new potatoes. **Elderflower trees** are covered with a froth of white flowers with a pungent scent. They can be used to make drinks (sparkling elderflower champagne is delicious) or to flavour food. Elderflower and gooseberries (also at their peak in June) are a perfect combination.

June is the start of the **soft fruit season** – as well as gooseberries, there are black and red currants, cherries, raspberries and loganberries. It's the time for summer puddings. Fresh peas, ready in June, are ideal for soups and risottos. Eat them soon after picking or they become starchy. July brings tasty French and broad beans, runner beans and globe artichokes. And fennel and shallots are coming in.

Aubergines appear in August but the season is short (they grow better in a Mediterranean climate). Courgettes are at their peak and tomatoes ripe, so there's the makings of **a good ratatouille**.

Broccoli (calabrese) is somewhat overshadowed by its purple sprouting winter relative but it is rich in vitamins and antioxidents and is also thought to fight cancer. Provided it is cooked properly (steaming is best) it is delicate and tasty. The thick stalks can be chopped up and cooked alongside the florets or used in stocks.

Fennel, with its **distinctive** aniseed flavour, can be sliced finely for salads, braised in a little stock or roasted, if blanched first. Use the fronds and stalks for making fish stock.

Summer

Chinese Pak Choi & Noodle Soup *(right)*

SERVES 4 ★
PREPARATION & COOKING TIME: 20 minutes
FREEZING: recommended

This clear soup full of vegetables and noodles is typically Chinese. The pak choi heads, now available in the bigger supermarkets, look like a thinner green version of a head of celery. Use just the vivid green stalks for the soup and save the greenery from the top for a salad or stir fry. Thread noodles are the fine ones, which you just soak in boiling water and they are ready to eat. The brown mushrooms used in this recipe are ideal because, when cooked, they stay fairly firm and have a good flavour.

1 litre (1¼ pints) well flavoured chicken stock (page 9)
1 teaspoon finely chopped fresh root ginger
1 small red chilli, de-seeded and chopped finely
juice of ½ lime (about 1 tablespoon)
1 tablespoon light soy sauce
50 g (2 oz) brown mushrooms (sometimes called Paris or chestnut mushrooms)
2 pak choi heads, finely sliced
150 g (5 oz) fine thread egg noodles
2 tablespoons chopped fresh coriander

1 Put the chicken stock, ginger, chilli, lime juice and light soy sauce in a roomy pan. Over a moderate heat, simmer for 5 minutes.
2 Stir in the mushrooms and the pak choi and continue cooking for another 5–7 minutes or until the green stems are cooked but not soggy.
3 Place the noodles in a bowl and pour boiling water over them. Stir to separate the strands and then drain off the water and divide the wet noodles between four warm bowls.
4 Top up with the soup and decorate each bowl with chopped coriander.

Asparagus & Pea Soup

SERVES 4
PREPARATION & COOKING TIME: 40 minutes
FREEZING: not recommended

This soup is almost as good made at any time of year with canned asparagus and frozen peas.

850 ml (1¼ pints) chicken stock (page 9)
450 g (1 lb) asparagus spears
225 g (8 oz) shelled fresh peas
1 fresh mint sprig
40 g (1½ oz) butter
40 g (1½ oz) plain flour
300 ml (½ pint) milk
salt and freshly ground black pepper
60 ml (4 tablespoons) cream, to serve

1 Into a large saucepan, put the stock, asparagus, peas and mint. Bring to the boil and simmer for 10–15 minutes, until tender.
2 Meanwhile, blend the butter and flour. Bring the milk to the boil and whisk walnut-sized pieces of the blended butter and flour into the milk. Continue cooking until the sauce has thickened.
3 Allow the soup to cool slightly and then purée it.
4 Mix the soup and sauce together. Reheat gently, without allowing it to boil. Adjust the seasoning.
5 Divide between individual bowls and serve each with a swirl of cream.

Borsch

SERVES 4 V
PREPARATION & COOKING TIME: 1 hour 15 minutes
FREEZING: recommended

1 large onion, grated
1 large potato, grated
450 g (1lb) raw beetroot, grated
300 ml (½ pint) tomato juice
575 ml (1 pint) water or vegetable stock (page 8)
1 teaspoon caraway seeds
salt, freshly ground black pepper and freshly grated nutmeg
150 ml carton of soured cream or natural yogurt, to serve

1 Put all the vegetables in large pan, with the tomato juice, stock or water and caraway seeds. Bring to the boil, cover and simmer for 45–60 minutes.
2 Season to taste with salt, pepper and nutmeg.
3 Serve as a coarsely textured soup or cool slightly and then liquidise until smooth.
4 Serve hot or cold, with a generous spoonful of cream or yogurt floating on top.

Cream of Mushroom Soup with Croûtons

SERVES 4 **V**
PREPARATION & COOKING TIME: 40 minutes
FREEZING: recommended for soup (not croûtons) after step 5

50 g (2 oz) butter
450 g (1 lb) mushrooms, chopped finely
1 onion, chopped finely
1 garlic clove, crushed (optional)
25 g (1 oz) plain flour
450 ml (16 fl oz) milk
450 ml (16 fl oz) vegetable (page 8) or chicken stock (page 9)
150 ml carton of single cream
salt and freshly ground black pepper

FOR THE CROÛTONS:
1 thick slice of day-old white bread, crusts cut off, cubed
oil, for frying

1 In a large pan, melt the butter. Sauté the mushrooms in the butter, with the onion and garlic, if using.
2 Add the flour and stir in well. Cook briefly. Add the milk and stock; stir well to make sure the flour is completely blended.
3 Bring to the boil and simmer for 15 minutes.
4 Meanwhile, make the croûtons. Heat the oil and fry the cubes of bread over a brisk heat for a few minutes, until browned on all sides. Remove with a slotted spoon and place on kitchen paper to drain. Keep warm.
5 Cool the soup a little and add the cream. Liquidise for a smoother finish.
6 For a thicker soup, add a little cornflour or arrowroot, blended with a little water.
7 Reheat the soup gently but do not allow it to boil. Check the seasoning and serve at once, with the croûtons.

Sorrel & Cucumber Soup

SERVES 6
PREPARATION & COOKING TIME: 25 minutes + 2 hours chilling
FREEZING: recommended

Sorrel has a sharp, lemony taste and used to be very popular in a sauce for poached salmon.

generous bunch of sorrel leaves, rinsed and picked over, torn up, stems discarded
thin fresh cucumber, chopped (the fat ones have rather big seeds)
1.1 litres (2 pints) chicken stock (page 9)
fat spring onions, chopped
1 garlic clove, sliced
150 ml carton of single cream
salt and freshly ground black pepper

1 Simmer the sorrel, cucumber, stock, spring onions and garlic together in a pan until the cucumber and spring onions are soft.

2 Allow this to cool and then reduce the soup to a purée.
3 Pour in the single cream, stir in well and season to taste. Chill for at least an hour or until ready to serve.
4 Serve cold, in small bowls.

Courgette & Mint Soup

SERVES 4 **V** (If using vegetable stock)
PREPARATION & COOKING TIME: 50 minutes
FREEZING: recommended at step 3

25 g (1 oz) butter
1 onion, chopped
450 g (1 lb) courgettes, chopped into chunks
700 ml (1¼ pints) chicken or vegetable stock (page 9 or 8)
a handful of fresh mint leaves
salt and freshly ground black pepper
4 tablespoons natural yogurt, to serve
4 small fresh mint sprigs or leaves, to garnish

1 Melt the butter in a large pan and cook the onion for 5 minutes over a gentle heat, until soft and transparent. Add the courgettes and cook for a further 5 minutes.
2 Add the stock and half the mint leaves. Cover the pan, bring to the boil and simmer for 20 minutes. Cool slightly
3 Add the remaining mint leaves and purée the soup. (Adding the mint in two batches preserves the flavour of the fresh herb in the finished soup.) Season to taste with salt and pepper.
4 If serving hot, reheat gently.
5 To serve cold, chill the soup for several hours.
6 Serve with a swirl of yogurt and a few mint leaves to garnish.

Courgette & Feta Soup

SERVES 4 **V**
PREPARATION & COOKING TIME: 35 minutes
FREEZING: recommended

2 tablespoons olive oil
1 large onion, chopped
2 garlic cloves, crushed
450 g (1 lb) courgettes, sliced
225 g (8 oz) potato, chopped
1 teaspoon chopped fresh parsley
700 ml (1¼ pints) vegetable stock (page 8)
80 g (3 oz) feta cheese
salt and freshly ground black pepper
chopped fresh parsley, to garnish

1 In a large pan, heat the oil and soften the onion and garlic.
2 Add the courgette and potato and sauté for about 10 minutes.
3 Add the parsley and stock, bring to the boil and cook for 15–20 minutes or until the vegetables are softened.
4 Allow the soup to cool slightly and then reduce to a purée.
5 Add the feta cheese and, off the heat, stir until melted.
6 Gently reheat the soup, without allowing it to boil. Check the seasoning and serve with a scattering of parsley on top.

Gazpacho

SERVES 4 ♥ ★
PREPARATION & COOKING TIME: 30 minutes
FREEZING: recommended

Outdoor tomatoes that are very ripe are the best choice for this soup; next-best are vine tomatoes or plum tomatoes.

6 tablespoons good quality extra-virgin olive oil
1 tablespoon finely chopped onion
2 fat garlic cloves, chopped finely and then crushed
2 red peppers, chopped roughly
1 yellow pepper, chopped roughly
7–8 very ripe tomatoes, chopped roughly
$^1/_2$ large cucumber, chopped roughly, or a sweetly-flavoured small
   cucumber
575 ml (1 pint) chicken stock (page 9)
2 fat pinches of caster sugar
2 teaspoons tomato purée
Tabasco or chilli sauce
white wine vinegar
a large handful of fresh herbs, e.g. basil, tarragon and chervil
snipped fresh chives, to garnish

1 Heat a tablespoon of the oil in a pan and gently fry the
   onion and garlic. Keep the lid on and shake the pan often
   to soften the onions. Set this pan aside to go cold.
2 Set aside a small piece each of red pepper and yellow
   pepper. Put the rest of the peppers, the tomatoes, and
   cucumber into a food processor or blender, with the
   remaining oil, chicken stock, sugar, tomato purée, 1–2
   shakes of Tabasco sauce, a dash of white wine vinegar, the
   cooked onion and garlic and the herbs.
3 Whiz to a smoothish purée. Pour through a nylon sieve.
4 Store in a fridge until needed.
5 Serve in small bowls, with a few bits of reserved and
   chopped red and yellow pepper and chives scattered over.

Tomato & Plum Soup *(above)*

SERVES 4 ♥
PREPARATION & COOKING TIME: 45 minutes
FREEZING: recommended

A sharp, bright red soup that is equally as good served hot or chilled.

1 tablespoon olive oil
1 onion, chopped
450 g (1 lb) red plums, stoned
450 g (1 lb) tomatoes, chopped
300 ml ($^1/_2$ pint) tomato juice
575 ml (1 pint) chicken stock (page 9)
fresh thyme sprig
salt and freshly ground black pepper
1 tablespoon chopped fresh parsley or 4 tablespoons crème fraîche

1 In a large pan, heat the oil and soften the onion, without
   browning.
2 Add all the other ingredients, except the chopped parsley
   and the crème fraîche.
3 Bring to the boil and simmer for 25 minutes or until the
   plums are soft.
4 Cool slightly and then remove the thyme sprig and
   liquidise until smooth.
5 Check the seasoning and then gently reheat or chill, as
   your prefer. Serve with a dollop of crème fraîche on each
   portion or, alternatively, for a healthier version, sprinkle
   each serving with chopped parsley.

Lettuce & Lovage Soup

SERVES 6 **V**
PREPARATION & COOKING TIME: 40 minutes
FREEZING: recommended

Lovage grows like a weed and seeds everywhere. The maddening thing is that the flavour of the leaves is so powerful you rarely need more than three of them; even this recipe needs only 25 g (1 oz). It's best to pick the young top leaves as the lower ones get very tough.

This recipe is based on the excellent book of soups by New Covent Garden Soup Company, though it has been altered slightly. They describe lovage as having an intense, celery-like flavour and say it was once called sea parsley. This great recipe also uses up that flush of lettuce which comes to all of us in summer. You'll get rid of 1.5 kg (3 lb 5 oz)! (Webb's Wonder is excellent but cos or Little Gem would work well too.)

25 g (1 oz) butter
175 g (6 oz) spring onions, chopped
250 g (9 oz) potatoes, chopped small
1.5 kg (3 lb 5 oz) crisp lettuce, chopped
575 ml (1 pint) vegetable stock (page 8)
30 ml (2 tablespoons) lemon juice
25 g (1 oz) young lovage leaves, hard stems removed, chopped
425 ml ($^3/_4$ pint) milk
300 ml carton of single cream
salt and freshly ground white pepper
tiny lovage leaves, to garnish

1 In a roomy pan, melt the butter and gently cook the spring onions, covered, and without burning, until soft. Add the potatoes, lettuce, vegetable stock and lemon juice and cover again.
2 Bring to the boil and then reduce the heat and simmer gently for about 15 minutes, until the vegetables are tender.
3 Cool a little and then reduce to a purée. Return the soup to a clean pan.
4 Stir in the lovage and simmer gently, covered, for a further 5 minutes.
5 Stir in the milk and cream, and season to taste with salt and white pepper.
6 Reheat gently and serve with one or two baby lovage leaves floating on each serving.

Green Vegetable Soup

SERVES 6 **V**
PREPARATION & COOKING TIME: 40 minutes
FREEZING: recommended

Not only does this soup taste delicious but it uses up broccoli stems, the parts you normally discard – though they are actually full of flavour – and asparagus stalks. So, if you are using just the tips of asparagus, for example in a pasta dish or to serve with grilled sole or plaice, this soup is good way to use up the leftover stems.

50 g (2 oz) butter
225 g (8 oz) asparagus stalks
450 g (1 lb) broccoli, stems only
1 leek, sliced
4 spring onions, chopped.
225 g (8 oz) shelled fresh, or frozen, peas
175 g (6 oz) french or green beans
1.1 litres (2 pints) vegetable stock (page 8)
1 fresh parsley sprig
1 fresh thyme sprig
salt and freshly ground black pepper

1 Melt the butter in a large pan. Put the asparagus stalks and the remaining vegetables in the pan. Cover and sweat for approximately 10 minutes.
2 Add the stock and herbs, bring to the boil and simmer for 10–15 minutes until the vegetables are tender. Remove the thyme sprig.
3 Allow to cool slightly and then liquidise until smooth. Return to the pan, check the seasoning and gently reheat before serving.

Tomato & Orange Soup

SERVES 6 ★
PREPARATION & COOKING TIME: 30 minutes
FREEZING: recommended

1 tablespoon oil
1 onion, chopped
2 celery sticks, chopped
6 large tomatoes, quartered and de-seeded
2 bay leaves
850 ml (1$^1/_2$ pints) chicken stock (page 9)
1 tablespoon cornflour
grated zest and juice of 1 orange
salt, and freshly ground black pepper
sugar
6 tablespoons cream, to serve

1 In a large pan, heat the oil and sauté the onion and celery for 3–4 minutes, until softened but not brown.
2 Add the tomatoes, bay leaves and stock.
3 Bring to the boil and simmer for 20 minutes or until the vegetables are tender.
4 Leave to cool for a moment. Remove the bay leaves. Purée the soup and then return to the pan.
5 Blend the cornflour with a little water and blend into the soup, stirring all the time until completely mixed in. Heat gently until slightly thickened.
6 Add the orange zest. Stir in the orange juice and season with salt, pepper and sugar to taste.
7 Divide between serving bowls and add a swirl of cream to each.

Red Pepper, Sweet Potato & Vine Tomato Soup

The hint of chilli powder and cumin makes this a warming soup for the cooler days of summer. Using vine tomatoes, although slightly more expensive, really enhances the flavour of the soup.

1 tablespoon olive oil
1 onion, chopped
2 garlic cloves, crushed
2 red peppers, de-seeded and cubed
250 g (9 oz) sweet potato, peeled and cubed
350 g (12 oz) vine tomatoes, de-seeded and chopped roughly
a pinch of chilli powder
$\frac{1}{2}$ teaspoon ground cumin
850 ml (1$\frac{1}{2}$ pints) vegetable stock
$\frac{1}{2}$ teaspoon sugar
freshly ground black pepper

TO GARNISH:
low fat plain yogurt
chopped fresh parsley

1 Heat the olive oil in a large saucepan and gently cook the onion and garlic for 5 minutes until softened but not browned. Stir in the red peppers, sweet potato and vine tomatoes along with the chilli powder and ground cumin. Cook for a further 5 minutes to soften the vegetables.
2 Pour in the stock, bring up to the boil, reduce the heat and then cover and leave to simmer for 20 minutes until the vegetables are tender.
3 Using a liquidiser or food processor, purée the soup in batches. Pass the soup through a sieve to remove any small pieces of tomato skin and return it to the rinsed-out saucepan. Stir in the sugar and check the seasoning, adding some freshly ground black pepper, if desired. Gently reheat the soup, then serve immediately in warmed bowls, garnishing with a swirl of yogurt and a sprinkling of chopped parsley.

Roasted Red Pepper & Tomato Soup

An interesting soup with a lovely colour and flavour; it can be served either hot or cold.

4 red peppers, cut in half lengthways and de-seeded
6 ripe tomatoes, skinned (see Note) and halved
1 tablespoon oil
5 ml (1 teaspoon) sugar
15 ml (1 tablespoon) chopped fresh basil
1 onion, chopped finely
1 garlic clove, chopped finely or crushed
575 ml (1 pint) vegetable stock (page 8)
salt and freshly ground black pepper
chopped fresh basil, to garnish.

1 Preheat the oven to Gas Mark 5/electric oven 190°C/fan oven 170°C.
2 Place the peppers, skin-side up, and the tomatoes, cut-side up, on a baking sheet. Drizzle with half the oil and sprinkle with the sugar and chopped basil. Roast in the oven for 30 minutes.
3 Meanwhile, in a large saucepan, sauté the onion and garlic in the remaining oil until soft but not browned.
4 Remove the skins from the peppers. Add the peppers, tomatoes and any juices to the saucepan, cover with the stock, and bring to the boil. Turn down the heat and simmer for 15 minutes.
5 Cool slightly and then liquidise until smooth.
6 Season to taste with salt and pepper and gently reheat. Serve garnished with chopped basil.

NOTE: To skin tomatoes, put them in a bowl and pour boiling water over them to cover. Leave for a minute or two and then make a small slit in one end and slip the skins off.

Minestrone Soup *(below)*

SERVES 4–6 ♥ ▼
PREPARATION & COOKING TIME: 1 hour
FREEZING: recommended

1 tablespoon olive oil
115 g (4 oz) pancetta or rindless back bacon, snipped into pieces
1 leek, sliced finely
1 carrot, diced
1 celery stick, sliced finely
1 large onion, chopped finely
400 g can of chopped tomatoes
1.4 litres (2¹/₂ pints) good-quality vegetable, ham or chicken stock
1 bay leaf
1 tablespoon tomato purée
¹/₂ x 410 g can of cannellini or butter beans, rinsed and drained
50 g (2 oz) small pasta, e.g. conchigliette
a handful of fresh basil leaves, torn roughly
175 g (6 oz) Savoy cabbage or spinach, shredded
sea salt and freshly ground black pepper

This timeless Italian soup is packed with goodness, probably providing at least two out of the five recommended daily portions of fruit and vegetables. Adding the cabbage right at the end ensures that it keeps its lovely green colour. All the minerals and vitamins that seep out of the vegetables during cooking are retained in the soup's liquid, together with their flavours.

1 Heat the oil in a large pan. Add the pancetta or bacon, leek, carrot, celery and onion. Toss them in the oil, cover pan with a lid and leave to 'sweat', over a low heat, for 10 minutes, without browning. Shake the pan occasionally.
2 Add the tomatoes, stock, bay leaf and tomato purée. Bring to the boil, cover, and simmer for 20 minutes.
3 Add the beans, pasta and basil. Season and return to the boil. Simmer for another 10 minutes, or until the pasta is cooked.
4 Three minutes before the end of the cooking time, add the cabbage to the pan, cover, and allow it to steam on top of the soup.
5 Stir through the cabbage and serve.

Fish Soup

SERVES 4 ♥
PREPARATION & COOKING TIME: 40 minutes
FREEZING: recommended

This is a low-fat soup but piquant and satisfying. If the taste is too sharp, add a little sugar.

2 onions, sliced
1 leek, white part only, sliced
3 fat garlic cloves, crushed
700 ml (1¼ pints) fish stock (page 8)
1 red pepper, de-seeded and chopped
450 g (1 lb) fresh tomatoes, skinned and chopped
1 tablespoon tomato purée
juice of 1 lemon and grated zest of ½ lemon
1 small cooking apple, cored and chopped
3 tablespoons dry white wine
a bouquet garni of 1 fresh thyme sprig, 1 fresh marjoram sprig and 3
   fresh parsley sprigs, tied with string or white cotton
450 g (1 lb) white fish, cut into bite-sized pieces
3 tablespoons chopped fresh parsley
salt and freshly ground black pepper

1 Soften the onion, leek and garlic in a little of the stock in a large pan over a medium heat for 10 minutes.
2 Add the stock, pepper, tomatoes, tomato purée, lemon zest and juice, apple and wine. Drop in the bouquet garni.
3 Bring to the boil, reduce the heat and simmer for 10 minutes.
4 Remove the bouquet garni. Add the fish and gently simmer for 5 minutes.
5 Adjust the seasoning and stir in most of the parsley.
6 Serve with the remaining parsley scattered on top.

Chicken Pesto Soup *(right)*

SERVES 4–6 ★
PREPARATION & COOKING TIME: 30 minutes
FREEZING: recommended, without pesto

This is Janet Melvin's recipe. She comments that it is colourful, satisfying and there is only one pan to wash at the end of the meal! This is a substantial soup, which can be served as a main course.

1 tablespoon oil
2 chicken leg portions, halved
1 large onion, chopped
2 tablespoons plain flour
1 litre (1¼ pints) chicken stock (page 9)
1 tablespoon tomato purée
80 g (3 oz) pasta shapes, e.g. twists, shells or quills
225 g (8 oz) broccoli, cut into small florets, soft part of stalk sliced
115 g (4 oz) french beans, sliced thickly
3 tablespoons pesto sauce
salt and freshly ground black pepper

1 Heat the oil in a large saucepan and fry the chicken pieces on both sides until browned, about 10 minutes.
2 Add the onion and continue to fry for a further 10 minutes, stirring occasionally.
3 Stir in the flour to combine with the juices.
4 Add the stock and tomato purée and season well. Stir well to make sure the flour is completely blended, bring to the boil, cover and simmer for 15 minutes.
5 Stir in the pasta and cook for 5 minutes.
6 Add the broccoli and beans and cook for a few more minutes, until the vegetables and pasta are tender but not soft.
7 Remove the chicken from the pan. When cool enough to handle, discard the skin and bones and cut the meat into thin strips. Return to the pan, together with the pesto sauce.
8 Stir well, reheat and serve immediately.

Mixed Melon & Tomato Salad with Mint

SERVES 8 ♥ V ★ ▼
PREPARATION TIME: 20 minutes
FREEZING: not recommended

This combination is so refreshing; serve it in the heat of summer as part of a mixed buffet or with poultry, ham or a soft cheese.

¹/₂ Piel de Sapo or honeydew melon, peeled and de-seeded
1 Charentais or cantaloupe melon, peeled and de-seeded
200 g (7 oz) cherry tomatoes
2 tablespoons chopped fresh apple mint
freshly ground black pepper

FOR THE DRESSING:
3 tablespoons fresh orange juice
1–3 teaspoons balsamic vinegar

1 Prepare the salad. Cut the flesh from both melons into 1-cm (¹/₂-inch) cubes, place in a bowl and stir in the cherry tomatoes and mint. Season with pepper. Cover and chill.
2 Prepare the dressing. Stir together the juice and vinegar to taste and season with pepper. Pour into a small non-metallic jug or bowl. Cover and chill.
3 Just before serving stir the dressing into the salad, or serve it separately.

Bruschetta

SERVES 4 ♥ V ★
PREPARATION & COOKING TIME: 15 minutes
FREEZING: not recommended

Bruschetta is a very simple and rustic dish. Eat as a starter or as a quick snack, where it makes an interesting and 'crunchy' alternative to a sandwich.

1 small French stick or a small ciabatta loaf
1 garlic clove
a little good quality olive oil
25 g (1 oz) fresh basil leaves
4 Italian plum tomatoes (on the vine are best for flavour), sliced thinly
salt and freshly ground black pepper

1 Cut the bread in half and split the halves again to make four portions. Grill on both sides until crispy.
2 Remove from the grill and immediately rub the garlic clove over the crusty surfaces, and then sprinkle over a little olive oil.
3 Lay three or four basil leaves on each piece of bread and top with the sliced tomatoes. Season with a little salt and pepper and eat immediately.

Beetroot & Ginger Pasta Salad

SERVES 4 ♥ V ★
PREPARATION & COOKING TIME: 25 minutes
FREEZING: not recommended

This salad can be served at any time of year – it makes a good winter salad served with cold meats and baked potatoes. But it is particularly good when made in the summer with deliciously sweet home-grown beetroot.

175 g (6 oz) pasta shapes such as farfalle or fusilli
1 tablespoon vegetable oil

FOR THE SALAD:
350 g (12 oz) cooked beetroot, diced
3 celery sticks, chopped
2 Comice pears cored, diced and coated in lemon juice
115 g (4 oz) seedless green grapes, halved
5-cm (2-inch) piece of fresh root ginger, grated finely
50 g (2 oz) Brazil nuts, chopped coarsely
2 tablespoons sunflower seeds

FOR THE DRESSING:
150 ml (¹/₄ pint) natural yogurt
2 tablespoons soured cream
2 tablespoons lemon juice
3 tablespoons horseradish sauce
salt and freshly ground black pepper
chopped fresh mint leaves, to garnish

1 Add the pasta and vegetable oil to a large saucepan of boiling, salted water and cook according to the packet instructions. Rinse under running cold water and drain well. Allow to cool completely.
2 In a large bowl stir together the beetroot, celery, pears, grapes, root ginger, nuts and seeds. Gradually add the cooked pasta stirring well.
3 Make the dressing: in a bowl mix together the yogurt, cream, lemon juice, horseradish sauce and seasoning.
4 Stir the dressing into the salad just before serving and sprinkle with chopped mint.

Warm Asparagus with Balsamic Dressing

SERVES 4 ♥ V ★ ▼
PREPARATION & COOKING TIME: 15 minutes
FREEZING: not recommended

English asparagus is the best, and is in season during May and June, but imported makes a good second choice. Trim the tough ends from the spears, and cut the lengths to fit your saucepan, about 18 cm (7 inches). Don't be put off by thinking that asparagus is difficult to cook – it's not! Use the best balsamic vinegar that you can afford.

20 (4–5 per person) asparagus spears, washed and trimmed
2–3 tablespoons walnut or hazelnut oil
2–3 tablespoons balsamic vinegar
50 g (1¼ oz) half fat Parmesan cheese, grated into shavings
Melba toast, to serve (page 28)

1 Bring a large saucepan of salted water to the boil, and drop in the asparagus spears, so that they lie lengthways in the pan, all facing the same way. Turn the heat down to a simmer.
2 Cook for about 8 minutes, then test the spears with the point of a sharp knife – they need to be just cooked. Put four layers of kitchen paper on a plate. Remove the asparagus from the pan with a slotted spoon and place on the kitchen paper to drain.
3 Arrange the spears (facing the same way) on four serving plates. Sprinkle over the oil and vinegar, then shave a little Parmesan over each portion, using the coarse blade of the grater. Serve while still warm with Melba toast.

Asparagus, Melted Cheese & Parma Ham Galette

SERVES 6 ★
PREPARATION & COOKING TIME: 30 minutes
FREEZING: recommended

This is a special tart for entertaining. Asparagus is always a luxury and combined with Parma ham, and creamy Pont L'Evêque cheese you have a quick, yet sumptuous dish. Petit Pont L'Evêque can be bought in a small, 220 g, box in which case you will need to use three quarters. Camembert or Brie could be substituted if they are more readily available.

FOR THE PASTRY:
225 g (8 oz) ready rolled puff pastry
1 egg, beaten

FOR THE FILLING:
115 g (4 oz) asparagus tips
5 ml (1 teaspoon) olive oil
1 teaspoon lemon juice
6 slices (approximately 80 g/3 oz) Parma or Serrano ham
175 g (6 oz) Petit Pont L'Evêque
salt and freshly ground black pepper

1 Preheat the oven to Gas Mark 6/electric oven 200°C/fan oven 180°C.
2 Trim the ends of the asparagus. Blanch the stems in boiling water for 2 minutes, drain and toss them in the olive oil and lemon juice. Season and leave to cool.
3 Cut each slice of ham lengthways. Wrap each asparagus stalk in a piece of ham – don't worry if you have a few stems spare, they can just be popped on the tart anyway.
4 Unroll the pastry from its packaging and lay it on a baking sheet. Using a sharp knife, score a line 1 cm (½ inch) from the edge. Prick the middle well with a fork, and brush it all over with the beaten egg.

5 Arrange the asparagus rolls on the pastry within the scored border; lay any spare asparagus tips in between. Remove and discard the edges of the cheese and thinly slice it. Arrange the cheese slices over the asparagus. Season with freshly ground black pepper.
6 Bake in the centre of the oven for 20–25 minutes, until the pastry is puffy and golden, and the cheese is bubbly and melted. Serve at once.

Smoked Mackerel & Rocket Pâté *(above)*

SERVES 4 ♥ ▽
PREPARATION & COOKING TIME: 15 minutes
   + 1 hour chilling
FREEZING: not recommended

This pâté is delicious as a starter or a light lunch. Serve with slices of wholemeal toast or warm wholemeal rolls and a salad garnish. The warm peppery flavour of rocket leaves complements the richness of the smoked mackerel perfectly.

50 g pack of rocket leaves
225 g (8 oz) smoked mackerel fillets, skinned and flaked
250 g tub of Quark
1 teaspoon horseradish sauce
a squeeze of fresh lemon juice
freshly ground black pepper

1 Place the rocket leaves, smoked mackerel, Quark and horseradish sauce into a food processor. Give several pulses to purée the ingredients, scraping round the sides of the bowl in between, to create a textured pâté.
2 Check the seasoning and add a generous squeeze of lemon juice and some freshly ground black pepper to taste.
3 Transfer to four individual ramekin dishes or one larger bowl, cover and chill for about 1 hour before serving.

Tomato Salsa

SERVES 4
PREPARATION & COOKING TIME: 15 minutes + 1 hour
  standing
FREEZING: not recommended

This just looks so healthy, and equally importantly, tastes wonderful. Visually vibrant, with its red, purple and green colours, the addition of lime juice and chilli makes the flavour 'zing'. Home-prepared salsa is a million miles away from its shop-bought counterpart – a sludgy, soft mass. Salsa's strong taste does tend to dominate, though, so serve it alongside less distinctive food, which it will complement, rather than compete with. It makes a delicious accompaniment grilled white fish or meat. Alternatively, serve as a dip with tortilla chips to scoop it up. Salsa is best eaten fresh, so aim to prepare it only a couple of hours before serving.

4 large ripe tomatoes (vine-ripened ones are best)
1/2 red onion, chopped very finely
2 fat green chillies, de-seeded and chopped very finely
2 tablespoons chopped fresh coriander
juice of 1 lime
a pinch of sugar
sea salt and freshly ground black pepper

1 Wash and dry the tomatoes. Quarter, remove core and
   seeds and chop the flesh finely.
2 Place in a bowl, with the red onion, chillies and coriander.
3 Stir in the lime juice and season with the sugar and salt
   and pepper to taste. Mix well to combine and set aside for
   an hour, to allow the flavours to mingle.

Sweet Red Pepper & Courgette Frittata

SERVES 4–6 ♥ v ★ ▼
PREPARATION & COOKING TIME: 30 minutes
FREEZING: not recommended

Full of flavoursome vegetables, this frittata makes a light meal served with a crisp green salad. Otherwise, allow it to cool, chill it and cut into wedges to make an excellent addition to a picnic for outdoor eating, or to a lunchbox as a change from sandwiches.

1 tablespoon olive oil
4 small new potatoes, unpeeled and cut into 1-cm (1/2-inch) dice
1 small red onion, sliced
1 garlic clove, chopped finely
1 red pepper, de-seeded and sliced
1 small courgette, cut into 5-mm (1/4-inch) slices
6 eggs, lightly beaten
150 g (5 oz) baby plum tomatoes, halved
freshly ground black pepper

1 Heat the oil in a large frying pan, at least 25 cm (10
   inches) in diameter, and add the cubed potatoes, red onion
   and garlic. Cook over a medium heat for about 10 minutes
   until the potatoes are just tender. Stir frequently to prevent
   the vegetables browning. Add the pepper and courgette
   and cook for another 5 minutes.
2 Pour the beaten egg into the pan and scatter in the
   tomatoes. Allow to cook gently for about 5 minutes,
   without stirring, until the egg is beginning to set.
3 Transfer the pan and place it underneath a medium hot
   grill for 2–3 minutes (taking care that the pan handle is
   away from the heat) until the frittata is completely set and
   lightly golden. Remove from the heat, allow to rest for a
   couple of minutes and then slide the frittata on to a
   warmed plate and cut it into four or six wedges for
   serving.

Chicken Timbales

SERVES 6 ▼
PREPARATION & COOKING TIME: 45 minutes
FREEZING: recommended

Serve these little timbales with mixed salad leaves. The timbales are lightly flavoured; if you prefer a stronger flavour replace the tomatoes with a small red pepper, de-seeded and finely chopped. Made into four timbales, these quantities would make a great light lunch dish, served with salad and new potatoes.

375 g (13 oz) skinless chicken fillets or pieces
6 mini plum tomatoes, skinned
4 spring onions, chopped finely
1–2 celery sticks (depending on size), chopped finely
1 teaspoon grated lemon zest
1 tablespoon chopped fresh parsley
1 teaspoon Worcestershire sauce
$^{1}/_{2}$–1 teaspoon mustard
1 egg, beaten
freshly ground black pepper
rocket leaves or fresh dill sprigs, to garnish

1 Preheat the oven to Gas Mark 4/electric oven 180°C/fan oven 160°C. Lightly grease six small ovenproof ramekin dishes (or cups).
2 Dice the chicken into pieces of 5–10 mm ($^{1}/_{4}$–$^{1}/_{2}$ inch) and place in a bowl.
3 Chop the tomatoes into small pieces, discarding any juice that comes out. Add to the chicken.
4 Stir the spring onions, celery, lemon zest, parsley and Worcestershire sauce into the chicken mixture.
5 Beat the mustard into the beaten egg (judge the amount depending on the strength of the mustard). Add this to the chicken mixture. Season with the pepper. Stir to mix well.
6 Spoon into the ramekin dishes, cover with foil and place the dishes on a baking sheet.
7 Bake for about 20 minutes until the mixture has set and any chicken juices are clear. Remove from the oven and allow to stand for 5 minutes, covered. Carefully tip off any juices. Turn out on to individual serving plates and garnish with the rocket or dill.

Warm Chicken & Mushroom Salad

SERVES 4 ♥
PREPARATION & COOKING TIME: 35 minutes
FREEZING: not recommended

An excellent, quick to prepare, light meal for serving on those chillier days during the summer when something warm is called for. Equally, it could be served in smaller portions and used as a starter for six people.

3 tablespoons extra virgin olive oil
1 red onion, sliced
1 garlic clove, chopped finely
150 g (5 oz) chestnut mushrooms, quartered
4 skinless, boneless chicken breasts, cubed
2 tablespoons clear honey
1 tablespoon coarse-grain mustard
2 tablespoons white wine vinegar
freshly ground black pepper
1 large bag of ready-prepared mixed salad leaves
$^{1}/_{2}$ cucumber, diced
100 g ($3^{1}/_{2}$ oz) cherry tomatoes, halved

1 Heat 1 tablespoon of the olive oil in a large pan and cook the sliced onion and garlic for 4–5 minutes until softened. Add the mushrooms to the pan and cook for a further 3–4 minutes. Remove the onions and mushrooms from the pan and set aside.
2 Add the remaining 2 tablespoons of oil to the pan and fry the cubes of chicken over a moderate heat until they are golden brown and cooked through. Add the honey, mustard and white wine vinegar, mixing well to coat the chicken with the dressing. Return the onion and mushrooms to the pan and cook for a further minute to warm through. Season with freshly ground black pepper.
3 Divide the salad leaves between four plates and scatter over the diced cucumber and cherry tomatoes. Top with the cooked chicken mixture and drizzle over any remaining warm dressing from the pan. Serve immediately.

Niçoise Salad

SERVES 4
PREPARATION & COOKING TIME: 40 minutes
FREEZING: not recommended

Make double the amount of French dressing. It will keep in the fridge in a screw top jar for at least three weeks.

100 g (3½ oz) French beans, topped, tailed and halved
2 Little Gem lettuces or 1 Cos lettuce
4 tomatoes, each cut into 8
½ small onion, sliced very finely
175 g can of tuna in brine, very well drained
2 hard boiled eggs, quartered
8–10 black or green olives
chopped fresh parsley, to serve

FOR THE FRENCH DRESSING:
4 tablespoons olive oil
1 tablespoon cider vinegar or tarragon vinegar
a good pinch of sugar
1 garlic clove, crushed
1 teaspoon French mustard
salt and freshly ground black pepper

1 Bring a small saucepan of water to the boil and add the beans. Bring back to the boil, boil for 1 minute, drain, and immediately rinse in cold water.
2 Wash and chop the lettuce into bite size chunks and arrange on a large serving dish. Add the tomatoes, beans, onion and the tuna, broken into chunks.
3 Lay the eggs and olives on top. Then, with very clean hands, gently mix the salad together.
4 Put all the dressing ingredients into a screw top jar and shake well.
5 When ready to serve, toss with the dressing and sprinkle with parsley.

Warm Potato Salad with Capers

SERVES 4 ★
PREPARATION & COOKING TIME: 30 minutes
FREEZING: not recommended

This potato salad is a little different and very easy to make. It can also be served cold.

450g (1lb) small waxy new potatoes, unpeeled
¼ red onion, chopped finely
1 tablespoon capers, drained and chopped
2 tablespoons olive oil
2 teaspoons dried dill
salt and freshly ground black pepper

1 Cut the potatoes into bite size pieces, cover with salted water and simmer for about 10 minutes until just soft.
2 Meanwhile, put the onion, capers, oil, dill, salt and pepper in a salad bowl.
3 Drain the potatoes well and put hot into the salad bowl with the other ingredients. Stir to mix, cover and leave until just warm.

Cucumber Mousse with Prawns

SERVES 6 ▼
PREPARATION & COOKING TIME: 35 minutes + 2 hours setting
FREEZING: not recommended

Set in ramekins these make a good dinner party starter – or serve in a soufflé dish as a great supper dish for three. Melba toast (page 28) would provide a crunchy accompaniment.

1 cucumber, topped, tailed and peeled
300 ml (½ pint) 'light' Greek-style natural yogurt
salt and freshly ground black pepper
freshly grated nutmeg
1 sachet powdered gelatine
1 vegetable stock cube

TO SERVE:
1 bunch of watercress, stems trimmed
175 g (6 oz) prawns, defrosted naturally (if frozen) and well drained
1 lemon, cut into 6 wedges

1 Grate the cucumber, either in a food processor or by hand over a large bowl. Stir in the yogurt, salt, pepper and grated nutmeg.
2 Put 300 ml (½ pint) water, the gelatine and stock cube in a small saucepan. Warm over a very low heat, stirring until it is melted and clear. Leave to cool for 5 minutes.
3 Add the gelatine to the cucumber mixture, stirring and mixing well. Taste to check the seasoning, and pour into a soufflé dish or six ramekins.
4 Leave in the fridge to set for 2 hours. Remove from the fridge an hour before eating. Serve with the watercress, prawns and lemon wedges.

Prawn, Fresh Tomato & Mozzarella Tartlets

MAKES 12
PREPARATION & COOKING TIME: 1 hour
FREEZING: not recommended

*These moreish little tartlets make ideal summer appetisers.
A simple green salad with plenty of watercress or rocket would
set these off superbly.*

1 garlic clove, peeled
1/4 teaspoon sea salt
1 tablespoon olive oil
4 medium tomatoes, skinned, de-seeded and chopped
1 small red chilli, de-seeded and chopped finely
a pinch of sugar
115 g (4 oz) fresh, peeled prawns
2 sheets 48 cm x 26 cm (19 inches x 10½ inches) filo pastry
40 g (1½ oz) butter, melted
80 g (3 oz) mozzarella cheese, cut into small cubes
50 g (2 oz) breadcrumbs
1 tablespoon chopped fresh parsley
freshly ground black pepper

1 Preheat the oven to Gas Mark 5/electric oven 190°C/fan
oven 170°C.
2 Crush the garlic and salt together in a pestle and mortar to
make a smooth purée. Heat the oil in a frying-pan. Sauté
the garlic with the tomatoes and chopped chilli for 8–10
minutes, until the mixture is reduced to a pulp. Season
with pepper and a pinch of sugar. Stir in the prawns.
3 Lay the sheets of filo on the work surface, one on top of
the other, making sure the edges match exactly. Arrange
the pastry so that the shortest edge is at the top. Cut it
from top to bottom into three equal strips. Now cut it in
half across the centre. You should have six pieces. Stack
these on top of each other and cut across twice to make
three equal squares.
4 Take a 12-hole patty tin. You will need three squares of
pastry for each hole. Take one square and brush it with
melted butter and place it in the patty tin. Do the same
with a second square, but lay it at an angle over the first.
Repeat with a third square, so that you have a sort of star
effect. Repeat with the remaining filo to make 12 tartlets.
5 Bake these in the oven for 6–8 minutes, or until just
golden.
6 Spoon the prawn and tomato mixture into the pastry
cases. Scatter cubes of mozzarella cheese over each one.
7 Stir the breadcrumbs into the remaining melted butter and
add the parsley. Sprinkle this over the top of tarts. Bake
the tartlets in the oven for 15–20 minutes, until the
breadcrumbs are crisp and golden and the cheese is melted.
Serve at once.

NOTE: Never reheat a dish containing prawns.

Crunchy Vegetable Saté Stir-fry

SERVES 4 **V** ★ ▼
PREPARATION & COOKING TIME: 30 minutes
FREEZING: not recommended

A tasty combination of crunchy stir-fried vegetables in a spicy peanut sauce makes a satisfying vegetarian main course. The golden rule for successful stir-frying is to ensure the vegetables are cut into pieces of approximately the same size, to ensure quick and even cooking.

80 g (3 oz) green beans, topped, tailed and cut into 5-cm (2-inch) pieces
115 g (4 oz) broccoli, sliced diagonally
2 tablespoons vegetable oil
2 garlic cloves, sliced
4 thin slices fresh root ginger
1 red chilli, de-seeded and sliced finely
115 g (4 oz) mange tout, topped and tailed
2 sticks celery, sliced diagonally
50 g (2 oz) courgettes, cut into strips
150 ml (¼ pint) vegetable stock (page 8)
4 tablespoons smooth peanut butter
50 g (2 oz) roasted salted peanuts
salt and freshly ground black pepper

1 Blanch the beans and broccoli in boiling, salted water for 30 seconds. Drain and refresh in cold water, drain again.
2 Heat the oil in a preheated wok or large frying pan, add the garlic, ginger and chilli and stir-fry to release the flavours.
3 Reduce the heat and add the mange tout to the pan, stir-fry for 1 minute. Add the celery, courgettes, broccoli and beans to the pan, and stir-fry for another minute until the vegetables are cooked but still crisp and bright green.
4 Stir in the vegetable stock and peanut butter, and heat through until bubbling. Add seasoning and the peanuts, and simmer for 2 minutes. Transfer to a serving dish and serve immediately.

Roast Halloumi Cheese Peppers

SERVES 4–6 **V**
PREPARATION & COOKING TIME: 1 hour
FREEZING: not recommended

Greek Halloumi cheese is a creamy-tasting chewy textured cheese that is most often served cooked. Here it is used to top differently coloured stuffed peppers for a light lunch. The peppers are stuffed with a spicy nut mixture flavoured with cayenne pepper. Cayenne is a pungent red, fiery-hot powder ground from the dried seeds and pods of red chillies.

6 small peppers, halved through the stalks and de-seeded
4 tablespoons olive oil
3 garlic cloves, crushed
16 fresh mint leaves, torn up
zest and juice of 1 lemon
3 tablespoons pine nut kernels
3 tablespoons flaked almonds
1 tablespoon cayenne pepper
225 g (8 oz) Halloumi cheese, sliced thinly
salt and freshly ground black pepper

1 Brush the inside and outside of the peppers with half the olive oil.
2 Place the peppers skin side down on a large baking sheet.
3 In a small bowl mix together the remaining olive oil, garlic, mint leaves, lemon zest and juice, pine nut kernels, almonds, cayenne and seasoning. Divide this between the peppers.
4 Scatter the cheese over the top of the peppers.
5 Bake at Gas Mark 6/electric oven 200°C/fan oven 180°C for 30–40 minutes, until the peppers are tender and charred at the edges.

Tomato, Spinach & Ricotta Lasagne *(below)*

SERVES 4–6 ♥ v ▼
PREPARATION & COOKING TIME: 1 hour 15 minutes
FREEZING: not recommended

8 sheets of lasagne
25 g (1 oz) reduced fat Cheddar cheese, grated
1 tablespoon grated Parmesan cheese
torn basil leaves, to garnish

FOR THE TOMATO SAUCE:
1 tablespoon olive oil
1 onion, chopped finely
2 garlic cloves, crushed
2 x 400 g cans of chopped tomatoes
1 tablespoon tomato purée
$\frac{1}{2}$ teaspoon dried basil
$\frac{1}{2}$ teaspoon sugar
150 ml ($\frac{1}{4}$ pint) vegetable stock (page 8)

FOR THE SPINACH LAYER:
450 g frozen spinach, defrosted
250 g tub of ricotta cheese
$\frac{1}{2}$ teaspoon ground nutmeg
freshly ground black pepper

Tomato, spinach and ricotta are classic flavourings to accompany pasta but they are normally used to create cannelloni. This is an easier to assemble version made into a lasagne. You can use ready-to-cook dried sheets of lasagne, but I think the fresh lasagne bought from the chiller cabinet gives a better result. Any left over can be frozen and used another time. Serve with a salad accompaniment.

1 Preheat the oven to Gas Mark 5/electric oven 190°C/fan oven 170°C.
2 To make the tomato sauce, heat the olive oil in a large saucepan and gently cook the onion and garlic until softened. Add the chopped tomatoes, tomato purée, dried basil, sugar and vegetable stock. Bring the mixture up to the boil, cover, then reduce the heat and simmer for 20–25 minutes until the sauce has slightly thickened.
3 Meanwhile, place the defrosted spinach in a sieve and, using the back of a wooden spoon, press against the spinach to remove as much of the excess water as possible. Turn the spinach into a bowl and mix in the ricotta, nutmeg and a good grinding of black pepper.
4 Pour half the tomato sauce over the base of a shallow ovenproof dish, measuring about 20 x 28 cm (8 x 11 inches). Place a layer of four lasagne sheets over the sauce. Spread over the spinach and ricotta mixture, then the last four sheets of lasagne. Cover with the remaining tomato sauce. Sprinkle over the reduced fat Cheddar cheese and the grated Parmesan.
5 Bake in the oven for 25–30 minutes until the cheese on top is melted and lightly browned and the lasagne is heated through. Serve immediately.

Artichoke, Salami & Mushroom Pizza (*opposite*)

SERVES 3
PREPARATION & COOKING TIME: 1 hour
FREEZING: not recommended

Pizzas are not difficult to make at home and have the advantage of tasting much fresher. As a compromise you could always buy a ready-made base and do your own topping. Rustica (crushed tomatoes) or passata (sieved tomatoes) are pure tomato, bottled, and make a ready-made, natural sauce. Serve with a mixed leaf salad.

FOR THE BASE:
225 g (8 oz) strong white bread flour
1 teaspoon easy-blend dried yeast
1/2 teaspoon coarse sea salt
1 tablespoon olive oil

FOR THE TOPPING:
2 teaspoons extra virgin olive oil
150 ml (1/4 pint) rustica or passata
1 garlic clove, chopped finely
15 g (1/2 oz) fresh basil leaves, a few sprigs reserved for garnish and the remainder torn
1/2 x 390 g can of artichoke hearts, drained and halved
115 g (4 oz) button mushrooms, wiped and sliced
25 g (1 oz) Italian salami with peppercorns slices, halved
125 g pack of buffalo mozzarella, drained, dried and sliced thinly
1/2 small red onion, sliced thinly and the rings separated
12 black olives
15 g (1/2 oz) Parmesan cheese shavings

1 In a mixing bowl, combine the flour, yeast and salt. Make a well in the centre and pour in the oil and 150 ml (1/4) pint of warm water. Mix to combine and then tip out on to a work surface and knead for 10 minutes by hand (5 minutes if you have a machine) until the dough is smooth. Place in an oiled polythene bag, in a warm place, for about 15 minutes, while you prepare the pizza topping.
2 Preheat the oven to Gas Mark 7/electric oven 220°C/fan oven 200°C. Grease a baking sheet.
3 Either roll out the dough on a lightly floured work surface or shape with your hands into a 30-cm (12-inch) round. Place on the greased baking sheet and brush the surface of the dough lightly with 1 teaspoon of the oil, to form a waterproof layer.
4 Smooth the tomato sauce evenly over the surface. Scatter with garlic and basil. Then top with the remaining ingredients, in the order they are listed.
5 Cover loosely with an oiled polythene bag and leave in a warm place for 15 minutes, to enable the dough to puff up slightly.
6 Remove the bag and drizzle the remaining teaspoon of oil over the pizza. Bake in the centre of the oven for 15–20 minutes. Check after 15 minutes and dab off any liquid that has come out of the mushrooms or tomato with a little kitchen paper. Return to the oven for a further 5 minutes if you like a more crisp pizza.
7 Serve with Parmesan shavings and basil leaves.

Pissaladière

SERVES 6
PREPARATION & COOKING TIME: 30 minutes + 1½ hours proving + 20–25 minutes cooking
FREEZING: recommended

Pissaladière combines elements of quiche and pizza, unsurprisingly as it is a native dish of Provence where the cuisine is greatly influenced by neighbouring Italy. Subtle variations in the dish occur according to regions – wine, tomatoes and garlic may or may not be included. Likewise the tart may be dough or pastry based.

FOR THE DOUGH:
225 g (8 oz) strong white bread flour
1/2 teaspoon salt
7 g sachet of easy-blend dried yeast
1 tablespoon olive oil
150 ml (1/4 pint) warm water

FOR THE FILLING:
4 tablespoons olive oil, plus extra for brushing
900 g (2 lb) Spanish onions, peeled, halved and sliced thinly
1 teaspoon fresh chopped thyme, or 1/2 teaspoon dried thyme
2 garlic cloves, crushed
350 g (12 oz) tomatoes, skinned, de-seeded and chopped
50 g can of anchovy fillets, drained and halved lengthways
12 black olives, stoned and halved
salt and freshly ground black pepper
fresh oregano, to garnish

1 For the dough, mix together the flour, salt and yeast. Stir in the oil and water and mix to a soft dough. Turn the dough out on to a work surface and knead for 10 minutes (5 minutes if you have a machine) until it feels smooth. Place in an oiled polythene bag and leave it in a warm place for about 1 hour, to double in size.
2 To make the filling, heat the oil in a large saucepan. Add the onions, thyme and garlic and sauté, covered, for 30 minutes. Stir the mixture occasionally, until it begins to soften. Remove the lid and continue cooking for a further 30 minutes until the liquid has evaporated, stirring occasionally. Season with salt and pepper. Cool the mixture slightly.
3 Preheat the oven to Gas Mark 7/electric oven 220°C/fan oven 200°C.
4 Push the dough into an oiled rectangular baking tin 28 cm x 23 cm (11 inches x 9 inches). Brush the surface with olive oil and then spread it with the onion mixture. Scatter chopped tomatoes over the top. Arrange the anchovy fillets in a diamond pattern and stud with halved olives. Prove in a warm place for 30 minutes before baking in the centre of the oven for 20–25 minutes. Serve scattered with fresh oregano leaves.

Courgette & Gruyère Flan

SERVES 4 **V**

PREPARATION & COOKING TIME: 40 minutes + 30 minutes
  chilling + 45–50 minutes cooking
FREEZING: recommended

FOR THE WHOLEMEAL PASTRY:
115 g (4 oz) wholemeal flour
1 teaspoon baking powder
25 g (1 oz) butter or block margarine
25 g (1 oz) lard or white vegetable fat

FOR THE FILLING:
15 g (¹/₂ oz) butter
1 small onion, halved and sliced thinly
225 g (8 oz) courgettes, sliced into 5-mm (¹/₄-inch) rings
1 teaspoon chopped fresh thyme
80 g (3 oz) Gruyère cheese, grated
2 large eggs
300 ml (¹/₂ pint) double cream
salt and freshly ground black pepper

Wholemeal pastry gives this flan a delicious flavour and nutty texture. Adding baking powder ensures a much lighter result than you would expect. This is a good recipe for the summer months when courgettes are at their best. Slices of this flan make great picnic fare. Alternatively, you could serve this warm with a tomato salsa (page 88).

1 For the pastry, mix the flour and baking powder together in a bowl. Rub in the butter and lard or vegetable fat. Stir in 2 tablespoons cold water and bring it all together to form a ball of dough.

2 On a lightly floured surface roll out the pastry and use it to line a deep 20-cm (8-inch) flan tin. Prick the base with a fork and chill for at least 30 minutes.

3 Preheat the oven to Gas Mark 6/ electric oven 200°C/fan oven 180°C. Place a baking sheet on the middle shelf.

4 For the filling, melt the butter in a frying-pan and add the onion and courgettes. Sauté for about 5 minutes, until the onion has softened and the courgettes have started to turn golden.

5 Bake the pastry case blind for 15 minutes. Remove the foil or paper and beans and return to the oven for a further 5 minutes.

6 Scatter the courgette mixture over the pastry base and sprinkle with the thyme and grated cheese. Whisk together the eggs, cream and seasoning, and pour this into the flan case. Bake in the oven for 30–35 minutes, until puffy and golden.

Tomato Tarte Tatin (*above*)

SERVES 6 **V** ▼
PREPARATION & COOKING TIME: 50 minutes
FREEZING: recommended

This is a savoury tarte tatin – really an upside down tomato pie. With good-flavoured tomatoes, it makes an unusual supper or light lunch dish.

225 g (8 oz) plain flour
1 heaped teaspoon baking powder
salt and freshly ground black pepper
50 g (2 oz) butter
150 ml (¼ pint) semi-skimmed milk
450 g (1 lb) plum tomatoes, or other good-flavoured vine tomatoes
2 tablespoons olive oil
1 teaspoon dried basil
8 fresh basil leaves, to garnish

1 Sieve the flour and baking powder into a large bowl. Season with salt and pepper. Rub in the fat using just your fingertips. Add the milk to make a soft dough, and set aside.
2 Meanwhile, skin the tomatoes (page 82) and cut each one into three thick slices.
3 Preheat the oven to Gas Mark 7/electric oven 220°C/fan oven 200°C.
4 Put the oil into a shallow, round ovenproof dish about 24-cm (9½-inches) in diameter. Lay the tomatoes on the bottom of the dish, sprinkle over the dried basil, salt and pepper.
5 Roll the dough out to fit over the tomatoes, put on top and tuck the edges inside the dish to seal. Cook in the oven for about 30 minutes until the crust is well risen and golden.
6 Remove from the oven, and release the edges with a knife. Leave to cool for 4 minutes, then turn upside down on to a serving dish. Scatter over the fresh, torn basil, and serve warm.

Summer Vegetable Risotto

SERVES 4 ♥ **V**
PREPARATION & COOKING TIME: 45 minutes
FREEZING: not recommended

Risottos make very simple yet elegant meals and are not as difficult to cook successfully as many believe. A basic risotto is a wonderful vehicle for all sorts of additions, and here a mixture of fresh summer vegetables have been used to help ensure a good supply of vitamins and antioxidants. Accompany with a crisp salad, if desired.

1 tablespoon olive oil
1 onion, chopped
2 garlic cloves, chopped
100 g (3½ oz) asparagus tips
1 courgette, sliced
350 g (12 oz) risotto rice
300 ml (½ pint) dry white wine
1 litre (1¼ pints) hot vegetable stock (page 8)
125 g (4½ oz) shelled broad beans, defrosted if using frozen
2 ripe tomatoes, de-seeded and chopped
2 tablespoons chopped fresh parsley
1 tablespoon roughly torn fresh basil
25 g (1 oz) Parmesan cheese, freshly grated
freshly ground black pepper

1 Heat the oil in a large frying pan and gently cook the onion and garlic for 3–4 minutes until softened but not coloured. Transfer to a plate using a slotted spoon. Add the asparagus tips and courgette slices to the pan and cook for 3–4 minutes. Remove to the plate and keep warm.
2 Add the risotto rice and cook for about 1 minute, stirring, to allow the grains to become coated with the oil. Pour in the wine, bring up to the boil, then reduce the heat and simmer gently, stirring until the wine has been absorbed.
3 Add half the hot vegetable stock and bring to the boil. Again, reduce the heat and simmer gently, stirring until the stock is absorbed. Add half of the remaining stock along with the broad beans. Bring to the boil and then allow to simmer gently until the liquid is absorbed.
4 Add the last of the stock and bring to the boil, Simmer gently until the stock is absorbed and the rice is tender. As a guide, the whole process of adding stock and simmering to cook the rice should take no more than about 25 minutes. If it has taken less time then the rice may not be thoroughly cooked but if it takes longer, then the rice is being overcooked. The consistency of the risotto should be thick and creamy with the grains of rice soft but still retaining a little bite.
5 Stir in the tomatoes, herbs and the reserved vegetables, along with the Parmesan and some freshly ground black pepper. Mix gently. Remove from the heat, cover the pan and leave to stand for 4–5 minutes to allow the flavours to mix. Serve on warmed plates.

Chick Pea Burgers
with Tomato Salsa *(above)*

SERVES 4 **V** ▼

PREPARATION & COOKING TIME: 40 minutes + 1 hour
  cooling
FREEZING: recommended

These spicy burgers make a great healthy alternative to meat
burgers, and can be served in a bun with salad if you prefer.

2 x 400 g cans of chick peas, rinsed and drained
2 tablespoons olive oil
1 small onion, chopped finely
1 garlic clove, crushed
1 red pepper, de-seeded and finely chopped
2 tablespoons chopped fresh coriander
1 fresh red chilli, de-seeded and finely chopped
salt and freshly ground black pepper
a little sunflower oil or cooking spray to fry the burgers
tomato salsa (page 88), to serve

1 Put the chick peas into a food processor, and pulse two or
  three times to lightly mix – you do not want them to be
  mushy but to retain some texture. Turn into a large bowl.
2 Heat the olive oil and gently fry the onion, garlic and
  pepper for 5 minutes to soften. Add to the chick peas, with
  the coriander, chilli, salt and pepper.
3 Stir to mix well and cool in the fridge for at least 1 hour,
  or overnight. Divide the mixture into eight and shape into
  burgers (you may need a little flour to do this).
4 Heat the sunflower oil or cooking spray in a non-stick
  frying pan and fry the burgers for 3 minutes on each side
  until they are golden and crispy.
5 Drain on kitchen paper. Serve warm with the tomato salsa.

Grilled Swordfish Steaks
with a Warm Tomato
& Herb Dressing

SERVES 4 ♥

PREPARATION & COOKING TIME: 50 minutes
FREEZING: not recommended

Swordfish, increasingly available although still fairly expensive,
makes an excellent choice for a dinner party main course. It is
meaty and substantial so can take quite robust flavourings.
This warm dressing with olive oil, lemon juice and fresh herbs
is an excellent accompaniment to the fish. Be careful not to
overcook the steaks, they only need 3–4 minutes on each side.
Serve with freshly boiled new potatoes and a green salad.

4 swordfish steaks (about 175 g/6 oz each)
olive oil for brushing
freshly ground black pepper

FOR THE DRESSING:
2 large tomatoes, peeled, de-seeded and chopped
2 shallots, chopped finely
1 garlic clove, crushed
2 tablespoons chopped fresh chives
2 tablespoons chopped fresh flat leaf parsley
1 tablespoon roughly torn fresh basil
115 ml (4 fl oz) extra virgin olive oil
zest and juice of 1 lemon
freshly ground black pepper

1 Combine the tomatoes, shallots, garlic, herbs, olive oil and
  the lemon zest and juice in a bowl. Give a good grinding
  of black pepper, stir well and set aside for 30 minutes to
  allow the flavours to mingle.
2 Preheat the grill until hot. Place the swordfish steaks on a
  grill rack and brush each side with a little olive oil and
  season with freshly ground black pepper. Put under the
  heat and grill for 3–4 minutes each side. Do not allow to
  overcook and dry out.
3 While the fish is grilling, transfer the dressing to a small
  saucepan and warm through gently for 2–3 minutes.
4 Serve the swordfish steaks with the warmed dressing
  drizzled over each one.

Provençal Fish Casserole *(above)*

SERVES 4
PREPARATION & COOKING TIME: 1 hour
FREEZING: recommended

Many traditional Provençal dishes feature generous amounts of garlic, this casserole uses just a couple of cloves, but if you prefer a stronger flavour add a couple more. Any firm-fleshed white fish such as monkfish or haddock can replace the cod.

2–3 tablespoons olive oil
2 large onions, chopped roughly
2 garlic cloves, chopped roughly
2 tablespoons coarsely chopped fresh parsley
450 g (1 lb) tomatoes, skinned and chopped roughly
115 ml (4 fl oz) dry white wine
1 teaspoon fresh or ½ teaspoon dried marjoram
4 cod steaks (approx 675 g/1½ lb total weight), skinned
50 g (2 oz) black olives
1 tablespoon tomato purée
salt and freshly ground black pepper
fresh parsley, to garnish

1 Heat the oil in a large deep frying pan and gently fry the onions, garlic and parsley over a low heat for 5–8 minutes.
2 Add the tomatoes. Mix well, and then stir in the wine, marjoram and seasoning.
3 Simmer, uncovered, for about 20 minutes.
4 Place the cod steaks in the pan and cover with the sauce. Add the olives and stir in the tomato purée. Cook, uncovered, over a very gentle heat for 20–25 minutes.
5 Serve garnished with fresh parsley.

Stuffed Layered Trout

SERVES 4
PREPARATION & COOKING TIME: 45 minutes
FREEZING: not recommended

Stuffed with tomatoes, spring onions, celery and almonds then wrapped in foil and baked until tender, this simple dish takes very little effort but looks and tastes wonderful. Serve to friends with buttered new potatoes and roasted vegetables as an alternative to a Sunday roast in summer.

4 rainbow trout, each weighing 300–350 g (11–12 oz) cleaned
4 firm tomatoes, sliced
8 spring onions, chopped
2 celery sticks, chopped
50 g (2 oz) wholemeal breadcrumbs
50 g (2 oz) flaked almonds
2 tablespoons finely chopped fresh parsley
4 tablespoons lemon juice

1 Wash the trout and dry with kitchen paper.
2 Place slices of tomatoes in the pocket of the fish.
3 In a small bowl place the spring onions, celery, breadcrumbs, almonds and parsley and mix well. Divide the mixture into four and fill the fish pockets with the stuffing.
4 Place each trout on a piece of buttered foil, sprinkle over the lemon juice and then seal.
5 Place in a baking dish and cook at Gas Mark 4/electric oven 180°C/fan oven 160°C for 30–35 minutes until the fish is cooked and tender.

Tuna Stacks

SERVES 4 ♥
PREPARATION & COOKING TIME: 1 hour 15 minutes
FREEZING: not recommended

Fresh tuna is a meaty fish and has quite a different flavour from the canned variety. This meal is cooked in one dish to combine the great flavours of the vegetables and fish, and only needs a simple accompaniment of crusty bread. Salmon steaks can be used as an alternative.

1 aubergine, sliced
1 onion, chopped
2 carrots, sliced thinly
2 courgettes, sliced
4 tomatoes, quartered
50 g (2 oz) butter
4 tuna steaks, approx 225–300 g (8–11 oz) each
salt and freshly ground black pepper

FOR THE TOPPING:
115 g (4 oz) wholemeal breadcrumbs
50 g (2 oz) Cheddar cheese, grated
1 cooking apple, cored and chopped finely

1 Place the aubergine, onion, carrots, courgettes and tomatoes into an ovenproof dish, season well.
2 Dot the vegetables with the butter, then place the tuna steaks on top of the vegetables.
3 In a small bowl combine the topping ingredients and spread evenly over the fish.
4 Bake at Gas Mark 4/electric oven 180°C/fan oven 160°C for 45–60 minutes until the vegetables and fish cooked.
5 Serve as a stack with the vegetables underneath the tuna.

Salmon with Crème Fraîche & Watercress Sauce

SERVES 4 ♥
PREPARATION & COOKING TIME: 35 minutes
FREEZING: not recommended

The delicate shade of this sauce is perfect against the brighter colour of the pink salmon. However, its rich nutritional value, from the antioxidants and minerals in the watercress, is even more attractive. Also, using half fat crème fraîche in the sauce means that the fat content is kept as low as possible

4 x 150 g (5 oz) pieces salmon fillet, skinned
1 tablespoon vegetable oil, plus extra for greasing
juice of ¹/₂ lemon

FOR THE SAUCE:
1 tablespoon vegetable oil
3 shallots, chopped finely
1 celery stick, trimmed and chopped finely
300 ml (¹/₂ pint) vegetable stock (page 8)
75 g (2³/₄ oz) watercress, rough stalks removed
150 ml (¹/₄ pint) half fat crème fraîche
freshly ground black pepper

1 Preheat the oven to Gas Mark 6/electric oven 200°C/fan oven 180°F.
2 To make the sauce, heat the oil in a pan and gently fry the shallots and celery for 4–5 minutes until softened. Pour in the stock, bring to the boil and bubble vigorously until the liquid is reduced by half.
3 Pour the mixture into a liquidiser and blend. Add the watercress and crème fraîche in stages, blending each time to create a smooth sauce. Return the sauce to the pan and reheat gently but do not allow to boil. Check the seasoning and add some freshly ground black pepper if required.
4 Place the salmon fillets on a lightly greased baking sheet and brush with the vegetable oil. Sprinkle over the lemon juice. Bake in the oven for 10–15 minutes until the salmon is cooked. Serve immediately accompanied by the sauce.

Fresh Tuna with Green Beans & Tomato *(below, left)*

SERVES: 2 ♥ ▼
PREPARATION & COOKING TIME: 40 minutes
FREEZING: not recommended

Fresh tuna is one of the oily fish that we should be eating at least once a week. If you prefer, cook the tuna steaks on a ridged griddle or in an oiled frying pan for 2–3 minutes on each side. This will only very slightly increase the fat content and the tuna will be firmer, drier and have more colour. Serve with boiled new potatoes in their skins.

¹/₂ teaspoon oil
1 small onion, chopped finely
2 tuna fish steaks, each about 1.5 cm (⁵/₈ inch) thick
2 tablespoons white wine or 1 tablespoon water mixed with 1 tablespoon fresh lime juice
200 g (7 oz) green beans, left whole if small (about 10 cm/4 inches long)
6 cherry tomatoes
¹/₂ tablespoon chopped fresh basil or ¹/₂ teaspoon dried basil
freshly ground black pepper

1 Heat the oil in a heavy-based small saucepan. Add the onion, cover and cook over a very low heat for 10–15 minutes, until the onion is softened and golden in colour.
2 Preheat the oven to Gas Mark 6/electric oven 200°C/fan oven 180°C and prepare a steamer for the beans.
3 Cover a baking sheet with foil and place the tuna steaks in the centre of this. Season well with black pepper and then lift the foil at the edges to form a 'wall'. Pour the wine or water over the fish and then fold the foil to make a loose parcel. Bake for 15 minutes, or until the steaks are tender.
4 Meanwhile, steam the beans until tender, about 8–10 minutes.
5 When the onion is ready, add the cherry tomatoes and cook with the lid on until the skins have split and the tomatoes are hot, 4–5 minutes. If using dried basil, add it now.
6 Divide the beans between two plates, spoon the tomato mixture over them and sprinkle with the fresh basil, if using.
7 Place a tuna steak on top or by the side of each portion of vegetables.

Broccoli & Smoked Salmon Roulade *(below)*

SERVES 4–6 ♥ ▼

PREPARATION & COOKING TIME: 50 minutes + 1 hour chilling

FREEZING: not recommended

Savoury roulades are as good to enjoy as the sweet varieties and make an excellent main course for a warm summer day. Equally, an individual slice of roulade with a small salad garnish would make a very acceptable starter to a meal.

225 g (8 oz) broccoli florets
4 eggs, separated
a generous pinch of grated nutmeg
freshly ground black pepper

FOR THE FILLING:
200 g (7 oz) smoked salmon slices
200 g (7 oz) low fat cream cheese
2 tablespoons low fat plain yogurt
2 ripe tomatoes, peeled, de-seeded and chopped finely
1 tablespoon snipped fresh chives

1 Preheat the oven to Gas Mark 7/electric oven 220°C/fan oven 200°C. Line a 33 x 23 cm (13 x 9 inch) Swiss roll tin with non-stick baking parchment.

2 Steam or gently simmer the broccoli florets until tender. Drain thoroughly, turn them on to a plate and chop finely. Place in a large mixing bowl with the egg yolks, the nutmeg and a grinding of black pepper. Mix well.

3 In a separate large bowl, whisk the egg whites until stiff but not dry. Stir 1 tablespoon of egg white into the broccoli mixture to loosen it slightly, then carefully fold in the remainder, taking care not to knock out any of the volume. Spread the broccoli mixture evenly into the prepared tin and bake in the oven for 10–12 minutes until firm and lightly golden.

4 Place a clean sheet of non-stick baking parchment on the work surface. Turn the roulade out on to the paper and leave to cool for 5 minutes. Peel off the lining paper and trim the edges of the roulade.

5 Carefully separate the slices of smoked salmon and lay them over the surface of the roulade. Mix together the cream cheese, yogurt, tomatoes and chives and spread in an even layer over the smoked salmon.

6 Using the sheet of baking parchment, roll up the roulade in the same way as a Swiss roll and, leaving it in the paper, chill in the fridge for about an hour to firm up. When ready to serve, remove the roulade from the paper and cut into thick slices.

Smoked Mackerel & Pasta Salad

SERVES 4 ♥ ★
PREPARATION & COOKING TIME: 25 minutes
FREEZING: not recommended

A colourful, crunchy salad and an interesting way to use smoked mackerel. Do remember that smoked fish have a higher salt content and so it is unlikely that you will need to add salt to the salad dressing – a good grinding of black pepper will be sufficient. Serve with some warmed crusty bread.

150 g (5 oz) dried fusilli pasta
4 smoked mackerel fillets, skinned and flaked
1 bunch of spring onions, trimmed and sliced
1 pink grapefruit, peeled and segmented
1 red apple, cored and chopped
2 celery sticks, trimmed and sliced
1 small bag of mixed salad leaves

FOR THE DRESSING:
115 ml (4 fl oz) extra virgin olive oil
4 tablespoons white wine vinegar
1 dessertspoon clear honey
1 tablespoon coarse grain mustard
freshly ground black pepper

1 Cook the pasta in a large pan of boiling water for 10 minutes, or according to the packet instructions, until 'al dente'. Drain and rinse thoroughly with cold water to cool the pasta quickly.
2 Put the pasta, mackerel, spring onions, grapefruit, apple and celery in a large mixing bowl and stir gently to combine.
3 Make the dressing by putting all the ingredients into a screw top jar and shaking vigorously, or place in a small bowl and whisk well. Pour the dressing over the salad ingredients and mix well.
4 Spread the salad leaves on a large serving plate and pile the salad mixture on top. Serve immediately.

Pasta with Chicken & Coriander

SERVES 4 ★
PREPARATION & COOKING TIME: 30 minutes
FREEZING: not recommended

Pasta and chicken breasts take very little preparation or cooking and are ideal ingredients for a wide variety of quick supper dishes. Here they are combined with sesame seeds, ginger and coriander for a subtle Thai flavour.

225 g (8 oz) dried pasta spirals
3 tablespoons sesame seeds
4 tablespoons olive oil
350 g (12 oz) skinless chicken breast, sliced
5-cm (2-inch) piece of fresh root ginger, diced finely
350 g (12 oz) leeks, cleaned and sliced thinly
3 tablespoons chopped fresh coriander
salt and freshly ground black pepper
fresh coriander leaves, to garnish

1 Bring a large saucepan of lightly salted water to the boil and cook the pasta spirals according to the packet instructions, until just tender. Drain the pasta.
2 In a small pan carefully dry fry the sesame seeds until just coloured, taking care not to burn them.
3 Heat the olive oil in a deep frying pan or wok, add the chicken and diced root ginger and cook for 5 minutes. Add the sliced leeks and cook for another minute. Cover the pan and continue cooking for a further 3–5 minutes until the chicken is cooked through.
4 Stir the drained pasta into the pan or wok with the chopped coriander and sesame seeds.
5 Season to taste, toss well and serve hot, garnished with coriander leaves.

Chicken with a Citrus Sauce & Roasted Vegetables

SERVES 4
PREPARATION & COOKING TIME: 10 minutes + 1 hour marinating + 50–60 minutes cooking
FREEZING: not recommended

The citrus flavours give a modern twist to chicken to produce a great lunchtime dish; served with roasted Mediterranean vegetables it is ideal for family meals or entertaining. You can serve the roasted vegetables as a dish on its own or with other main courses.

4 chicken portions
grated zest and juice of 1 lemon
grated zest and juice of 1 lime
2 tablespoons olive oil
1 garlic clove, crushed
3 tablespoons orange marmalade
1 teaspoon dried mixed herbs
1 tablespoon chopped fresh parsley

FOR THE ROASTED VEGETABLES:
1 medium aubergine, sliced thickly
2 small courgettes, topped, tailed and halved lengthways
1 red pepper, quartered and de-seeded
1 yellow pepper, quartered and de-seeded
2 small red onions, quartered
4 garlic cloves, unpeeled
3 tablespoons olive oil
2 tablespoons chopped fresh thyme
115 g (4 oz) cherry tomatoes
salt and freshly ground black pepper

1 Place the chicken portions in a shallow ovenproof dish.
2 In a small jug mix together the remaining ingredients for the chicken.
3 Pour the mixture over the chicken portions, cover and leave to marinate for 1 hour, basting occasionally.
4 Uncover and bake at Gas Mark 6/electric oven 200°C/fan oven 180°C for 50–60 minutes until crispy, golden and cooked through.
5 For the roasted vegetables, place the aubergine, courgettes, peppers, onions and garlic in a roasting tin.
6 Drizzle the olive oil over the vegetables, sprinkle the thyme over and season well.
7 Place the tin in the oven 15 minutes into the chicken's cooking time.
8 After 30 minutes, add the tomatoes and cook for a further 10–15 minutes, until the vegetables are charred and tinged brown. Serve with the chicken.

Mediterranean Lamb

SERVES 4
PREPARATION & COOKING TIME: 20 minutes + 1 hour marinating + 50–60 minutes cooking
FREEZING: recommended

The flavours of this dish are reminiscent of Greek holidays – the lamb is marinated in a spicy yogurt mixture and then gently simmered in a tomato sauce. Serve with plain boiled rice and a green salad.

225 g (8 oz) Greek yogurt
zest of 1 lemon
2 garlic cloves, crushed
3 tablespoons olive oil
1 teaspoon ground cumin
675 g (1½ lb) tenderloin of lamb, cubed
1 onion, sliced thinly
150 ml (¼ pint) dry white wine
1 lamb stock cube, crumbled
400 g can of chopped tomatoes
1 tablespoon tomato purée
1 teaspoon caster sugar
2 bay leaves
1 tablespoon fresh oregano
80 g (3 oz) stoned black olives
175 g (6 oz) artichoke hearts
salt and freshly ground black pepper
6 mint leaves, chopped finely

1 Spoon 3 tablespoons of the Greek yogurt into a bowl and stir in the lemon zest, garlic, 1 tablespoon of the oil, seasoning and cumin. Place the lamb in the marinade and coat well. Place in the fridge for at least 1 hour to marinate.
2 Heat the remaining oil in a large frying pan and fry the onion over a gentle heat until tender. Add the meat and fry until browned on all surfaces.
3 Pour the wine into the frying-pan and stir well. Add the stock cube, tomatoes, tomato purée, sugar, bay leaves and oregano.
4 Cover the pan and simmer very gently until the meat is tender for about 50–60 minutes.
5 Stir in the olives and artichoke hearts and cook for 10 minutes.
6 Serve with the remaining Greek yogurt mixed with the chopped mint leaves.

Braised Pork with Fennel

SERVES 4
PREPARATION & COOKING TIME: 1 hour
FREEZING: recommended

A simple pork casserole made with just six ingredients, but full of taste. The subtle flavour of the fennel enhances the pork and adds a sweetness to the finished dish. Serve with roasted sweet potatoes.

2 tablespoons sunflower oil
4 pork steaks, approx 175–225 g (6–8 oz) each
225 g (8 oz) fennel bulb
1 red pepper, de-seeded and diced
225 g (8 oz) mushrooms wiped and quartered
400 g can chopped tomatoes
salt and freshly ground black pepper

1 Heat the oil in a frying pan and brown the steaks on both sides. Place in a large shallow roasting dish.
2 Thinly slice the fennel and reserve any feathery leaves for garnish.
3 Cook the fennel slices in the frying pan until softened and place on top of the pork in the dish.
4 Fry the pepper and mushrooms until soft for about 5 minutes, stir in the tomatoes and bring to the boil. Add seasoning. Pour the sauce over the pork in the dish and cover with a lid or foil.
5 Cook at Gas Mark 6/electric oven 200°C/fan oven 180°C for 25–30 minutes until the pork is cooked through and the vegetables are tender.
6 Serve garnished with the feathery fennel leaves.

Spicy Kebabs *(left)*

MAKES 6 kebabs
PREPARATION & COOKING TIME: 30 minutes + 1 hour chilling + 15–20 minutes cooking
FREEZING: not recommended

Each type of meat in this colourful dish has its own special flavouring ingredient – the lamb is enhanced with crushed garlic cloves; the minced pork is combined with coriander seeds and the steak is flavoured with horseradish sauce. Serve with dips such as tzatziki with the lamb, tomato salsa (page 88) with the steak and pesto dip with the pork, and a selection of salads for easy summer entertaining.

350 g (12 oz) lean lamb, minced
350 g (12 oz) lean pork, minced
350 g (12 oz) lean steak, minced
1 large onion, grated
3 garlic cloves, crushed
1 tablespoon coriander seeds, crushed
3 tablespoons horseradish sauce
9 tablespoons finely chopped fresh mint
9 tablespoons sesame seeds, toasted
6 tablespoons poppy seeds
salt and freshly ground black pepper

1 Place each of the minced meats into a separate bowl, divide the grated onion between each and season well.
2 To the minced lamb add the crushed garlic cloves; to the minced pork add the coriander seeds; to the minced steak add the horseradish sauce.
3 Mix each of the meats thoroughly working in the flavourings.
4 Divide each mixture into eight evenly sized small balls.
5 Roll the lamb balls in the mint; the pork balls in the sesame seeds and the steak balls in the poppy seeds. Make sure each ball is evenly covered.
6 Thread four of each type of meatball on to six thin skewers and chill in the fridge for 1 hour.
7 Cook the kebabs under a hot grill: cook the pork kebabs for 12–15 minutes; the lamb kebabs for 10–12 minutes and the steak kebabs for 10 minutes, turning the skewers frequently during cooking.

Cherry & Almond Tart

SERVES 8
PREPARATION & COOKING TIME: 20 minutes + 30 minutes
    chilling + 50 minutes cooking
FREEZING: recommended

*Amaretto liqueur is the secret of success here, as it is more
subtle than the rather harsh-flavoured almond essence often
used in this tart. Delicious offered at teatime or as a dessert, it
can be served hot or cold. I would serve this in a very English
way with some freshly made custard.*

FOR THE PASTRY:
sweet rich shortcrust pastry made with 115 g (4 oz) flour (page 10)
FOR THE FILLING:
115 g (4 oz) unsalted butter, softened
115 g (4 oz) caster sugar
115 g (4 oz) ground almonds
25 g (1 oz) self-raising flour
2 large eggs, beaten
1 tablespoon amaretto liqueur
225 g (8 oz) stoned sweet red or black cherries
15 g (½ oz) flaked almonds

1 Line a 20-cm (8-inch) loose-bottomed, deep flan tin with
  the sweet rich shortcrust pastry. Chill for 30 minutes.
2 Preheat the oven to Gas Mark 5/electric oven 190°C/fan
  oven 170°C. Place a baking sheet just above the middle
  shelf.
3 On the heated baking sheet, bake the pastry case blind for
  15 minutes, then remove the foil or paper and beans and
  return it to the oven for a further 5 minutes.
4 Meanwhile, cream together the butter and sugar. Combine
  the ground almonds and flour. Beat this into the creamed
  mixture alternately with the eggs. Add the amaretto.
5 Scatter the cherries over the pastry base. Spoon over the
  almond filling and smooth it out. Sprinkle the top with
  flaked almonds and bake for approximately 30 minutes,
  until risen and just firm to the touch.

Apricot & Almond Crumble

SERVES 6
PREPARATION & COOKING TIME: 20 minutes + 25 minutes
    cooking
FREEZING: recommended

*This is a different way of making a crumble and it has the
benefit of being speedy to prepare. The end result is a rather
rustic one and the inclusion of the almonds in the crumble gives
a lovely crunchy, nutty taste.*

675 g (1½ lb) fresh ripe apricots
25 g (1 oz) granulated sugar
175 g (6 oz) plain flour
80 g (3 oz) caster sugar
50 g (2 oz) blanched almonds, chopped roughly
50 g (2 oz) butter, melted

1 Preheat the oven to Gas Mark 4/electric oven 180°C/fan
  oven 160°C.
2 Cut the apricots in half, remove the stones and place them,
  cut-side down, in the bottom of a greased 1.1-litre (2-pint)
  buttered pie dish. Sprinkle the granulated sugar over the
  apricots.
3 Combine the flour, caster sugar and almonds in a bowl,
  pour in the butter and stir to form a rough crumble. Spoon
  evenly over the apricots and bake in the oven for 25
  minutes, until the crumble is golden brown.
4 Serve warm, with custard, cream or vanilla ice cream.

Raspberry & Vanilla Ice Cream Gâteau *(right)*

SERVES 6–8
PREPARATION & COOKING TIME: 30 minutes + 1 hour
    cooking + 8 hours freezing
FREEZING: essential

*This dessert makes an impressive finale to a summer dinner
party or barbecue. It is actually very straightforward and can
be made several days before it is needed. You could change the
ice cream, sorbet and fruit to suit your preferences or what is
available.*

4 large egg whites
225 g (8 oz) caster sugar
700 ml (1¼ pints) vanilla ice cream, softened slightly
700 ml (1¼ pints) raspberry sorbet, softened slightly
300 ml (½ pint) double cream, whipped
fresh raspberries to decorate

1 Preheat the oven to Gas Mark 2/electric oven 150°C/fan
  oven 130°C. Mark three 20-cm/8-inch circles on baking
  parchment, cut out and place the circles on three baking
  sheets.
2 Place the egg whites in a large bowl and whisk on full
  speed until stiff but not dry. Add the sugar, a teaspoon at a
  time, continuing to whisk at full speed. Divide the
  meringue between the three circles and spread evenly with
  a palette knife.
3 Bake in the oven for 1 hour; the meringue is cooked when
  the baking parchment will easily peel away from the
  meringue and the bases make a hollow sound when tapped
  lightly, so test for this but don't peel off the paper. Turn off
  the oven, leave the door half open and leave the meringues
  in the oven until they are completely cold.
4 To assemble, peel off the baking parchment from two of
  the meringue circles. Place the third meringue disc in the
  base of a 20-cm/8-inch springform cake tin. Spoon the
  vanilla ice cream evenly over the meringue. Top with the
  second meringue disc, cover with the raspberry sorbet and
  top with the final meringue disc, smooth-side upwards;
  press down firmly. Cover and freeze for at least 8 hours.
5 To serve, remove the sides and base of the tin as well as
  the paper from the base. Spread the whipped cream over
  the surface and pile the raspberries into the centre.

Raspberry & White Chocolate 'Chifle' *(above)*

SERVES 8
PREPARATION TIME: 30 minutes + 1 hour chilling
FREEZING: not recommended

This dessert is called a 'chifle' because it is a cross between a cheesecake and a trifle. Raspberries and white chocolate go so well together, but you could alter the fruit to suit your taste and what is available. Care needs to be taken when melting the chocolate as white chocolate is not as stable as dark.

4 trifle sponges
3 tablespoons brandy or kirsch
225 g (8 oz) fresh or frozen and thawed raspberries
500 g carton of custard
250 g cream cheese
50 g (2 oz) caster sugar
115 g (4 oz) white chocolate, melted and cooled
300 ml (¹/₂ pint) whipping cream, whipped
fresh raspberries and mint leaves, to decorate

1 Cut the sponges into small pieces and place in the bottom of a glass serving bowl. Sprinkle the brandy or kirsch over. Spoon the raspberries over the sponges.
2 Divide the custard between two large bowls. Add the cream cheese and half the sugar to one and mix thoroughly. Add the chocolate and remaining sugar to the other and mix well. Add half the cream to the chocolate mixture and fold in thoroughly.
3 Spoon the cream cheese mixture on to the raspberries, levelling the surface, and then repeat with the chocolate mixture. Spread the remaining cream on top. Pile some fresh raspberries in the middle and chill for at least 1 hour or until ready to serve. Decorate with fresh mint.

Raspberry, White Chocolate & Vanilla Tart *(above)*

SERVES 6
PREPARATION & COOKING TIME: 25 minutes + 1 hour chilling + 20–25 minutes cooking
FREEZING: not recommended

'Truly scrumptious' is probably a fair description of this tart. It looks stunning, is simple to make and tastes divine! It epitomizes summer dining – light, yet rich in flavour. The colours in this tart are really vibrant.

FOR THE PASTRY:
sweet rich shortcrust pastry made with 115 g (4 oz) flour (page 10)

FOR THE FILLING:
150 g (5 oz) white chocolate (the drops are good for this)
250 g tub of mascarpone
200 g tub of plain fromage frais
¹/₄ teaspoon vanilla extract
225 g (8 oz) fresh raspberries
1¹/₂ tablespoons redcurrant jelly

1 Line a 23-cm (9-inch) loose-bottomed, shallow flan tin with the pastry. Chill for 1 hour.
2 Preheat the oven to Gas Mark 5/electric oven 190°C/fan oven 170°C. Place a baking sheet in the centre of the oven.
3 On the heated baking sheet, bake the pastry case blind for 15 minutes. Remove the foil or paper and beans and continue cooking for a further 5–10 minutes, until the pastry is cooked through.
4 Melt the chocolate in a bowl over a pan of barely simmering water.
5 Meanwhile, beat together the mascarpone, fromage frais and vanilla, until smooth. Stir in the melted chocolate. Spoon the mixture into the pastry case. Level the surface.
6 Scatter the raspberries over the top and brush with warmed redcurrant jelly.

Lemon & Raspberry Delight

SERVES 4 ▼
PREPARATION & COOKING TIME: 30 minutes + 45 minutes
  cooking
FREEZING: not recommended

*The lemon mixture separates into the lightest of sponges with
a lemon sauce underneath that combines with the raspberries
to make a delightful dessert. It's best served warm but can also
be made in advance and served at room temperature. Vary the
fruit by using the same amount of strained, lightly stewed,
sweetened rhubarb or gooseberries.*

225 g (8 oz) fresh or thawed frozen raspberries
25 g (1 oz) sunflower or olive oil spread
110 g (4 oz) caster sugar
grated zest and juice of 1 lemon
25 g (1 oz) plain flour
150 ml (¼ pint) skimmed milk
1 egg, separated, plus 1 egg white

1 Preheat the oven to Gas Mark 4/electric oven 180°C/fan
  oven 160°C. Prepare a bain-marie (a roasting tin half filled
  with cold water is ideal).
2 Spoon the raspberries over the base of an ovenproof dish.
3 Cream together the spread, half the sugar and the lemon
  zest.
4 Mix together the remaining sugar with the flour.
5 Beat the lemon juice into the creamed mixture. The
  mixture will curdle.
6 Whisk together the milk and the egg yolk. Gradually beat
  this into the creamed mixture, alternating it with the flour
  mixture. The mixture will remain curdled.
7 Using a clean whisk, whisk the egg whites together until
  soft peaks just hold.
8 Fold the egg whites into the lemon mixture. Pour the
  mixture over the raspberries.
9 Place the dish into the bain-marie and then put that in the
  middle of the oven. Bake for about 45 minutes, until it is
  golden brown and the top is set.

Baked Nectarine & Blueberry Tart

SERVES 8
PREPARATION & COOKING TIME: 30 minutes + 1 hour
chilling + 30–35 minutes cooking
FREEZING: not recommended

*This is a wonderful summertime flan that can be made the
night before and assembled on the day. You can substitute
peaches for the nectarines. Fresh raspberries would go well in
place of the blueberries – but do not bake them. Walnut pastry
sounds difficult to make, but it is not at all, and if you omit the
sugar it would be ideal for use in any savoury flan.*

FOR THE WALNUT PASTRY:
50 g (2 oz) unsalted butter
115 g (4 oz) plain flour
25 g (1 oz) walnuts, ground
2 tablespoons caster sugar
1 large egg yolk

FOR THE FILLING:
3 ripe nectarines
juice of 1 lemon
115 g (4 oz) blueberries
50 g (2 oz) caster sugar
250 g tub of mascarpone
150 ml (¼ pint) double cream
¼ teaspoon vanilla essence
2 tablespoons icing sugar

1 First make the walnut pastry. Rub the butter into the flour
  until the mixture resembles fine breadcrumbs. Stir in the
  ground walnuts and sugar. Add the egg yolk and 1 tablespoon
  cold water. Bring together to form a smooth dough.
2 Roll out the dough on a lightly floured surface. Use it to
  line a 20-cm (8-inch) round, loose-bottomed, deep flan tin.
  Prick the base all over with a fork, cover, and chill for
  about 1 hour.
3 Preheat the oven to Gas Mark 5/electric oven 190°C/fan
  oven 170°C.
4 Cut the nectarines into quarters and discard the stones.
  Place them in a non-metallic baking dish and sprinkle with
  lemon juice. Spoon the sugar evenly over the fruit and
  bake towards the top of the oven for 20 minutes. Now stir
  the nectarines to coat them with the juices, and sprinkle
  the blueberries over the top. Return to the oven for a
  further 5 minutes, until the nectarines are tinged golden.
  Remove from the oven and allow to cool.
5 Increase the oven temperature to Gas Mark 6/electric oven
  200°C/fan oven 180°C and put a baking sheet on the
  middle shelf. On the warmed baking sheet, bake the pastry
  case blind for 15 minutes. Remove the foil and beans and
  cook for a further 5–10 minutes until crisp and golden.
  Leave to cool.
6 When you are ready to assemble the tart whisk together
  the mascarpone, cream, vanilla and sugar until you have a
  thick and smooth mixture. Spread this over the base of the
  pastry shell. Pile the baked fruits on top and spoon over
  any juices just prior to serving.

Gooseberry & Elderflower Cobbler

SERVES 6
PREPARATION & COOKING TIME: 40 minutes + 40 minutes cooking
FREEZING: recommended

You don't often get cobblers these days, which is a shame as they are so delicious and very satisfying. They look impressive and would therefore be suitable for serving at a summer dinner party or Sunday lunch.

625 g (1 lb 6 oz) gooseberries, topped and tailed
115 g (4 oz) caster sugar, or to taste
a knob of unsalted butter
2–3 tablespoons elderflower cordial

FOR THE COBBLER:
225 g (8 oz) self-raising flour
a pinch of salt
100 g (3½ oz) unsalted butter, cubed
50 g (2 oz) caster sugar
1 large egg, beaten
4 tablespoons milk, plus extra
demerara sugar, for sprinkling

1 Place the gooseberries, sugar and butter in a saucepan and cook over a very gentle heat until the butter has melted. Add the cordial and raise the heat a little. Bring to the boil and simmer for 1 minute. Transfer to a greased ovenproof dish – approximately 27 x 17 cm (11 x 6½ inches) and 8 cm (3 inches) deep.
2 Preheat the oven to Gas Mark 6/electric oven 200°C/fan oven 180°C.
3 To make the cobbler topping, sift the flour and salt into a large bowl, add the butter and rub in until the mixture resembles breadcrumbs. Add the sugar, stir in and add the egg and two-thirds of the milk. Bring the mixture together using a knife, adding a little more milk if needed. Roll out the mixture on a floured surface to 1 cm (½ inch) thick and cut into 4-cm (1½-inch) rounds. Arrange the scones on top of the gooseberries, brush with a little milk and sprinkle with the demerara sugar. Bake for 15 minutes.
4 Reduce the temperature to Gas Mark 4/electric oven 180°C/fan oven 160°C and continue to cook for another 20–25 minutes, until the scones are cooked and golden brown.
5 Serve hot or warm, with custard or thick cream.

Gooseberry Flan with Elderflower Custard

SERVES 8
PREPARATION & COOKING TIME: 25 minutes + 1 hour chilling + 50 minutes cooking
FREEZING: not recommended

This custard is to die for! It has such a melt-in-the-mouth texture. It is almost an upside-down crème caramel with caramel being poured over the gooseberries and the custard on top. Do not be alarmed by the amount of liquid the gooseberries produce, it all reduces to a caramel.

FOR THE PASTRY:
pâte sucrée made using 115 g (4 oz) flour (page 10)

FOR THE FILLING:
80 g (3 oz) unsalted butter
50 g (2 oz) granulated sugar
450 g (1 lb) fresh or frozen gooseberries, topped and tailed
2 large eggs, plus 2 large yolks
25 g (1 oz) caster sugar
300 ml (½ pint) double cream
2 tablespoons elderflower cordial

1 Line a 20-cm (8-inch) loose-bottomed, deep flan tin with the pâte sucrée. Chill for 1 hour.
2 Preheat the oven to Gas Mark 5/electric oven 190°C/fan oven 170°C. Place a baking sheet in the middle of the oven.
3 On the warmed baking sheet, bake the pastry case blind for 15 minutes. Remove the foil or paper and beans and continue cooking for a further 5–10 minutes.
4 Melt the butter in a medium saucepan and stir in the granulated sugar. Stir until the sugar is dissolved and then add the gooseberries. Simmer for about 10 minutes, until the fruit is just tender.
5 Using a slotted spoon remove the gooseberries. Turn the heat up and boil rapidly until the liquid has reduced and caramelised. Spoon the gooseberries into the pastry case and pour over the caramel.
6 Beat together the eggs, yolks, caster sugar, cream and elderflower cordial. Pour this over the gooseberries. Bake for about 30 minutes, or until just set. Leave to cool slightly and serve warm.

Summer Fruit Roulade (right)

SERVES 6–8

PREPARATION & COOKING TIME: 40 minutes + 10 minutes
   cooling

FREEZING: recommended

*Many people think that roulades are difficult to make – they
are not, as long as you follow the method carefully. Roulades
are well worth the effort because they look so impressive.
A fruit coulis, such as raspberry, would make a perfect
accompaniment to this dessert.*

FOR THE ROULADE:

4 large eggs

115 g (4 oz) caster sugar, plus extra

115 g (4 oz) plain flour

1/2 teaspoon baking powder

25 g (1 oz) butter, melted and cooled

grated zest of 1 orange

FOR THE FILLING:

300 ml (1/2 pint) double cream, whipped

175 g (6 oz) summer fruit, such as raspberries, strawberries and
   redcurrants, prepared as necessary

1 Preheat the oven to Gas Mark 5/electric oven 190°C/fan
   oven 170°C. Line a 30 x 23 cm (12 x 9 inch) Swiss roll tin
   with baking parchment or greased greaseproof paper.

2 Place the eggs and sugar in a large bowl and whisk until
   the mixture becomes thick and creamy and the whisk
   leaves a heavy trail when lifted. Sift the flour and baking
   powder together and then sift over the egg mixture. Fold
   in the flour quickly with a metal spoon, followed by the
   butter and the orange zest. Pour into the prepared tin and
   gently spread into the corners until the surface is even.
   Bake in the oven for about 15 minutes until the surface is
   golden brown and springs back when gently pressed and
   the sides have begun to shrink back from the sides.

3 While the cake is cooking, cut a piece of greaseproof paper
   slightly larger than the tin and sprinkle generously with
   caster sugar. When cooked, invert the cake immediately on
   to the sugared paper, trim the edges and fold over one of
   the short edges by 2.5 cm (1 inch). Roll up the roulade,
   with the paper inside, and fold back the top of the paper
   so that it doesn't stick to the cake as it cools. Leave to cool
   for about 10 minutes. Unroll carefully and remove the
   paper.

4 Spread most of the cream over the roulade, but not right
   to the edges, and scatter over the fruit, reserving a few
   perfect berries to decorate. Roll up the filled roulade and
   transfer to a serving platter, preferably an oval one. Spoon
   the remaining cream into a piping bag and pipe rosettes on
   top of the roulade. Decorate with some more fruit and
   serve straight away.

Strawberries Romanov

SERVES 4–6
PREPARATION TIME: 30 minutes + 2 hours chilling
FREEZING: not recommended

This version of a classic dessert contains less alcohol than the original and uses gelatine to set the mixture a little so that the end result is less sloppy and will last a lot longer, allowing you to prepare it well in advance.

450 g (1 lb) fresh strawberries, preferably English
2 tablespoons port
1 tablespoon Cointreau or Grand Marnier
11.7 g sachet of gelatine
1 tablespoon icing sugar
300 ml (¹/₂ pint) whipping cream, whipped lightly
fresh mint leaves, to decorate

1 Wash the strawberries and remove the stalks and set aside a few perfect small ones to decorate. Cut 175 g (6 oz) of them into pieces and purée. Pass the purée through a nylon sieve. Cut the remaining strawberries into even-sized pieces and divide between glass dishes.
2 Place the port and liqueur in a bowl, sprinkle over the gelatine and leave to soak for a minute or two. Dissolve in a bowl of hot water, stirring, or place in a microwave for about 30 seconds on high. Stir well and allow to cool.
3 Meanwhile, fold the icing sugar into the strawberry purée. Whisk the gelatine into the strawberry mixture and then fold in the whipped cream. Spoon over the strawberries.
4 Chill for at least 2 hours. Just before serving, decorate with strawberries, sliced if necessary, and mint leaves.

NOTE: Replace the gelatine with Vegegel if you are vegetarian.

Strawberry Pavlova *(left)*

SERVES 6 ▼
PREPARATION & COOKING TIME: 25 minutes + 1 hour cooking
FREEZING: not recommended

Almost everyone loves this traditional dessert, which conjures images of summer days. Pavlova need not be decadent: choose your filling according to the tastes you enjoy and the varying fat contents. Other fruits can be used, try green and black grapes with mandarins in the winter.

FOR THE PAVLOVA:
3 egg whites
175 g (6 oz) caster sugar
¹/₄ teaspoon vanilla essence
¹/₂ teaspoon lemon juice or wine vinegar
2 teaspoons cornflour

FOR THE FILLING:
425 ml (³/₄ pint) half-fat crème fraîche, half-fat Greek yogurt or natural fromage frais (not low fat)

FOR THE TOPPING:
500 g (1 lb 2 oz) strawberries, sliced if large

1 Ensure your mixing bowl and whisk are free from grease by washing in very hot soapy water and drying on a clean tea towel. This will help produce a good meringue mixture.
2 Grease a baking sheet and cover with a sheet of baking parchment (or use greaseproof paper and grease the top of it). If it helps, draw a circle 20 cm (8 inches) in diameter on the paper.
3 Preheat the oven to Gas Mark 2/electric oven150°C/fan oven 130°C.
4 Place the egg whites in the bowl and whisk until they are very stiff and the mixture holds firm peaks when the whisk is taken out.
5 Add the caster sugar 1 tablespoon at a time, whisking well between each addition. Carefully fold in the vanilla essence, lemon juice or vinegar and cornflour.
6 Spoon the meringue on to the lined baking sheet to form a 20-cm (8-inch) circle, piling the mixture up around the edge to form a shell. Bake for an hour until the meringue is a pale biscuit colour with a crisp outside and a marshmallow texture inside. Leave it to cool on the baking sheet.
7 Remove the paper when cold; a pavlova meringue usually cracks a little as it cools. At this stage it can be stored for 2–3 days in an airtight container.
8 Place the pavlova on a flat serving dish. Fill with your choice of filling and pile the strawberries on top.

Strawberry Shortcake

SERVES 8
PREPARATION & COOKING TIME: 25 minutes + 30 minutes
   chilling + 15 minutes cooking
FREEZING: not recommended

This is a very easy pudding, ideal for hot, sunny days when you would rather be outside than baking in the kitchen. Make the base the night before and assemble this when required. Raspberries work equally well and can be substituted for the strawberries when they are plentiful.

FOR THE SHORTBREAD:
115 g (4 oz) unsalted butter
75 g (6 oz) self-raising flour
50 g (2 oz) golden caster sugar
1 large egg yolk

FOR THE FILLING:
150 ml (¼ pint) double cream
200 g carton of Greek yogurt
1 tablespoon icing sugar, sifted, plus extra for dusting
a few drops of vanilla essence
450 g (1 lb) strawberries

1 To make the shortbread, rub the butter into the flour, until it resembles fine breadcrumbs. Stir in the sugar and add the egg yolk. Using your hands, mix everything together until the mixture forms a ball.
2 Press pieces of the dough evenly over the base of a greased 23-cm (9-inch) loose-bottomed flan tin, and prick it all over with a fork. Chill for 30 minutes.
3 Preheat the oven to Gas Mark 4/electric oven 180°C/fan oven 160°C. Place a baking sheet on the centre shelf of the oven.
4 Bake the shortbread on the heated baking sheet for about 15 minutes, or until just lightly coloured. Cool in the tin, and then carefully turn it out on to a serving plate, gently prising it off its base.
5 Pour the cream, yogurt, icing sugar and vanilla essence into a bowl and whisk them together until the mixture leaves a trail. Spread this over the shortcake pastry base.
6 Remove the stalks from the strawberries and arrange them on top of the creamy mixture. Dust with icing sugar to serve.

Strawberry Cheesecake

SERVES 10–12
PREPARATION TIME: 40 minutes + 3–4 hours chilling
FREEZING: not recommended

This would make a stunning dessert for a summer dinner party or buffet. The strawberries could be replaced with raspberries.

FOR THE BASE:
80 g (3 oz) butter, melted
1 tablespoon golden syrup
225 g (8 oz) amaretti biscuits, crushed

FOR THE CHEESECAKE:
420 g can of strawberries in light syrup
11.7 g sachet of gelatine
2 x 250 g tubs of ricotta cheese
250 g tub of mascarpone cheese
50 g (2 oz) caster sugar
2 medium eggs, separated

FOR THE TOPPING:
3 tablespoons strawberry conserve
2 tablespoons amaretto liqueur
175 g (6 oz) fresh strawberries

1 Lightly grease a 20-cm (8-inch) springform tin and make the base by combining the first three ingredients. Press them into the tin with a potato masher and chill while you make the top.
2 Drain the strawberries, reserving 150 ml (¼ pint) of the syrup. Place the syrup in a bowl, sprinkle over the gelatine and leave to soak for a minute. Stand in a bowl of hot water and stir until dissolved, or microwave on high for 1 minute and then set to one side to cool.
3 Liquidise the canned strawberries. In a large bowl, beat the strawberry purée with the cheeses, sugar and egg yolks. Add the cooled gelatine.
4 Whisk the egg whites stiffly and fold them into the strawberry mixture – it is best to fold in 1 tablespoon of the whites to loosen the mixture before adding the remainder. Spoon over the biscuit base and chill for 3–4 hours, until set.
5 Warm the conserve and liqueur together over a gentle heat and then sieve to make a clear glaze. Cut or slice the fresh strawberries and arrange on top of the cheesecake in an attractive pattern. Brush the glaze over the strawberries.

Strawberry & Lime
Angel Cheesecake *(above)*

SERVES 8 ♥ ▼

PREPARATION & COOKING TIME: 1 hours 15 minutes +
   2 hours setting

FREEZING: not recommended

*Strawberry and lime combine to make a wonderfully refreshing
flavour to this cheesecake as well as providing plenty of vitamin
C. Using Quark and very low fat Greek yogurt makes this a
'healthy option' dessert.*

FOR THE SPONGE:

2 eggs

75 g (2¼ oz) caster sugar

50 g (2 oz) self-raising flour

icing sugar, for dusting

FOR THE FILLING:

2 x 250 g cartons of Quark

150 g pot of no fat Greek yogurt

75 g (2¼ oz) caster sugar

zest and juice of 2 limes

1 sachet of gelatine powder (page 110)

400 g (14 oz) fresh strawberries, hulled

1 Preheat the oven to Gas Mark 4/electric oven 180°C/fan
   oven 160°C. Lightly grease and line with greaseproof
   paper the base of a 20-cm (8-inch) loose bottomed cake tin
   or springform tin.

2 To make the sponge, break the eggs into a large bowl and
   add the caster sugar. Whisk with an electric hand mixer
   until the mixture is thick, light in colour and creamy.
   When the whisk is lifted out of the mixture, a trail should
   be left across the surface.

3 Sift the flour on to the surface of the whisked mixture and
   fold in carefully, using a large metal spoon. Turn the
   mixture into the prepared cake tin and spread out evenly.
   Bake in the oven for 20–25 minutes until the sponge is
   risen, lightly golden and just beginning to shrink from the
   sides of the cake tin. Turn out and leave to cool on a wire
   rack.

4 Wash out the cake tin, dry, and line the sides and base with
   greaseproof paper.

5 For the filling, place the Quark and Greek yogurt in a
   large bowl and stir in the caster sugar and the lime zest.
   Pour the lime juice into a small bowl and sprinkle over the
   gelatine powder. Leave for 5 minutes to 'sponge', then
   stand the bowl over a pan of gently simmering water until
   the gelatine granules have dissolved completely. Set it aside
   to cool slightly.

6 Using a sharp knife, carefully split the cold cake in half
   horizontally and place the base back in the tin, cut side up.
   Thinly slice five or six equal sized strawberries lengthways
   and place the slices around the edge of the cake tin.
   Reserve at least four strawberries for decoration and finely
   chop the rest. Stir the chopped strawberries and the cooled
   gelatine into the cheese mixture and stir to combine well.

7 Carefully spoon the cheesecake mixture into the tin, taking
   care not to knock over any of the strawberry slices around
   the edge. Level the surface of the cheese mixture and place
   the remaining sponge layer on top with the cut side down
   on to the cheese. Cover the tin with clingfilm and leave in
   the fridge for 1½–2 hours to set.

8 To serve, remove from the cake tin and carefully peel off
   the greaseproof paper. Transfer to a serving plate, dust the
   top with icing sugar and decorate with the reserved
   strawberries.

Strawberry & Orange Meringue Roulade with Fresh Strawberry Sauce *(below)*

SERVES 8 ♥ ▼
PREPARATION & COOKING TIME: 1 hour 10 minutes
FREEZING: not recommended

Roulades make an elegant dessert for a dinner party and are not as difficult to make as you may think. Filled with low fat Greek yogurt and served with a fruit sauce instead of pouring cream, this is a delicious low fat version. In the winter, when strawberries are not so flavoursome, a large ripe mango could be used as a substitute.

3 large egg whites
175 g (6 oz) caster sugar
1 level teaspoon cornflour
1 teaspoon malt vinegar
1 teaspoon vanilla essence
grated zest and juice of 1 large orange
400 g (14 oz) ripe strawberries, hulled and sliced
500 g pot of low fat Greek yogurt
1–2 tablespoons icing sugar

1 Preheat the oven to Gas Mark 2/electric oven 150°C/fan oven 130°C. Line a 33 x 23 cm (13 x 9 inch) Swiss roll tin with non-stick baking parchment.

2 Place the egg whites in a large bowl and beat with an electric whisk until stiff but not dry. Gradually whisk in the caster sugar until the mixture is thick and shiny and meringue-like. Finally, whisk in the cornflour, vinegar, vanilla essence and the grated orange zest.

3 Transfer the meringue mixture to the prepared tin, spread it out and level gently. Place in the oven and bake for 25–30 minutes until the surface of the meringue is golden and just firm.

4 Remove the meringue from the oven and cover with a clean, damp tea towel for 10 minutes.

5 Place a length of non-stick baking parchment, larger than the area of the meringue, on the work surface. Turn the roulade out of the tin and on to the baking parchment. Spread the yogurt over the meringue, then scatter over half the sliced strawberries. Use the edge of the paper to help roll up the meringue into a roulade and place on the serving dish.

6 Liquidise the remaining strawberries with the orange juice and then pass through a sieve to remove the seeds. If necessary, stir in 1–2 tablespoons of icing sugar to sweeten the fruit sauce. Serve the roulade in slices, accompanied by the strawberry sauce.

Blackcurrant Kissel

SERVES 4 ★ ▼
PREPARATION & COOKING TIME: 25 minutes
FREEZING: recommended

Kissels are traditional Russian desserts made with soft fruit. This blackcurrant version is a favourite, but create your own with other fruits. Kissel can be served warm or cold.

450 g (1 lb) fresh or thawed frozen blackcurrants
55 g (2 oz) light soft brown sugar
2 teaspoons grated orange zest
juice of 1 orange
4 tablespoons red wine or blackcurrant juice mixed with water
1–1¹/₂ tablespoons arrowroot
3 tablespoons cold water
1 tablespoon caster sugar
1 tablespoon flaked almonds, toasted

1 Place the blackcurrants, sugar, orange zest, juice and wine in a pan on a low heat. Cover and slowly bring to the boil. Simmer for 10 minutes or until the fruit is just tender.
2 Mix the arrowroot with the cold water to make a smooth paste; if the fruit has created a lot of juice use the larger amount. Stir the paste into the fruit and simmer gently, stirring constantly until the mixture thickens.
3 Pour into a serving dish and sprinkle with a little caster sugar to prevent a skin forming on the top.
4 Sprinkle the almonds over the kissel.

Summer Fruits with White Chocolate Sauce *(above)*

SERVES 6 ★
PREPARATION TIME: 5–10 minutes
FREEZING: not recommended

It's wonderful to have a simple, sophisticated dessert up your sleeve when you're either very busy or have unexpected guests. This fits the bill perfectly. You'll have guests guessing how you made the sauce! It's best to thaw the fruits in a single layer on a plate lined with kitchen paper.

500 g bag of frozen summer fruits, defrosted
150 g (5¹/₂ oz) white chocolate, broken into pieces
300 ml (10 fl oz) soured cream

1 Divide the fruit between six wine glasses or sundae dishes.
2 Melt the chocolate by placing it in a bowl set over a pan of barely simmering hot water, stirring from time to time. Remove from the heat and allow to cool.
3 Stir a spoonful of the cream into the melted chocolate and mix well. Add the remaining cream and mix thoroughly. Spoon over the fruit and serve.

Blackcurrant & Cracked Caramel Tart

SERVES 8
PREPARATION & COOKING TIME: 25 minutes + 1 hour
   chilling + 25 minutes cooking
FREEZING: not recommended

This would make a spectacular finale to any meal – the shafts of transparent golden caramel resemble modern architectural sculptures as they rise above a smooth, creamy filling with a sharp fruity base. All the layers can be made in advance, but the tart needs to be assembled near to serving time as, after a few hours, the golden spires will start to dissolve back to their liquid state. If using frozen blackcurrants there is no need to add any water when cooking.

FOR THE PASTRY:
pâte sucrée pastry made using 115 g (4 oz) plain flour (page 10)

FOR THE FILLING:
350 g (12 oz) blackcurrants
50 g (2 oz) light muscovado sugar
200 g tub of plain Greek yogurt
150 ml (¼ pint) double cream
¼ teaspoon vanilla essence

FOR THE CARAMEL:
80 g (3 oz) granulated sugar
80 ml (3 fl oz) water

1 Line a 20-cm (8-inch) loose-bottomed, deep flan tin with the pâte sucrée. Chill for 1 hour.
2 Preheat the oven to Gas Mark 5/electric oven 190°C/fan oven 170°C. Place a baking sheet in the centre of the oven.
3 On the warmed baking sheet, bake the pastry case blind for 15 minutes. Remove the foil or paper and beans and continue cooking for a further 5–10 minutes, until the pastry is cooked through and golden in colour.
4 Gently heat the blackcurrants in a medium saucepan with the muscovado sugar and 2 tablespoons water for about 5 minutes, or until the fruit just softens, and the juices start to run. Cool and strain.
5 For the caramel, place the granulated sugar in a small saucepan with the water. Gently heat to dissolve the sugar. Increase the heat and boil rapidly for about 15 minutes, until the syrup turns to a golden caramel. Pour it out on to a small baking tin lined with baking parchment. Cool until the caramel becomes brittle.
6 Place the yogurt, cream and vanilla essence in a bowl and beat gently until the mixture is smooth and just able to hold its shape.
7 Spoon the blackcurrants over the pastry base. Cover with the yogurt and cream filling. Break up the caramel roughly into jagged triangular shapes and arrange at various angles over the surface of the tart.

Tiramisù Ice Cream Terrine

SERVES 6–8
PREPARATION TIME: 30 minutes + 3–4 hours freezing
FREEZING: essential

Tiramisù is an extremely popular dessert. This variation looks impressive served as a terrine and is useful to have in the freezer for when you have unexpected guests. It's best served with a bowl of summer berries, such as raspberries.

500 g carton of custard
250 g tub of mascarpone cheese
75 ml (5 tablespoons) Marsala or sweet sherry
50 g (2 oz) chocolate-coated coffee beans or plain chocolate pieces
2½ tablespoons freshly ground coffee
40 g (1½ oz) caster sugar
2 tablespoons brandy
about 36 sponge fingers
150 ml (¼ pint) double cream, whipped
cocoa powder and chocolate-coated coffee beans, to decorate

1 Place the custard, mascarpone and Marsala or sherry in a bowl and mix thoroughly. Fold in the chocolate-coated coffee beans or chocolate pieces and set aside.
2 To make the coffee, add 250 ml (9 fl oz) of boiling water to the ground coffee in a cafetière or jug, leave to brew and then strain into a bowl. Add the sugar and brandy.
3 Line a lightly oiled 1 kg (2¼ lb) loaf tin with clingfilm. Dip a third of the sponge fingers into the coffee mixture and place side by side in the base of the tin. Spoon half of the mascarpone mixture on top and then repeat the layers, finishing with the sponge fingers. You will probably need to fill some gaps with pieces of sponge fingers on the top layer.
4 Freeze until solid – this will probably take 3–4 hours.
5 Invert it on to a plate and decorate the top surface with the cream – if you are feeling creative, you could pipe it on top – and then finish with the beans and cocoa, sifted. Return it to the freezer and leave until the cream is frozen. Wrap it in a freezer bag and return to the freezer. Place in the fridge for 30 minutes to allow it to soften a little before serving.

White Chocolate Terrine with Summer Fruit Coulis *(above)*

SERVES 8
PREPARATION TIME: 25 minutes + 2–3 hours chilling
FREEZING: recommended

*This dessert looks stunning whether it is left whole or sliced
on to dessert plates and surrounded by the coulis. The coulis
complements the white chocolate beautifully, both in taste
and appearance.*

200 g (7 oz) good-quality white chocolate, such as Lindt, broken
  into pieces
11.7 g sachet of gelatine
500 g tub of Greek yogurt
1 teaspoon vanilla essence
300 ml (½ pint) whipping cream, whipped to soft peaks

FOR THE COULIS:
500 g (1 lb 2 oz) packet of frozen summer fruit, thawed and drained
115 g (4 oz) caster sugar
45ml (3 tablespoons) kirsch
fresh mint leaves, to decorate

1 Melt the chocolate by placing it in a bowl over a pan of
   hot water and stirring occasionally until it has melted.
   Allow to cool.
2 Meanwhile, dissolve the gelatine by sprinkling it over 3
   tablespoons of water, leaving it to go 'spongy' for a minute
   and then either placing in a bowl of hot water or in the
   microwave on full power for 30 seconds. Allow to cool.
3 Combine the yogurt and vanilla in a large bowl and fold in
   the melted chocolate. Pour in the melted gelatine in a
   steady stream, while stirring. Finally, fold in the whipped
   cream and mix thoroughly. Spoon into a 900 g (2 lb) loaf
   tin that has been lightly oiled and lined with clingfilm.
   Chill for 2–3 hours, until set and firm.
4 Heat the summer fruits and sugar over a gentle heat until
   the sugar has dissolved and then pass the mixture through
   a nylon sieve into a bowl. Stir in the kirsch and then taste
   to ensure it is to the required sweetness.
5 Invert the terrine on to a serving platter, preferably oval in
   shape, decorate with the mint leaves and pour the coulis
   into a jug. If wished, you could slice the terrine on to the
   dessert plates and surround with the coulis.

Double Chocolate Mousse Tartlets

SERVES 4
PREPARATION & COOKING TIME: 40 minutes + 50 minutes chilling + 25 minutes cooking
FREEZING: recommended

These tartlets look so attractive with their contrasting colours: the pale pastry is topped with a layer of dark chocolate with a filling of white chocolate. A raspberry coulis would be a delicious accompaniment to this elegant dessert.

FOR THE PASTRY:
175 g (6 oz) plain flour
25 g (1 oz) cornflour
80 g (3 oz) butter, diced
50 g (2 oz) icing sugar
1 egg and 1 egg yolk

FOR THE MOUSSES:
115 g (4 oz) plain chocolate
175 g (6 oz) white chocolate, broken into pieces
3 tablespoons milk
2 teaspoons gelatine (page 110)
225 ml (8 fl oz) double cream, whipped to soft peaks
2 egg whites
2 drops lemon juice
cocoa powder, for dusting

1 Place the flour, cornflour, butter and icing sugar in a food processor and process until the mixture resembles breadcrumbs. Add the egg and egg yolk, together with 1 teaspoon of cold water and process until a dough forms. Wrap the dough in clingfilm and place in the fridge for 30 minutes.

2 Divide the dough into six pieces and roll each piece out on a floured surface to fit six 10-cm (4-inch) loose-bottomed flan tins. Prick the bases with a fork and trim the edges. Line the pastry cases with baking parchment or foil and fill with baking beans. Chill for a further 20 minutes.

3 Preheat the oven to Gas Mark 4/electric oven 180°C/fan oven 160°C. Bake blind for 10 minutes, remove the parchment or foil and beans and return to the oven for a further 10–15 minutes, until the pastry is golden brown and cooked. Cool completely on a wire rack.

4 Melt the plain chocolate and brush the insides of the pastry cases with it – it's better to brush a thin layer and then repeat rather than brushing one thick layer. Leave to set.

5 Place the white chocolate and milk in a bowl and set the bowl over a pan of barely simmering hot water. Stir occasionally until the chocolate has melted. Allow to cool. In a small dish, sprinkle the gelatine over 1 tablespoon of cold water and leave for the mixture to go spongy. Dissolve the gelatine by setting the bowl in a larger bowl of hot water or place in the microwave for 10 seconds. Stir until no crystals are visible. Allow to cool.

6 Add the gelatine to the white chocolate mixture and mix well. Fold in the whipped cream. Whisk the egg whites with the lemon juice until they are stiff. Add a spoonful of the whisked egg whites to the chocolate mixture and mix it in. Fold in the remaining egg whites using a figure-of-eight action.

7 Spoon the mousse into a piping bag fitted with a star nozzle and pipe the mixture into the tart cases (alternatively simply spoon the mousse into the cases). Dust the tartlets with sifted cocoa powder.

Roast Pineapple with Mango Yogurt Sauce

SERVES 4
PREPARATION & COOKING TIME: 40 minutes
FREEZING: not recommended

Roasting the pineapple gives it a delicious flavour and texture. The sauce complements it beautifully. It's hard to believe that it is so simple to prepare such a lovely dessert.

1 ripe pineapple
3 tablespoons light muscovado sugar
50 g (2 oz) unsalted butter

FOR THE SAUCE:
1 large, ripe mango
200 g tub of Greek-style yogurt
25 g (1 oz) caster sugar
3 drops of vanilla extract
4 small fresh mint sprigs, to decorate

1 Preheat the oven to Gas Mark 6/electric oven 200°C/fan oven 180°C.

2 Peel the pineapple and remove any 'eyes'. Cut it lengthways into four wedges and then cut each wedge into triangular slices. Arrange these slices in a single layer in a large roasting tin, sprinkle over the sugar and then dot with the butter. Roast for 20 minutes.

3 Meanwhile, make the sauce. Peel the mango, remove the stone, cut into chunks and purée. Place in a bowl and whisk with the yogurt, sugar and vanilla extract. Spoon the sauce into a small bowl.

4 To serve, arrange the pineapple on serving plates, place a mint sprig in the centre and allow your guests to help themselves to the mango sauce.

Blueberry Muffins (*above*)

MAKES 12 'man-sized' muffins ♥
PREPARATION & COOKING TIME: 50 minutes
FREEZING: recommended

These are the real McCoy, larger than life, American style! Muffins are good for packed lunches and also make a great pudding, served warm, with custard. They are very easy to make, as they only require mixing, so why not let the children have a go – they are the next generation of cooks, after all – and what an achievement to see that they can make even better-tasting muffins than the supermarket!

80 g (3 oz) butter or margarine
225 g (8 oz) plain flour
2 teaspoons baking powder
$^{1}/_{2}$ teaspoon bicarbonate of soda
115 g (4 oz) golden granulated sugar, plus 2 teaspoons for sprinkling
225 ml (8 fl oz) natural 'bio' yogurt
1 large egg, beaten
$^{1}/_{2}$ teaspoon vanilla essence
175 g (6 oz) blueberries, washed and dried

1 Preheat the oven to Gas Mark 4/electric oven 180°C/fan oven 160°C. Set out 12 paper muffin cases on a baking sheet, or use to line large bun tins if you have them.
2 Melt the butter or margarine and allow to cool slightly.
3 Sift the flour, baking powder and bicarbonate of soda into a large bowl.
4 Stir in the sugar. Make a well in the centre of the dry ingredients and add the butter, yogurt, beaten egg and vanilla extract. Stir to just combine. The mixture will look lumpy – this is fine – over mixing will make the muffins heavy and tough.
5 Carefully fold in the blueberries, taking care not to break them up. Divide between muffin cases and sprinkle a little sugar over the top of each.
6 Bake in the centre of the oven for about 30 minutes, until the muffins are risen and crisp on the top. Cool on a wire rack or eat warm.

Raspberry Buns (*below*)

MAKES 10 ★
PREPARATION & COOKING TIME: 30 minutes
FREEZING: not recommended

These are quick and easy to prepare, so are great for children to make. They are best eaten fresh – not difficult when children are around.

sieve together: 225 g (8 oz) self-raising flour and a pinch of salt
80 g (3 oz) margarine, chilled
80 g (3 oz) caster sugar
2 eggs
raspberry jam

1 Place the flour and salt into a mixing bowl and rub in the margarine until the mixture resembles fine breadcrumbs. Stir in the sugar.
2 Make a well in the centre of the mixture, add the eggs and mix well to form a stiff dough.
3 Turn the dough on to a lightly floured surface and form it into a roll. Cut the roll into 10 pieces and shape each into a ball.
4 Place the balls on to a lightly greased baking sheet, ensuring there is space between each.
5 Make a hole in the middle of each ball and fill with a little raspberry jam; close the hole carefully and dust the tops with a little sugar.
6 Bake at Gas Mark 6/electric oven 200°C/fan oven 180°C for 15–20 minutes until the buns are golden-brown. Leave to cool on the tray for 5 minutes before transferring them on a wire rack to cool completely.
7 The buns will keep fresh if stored in an airtight container for 2–3 days.

Apricot, Polenta & Ricotta Cake

MAKES 12–16 slices
PREPARATION TIME: 30 minutes soaking time + 15 minutes
COOKING TIME: 1½–2 hours
FREEZING: not recommended

This Italian cake, which has a sand-like, moist texture is flavoured with almond and apricots. Polenta is a coarse, golden flour and ricotta is a fragrant Italian cheese with a delicate, smooth flavour, made from ewe's milk whey left over after other cheeses have been produced.

175 g (6 oz) ready-soaked dried apricots, chopped coarsely
3 tablespoons amaretto liqueur
sieve together: 115 g (4 oz) self-raising flour and 115 g (4 oz) self-raising wholemeal flour and 1 teaspoon baking powder and 1 tablespoon ground cinnamon
175 g (6 oz) polenta
225 g (8 oz) caster sugar
250 g (9 oz) ricotta cheese
115 g (4 oz) butter, melted
200 ml (7 fl oz) warm water
80 g (3 oz) walnut pieces, chopped

1 Place the apricots in a bowl, add the liqueur and allow to soak for at least 30 minutes.
2 In a large bowl, place the flours, baking powder, ground cinnamon, polenta and sugar.
3 In another bowl, whisk together the ricotta cheese, melted butter and water. Then whisk this into the flour mixture until well blended.
4 Stir in the apricots, any remaining liqueur and the chopped nuts.
5 Spoon the mixture into a greased and lined 20-cm (8-inch) round cake tin.
6 Bake at Gas Mark 3/electric oven 170°C/fan oven 150°C for 1½–2 hours until the cake is pale golden in colour and a skewer inserted into the centre of the cake comes out clean.
7 Remove the cake from the oven and leave to cool in the tin for 30 minutes before placing it on a wire rack to cool completely.

Passion Cake Squares

MAKES 12 squares ♥
PREPARATION & COOKING TIME: 1 hour
FREEZING: recommended

Passion cake or, to give it its more ordinary name, carrot cake is one of those cakes which seem to be very indulgent but actually is fairly healthy. With vegetable oil instead of butter in the cake mix and Quark for the topping, then plenty of fibre, vitamins and minerals from the fruit, wholemeal flour and nuts, the whole thing is not quite as naughty as it sounds.

125 g (4½ oz) self-raising white flour
125 g (4½ oz) self-raising wholemeal flour
2 teaspoons baking powder
1 teaspoon ground mixed spice
½ teaspoon ground nutmeg
125 g (4½ oz) soft light brown sugar
150 g (5 oz) carrots, grated
grated zest and juice of 1 orange
50 g (2 oz) pecan nuts, chopped roughly, plus 12 to decorate
200 ml (7 fl oz) sunflower oil, plus extra for greasing
2 eggs, beaten lightly
2 ripe bananas, mashed

FOR THE TOPPING:
250 g tub of Quark
75 g (2½ oz) icing sugar, sieved
2 teaspoons orange juice

1 Preheat the oven to Gas Mark 4/electric oven 180°C/fan oven 160°C. Grease a 28 x 19 cm (11 x 7½ inch) baking tin with sunflower oil and base line with greaseproof paper.
2 Place all the ingredients for the cake in a large mixing bowl and beat well until thoroughly combined. Transfer the mixture into the prepared baking tin and bake in the oven for 30–35 minutes until firm on the top and a skewer inserted in the middle comes out clean.
3 Remove the cake from the tin, peel off the greaseproof paper and leave to cool on a wire rack.
4 To make the topping, put the Quark, icing sugar and orange juice into a bowl and mix well together until smooth and creamy. Spread evenly over the top of the cake and swirl with a knife to create an interesting effect. Cut the cake into 12 squares and place a pecan nut in the centre of each square.
5 The cake will keep for several days in an airtight container in the fridge.

Cakes & Bakes

Biscotti

MAKES 14
PREPARATION & COOKING TIME: 50 minutes

These are crisp, dry Italian cookies that look a bit like slices of toasted bread. They are delicious when dipped in coffee.

sieve together: 275 g (10 oz) plain flour and 1 teaspoon baking powder
150 g (5 oz) caster sugar
2 whole eggs, plus 1 egg yolk
1 teaspoon vanilla essence
115 g (4 oz) whole blanched almonds
icing sugar, to dust (optional)

1 Place the flour, baking powder, sugar, eggs and egg yolk, vanilla essence and almonds in a bowl.
2 Using a wooden spoon, mix the ingredients together until the mixture forms a soft dough. Knead the dough gently on a lightly floured surface until it is smooth.
3 Shape the dough into a log and place on a greased baking sheet, then flatten to a thickness of 2.5 cm (1 inch). Dust the top with flour.
4 With a sharp knife, cut two-thirds through the dough to make 14 slices.
5 Bake at Gas Mark 4/electric oven 180°C/fan oven 160°C for 15–20 minutes until light golden and firm. Remove from the oven and, while still warm, completely cut through the biscotti to make individual slices.
6 Place the slices cut side up on a baking sheet. Return to the oven and continue baking for 10–15 minutes until golden.
7 Cool the biscotti on a wire rack. If required, dust with icing sugar.

Cappuccino Bars *(below)*

MAKES 12–16 bars
PREPARATION & COOKING TIME: 1 hour

These chocolate bars with coffee flavouring are enhanced by the milk chocolate icing.

2 tablespoons coffee concentrate
1 tablespoon cocoa powder
225 g (8 oz) butter, softened
225 g (8 oz) caster sugar
4 eggs
sieve together: 225 g (8 oz) self-raising flour and 1 teaspoon baking powder

FOR THE FROSTING
115 g (4 oz) milk chocolate
50 g (2 oz) butter, softened
3 tablespoons milk
175 g (6 oz) icing sugar, sieved

1 In a large bowl, blend together the coffee liquid and the cocoa powder. Add all the remaining cake ingredients and, using a wooden spoon, mix together until well combined; this should take about 2–3 minutes. It is important not to overbeat the mixture.
2 Spoon the mixture into a shallow (4 cm/1½ inches) greased and lined 18 x 28 cm (7 x 11 inch) tin; smooth the top.
3 Bake at Gas Mark 4/electric oven 180°C/fan oven 160°C for 35–45 minutes until well risen and firm to the touch. Cool in the tin for 10 minutes, and then turn out on to a wire rack to cool completely.
4 To make the frosting, melt the chocolate, butter and milk in a bowl over a pan of simmering water. Remove the bowl from the heat; beat in the icing sugar until smooth. When cold spread over the top of the cake, and cut the cake into bars.

120

Fruit Pizza (right)

MAKES a 30-cm (12-inch) pizza
PREPARATION TIME: 55 minutes + rising
FREEZING: recommended (base only)

This fun dessert makes a change from a savoury version. It evolved from having a quantity of fruit left over following a food photography session. The fruits can be varied according to the season.

225 g (8 oz) strong white flour
¹/₂ teaspoon salt
25 g (1 oz) margarine
¹/₂ sachet easy-blend yeast
1 teaspoon caster sugar
1 egg
115 ml (4 fl oz) hand-hot milk

FOR THE TOPPING:
6 tablespoons apricot jam, warmed
1 peach, sliced
115 g (4 oz) strawberries, sliced
1 orange, sliced in circles
1 kiwi fruit, sliced
2 tablespoons icing sugar, sifted

1 Sift the flour and salt into a bowl. Rub in the margarine until the mixture resembles fine breadcrumbs. Stir in the yeast and sugar. Add the egg and milk and mix to form a soft dough.
2 Turn the dough on to a floured surface and knead well until the dough is smooth and elastic.
3 Place the dough in a clean, greased bowl, cover and leave to rise until doubled in size.
4 Preheat the oven to Gas Mark 6/electric oven 200°C/fan oven 180°C.
5 When the dough has risen, knock it back. Roll into a 30 cm (12-inch) round and place on a greased baking tray. Bake for 10 minutes.
6 Remove from the oven, spread with apricot jam and place the fruit on top. Continue cooking for a further 15 minutes. Sprinkle with icing sugar in the last 5 minutes for a glazed finish.

Brioches

MAKES 8 small brioches or 1 large one
PREPARATION & COOKING TIME: 35 minutes + rising
FREEZING: recommended

A French sweet bread/cake, brioches can be baked whole in a deep round fluted tin or as individual cakes. We have enjoyed these for breakfast, served with unsalted butter and conserves. They can form the basis of a savoury dish, if you hollow the centre out and use the 'shell' to hold a savoury filling, or try slicing, buttering and layering into ramekin dishes to make individual bread and butter puddings.

225 g (8 oz) strong white flour
¹/₂ teaspoon salt
115 g (4 oz) unsalted butter
1 teaspoon easy-blend yeast
25 g (1 oz) caster sugar
3 eggs, beaten
50 ml (2 fl oz) hand-hot milk

1 Sift the flour and salt into a mixing bowl. Rub in the butter.
2 Stir in the yeast and sugar. Add the eggs and enough milk to make a very soft dough.
3 Cover and leave to rise for 2 hours.
4 Knead gently on a well floured surface and divide into eight pieces.
5 Take a small ball from each piece to form the 'hat'. Form the rest into buns and place in greased fluted tins. Cut a cross in the top and place the 'hat' on top. Leave to prove for 20 minutes.
6 Preheat the oven to Gas Mark 7/electric oven 220°C/fan oven 200°C.
7 Bake for 15–20 minutes, until golden. Place on a wire rack to cool.

Sun-Dried Tomato, Olive & Basil Foccacia

MAKES 1 round loaf
PREPARATION & COOKING TIME: 15–20 minutes + rising +
  20-25 mintes cooking
FREEZING: recommended

A traditional flat bread from the northern shores of the Mediterranean.

350 g (12 oz) strong white flour
1¹/₂ teaspoons salt
1 sachet of easy-blend yeast
8 sun-dried tomatoes, chopped
12 stoned olives, halved
8 fresh basil leaves, chopped roughly
200 ml (7 fl oz) hand-hot water
5–6 tablespoons extra-virgin olive oil

1 Sift the flour and salt into a large bowl. Add the yeast, tomatoes, half the olives and most of the basil.
2 Gradually stir in the water and 3 tablespoons of the olive oil to make a soft dough.
3 Turn on to a floured surface and knead the dough until smooth and elastic.
4 Shape into a 25-cm (10-inch) round, place on a greased baking sheet and prick all over with a fork. Cover with greased clingfilm and leave in a warm place until doubled in size.
5 Preheat the oven to Gas Mark 7/electric oven 220°C/fan oven 200°C.
6 When risen, remove the clingfilm and gently press the remaining olives into the dough.
7 Trickle the rest of the olive oil over the dough, spreading it lightly with your fingers. Sprinkle over the rest of the basil and a little salt.
8 Bake in the preheated oven for 20–25 minutes, until golden and hollow-sounding when the base is tapped. Transfer to a wire rack to cool.

Sunflower Ciabatta

MAKES 1 oval loaf
PREPARATION & COOKING TIME: 15–20 minutes + rising +
  20–25 minutes cooking
FREEZING: recommended

An Italian bread with a light texture, ciabatta is delicious served with cold poached salmon and salad or used as a base for pizzas.

250 g (9 oz) strong white flour
¹/₂ teaspoon salt
1 teaspoon easy-blend yeast
1 teaspoon sugar
25 g (1 oz) sunflower seeds
1¹/₂ tablespoons olive oil
175 ml (6 fl oz) hand-hot water

1 Sift the flour and salt into a bowl. Add the yeast, sugar and sunflower seeds.
2 Add the oil and enough water to form a soft dough.
3 Turn on to a lightly floured surface and knead until smooth.
4 Place in a clean, greased bowl, cover and leave to rise until doubled in size.
5 Knock back and shape into an oval.
6 Place on a greased baking sheet and leave to prove for 30 minutes.
7 Preheat the oven to Gas Mark 7/electric oven 220°C/fan oven 200°C.
8 Bake the loaf for 20–25 minutes or until golden and the base sounds hollow when tapped. Transfer to a wire rack to cool.

Savoury Swirls with Tomato & Basil

MAKES 9 pieces
PREPARATION & COOKING TIME: 25–30 minutes + rising +
  25–30 minutes cooking
FREEZING: recommended

These were inspired by our traditional Chelsea Buns, but have a savoury filling.

225 g (8 oz) strong white flour
¹/₂ teaspoon salt
25 g (1 oz) margarine
¹/₂ sachet easy-blend yeast
1 egg, beaten
5 tablespoons hand-hot milk

FOR THE FILLING:
3 tablespoons tomato purée
10 fresh basil leaves, chopped

1 In a large bowl, sift together the flour and salt. Rub in the margarine and add the yeast. Stir in the egg and milk to give a soft dough.
2 Turn on to a floured surface and knead for 8–10 minutes, until the dough is smooth, elastic and no longer sticky.
3 Place the dough in a clean, greased bowl, cover and leave to rise until doubled in size.
4 Transfer the risen dough to a lightly floured surface. Knock back and knead.
5 Roll the dough into a rectangle 30 x 23-cm (12 x 9 inches). Spread with tomato purée and sprinkle on the chopped basil.
6 Roll up the dough like a Swiss roll, starting at the longest side. Cut into nine equal pieces and place on a greased baking sheet, cut-side down, to form a square, about 1 cm (½ inch) apart. Cover and leave to prove for about 30 minutes, until well risen.
7 Preheat the oven to Gas Mark 6/electric oven 210°C/fan oven 190°C.
8 Bake for 25–30 minutes, until golden brown. Place on a wire rack to cool.

Olive & Cheese Bread Ring *(above)*

MAKES 8–10 pieces

PREPARATION & COOKING TIME: 35–40 minutes + rising +
25–30 minutes cooking

FREEZING: recommended

*This bread is a fusion of Mediterranean and traditional
English flavours. It's delicious served with a green salad
or a summer soup.*

250 g (9 oz) strong white bread flour
¹/₂ teaspoon salt
1 teaspoon caster sugar
¹/₂ sachet easy-blend yeast
100 ml (3¹/₂ fl oz) hand-hot milk
1 egg, beaten
50 g (2 oz) butter

FOR THE FILLING:
50 g (2 oz) stoned olives, sliced
115 g (4 oz) Cheddar cheese, grated
1 egg, beaten
salt and freshly ground black pepper
sesame seeds, to decorate

1 Prepare the dough by mixing together the flour, salt, sugar
and yeast in a bowl.
2 Mix together the warmed milk and beaten egg. Add to the
dry ingredients and beat well.
3 Turn the dough on to a floured board and knead until
smooth and elastic. Place in a clean, greased bowl and
leave in a warm place to rise until doubled in size.
4 Turn the dough on to a floured surface and roll into a
rectangle about 15 x 30 cm (6 x 12 inches).
5 Cover the bottom two-thirds of the dough with half the
butter, chopped into small pieces.
6 Fold the top third over the centre third and then the
bottom third over that. Seal the edges.
7 Turn the dough a quarter-turn and repeat with the rest of
the butter.
8 Place the dough on a plate, cover and chill for 20 minutes.

MAKING THE RING
1 Mix together the filling ingredients, saving a little egg for
glazing.
2 Roll the dough into an oblong about 30 x 20 cm (12 x 8
inches).
3 Spread the filling over the surface.
4 Roll the dough from the longest edge like a Swiss roll.
5 Shape this into a ring. Place on a greased baking sheet.
6 Make a series of cuts evenly into the ring and brush with
egg. Sprinkle with sesame seeds. Leave in a warm place to
rise for about 30 minutes.
7 Preheat the oven to Gas Mark 7/electric oven 220°C/fan
oven 200°C.
8 Bake for 25–30 minutes, until golden brown. Transfer to a
wire rack to cool.

Naan (above)

MAKES 4 naan breads
PREPARATION & COOKING TIME: 10–15 minutes + rising +
  10–15 minutes cooking
FREEZING: recommended

*Naan is the Persian word for bread and is commonly used in
India and many Asian countries. These are flat breads with a
crisp crust usually served with Indian meals.*

300 g (11 oz) strong white flour
1 teaspoon salt
1 teaspoon baking powder
1½ teaspoons easy-blend yeast
3 tablespoons natural yogurt
1½ tablespoons sunflower oil
150 ml (¼ pint) hand-hot water

1 Sift together the flour, salt and baking powder into a
  mixing bowl.
2 Stir in the yeast. Add the yogurt, oil and water to form a
  soft dough.
3 Knead until smooth and elastic.
4 Place in a clean, greased bowl, cover and leave to rise until
  doubled in size.
5 Knock back, divide the dough into four and roll each piece
  into an oval 20 x 15 cm (8 x 6 inches). Leave to prove for
  15 minutes.
6 Preheat the grill until very hot and cook the breads under
  the grill for 3–4 minutes on each side, or until golden and
  puffy.

Mixed-flour Rolls (opposite)

MAKES 6 rolls
PREPARATION & COOKING TIME: 20–25 minutes + rising +
  10–15 minutes cooking
FREEZING: recommended

*Flours can be mixed to give different textures to these rolls.
Combining strong brown and strong white flour will give a soft
bread texture; strong white and country-grain will give a soft
texture with a nutty flavour and strong wholemeal and
country-grain will give a coarser texture and a stronger nutty
flavour.*

250 g (9 oz) mixture of strong brown flour and strong white flour or
  250 g (9 oz) mixture of strong white flour and country-grain
  flour or 250 g (9 oz) mixture of strong wholemeal flour and
  country-grain flour
1 teaspoon salt
25 g (1 oz) butter
1 teaspoon sugar
1 teaspoon easy-blend dried yeast
175 ml (6 fl oz) hand-hot milk

1 Sift the flour and salt into a bowl. Rub in the butter.
2 Stir in the sugar and yeast. Add enough milk to form a soft
  dough. You may need more milk if using wholemeal flour.
3 Turn the dough on to a floured surface and knead well
  until the dough is smooth and elastic.
4 Place the dough in a clean, greased bowl, cover and leave
  to rise until doubled in size.
5 Preheat the oven to Gas Mark 7/electric oven 220°C/fan
  oven 200°C.
6 Knock back and divide the dough into six. Form into rolls
  (see below). Place on a greased baking sheet and leave to
  prove for 30 minutes.
7 Bake for 10–15 minutes. Transfer to a wire rack to cool.

SHAPING ROLLS

TWIST Form the dough into a sausage 30 cm (12 inches)
long, fold in half and twist around itself.
PLAIT Divide the dough into three pieces. Form each into a
sausage 12 cm (5 inches) long and plait together.
KNOT Form the dough into a sausage 24 cm (9½ inches)
long and tie it into a knot.
COTTAGE ROLLS Take a small piece from the dough and roll
it into a ball. Form the larger piece into a round and place
the smaller ball on top. Push a floured wooden spoon handle
through the top to form an indentation.
'S' SHAPE Form the dough into a sausage 18 cm (7 inches)
long and bend into an 'S' shape, so the inside edges touch
each other.
COBURG Form the dough into a flattened ball and cut a
cross in the top, using a sharp knife.
HEDGEHOG Form the dough into an oval, making one end
more pointed to form the nose. Using a pair of scissors, snip
the dough to give the appearance of spines. Currants can be
used for eyes, if you like.
BAP Form the dough into a ball, place on a baking tray and
flatten with the palm of your hand. Dust with flour before
baking.

Traditional Raspberry Jam *(right)*

MAKES about 2.2 kg (5 lb)
PREPARATION & COOKING TIME: 40 minutes

This must be one of the all-time favourites and so easy to make. It can be rather expensive if you have to buy the fruit, which is why there are some variations included here with some less expensive partners. The nectarine version is particularly good and is similar to the peach version sent in by Christine Sherriff. They all have a beautiful aroma and the taste is delectable. Use to fill a freshly made sponge cake or team it up with fromage frais or flavoured mascarpone cheese for a special teatime treat or party pudding.

1.3 kg (3 lb) raspberries, washed and drained well if necessary
1.3 kg (3 lb) granulated sugar

1 Place the raspberries in a large pan and simmer gently for about 10 minutes, until the raspberries are tender and the juice is extracted.
2 Remove from the heat and add the sugar, stirring until it is completely dissolved.
3 Put the pan back on the heat and bring to the boil. Boil rapidly for about 5 minutes and then remove any scum and test for a set (see page 12).
4 Pour into cooled, sterilised jars and then seal and label (see pages 12 and 13).

RASPBERRY & NECTARINE (OR PEACH) JAM: Replace half of the raspberries with 675 g (1¹/₂ lb) chopped nectarines or peeled peaches and add 150 ml (¹/₄ pint) of water and 2 tablespoons of lemon juice. Cook the nectarines or peaches first with the water and lemon juice until soft – about 5 minutes. Add the raspberries and simmer for a further 5 minutes. Continue as above.

RASPBERRY & RHUBARB JAM: Again, replace half the raspberries with rhubarb and add 150 ml (¹/₄ pint) of water. Cook for about 15 minutes before adding the raspberries. Continue as above.

Mixed Berry Jam

MAKES about 675 g (1¹/₂ lb)
PREPARATION & COOKING TIME: 50 minutes

This recipe needs no added sugar but, instead, uses apple juice in concentrated form, which you can buy from healthfood shops. It is suitable for some diabetics but, obviously, individual diabetics' dietary needs vary greatly. It is not a true preserve as it is too low in sugar to prevent moulds from growing. Store in a refrigerator.

225 g (8 oz) strawberries, fresh or frozen, hulled
225 g (8 oz) blackberries, fresh or frozen
225 g (8 oz) gooseberries
225 g (8 oz) apple juice concentrate, weighed in a plastic container

1 Liquidise half the fruit and place in a saucepan, with the whole fruit.

2 Simmer gently until the gooseberries are cooked – about 15–20 minutes.
3 Add the apple juice and boil for 15 minutes or until you achieve a set (see page ??). Remove any scum (see page ??).
4 Pour into cooled, sterilised jars and cover. Label and store for up to 6 months. Once open, store in the fridge and use within 2 weeks.

Tutti Frutti Jam

MAKES about 2.7 kg (6 lb)
PREPARATION & COOKING TIME: 1 hour 10 minutes

This is a particular favourite and very fruity, as the name suggests. It first appeared in a WI Home Skills book written by Olive Odell in the late 70s. There are also several variations, known by names such as 'Midsummer Jam', and 'Four-Fruit Jam' (see below). The success of the jam is in the combination of high, medium and low pectin content of the different fruit. Make sure you cook the currants until they are really soft as, once the sugar is added, you're at the point of no return! The best way to strip the currants from the stem is to hold the stalk in one hand and use a fork to slide down the stem and strip away the fruit.

450 g (1 lb) blackcurrants, stripped from stalks
450 g (1 lb) redcurrants, stripped from stalks
450 g (1 lb) strawberries, hulled
450 g (1 lb) raspberries, hulled
1.8 kg (4 lb) granulated sugar

1 Place the blackcurrants and redcurrants in a large preserving pan with 150 ml (¼ pint) of water. Bring to the boil and then gently simmer for about 15–20 minutes, ensuring that the skins of the currants are soft.
2 Add the strawberries and raspberries and simmer for a further 10 minutes.
3 Add the sugar, stirring until dissolved. Bring to the boil and boil rapidly until setting point is reached (see page 12).
4 Remove any scum from surface of jam, if necessary (page 12). Pour into cooled, sterilised jars and seal (see page 13).

MIDSUMMER JAM: Replace the blackcurrants with gooseberries.
FOUR-FRUIT JAM: Replace the redcurrants with gooseberries.

Microwave Strawberry Jam with Apple

MAKES: about 1.1 kg (2¼ lb)
PREPARATION & COOKING TIME: about 50 minutes

This quick microwave version of strawberry jam is delicious. You can't really taste the apple – the strawberry flavour shines through.

115 g (4 oz) prepared weight peeled and chopped cooking apple
675 g (1½ lb) strawberries
675 g (1½ lb) granulated sugar

1 Place the apples in a large bowl. Cover with cling film and puncture a couple of times. Cook on full power for 5 minutes. Remove the cover and mash the apple.
2 Add the strawberries and stir. Cook on full power for 5 minutes and then stir and mash the fruit. Cook on full power for a further 10 minutes.
3 Add the sugar and stir to dissolve. Continue to cook for 2 minutes on full and stir well. Remove any scum (see page 12).
4 Cook for 3 minutes and test for a set (see page 12). Continue cooking for 1 minute and testing in the intervals, if necessary, until setting point is reached.
5 Pour into cooled, sterilised jars, seal and label (see pages 12 and 13).

Rhubarb & Blackcurrant Jam

MAKES about 2.2 kg (5 lb)
PREPARATION & COOKING TIME: 1 hour

Midge Thomas devised this delicious combination of fruits when teaching cookery at Denman College on the WI Markets courses.

900 g (2 lb) blackcurrants, washed and stalks removed
675 g (1½ lb) rhubarb, washed and sliced
1.5 kg (3 lb 5 oz) sugar

1 Place the fruit and 425 ml (¾ pint) of water in a large preserving pan. Bring to the boil and then gently simmer until the fruit is quite soft – about 20 minutes. Remove from the heat.
2 Add the sugar and stir until dissolved.
3 Return to the heat and bring to the boil. Boil rapidly until setting point is reached. Remove any scum (see page 12). Test for a set after 5–10 minutes.
4 Pour into cooled, sterilised jars, seal and label (see pages 12 and 13).

Ratatouille Chutney (opposite, left)

MAKES about enough to fill four 450 g (1 lb) jars
PREPARATION TIME: about 45 minutes
COOKING TIME: about 2–2¹⁄₂ hours

A paticular favourite, this is a strong and hot chutney.

900 g (2 lb) tomatoes, skinned and chopped
450 g (1 lb) spanish onions, chopped
450 g (1 lb) courgettes, sliced thinly
1 large green pepper, sliced
1 large red pepper, sliced
1 aubergine, diced
2 large garlic cloves, crushed
1 tablespoon salt
1 tablespoon cayenne pepper
1 tablespoon paprika
1 tablespoon ground coriander
300 ml (¹⁄₂ pint) malt vinegar
350 g (12 oz) granulated sugar

1 Place the tomatoes, onions, courgettes, peppers, aubergine and garlic in a large pan. Add the salt, cayenne and paprika and coriander. Cover and cook gently, stirring occasionally, until the juices run.
2 Bring to the boil, reduce the heat, uncover and simmer for 1–1¹⁄₂ hours or until the vegetables are soft but still recognisable as shapes, and most of the water from the tomatoes has evaporated.
3 Add the vinegar and sugar, stirring to dissolve the sugar. Continue to cook for 1 hour or until the chutney is thick and there is no free vinegar on top.
4 Spoon while still hot into cooled, sterilised jars and seal with vinegar-proof covers (see pages 12 and 13). Label and store for at least 2 months to mature

Nectarine Chutney (opposite, right)

MAKES about 1.3 kg (3 lb)
PREPARATION TIME: 30 minutes
COOKING TIME: about 1³⁄₄ hours

This recipe comes from New Zealand and goes well with lamb. It is quite strongly flavoured with rosemary, so you could reduce the amount by up to a half. The recipe states that it can be made with any fruit.

1.1 kg (2¹⁄₄ lb) nectarines, about 12 fruits, stoned and quartered
675 g (1¹⁄₂ lb) red onions, sliced finely
4 garlic cloves, chopped roughly
1 lemon, halved and pips removed, sliced finely
2 tablespoons chopped fresh rosemary
1 teaspoon cumin seeds
1 teaspoon fennel seeds
250 ml (9 fl oz) cider vinegar
500 g (1 lb 2 oz) demerara sugar

1 Preheat the oven to Gas Mark 6/electric oven 200°C/fan oven 180°C.
2 Put all the ingredients except the sugar into a large roasting tin. Mix well and roast for 1¹⁄₄ hours, stirring occasionally.
3 When the mixture starts to reduce and colour, add the sugar. Cook for a further 30 minutes, stirring twice during this period. The chutney should be fairly dry and any liquid should be quite syrupy and jam-like. The shapes of the fruit should still be discernible.
4 Spoon into cooled, sterilised jars and cover with vinegar-proof lids (see pages 12 and 13). Label and store. This could be used straightaway but the flavour will mature on keeping.

Brandied Grape & Apricot Jam (pictured opposite, in the spoon)

MAKES about 1.3 kg (3 lb)
PREPARATION TIME: 20 minutes + 2–3 hours standing
COOKING TIME: about 40 minutes

This recipe is from Joan Brown, stalwart of Scotton and District WI and of Gainsborough and District WI Market, and was a prizewinner in the Lincolnshire Show in the 1970s. She suggests that it is delicious served with cold meats and that peaches can be used instead of apricots. Similar jams made with grapes, lemon, nuts and brandy, are part of the traditional Middle-Eastern welcoming ceremony, eaten with a spoon and accompanied by a glass of cold water.

225 g (8 oz) black grapes, halved and pips removed
225 g (8 oz) green grapes, halved and pips removed (or use 450 g/ 1 lb seedless grapes, halved, instead of both black and green grapes)
450 g (1 lb) apricots, halved and stoned
900 g (2 lb) granulated sugar
juice of 1 lemon
50 g (2 oz) blanched almonds, chopped (optional)
5 tablespoons brandy

1 Place the fruit in a preserving pan, with the sugar. Leave to stand for 2–3 hours.
2 Slowly bring to the boil, stirring until the sugar is dissolved.
3 Add the lemon juice and then boil rapidly until setting point is reached. Remove any scum (see page 12). Add the almonds, if using, and the brandy.
4 Pour into cooled, sterilised jars and seal (see pages 12 and 13). Label and store.

NOTE: Apricot and almond is a favourite combination but other nuts can be added to jam: how about walnuts with plum jam? Or stir toasted pine nut kernels into raspberry jam.

Peach Marmalade

MAKES about 1.3 kg (3 lb)
PREPARATION & COOKING TIME: 1½ hours

This preserve was served to Doreen Hancock of Willingham-by-Stow WI for breakfast with croissants on a twinning trip to France. Her hostess very kindly gave her the recipe. It is a lovely colour and tastes great. The ratio of sugar to fruit is not in the usual proportion and this makes the preserve unsuitable for long keeping.

2 oranges, chopped (or sliced, if you prefer larger pieces of peel)
800 g (1¾ lb) sugar
115 ml (4 fl oz) water
1.3 kg (3 lb) peaches, skinned and chopped
juice of 1 lemon

1 In a large pan, cook the oranges with 200 g (7 oz) of the sugar and the water, until they are soft.
2 Add the peaches, with the rest of the sugar and the lemon juice. Stir until the sugar is dissolved and then bring to the boil.
3 Cook to setting point – about 15 minutes. Remove any scum (see page 12).
4 Pour immediately into cooled, sterilised jars and seal (see pages 12 and 13). Label and store in a cool and dry place for up to 6 months. Once opened, store in the fridge and use within 3–4 weeks.

Gooseberry Curd

MAKES about 1.4 kg (3 lb) ★
PREPARATION & COOKING TIME: 25 minutes

Gooseberries make a lovely tangy curd. Some people prefer to keep in the skins and seeds of the fruit rather than have a smooth curd. If you're not going to sieve it, though, you need to top and tail the fruit.

900 g (2 lb) gooseberries
450 g (1 lb) granulated sugar
115 g (4 oz) butter, preferably unsalted
4 eggs, beaten

1 Place the gooseberries and 2–3 tablespoons of water in a large bowl and cover with pierced clingfilm. Microwave on full power for 10–15 minutes or until very soft. Rub through a sieve to remove skins and seeds.
2 Return to the bowl and add the sugar and butter. Cook on full power for 2 minutes or until the butter is melted and the sugar is dissolved.
3 Add the eggs and stir well. Cook, stirring frequently, until the mixture is thick and will coat the back of a spoon.
4 Strain this again, to remove any bits of cooked egg. Pour into cooled, sterilised jars and seal with a waxed disc (see pages 12 and 13). Cover with cellophane and store in the fridge for up to 6 weeks. Once opened, use within 2 weeks.

Apricot & Honey Conserve

MAKES about 450 g (1 lb)
PREPARATION & COOKING TIME: 10 minutes

225 g (8 oz) honey
225 g (8 oz) apricots
4 teaspoons lemon juice
½ teaspoon ground cinnamon
2 tablespoons brandy

This is a very quick and easy recipe from Simply Good Food, a book published by the NFWI Wales following their 'Lose Weight Wales' campaign in the 1990s. About 2,500 individual WI members and their families became fitter and healthier through following the campaign and the cookbook was devised to help them achieve their aims.

1 Process all the ingredients together. Store in a sterilised jar (see pages 12 and 13) with an airtight top for up to 6 months. Once opened, use within 2–3 weeks.

Near-Miss Jam Wine

MAKES enough to fill five or six 75 cl bottles
PREPARATION TIME: about 15 minutes + 24 hours + 5 days + 3 weeks + 6 months + 3 months

This great idea comes from Ann Creasey. Ann says it certainly saves face, as well as the jam. All the ingredients are available from home-brewing shops and some pharmacies.

1.3 kg (3 lb) any fruit jam with soft set or no set
1 teaspoon pectin-destroying enzyme (see note)
2 teaspoons citric acid
225 g (8 oz) raisins, minced or processed
675 g (1½ lb) sugar
1 teaspoon grape tannin
1 teaspoon brewer's yeast
1 yeast nutrient tablet
1 Camden tablet, crushed

1 Put the jam into a sterilised plastic bucket and pour over 4.5 litres (1 gallon) of boiling water. Leave to cool.
2 Add pectin-destroying enzyme and citric acid. Leave for 24 hours.
3 Add the minced raisins, sugar, tannin, yeast and yeast nutrient tablet. Stir well to dissolve the sugar. Cover and leave to ferment for about 5 days, giving it a stir each day.
4 Strain the mixture through a nylon sieve or muslin into a fermentation jar. Fit an airlock and leave to ferment out, i.e. until the bubbling stops – about 3 weeks.
5 When fermentation is finished and the wine is clear, rack into a clean jar for 6 months storage, adding the crushed Camden tablet to prevent further fermentation.
6 Bottle after another 3 months.

NOTE: Using pectin-destroying enzyme – Pectinol or Pektolase – is most important, since the high level of pectin that jam contains would otherwise prevent the wine from clearing.

Elderflower Cordial

MAKES 575 ml (1 pint)
PREPARATION & COOKING TIME: 20 minutes + 24 hours infusion

This keeps well in the fridge for several months, although it may not last that long.

6–8 elderflowers
575 ml (1 pint) water
450 g (1 lb) caster sugar
2 teaspoons citric acid or cider vinegar
juice and grated zest of 1 lemon

1 Bring the sugar and water gently to the boil and stir until the sugar is dissolved.
2 Put the elderflowers in a bowl and pour the sugar solution over them. Stir in the citric acid or cider vinegar, the lemon juice and zest. Cover and leave for 24 hours to infuse.
3 Strain through muslin and bottle into sterilised containers (see page 12).

Gooseberry Chutney

MAKES about 2 kg (4½ lb)
PREPARATION & COOKING TIME: 1 hour 45 minutes

This recipe comes from Gill Worrell, of Marton WI and Gainsborough WI Market. Gill quickens up the process by cooking the gooseberries and onions in the microwave first, which will obviously reduce the total cooking time considerably. Gill always uses sultanas rather than raisins and the lighter brown sugar. Gill also makes the chutney with red gooseberries, which produce a good colour. You could substitute tarragon vinegar for half the malt vinegar, for a different flavour.

1.3 kg (3 lb) gooseberries
225 g (8 oz) onions
225 g (8 oz) sultanas
20 g (¼ oz) salt, or less if preferred
450 g (1 lb) sugar
850 ml (1½ pints) malt vinegar
1 tablespoon allspice berries
1 tablespoon ground ginger
¼ teaspoon cayenne pepper

1 Place all the ingredients in a large preserving pan. Bring to the boil and then reduce the heat and simmer, uncovered, until the chutney is of a thick and pulpy consistency, about 45 minutes.
2 Spoon into cooled, sterilised jars and seal with a vinegar-proof cover (see pages 12 and 13). Label and store for at least 4–6 weeks before using.

Cumberland Bean Pickle

MAKES about six 450 g (1 lb) jars
PREPARATION & COOKING TIME: 1 hour

There are several versions of this available and sometimes it is, mistakenly, called a chutney. It uses similar ingredients to piccalilli, in which the raw vegetables are brined and then cooked and mixed in a hot spiced sauce. In this pickle, however, the vegetables are simply cooked in lightly salted water before being mixed with the sauce. This was given by Kathryn Wall of the Clwyd–Flint WI Federation.

900 g (2 lb) prepared weight trimmed and thinly sliced runner beans
450 g (1 lb) onions, sliced finely
a pinch of salt
425 ml (¾ pint) white malt vinegar
50 g (2 oz) plain flour (some recipes use cornflour)
1 tablespoon mustard powder
½ teaspoon freshly ground black pepper
½ teaspoon ground turmeric
150 g (5 oz) white sugar

1 Put the beans and onions in a pan with a pinch of salt and just enough water to cover. Bring to the boil and then simmer until tender – about 20 minutes.
2 In another large pan, mix together a tablespoon of vinegar, the flour and the spices to a smooth paste. Start to heat gently, adding the rest of the vinegar very carefully bit by bit, as you would for a roux sauce, ensuring that there are no lumps.
3 Simmer gently for 2–3 minutes, until the flour is cooked.
4 Add the sugar and stir well to make sure it is dissolved. Bring the sauce to the boil. It should be thick and shiny.
5 Drain the beans and onions and add to the sauce. Stir well and bring the mixture back to the boil. Continue cooking for about 10 minutes.
6 Spoon the mixture into cooled, sterilised jars and seal with a vinegar-proof cover (see pages 12 and 13). Label and store.

CARROT & RUNNER BEAN PICKLE: Add 450 g (1 lb) of peeled and sliced carrots and cook along with the beans and onions.
Add more sugar if you prefer a sweeter pickle. Also works well with broad beans and french beans.

Raspberry Vinegar

MAKES 1.1 litres (2 pints)
PREPARATION & COOKING TIME: 35 minutes + 3–6 days
  standing

*Fruit vinegars are very easy to make, even if you do have to
wait a few days for the initial stage to be completed. The
unsweetened vinegar can be used in salad dressings, sauces or
drinks. The sweetened version is an excellent remedy for a sore
throat (taken neat and hot) and can be used to make summer
drinks, or pour it on freshly-made pancakes for one of the best
puddings ever. You can also use blackberries, gooseberries
(chopped roughly), blueberries or blackcurrants, or with
strawberries and with a mixture of berries.*

450 g (1 lb) raspberries, washed only if absolutely necessary and
  then drained well
575 ml (1 pint) wine or cider vinegar
sugar (see step 3)

1 Place the fruit in a glass, china or earthenware bowl and
  pour the vinegar over it. Cover the bowl with a cloth and
  leave to stand in a cool place for 4–6 days, stirring each
  day. Pop a plate over the top to save anyone inadvertently
  placing anything on it.
2 Strain off and measure the liquid. For the unsweetened
  version, strain the vinegar through a jelly bag or filter.
  Pour into sterilised bottles and seal (see pages 12 and 13).
3 For the sweetened version, weigh 450 g (1 lb) of sugar for
  each 575 ml (1 pint) of vinegar. Put the liquid into a large
  pan and heat gently. Add the sugar and stir until it is
  completely dissolved. Bring to the boil and boil for 10
  minutes. Pour into sterilised bottles and cork or seal with
  screw top. Leave to mature for at least 2 weeks before
  using.

Gooseberry Mint Jelly (*opposite*)

MAKES about 1.1 kg (2¼ lb)
PREPARATION & COOKING TIME: 1–1½ hours + draining
  overnight

*This recipe was supplied by Judith Wilson. It's a very useful
alternative to jelly made with apples, as the mint supply can be
a bit sparse by the apple season. It works best with under-ripe
or just-ripe gooseberries. Judith says that the recipe works
equally well with cooking apples.*

1.3 kg (3 lb) gooseberries, washed and dried but no need to top and
  tail
1 bunch of fresh mint
425 ml (¾ pint) vinegar
granulated sugar (see step 4)
2 tablespoons finely chopped fresh mint

1 Put the gooseberries in a heavy-based pan with enough
  water to cover them. Add the bunch of mint and then
  bring to the boil and simmer until the gooseberries are soft
  – about 30 minutes.
2 Add the vinegar and cook for a further 5 minutes.
3 Remove from the heat, put the contents of the pan into a
  jelly bag and allow to drip into another container
  overnight.
4 Measure the liquid and put in a pan with sugar, allowing
  450 g (1 lb) of sugar to each 575 ml (1 pint) of liquid.
5 Heat gently until the sugar has dissolved and then boil
  briskly until setting point is reached – about 15 minutes
  (see page ??). Remove any scum (see page ??).
6 Turn off the heat and cool slightly before stirring in the
  chopped mint.
7 Pot into small cooled, sterilised jars, cover and label (see
  pages 12 and 13).

NOTE ON HERBS IN JELLIES: Herb jellies are given extra
appeal if you include either some of the chopped herb in the
jelly or suspend a sprig in it. However, there can sometimes
be a problem with the chopped herb or sprig rising in the jar.
Terry Clarke seems to have solved this by using the prepared
herb wet, but not soaking, and adding it after setting point is
reached. Terry freezes finely chopped mint specifically for
this purpose.

about 4.5 kg (10 lb) green walnuts

FOR THE BRINE:
450 g (1 lb) salt and 4.5 litres (8 pints) water, or 50 g (2 oz) salt per
  575 ml (1 pint) water

FOR THE SWEETENED SPICED VINEGAR:
1.7 litres (3 pints) malt vinegar
450 g (1 lb) brown sugar
1¹/₂ teaspoons salt
1 teaspoon pickling spice
1 teaspoon black peppercorns
¹/₂ teaspoon whole cloves

1 To make the brine, stir the salt into the water until the salt
   has dissolved.
2 Once you have picked your walnuts, put on a pair of
   rubber gloves. This is vital because walnuts will produce a
   brown stain which give the fingers the appearance of those
   of a 40-a-day smoker! Take a fork and prick each walnut
   three or four times. Put them in a jar and cover them with
   the brine overnight. Repeat the process for three days,
   using fresh salt water each time.
3 Rinse the walnuts in clean water to remove excess salt. The
   walnuts should then be placed on a tray outside or in a
   window to dry until they blacken. This takes about a day.
4 To make the spiced vinegar, put all the ingredients in a pan
   and bring to the boil. Boil for 5–10 minutes. Once the
   walnuts are black, place them in a sterilised jar and cover
   with the sweetened spiced vinegar. Seal and label (see pages
   12 and 13). They will take about 6 months to become
   mature enough.

NOTES: The walnuts can be covered with unsweetened spiced
vinegar, if preferred. It's an idea to make several smaller jars
and fill with different aromatic flavourings. Chillies, peppers
and sugar are all possible.

Dylan's Pickled Walnuts

MAKES enough to fill two 1.3 kg (3 lb) jars
PREPARATION & COOKING TIME: 1 hour + 3 days brining

*This recipe was supplied by Dylan Roys, of BBC Radio
Lincolnshire. He has covered many a WI event and WI Market
all around Lincolnshire and we receive excellent coverage of
our activities in the Federation. This recipe came about
following Dylan's trip out to see Bill, 'The Fulbeck Walnut
Man'. Dylan says: 'I've always been a big fan of pickled
walnuts although I must admit they are an acquired taste.
Mother once had a huge sweet jar which lasted many years and
they improved with age.*

*'Anyone looking for pickled walnuts in the shop will know
how expensive they are, which is a pity because they are so
easy to put down. The shop-bought ones are also a pale
imitation of the real home-pickled ones. There are many recipes
but on a recent trip out with my mate Bill, he gave me some
good tips. Walnuts need to be picked in the green before the
shell inside has formed. Bill tells me Wimbledon week is a good
bet. Not every year will produce a good crop of walnuts so
make enough to last through a bad season.'*

*Another recipe for pickled walnuts came from Margaret
Hanford, who says that her neighbour has a huge walnut tree
in his garden. He reckons the latest date for picking is 12th
July. Margaret very kindly sends quantities for the brine and a
sweetened spiced vinegar but otherwise the method is exactly as
Dylan outlines.*

September marks the **beginning of harvest time** and there is still plenty of fruit to be had. The second crop of raspberries runs from September to the first frosts and, in cooler areas, blackberries are around until November. Make the most of the season's apples, combining them with blackberries in a scrumptious pie. Raspberries can be turned into raspberry vinegar to use through the winter months.

Sweet, juicy dessert plums like the late summer heat and follow the berry season from August through September into October, with damsons following in the latter two months.

Autumn is the season for wild mushrooms – a real gourmet treat but expensive due to the expertise required in finding and identifying them.

Perhaps the most vivid image of autumn is the **pumpkin**. Gloriously coloured squashes and pumpkins are an American import but are now popular here. There are plenty of other vegetables on offer including Brussels sprouts, Savoy cabbage, red cabbage, cauliflower, Jerusalem artichokes, parsnips, celeriac, celery and chicory.

Our native apples – such as Discovery, Cox's orange pippin and Egremont russet – are much tastier and have two to five times more **vitamin C** than imported varieties, so try to seek them out.

Autumn

Artichoke & Spinach Soup with Hazelnuts *(right)*

SERVES 4–5
PREPARATION & COOKING TIME: 1 hour 10 minutes
FREEZING: recommended, without hazelnuts

This soup is made with the knobbly Jerusalem artichokes rather than globe artichokes (which aren't related in any way). Don't miss out the hazelnuts – they are perfect with the soup.

40 g (1½ oz) butter
1 small onion, sliced finely
350 g (12 oz) Jerusalem artichokes, scrubbed and sliced finely
575 ml (1 pint) chicken stock (page 9)
175 g (6 oz) young spinach leaves
300 ml (½ pint) milk
80 g (3 oz) whole skinned hazelnuts, toasted, if wished, and slivered (see Note)
salt and freshly ground black pepper
freshly grated nutmeg

1 Take a roomy pan and melt the butter. Fry the onion very gently until transparent and soft but not brown.
2 Stir in the artichokes. Continue to sweat the vegetables, covered, and shaking the pan well from time to time, for about 10 minutes.
3 Pour in the stock and add pepper and salt plus some freshly grated nutmeg to taste. Bring to the boil and then reduce the heat and simmer gently, stirring often, for about 20–25 minutes or until the artichokes are really soft.
4 Now rinse the spinach leaves and discard the tough stems and any slightly yellow leaves. Add the spinach to the soup and remove the pan from the hob. The spinach cooks enough in the residual heat of the pan and retains its colour.
5 Allow to cool a little and then reduce the soup to a purée. Stir in the milk and then gently reheat, without boiling. Serve hot, with the slivered hazelnuts sprinkled on top.

NOTE: The best way to sliver the hazelnuts is with the slicing disc on your food processor.

Stilton & Pear Soup

SERVES 4
PREPARATION & COOKING TIME: 1 hour
FREEZING: recommended

This delicious recipe was supplied by a farmer's wife, Liz Pexton. Her husband is a driving force in the NFU. Their farm is near Driffield in East Yorkshire.

15 g (½ oz) butter
1 onion, finely chopped
4 ripe pears, peeled, cored and chopped
850 ml (1½ pints) chicken stock (page 9)
115 g (4 oz) Stilton cheese, crumbled
juice of ½ lemon (about 1½ tablespoons)
salt and freshly ground black pepper
snipped fresh chives, to garnish

1 Melt the butter in a roomy pan and cook the onion slowly. Do not let it brown.
2 Add the pears, stock and seasoning. Simmer until the pears are tender (simmering time will depend on the type and ripeness of the pears).
3 Remove the pan from the heat and leave to cool a little. Then purée the soup until it is smooth. Return the pan to the heat and reheat gently.
4 Add the crumbled Stilton and stir until it melts. Add the lemon juice to taste and adjust the seasoning.
5 Serve hot, with some snipped chives on each bowl.

Mussel Soup *(right)*

SERVES 4
PREPARATION & COOKING TIME: 1 hour
FREEZING: not recommended

This a real treat on a special occasion, and is a complete meal in itself. Mussels are particularly plentiful around Caernarfon and Bangor in North Wales and they are reputed to be some of the finest harvested in this country.

2 kg (4½ lb) fresh mussels
300 ml (½ pint) dry white wine
2 bay leaves
6 black peppercorns
25 g (1 oz) butter
1 large onion, chopped
4 garlic cloves, crushed
300 ml (½ pint) milk
150 ml carton of cream
2 tablespoons chopped fresh parsley
salt and freshly ground black pepper

1 Wash the mussels several times to remove any sand. Remove the 'beards' and discard any mussels that are not closed
2 Put the wine in a large saucepan, with the bay leaves and the peppercorns, and bring to the boil. Add the mussels, cover with a tightly fitting lid and cook on a high heat for 3–4 minutes, shaking the pan to ensure they all cook.
3 Drain and reserve the liquor and remove the mussels from their shells. Discard any mussels that have not opened.
4 Melt the butter in the pan and soften the onion and garlic.
5 Add the strained mussel liquor and the milk. Bring to the boil and then reduce the heat and leave to simmer until the onions and garlic are cooked
6 Adjust the seasoning. Add the mussels, cream and parsley. Reheat gently, without boiling and serve immediately.

Curried Parsnip Soup

SERVES 4 **V**
PREPARATION & COOKING TIME: 1 hour 15 minutes
FREEZING: recommended

1 tablespoon oil
450 g (1 lb) parsnips, sliced
1 onion, chopped
1 teaspoon curry powder
700 ml (1¼ pints) vegetable stock (page 8)
150 ml (¼ pint) milk
salt and freshly ground black pepper
chopped fresh parsley, to garnish

1 In a large pan, heat the oil and fry the parsnips and onion for 10 minutes, without letting them brown.
2 Add the curry powder and cook for 2–3 minutes. Add the stock, milk and seasoning and simmer for 45 minutes.
3 Allow to cool slightly and then reduce to a purée.
4 Return to the clean pan and reheat gently. Serve piping-hot, sprinkled with parsley.

Carrot & Ginger Soup

SERVES 4 **V**
PREPARATION & COOKING TIME: 25 minutes
FREEZING: recommended

350 g (12 oz) carrots, sliced
575 ml (1 pint) vegetable stock (page 8)
a knob of fresh root ginger, crushed
40 g (1½ oz) butter
2 onions, sliced
1 teaspoon ground ginger
1 teaspoon grated orange zest
2 tablespoons orange juice
salt and freshly ground blackpepper
60 ml (4 tablespoons) whipping cream, whipped, to serve

1 Place the carrots, stock and fresh root ginger in a pan. Bring to the boil and simmer for 15 minutes. Discard the ginger.
2 Meanwhile, melt the butter in a saucepan; add the onion and fry gently until soft.
3 Stir in the ground ginger and orange zest and then add the cooked carrots and their cooking stock. Cover the pan, bring to the boil and simmer for 10 minutes.
4 Allow to cool slightly and then purée the soup. Return the purée to the pan, add the orange juice and season to taste with salt and pepper.
5 Reheat the soup. Serve in individual bowls with a spoonful of the whipped cream floating on top.

Roasted Pumpkin Soup *(below)*

SERVES 4–6
PREPARATION & COOKING TIME: 1 hour 20 minutes
FREEZING: recommended

Roasting the pumpkin first develops its naturally sweet flavour. This is a wonderfully satisfying autumnal soup that can be served with granary bread as a warming supper or lunch.

1.8 kg (4 lb) pumpkin, unpeeled, quartered and de-seeded
4 tablespoons sunflower oil
1 teaspoon ground nutmeg, plus extra for seasoning
2 medium onions, sliced
700 ml (1¼ pints) vegetable stock (page 8)
425–575 ml (¾–1 pint) milk
salt and freshly ground black pepper

1 Place the prepared pumpkin on a roasting tray, brush with half the sunflower oil and sprinkle with the nutmeg. Roast at Gas Mark 6/electric oven 200°C/fan oven 180°C for 30–40 minutes until soft.
2 Remove the pumpkin from the oven and carefully peel the skin away from the flesh. Dice the flesh.
3 In a large pan gently cook the onions in the remaining sunflower oil until soft but not coloured, stir in the stock and the pumpkin and cook for 15 minutes.
4 Allow the soup to cool for a few minutes and then liquidise until smooth or push through a fine sieve.
5 Return the soup to a clean pan and stir in enough milk until the desired consistency is reached. Reheat gently, season to taste and add a little extra nutmeg if necessary.

Pumpkin & Apple Soup with Mint

SERVES 7–8 **V**
PREPARATION & COOKING TIME: 1½ hours
FREEZING: recommended

This recipe comes from Australia, where pumpkins are used a lot for soup. This recipe works with any kind of pumpkin and the soup is a lovely orange colour.

80 g (3 oz) butter
2 large onions, sliced
1 kg (2 lb 2 oz) peeled and de-seeded pumpkin flesh, chopped
1 large carrot, chopped
1 large ripe tomato, chopped
1 Granny Smith apple, peeled, cored and chopped
½ teaspoon salt
½ teaspoon curry powder
1.1 litres (2 pints) water
freshly ground black pepper
3 tablespoons chopped fresh mint, to garnish

1 In a very large pan, melt the butter and sweat the onion for at least 10 minutes. This is best done with the lid on but you must keep shaking and stirring as well.
2 Add everything else except the mint. Stir well. Bring to the boil and then reduce the heat and leave to a simmer for about 45 minutes or until all the vegetables are soft.
3 Remove the pan from the heat, leave to cool for a little and then reduce the contents to a purée, which you will have to do in batches.
4 If the purée is too thick, add a little more water. Taste and adjust the seasoning.
5 Serve hot and scatter the mint generously over the surface of each serving.

Butter Bean & Celeriac Soup

SERVES 4
PREPARATION TIME: 12 hours soaking + 20 minutes
  + 1¾ hours cooking
FREEZING: recommended

225 g (8 oz) dried butter beans, soaked for 12 hours
1 litre (1¾ pints) vegetable stock (page 8)
2 onions, chopped
1 celeriac, peeled and chopped
1 teaspoon caraway seeds
2 tablespoons chopped fresh parsley
575 ml (1 pint) milk
salt and freshly ground black pepper

1 Drain the beans, rinse well, and transfer to a large pan. Pour in the stock, bring to the boil and cook for 1 hour.
2 Add the onion, celeriac, caraway seeds and parsley and simmer until the beans are tender (about another 45 minutes).
3 Allow to cool a little and then purée the soup. Add the milk, adjust the seasoning, and reheat gently, without boiling, before serving.

Sweet Potato & Orange Soup

SERVES 4 V ★
PREPARATION & COOKING TIME: 20 minutes
FREEZING: recommended

This soup is refreshing, slightly sweet and a delightful colour; it's the ideal remedy for jaded appetites. The soup can be cooked in the microwave.

25 g (1 oz) butter
1 onion, chopped
450 g (1 lb) sweet potatoes, peeled and grated
2 celery sticks, very finely chopped
850 ml (1½ pints) vegetable stock (page 8)
2 fresh thyme sprigs
grated zest and juice of 1 orange
1 tablespoon chopped fresh parsley
salt and freshly ground black pepper

1 Melt the butter in a large pan and then soften the onion, without browning
2 Add the sweet potatoes, celery, stock, thyme and orange zest. Bring to the boil and simmer for 10 minutes.
3 Remove the thyme and stir in the orange juice and parsley. Reheat gently, check the seasoning and serve immediately.

Split Pea & Ham Soup

SERVES 4
PREPARATION & COOKING TIME: 1½ hours
FREEZING: recommended

An old favourite, enhanced by the addition of a little nutmeg.

1 tablespoon oil
1 large onion, chopped
1 garlic clove, crushed or chopped
¼ teaspoon freshly grated nutmeg
175 g (6 oz) gammon, chopped small
175 g (6 oz) dried split peas
850 ml (1½ pints) vegetable or chicken stock (page 8 or 9)
½ teaspoon sugar
150 ml carton of single cream
salt and freshly ground black pepper
chopped fresh parsley, to garnish

1 Heat the oil in a large saucepan, add the onion and garlic and sauté for 5 minutes, stirring occasionally. Add the nutmeg and gammon and cook for a further 5 minutes.
2 Add the peas and stock. Bring to the boil, cover and simmer for 45 minutes or until the peas are mushy.
3 Stir in the sugar and cream and heat through gently. Season to taste with salt and pepper. Sprinkle with parsley to serve.

Chilli Bean Soup

SERVES 4–6
PREPARATION & COOKING TIME: 50 minutes
FREEZING: recommended, without the sausage slices

1 tablespoon oil
1 large onion, chopped
2 carrots, diced
425 g can of kidney beans, drained
1 teaspoon chilli powder
225 g can of chopped tomatoes
1 tablespoon tomato purée
850 ml (1½ pints) chicken stock (page 9)
salt and freshly ground black pepper
sliced spicy sausage, to serve

1 Heat the oil in a large saucepan. Add the onion and carrot and sauté over a medium heat until the vegetables are soft but not browned. Stir occasionally.
2 Add the kidney beans and chilli powder. Cook for 1 minute.
3 Add the tomatoes, tomato purée, stock and seasoning. Bring to the boil, reduce the heat, cover and simmer for 20 minutes.
4 Allow to cool slightly and then purée half the soup until coarsely chopped.
5 Return to the remaining soup in the pan and reheat.
6 Serve each portion with a few small slices of spicy sausage.

Cabbage Soup

SERVES 8
PREPARATION & COOKING TIME: 50 minutes
FREEZING: recommended

Although cabbage is available all year round, this soup is an excellent way of using a glut of cabbage, courgettes, fennel and spinach from the garden. Add a variety of green vegetables in season and flavourings to suit your own taste.

6 large onions, chopped
2 large green peppers, chopped
1 head of celery, chopped
1 green cabbage, shredded
2 x 400 g cans of tomatoes
40 g can of tomato paste
vegetable stock (page 8)

FLAVOURINGS:
(use some of the following):
1 lemon grass stem
3 garlic cloves, crushed
7.5-cm (3-inch) piece of fresh root ginger, grated
2 teaspoons caraway seeds
dried mixed herbs.
2 chillies, de-seeded and sliced thinly

1 Put all the ingredients into a large pan, such as a preserving pan.
2 Add enough boiling stock to come halfway up the vegetables.
3 Add any flavourings you like, bring to the boil and simmer until the vegetables are tender, about 30 minutes.
4 Cool and freeze in individual portions.

NOTE: Other vegetables can also be added to provide variety; try courgettes, bean sprouts, fennel or spinach.

Barley Broth with Chicken

SERVES 4
PREPARATION & COOKING TIME: 2 hours 20 minutes
FREEZING: not recommended

Barley was often added to soup in the past, and it gives a lovely texture.

1 tablespoon oil
4 chicken drumsticks
1 onion, chopped finely
1 carrot, chopped small
1 celery stick, chopped small
1 leek, sliced finely
2 potatoes, chopped small
1.1 litres (2 pints) chicken stock (page 9)
40 g (1½ oz) pearl barley
1 fresh thyme sprig and 1 bay leaf
4 tablespoons chopped fresh parsley
salt and freshly ground black pepper

1 In a large pan, heat the oil and fry the drumsticks hard until they are well browned all over. Use tongs to remove the chicken to a plate and set this aside. Lower the heat a little.
2 Now add the onion, carrot, celery, leek and potato to the pan and sweat the vegetables, covered, shaking the pan occasionally, for about 10 minutes; you may need to add a little more oil.
3 Then add everything else, including the chicken but reserving 1 tablespoon of chopped parsley. Bring to the boil and then reduce the heat to a simmer.
5 Cook for about 2 hours. Stir often.
6 Remove the chicken to a plate and fish out the bay leaf and sprig of thyme. When the chicken is cool enough to handle, separate the meat from the skin and bones. Chop it and return it to the broth.
7 Adjust the seasoning and serve hot, with the rest of the parsley scattered on top.

Mushroom Soup Thickened with Toast

SERVES 5–6 **V**
PREPARATION & COOKING TIME: 45 minutes
FREEZING: recommended, after step 6

This soup is thickened with toast, as an alternative to flour or egg.

2 thick slices of white bread, crusts removed
50 g (2 oz) butter
400 g (14 oz) chestnut (Paris) mushrooms, chopped, or ordinary mushrooms if these are not available
1 fat garlic clove
450 ml (16 fl oz) double cream
150 ml (¼ pint) vegetable or chicken stock (page 8 or 9)
salt and freshly ground black pepper
oil, for frying

1 Toast the bread thoroughly. When it is cold and dry, put it in the food processor and reduce it to a fine powder.
2 Melt the butter in a roomy pan. Set aside four small mushrooms and add the remaining mushrooms to the pan. Grate the clove of garlic straight into the pan, using the coarse side of a metal grater.
3 Cook the mushrooms and garlic until soft. If the mushrooms stick, add a dash of water, stirring often.
4 Add the cream and stock to the pan and continue to simmer for about 10 minutes.
5 While this is cooking, slice the reserved mushrooms downwards into four slices and fry in oil until they are soft. Set aside and keep warm.
6 Allow the soup to cool briefly and then blend the soup until smooth. Season to taste and then stir in enough of the powdered toast to give the consistency you like.
7 Serve piping hot, topping each bowlful with a couple of slices of fried mushrooms

Roasted Root Vegetable Soup

SERVES 6 ♥

PREPARATION & COOKING TIME: 35 minutes + 30 minutes
  marinating
  + 1 hour cooking
FREEZING: recommended

Roasting the vegetables for the soup is well worth the effort. It gives the soup a very different flavour from a soup made with the same raw vegetables. Vary the vegetables according to your taste and what is available.

This recipe was sent in by Sîan Cook, author of the WI Book of Vegetarian Cuisine *and* Best-Kept Secrets of the WI: Puddings and Desserts.

450 g (1lb) celeriac, cut into wedges
1 large parsnip, quartered lengthways
2 carrots, halved lengthways
8 shallots
1 large sweet potato, cut into 8
3 tablespoons olive oil
1 tablespoon chopped fresh parsley
1 tablespoon fresh thyme leaves
850 ml (1½ pints) vegetable stock (page 8)
salt and freshly ground black pepper
90 ml (6 tablespoons) single cream or natural yogurt, to serve

1 Toss the vegetables in the oil and sprinkle with the herbs and salt and pepper. Marinate for at least half an hour.
2 Preheat the oven to Gas Mark 8/electric oven 220°C/fan oven 200°C. Roast the vegetables for 45 minutes, until the vegetables are beginning to brown.
3 Transfer to a large saucepan. Add the stock, bring to the boil and simmer for 15 minutes or until the vegetables are tender.
4 Liquidise the soup. Return to the pan and gently reheat. Check the seasoning.
5 Transfer to six bowls and serve each with a swirl of cream or yogurt.

Seriously Spicy Lentil Soup

SERVES 6 ♥ ♥ ▼

PREPARATION & COOKING TIME: 45 minutes
FREEZING: recommended

A wonderfully robust soup based on the traditional Indian dhal, with the lentils providing useful amounts of soluble fibre. The quantity of chilli powder in the recipe gives a medium spiciness and heat, but adjust it according to your own taste.

1 tablespoon vegetable oil
1 onion, chopped
1 red pepper, de-seeded and diced
2 garlic cloves, crushed
2.5-cm (1-inch) piece fresh root ginger, peeled and chopped finely
½ teaspoon chilli powder
½ teaspoon turmeric powder
½ teaspoon ground coriander
225 g (8 oz) split red lentils
850 ml (1½ pints) vegetable stock (page 8)
400 g tin of chopped tomatoes
1 tablespoon tomato purée
freshly ground black pepper

TO GARNISH:
low fat plain yogurt
fresh coriander leaves

1 Heat the vegetable oil in a large saucepan and gently fry the chopped onion for 3–4 minutes until softened but not coloured. Stir in the diced red pepper and crushed garlic and cook for a further 3–4 minutes.
2 Add the ginger, chilli powder, turmeric, ground coriander and lentils. Stir well to coat with the oil. Add the vegetable stock, chopped tomatoes and tomato purée, stir and bring up to the boil. Reduce the heat, cover the pan and simmer the soup for 20–25 minutes, stirring occasionally, until the lentils are cooked.
3 Liquidise or process half the soup to give a chunky texture. If you prefer a smoother textured soup, then purée the whole amount. Reheat the soup, adjusting the seasoning to taste. Ladle into warmed bowls and garnish with a swirl of yogurt and some fresh coriander leaves.

French Onion Soup *(right)*

SERVES 6
PREPARATION & COOKING TIME: 2½ hours
FREEZING: recommended, after step 5

This soup, supplied by the chef, Steven Jackson, is superb: not at all quickly made but worth the effort and expense.

FOR THE SOUP:
115 g (4 oz) butter
2 kg (4 lb 8 oz) large onions, sliced as thinly as possible, slices cut into short lengths
1 tablespoon plain flour
1.5 litres (2¾ pints) rich and jellied beef stock – the best quality you can manage (you could use fresh stock from the supermarket, or canned consommé)
150 ml (¼ pint) dry white wine
salt and freshly ground black pepper
brandy or Calvados

FOR THE CROÛTES:
1 garlic clove, crushed
50 g (2 oz) butter, softened
1 teaspoon chopped fresh parsley
175 g (6 oz) Gruyère cheese, grated finely
1 small baguette

1 You will need a pan big enough to take all the soup ingredients.

2 First, melt the butter in the pan and add the onions. Stir well and then turn the heat to the lowest setting and cover the onions with a circle of dampened greaseproof paper. Allow the onions to soften for about an hour, stirring frequently.

3 Now remove the paper and turn up the heat. Stir constantly and allow the onions to brown evenly.

4 Sprinkle the flour over the onions and stir and cook this roux for a couple of minutes.

5 Add the stock, a little at a time, stirring without stopping. As the soup thickens, add the wine plus a splash of brandy or Calvados. Allow this to simmer for about a further hour. Check the seasoning.

6 Meanwhile, preheat the oven to Gas Mark 7/ electric oven 220°C/fan oven 200°C. To make the garlic butter, add the garlic and parsley to the butter and beat well.

7 Cut the bread into enough 2.5-cm (1-inch) thick slices to cover the surface of the soup. Spread the bread with the garlic butter and dip each slice into the grated cheese. Set the bread slices, cheesy-side up, on a baking sheet. Bake for about 10–15 minutes or until the cheese is bubbly and golden. Leave the bread to cool and then break the slices into bite-size pieces.

8 Have ready six fairly large soup bowls that will stand up to being put under a hot grill or in the oven, and warm them up. Check that the soup is very hot and then divide it between the bowls. Then place the cheesy toasts on the surface and sprinkle over the rest of the cheese. Place the bowls under a grill or in the oven and bake or grill until the cheese melts and bubbles. Serve at once.

Red, White & Blue Salad *(above)*

SERVES 6 **V** ★
PREPARATION TIME: 20 minutes
FREEZING: not recommended

*This patriotic salad uses all three varieties of Cheshire cheese –
red, white and blue. Combined with apples and pears it makes
a colourful and tasty main course. Serve with sun-dried tomato
bread to complete the meal.*

175 g (6 oz) blue Cheshire cheese, diced
115 g (4 oz) seedless black grapes, quartered
115 g (4 oz) seedless green grapes, quartered
1 round lettuce, shredded coarsely
2 firm Comice pears, cored and sliced
175 g (6 oz) white Cheshire cheese, crumbled
2 red apples, cored and diced
175 g (6 oz) red Cheshire cheese, grated

FOR THE DRESSING:
4 tablespoons vegetable oil
2 tablespoons apple juice
salt and freshly ground black pepper

1 Arrange the blue Cheshire cheese and black and green
  grapes in the base of a large salad dish.
2 Top with a layer of lettuce and arrange the pear slices on
  top of the lettuce.
3 Sprinkle over the white Cheshire cheese and add another
  layer of lettuce. Arrange the diced apple on top and
  sprinkle with the red Cheshire cheese.
4 Whisk all the dressing ingredients together and drizzle over
  the salad just before serving.

Hot Potato & Chicken Salad

SERVES 4
PREPARATION & COOKING TIME: 35 minutes
FREEZING: not recommended

*The freshly cooked hot potatoes and chicken slightly wilt the
leaves in this main course salad, while the zesty lime and
balsamic dressing give it a real zing. Serve straight away, with
crusty white bread to mop up the juices.*

450 g (1 lb) potatoes, diced
4 boneless, skinless chicken breasts
2 tablespoons sunflower oil
2 tablespoons sesame seeds
225 g (8 oz) salad leaves
10 cherry tomatoes, halved

FOR THE DRESSING:
4 tablespoons olive oil
2 tablespoons balsamic vinegar
zest and juice of 1 lime
salt and freshly ground black pepper

1 Place the potatoes in a pan of salted water and bring to the
  boil. Reduce the heat to a simmer, cover the pan and cook
  for 15 minutes until the potatoes are tender. Drain.
2 Slice the chicken breasts into strips. Heat the sunflower oil
  in a frying pan, add the chicken strips for 4-5 minutes or
  until cooked. Place on kitchen paper to drain.
3 In a small pan carefully dry fry the sesame seeds until just
  coloured, take care not to burn them.
4 Whisk together the dressing ingredients in a small jug.
5 Place the salad leaves and tomatoes in a serving bowl. Add
  the potatoes, chicken and sesame seeds and pour over the
  dressing, toss all the ingredients together to mix
  completely. Serve immediately.

Smoked Chicken Waldorf (below)

SERVES 4 ★ ▼
PREPARATION TIME: 20 minutes
FREEZING: not recommended

This is a take on the classic Waldorf salad in which French dressing has been substituted for mayonnaise and the amount of nuts reduced. Smoked chicken has a really good flavour, but you could substitute cold cooked chicken if preferred.

1 head of celery, trimmed and cut into chunks
2 red skinned apples, quartered and cored
50 g (13/4 oz) walnut pieces
100 g (3½ oz) smoked chicken breast, cut into bite size pieces
3 tablespoons French dressing
2 tablespoons chopped fresh parsley, to garnish

1 Put the celery in a large bowl. Cut the apple quarters in half again, and cut each piece into four or five chunks. Add to the celery.
2 Add the walnuts, chicken and French dressing, and stir to mix well. Pile in a pretty dish, sprinkle over the parsley and serve immediately.

Warm Chicken Liver Salad

SERVES 4
PREPARATION & COOKING TIME: overnight defrosting
  + 35 minutes
FREEZING: not recommended

This also makes a good supper dish for two people. Using curly endive lettuce adds an interesting flavour and texture.

2 x 225 g tubs of frozen chicken livers, defrosted overnight
salt and freshly ground black pepper
1 tablespoon olive oil
125 g (4½ oz) curly endive or mixed salad leaves
2 tablespoons good quality balsamic vinegar
1 tablespoon chopped fresh parsley

1 Drain the chicken livers in a sieve for 20 minutes, trim well and cut into bite-size pieces. Put on kitchen paper to dry and season with salt and pepper.
2 Heat a small non-stick frying pan, add the oil and fry the livers for 8–10 minutes until golden and crispy on all sides.
3 Meanwhile, divide the endive or salad leaves between four plates. Remove the livers from the frying pan with a slotted spoon and scatter over the lettuce.
4 Put the pan back on the heat, add the balsamic vinegar, bring up to the boil and pour the juices over the salad.
5 Sprinkle over the parsley and serve immediately.

Moroccan Couscous Salad

SERVES ∨ ▼
PREPARATION & COOKING TIME: 40 minutes + cooling
FREEZING: not recommended

This salad is extremely versatile because you can also serve it warm – it goes particularly well with lamb, grilled or casseroled. It keeps well, too. If making a day in advance, then prepare to the end of step 3. Adding the herbs and pine nut kernals on the day ensures that the herbs keep their fresh greenness and the nuts their bite.

225 g (8 oz) couscous
2 rounded tablespoons sultanas
3 tablespoons extra virgin olive oil
1 large onion, chopped
¼ teaspoon each paprika, ground cumin, ground ginger and ground cinnamon
⅛ teaspoon cayenne pepper
¼ teaspoon coarse sea salt, ground
juice of 1 small lemon
2 rounded tablespoons each chopped fresh mint and parsley
2 tablespoons pine nut kernels, toasted

1 Place the couscous and sultanas in a bowl and pour over 300 ml (½ pint) of boiling water. Cover with a clean tea towel and leave to stand for 20 minutes, until all the water has been absorbed.
2 Meanwhile, heat 1 tablespoon of the oil in a frying pan. Add the onion and fry until soft and golden. Stir in the spices and cayenne and cook for 1 minute.
3 Add the salt to the couscous and fork through, to separate the grains. Stir in the remaining olive oil and the lemon juice. Leave to cool completely before adding the spicy onion mixture.
4 Just prior to serving, mix in the chopped mint and parsley with the toasted pine nut kernels.

Lettuce & Celery with a Creamy Dressing

SERVES 4 ∨ ★ ▼
PREPARATION TIME: 10 minutes
FREEZING: not recommended

This creamy dressing is a simple variation on 'regular' salad dressing, but is quite different and delicious!

2 Little Gem lettuces or 1 Cos lettuce
4 leafy celery sticks, chopped into chunks
2 tablespoons low fat crème fraîche
1 teaspoon Dijon mustard
1 teaspoon caster sugar
salt and freshly ground black pepper
2 tablespoons good quality olive oil
2 tablespoons tarragon vinegar

1 Cut the lettuce into thick slices, and put with the celery in a deep salad bowl.
2 In a small bowl, blend together the crème fraîche, mustard, sugar, salt and pepper. Using a small whisk, beat in the olive oil, drop by drop.
3 When all the oil has been absorbed, stir in the vinegar until the dressing has the consistency of thick cream.
4 Pour over the lettuce and celery, toss well to mix, and serve immediately.

Mushroom Pâté

SERVES 4 ∨ ▼
PREPARATION & COOKING TIME: 30 minutes soaking + 20 minutes + chilling
FREEZING: not recommended

The dried mushrooms give this dark pâté a wonderfully strong flavour. Serve with fingers of toast.

40 g packet of porcini mushrooms
spray oil
125 g (4½ oz) chestnut mushrooms, wiped and sliced
1 garlic clove, chopped
110 g (4 oz) light cream cheese
2 teaspoons lemon juice
freshly ground black pepper
a few drops of Tabasco sauce
freshly grated nutmeg
chopped fresh parsley, to garnish

1 Soak the porcini mushrooms in 100 ml (3 ½ fl oz) hot water for at least 30 minutes.
2 Coat the base of a frying pan with about 4 sprays of oil. Heat the oil and stir-fry the chestnut mushrooms with the garlic for 1 minute. Remove from the pan.
3 Fry the soaked mushrooms for 1 minute to dry them.
4 Put the cheese and lemon juice into a small processor or liquidiser. Add most of the chestnut mushrooms, reserving a few for garnish, the porcini mushrooms and the garlic. Process until the mixture is smooth.
5 Season to taste with black pepper, Tabasco and nutmeg. Spoon into a serving dish and chill.
6 Remove from the refrigerator 30 minutes before serving, to allow the flavours to develop.
7 Serve garnished with the reserved sliced mushrooms and a little chopped parsley.

Fruity Rice Salad

SERVES 3 V V

PREPARATION & COOKING TIME: 45 minutes
FREEZING: not recommended

Brown rice has a lovely nutty flavour, which complements the fruit in this starter. It would also be suitable as a lunch dish, served with slices of chicken.

110 g (4 oz) long-grain brown rice
1 eating apple
2 teaspoons lemon juice
1 orange
6 ready-to-eat prunes, quartered
2 teaspoons sunflower seeds, toasted
1–2 tablespoons low fat natural yogurt
freshly ground black pepper
lettuce leaves, e.g. Little Gem, to serve
2 teaspoons walnut pieces, to garnish

1 Cook the rice according to the packet instructions, until it is tender but still has a little bite to it, about 25 minutes. Drain, rinse in cold water and drain again.
2 Core and slice the apple and then halve across the slices. Toss the slices in lemon juice to prevent browning.
3 Peel and segment the orange, removing as much pith as possible and retaining any juice.
4 Toss together the rice, fruit and sunflower seeds.
5 Make the dressing by combining the yogurt and reserved orange juice. Season to taste with pepper.
6 Just before serving, toss the salad in the dressing.
7 Serve on lettuce leaves, garnished with the walnut pieces.

Guacamole *(left)*

MAKES 425 ML (³/₄ PINT) V
PREPARATION: 15 minutes + 30 minutes standing
FREEZING: not recommended

This traditional Mexican dip is widely available in supermarkets, a velvety, bright green concoction that is far removed from this 'zingy', chunky, home-made version. Do not prepare too far in advance, though, as the avocado tends to turn slightly brown on standing.

2 ripe avocados
juice of 1 lime
2 ripe tomatoes, skinned, de-seeded and chopped finely
¹/₂ small red onion, grated
1 small garlic clove, crushed
1 fat green chilli, de-seeded and chopped very finely
2 tablespoons chopped fresh coriander
a pinch of sugar
sea salt

1 Halve the avocados and remove the stones. Scoop out the flesh into a bowl, making sure that you include the greenest part nearest the skin. Pour over the lime juice and mash well, using a fork. You should end up with a slightly lumpy mixture.
2 Stir in the remaining ingredients and season to taste with sugar and salt.
3 It is exposure to air that causes avocado to brown, so cover with clingfilm, ensuring that it actually touches the guacamole's surface. Leave to stand for half an hour to allow the flavours time to mingle.
4 Serve with crisp sticks of raw vegetables and strips of pitta bread. Any left over should be stored in the fridge, but will tend to discolour

Autumn

147

Mushroom Brioches *(left)*

SERVES 4 V
PREPARATION & COOKING TIME: 40 minutes
COOKING TIME: 25 minutes
FREEZING: not recommended

Brioches rolls make an unusual and attractive shell for this rich mushroom filling. Any combination of mushrooms can be used – look out for packets of mixed exotic mushrooms in supermarkets. Serve the brioches straight from the oven with potato wedges and salad leaves.

2 tablespoons olive oil
1 red onion, sliced
1 red pepper, de-seeded and diced
1 garlic clove, crushed
175 g (6 oz) brown chestnut mushrooms, sliced
115 g (4 oz) button mushrooms, halved
50 g (2 oz) shiitake mushrooms
150 ml (¼ pint) red wine
150 ml (¼ pint) vegetable stock
2 tablespoons cranberry sauce
4 brioches rolls
salt and freshly ground black pepper

1 Heat half the oil in a frying pan and cook the onion, red pepper and garlic over a gentle heat until soft and cooked.
2 Add the remaining oil to the pan and gently fry the mushrooms until soft and browned.
3 Stir in the red wine, stock, cranberry sauce and seasoning and simmer for 10–15 minutes until reduced to a thick syrup.
4 While the sauce is reducing, slice the tops from the brioche rolls and using a spoon scoop out the bread from inside. Bake them at Gas Mark 6/electric oven 200°C/fan oven 180°C for 5 minutes to crisp the shells.
5 Spoon the mushroom mixture into the brioches shells and serve immediately.

Tagliatelle with Wild Mushrooms

SERVES 4 V ★ ▼
PREPARATION & COOKING TIME: 25 minutes
FREEZING: not recommended

You often see 'exotic' or 'wild' mushrooms in the supermarket, this is a good opportunity to try them. They have a lot more flavour than regular mushrooms, but if you can't find them, any other mushrooms will do.

350 g (12 oz) tagliatelle
4 tablespoons olive oil
2 fat garlic cloves, sliced thinly
175 g (6 oz) wild mushrooms, chopped roughly
salt and freshly ground black pepper
2 tablespoons chopped fresh parsley

1 Cook the pasta in a large saucepan of boiling salted water until just soft (al dente).
2 Meanwhile, heat the oil in a small saucepan and fry the garlic slices until just beginning to brown.
3 Add the mushrooms to the garlic and cook for 4–5minutes until the mushrooms soften and release their juices. Season with salt and pepper.
4 Drain the pasta, return to the saucepan and pour over the mushroom mixture. Stir to mix and sprinkle in the parsley. Serve immediately.

Vegetable Couscous

SERVES 6 ❥ ▼
PREPARATION & COOKING TIME: 1½ hours
FREEZING: not recommended

Traditionally in Morocco a selection of seven vegetables is used in this dish – seven is considered to be a lucky number. Choose any seven from those listed below, the choice is yours. The secret is to cook whichever vegetables you select in the right order, so follow the sequence of cooking given here.

400 g can of chopped tomatoes
1 vegetable stock cube
1 garlic clove, crushed
1–2 dried red chillies, more if you like it really hot
salt and freshly ground black pepper
175 g (6 oz) couscous
2 tablespoons chopped fresh parsley

FOR THE VEGETABLES:
225 g (8 oz) small new potatoes, scrubbed and halved lengthways
2 carrots, cut into large sticks
1 small white cabbage, cut into 8 and the core removed
1 onion, cut into chunks
1 turnip, cut into chunks
1 parsnip, cut into chunks
175 g (6 oz) shelled fresh broad beans
4 celery sticks, scrubbed and cut into chunks
1 small aubergine, cut into chunks
1 small sweet potato, peeled and cut into chunks
½ butternut squash, peeled, seeds removed and cut into chunks

1 Put the tomatoes, 300 ml (½ pint) water, the stock cube, garlic, chillies, salt and pepper in a large saucepan and bring to the boil.
2 Add the vegetables in rotation, starting with the new potatoes, carrots, cabbage and onion. Cover and simmer for 10 minutes.
3 Next add the turnip, parsnip, broad beans and celery, and cook for a further 10 minutes.
4 Lastly add the aubergine, sweet potato and squash and cook for another 10 minutes.
5 Meanwhile, make up the couscous. Place in a bowl and pour boiling water to come just above the surface. Cover with a clean tea towel and leave to stand for 20 minutes. Graze with a fork and season to taste. Turn on to a large serving plate. Using a slotted spoon, pile the vegetables into the centre of the dish.
6 Ladle over a little of the spicy stock and sprinkle with the chopped parsley. Serve the rest of the stock separately in a sauce boat.

Red Onion & Goat's Cheese Pizza Tart

SERVES 4
PREPARATION & COOKING TIME: 20 minutes + 45 minutes proving + 45–55 minutes cooking
FREEZING: recommended

The combination of red onion, balsamic vinegar and goat's cheese is now an established one. Serve as a light lunch or supper dish, or cut into bite-sized pieces and offer as appetisers.

FOR THE DOUGH BASE:
175 g (6 oz) plain flour
1 teaspoon easy-blend yeast
¼ teaspoon salt
1 large egg, beaten
2 tablespoons extra virgin olive oil

FOR THE TOPPING:
1 tablespoon olive oil
2 medium red onions, halved and sliced thinly
2 teaspoons chopped fresh thyme, plus extra to garnish
2 tablespoons balsamic vinegar
2 teaspoons granulated sugar
120 g roll of goat's cheese
salt and freshly ground black pepper

1 Preheat the oven to Gas Mark 6/electric oven 200°C/fan oven 180°C.
2 Combine the flour, yeast and salt. Make a well in the centre, add the egg, 50 ml (2 fl oz) warm water and oil, and mix to form a dough. Turn out the dough and knead for 5 minutes until smooth. Place in an oiled polythene bag, seal and leave in a warm place to prove for about 45 minutes.
3 For the topping, heat the oil and sweat the onions and thyme over a medium heat, uncovered, for 25–30 minutes, until softened.
4 Add the vinegar and sugar, increase the heat, and boil for about 5 minutes, until the mixture is syrupy and the onions start to caramelise. Season to taste.
5 Using your fingertips, press the risen dough into the base of a greased shallow baking tin, measuring 25 x 17 cm (10 x 6½ in). Spread the onion mixture over the surface.
6 If using hard goat's cheese, discard the ends, and slice it thinly into 12 rounds. Dot the slices over the onion mixture.
7 Bake in the centre of the oven for about 20 minutes until risen and golden. Scatter a few stalks of thyme over the top and serve at once.

Farmhouse Potato Pie

SERVES 4 **V**
PREPARATION & COOKING TIME: 25 minutes + 30 minutes
   chilling + 45–60 minutes cooking
FREEZING: recommended

This is a real Cinderella dish! The pastry base uses potato,
which makes a lovely soft dough to handle and, when cooked,
browns to a chip-like golden colour. If you do not have a
microwave, boil the potatoes for the filling in advance, adding
an extra one for the pastry.

FOR THE POTATO PASTRY:
1 medium (115 g/4 oz) floury potato
115 g (4 oz) plain flour
1 teaspoon baking powder
a pinch of salt
40 g (1½ oz) butter
40 g (1½ oz) lard
1 large egg yolk

FOR THE FILLING:
350 g (12 oz) potatoes, peeled
1 tablespoon olive oil
25 g (1 oz) butter
450 g (1 lb) onions, chopped
1 garlic clove, peeled
¼ teaspoon salt
45 ml (3 tablespoons) double cream
1 teaspoon Dijon mustard
125 g (4½ oz) Cheddar cheese, grated
3 tablespoons chopped fresh parsley
freshly ground black pepper

1 To make the pastry, wash the potato and wrap it in a piece
   of kitchen paper. Microwave on high for 4 minutes,
   turning it half way through cooking. Allow it to cool
   before removing its skin and mashing with a fork, until as
   smooth as possible.
2 Combine the flour, baking powder and salt in a bowl. Rub
   in the butter and lard. Stir in the mashed potato. Add the
   egg yolk and bring it all together to form a ball of dough.
3 Roll out the dough on a lightly floured surface and use it
   to line a deep 20-cm (8-inch) loose-bottomed flan ring.
   Prick the base with a fork and chill for at least 30 minutes.
4 Preheat the oven to Gas Mark 7/electric oven 220°C/fan
   oven 200°C. Place a baking sheet on the middle shelf.
5 To make the filling, boil the potatoes for about 15
   minutes, until just tender. Drain and slice them thinly.
6 Meanwhile, heat the oil and butter in a pan and sauté the
   onion for 10–15 minutes, until it is transparent and
   softened – do not allow it to brown.
7 Using a pestle and mortar, pound the garlic and salt to a
   creamy consistency. Add the cream, mustard and pepper to
   the garlic purée.
8 Layer the potato, onion, grated cheese and parsley in the
   pastry case, reserving 25 g (1 oz) cheese for the top. Pour
   in the garlicky cream mixture.
9 Sprinkle the top with the remaining grated cheese. Place
   the tin on the heated baking sheet and cook for 25–30
   minutes, until the pastry is crisp and the top is golden.

The Great English Breakfast Quiche *(right)*

SERVES 4
PREPARATION & COOKING TIME: 20 minutes + 30 minutes
   chilling + 30 minutes cooking
FREEZING: not recommended

Imagine those favourite cooked breakfast ingredients, all
encapsulated in a quiche. What's more, it has a case made of
sliced bread which, when cooked, is crispy just like fried bread.
This would make an ideal brunch or a Sunday night supper
dish.

FOR THE BREAD CASE:
6 medium slices of bread from a square cut white loaf
40 g (1½ oz) butter, softened

FOR THE FILLING:
1 teaspoon sunflower oil
175 g (6 oz) good quality pork chipolatas, cut into bite-sized pieces
80 g (3 oz) lean streaky bacon, snipped
80 g (3 oz) button mushrooms, wiped
50 g (2 oz) cherry tomatoes, halved
2 large eggs, beaten
300 ml (½ pint) milk
salt and freshly ground black pepper

1 Remove and discard the crusts from the bread. Spread the
   slices thinly with some of the butter and arrange them,
   butter side down, in a 20-cm (8-inch) square or 23-cm
   (9-inch) round cake tin. Make sure that the bread is
   pressed together well so that there are no gaps for the
   liquid to disappear down. Spread the remaining butter
   over the inside of the bread case to form a seal. Chill for
   30 minutes.
2 Preheat the oven to Gas Mark 5/electric oven 190°C/fan
   oven 170°C.
3 Heat the oil in a frying pan and add the sausage pieces.
   Fry them over a medium-high heat for 3–4 minutes, until
   browned. Add the bacon and fry for a couple of minutes
   until crisp. Now add the mushrooms to the pan (halve any
   large ones) and cook for 1 minute.
4 Remove any excess fat with kitchen paper and scatter the
   fried ingredients over the base of the quiche. Arrange the
   tomato halves on top.
5 Whisk together the eggs and milk and season with salt and
   pepper. Pour into the bread case.
6 Bake in the middle of the oven for about 30 minutes, or
   until the quiche is puffy and golden. Serve at once.

Hake Baked en Papillote

SERVES 4 ♥ ★ ▼

PREPARATION & COOKING TIME: 20 minutes
FREEZING: not recommended

*This is a really good way of cooking fish: the sealed foil
'packets' keep in the flavours, and save on the washing up.
You can substitute sliced tomatoes, chopped coriander or a
little garlic for the olives – experiment as much as you want.*

4 x 175 g (6 oz) portions of hake or haddock, skinned
12 black olives, stoned and chopped roughly
finely grated zest of 1 lemon
freshly ground black pepper
a little olive oil
4 fresh bay leaves (optional)

1 Preheat the oven to Gas Mark 5/electric oven 190°C/fan
  oven 170°C.
2 Lay each portion of fish on a large square of aluminium
  foil, sprinkle on the chopped olives and lemon zest and
  season with pepper.
3 Put on a flat baking sheet, sprinkle a little olive oil over
  each one and top with a bay leaf, if using. Scrunch up each
  foil parcel tightly.
4 Bake in the preheated oven for 15 minutes.
5 Serve the wrapped parcels as they are – open them up on
  your plate and let the juices run out.

Plaice with a White Wine Sauce

SERVES 4

PREPARATION & COOKING TIME: 50 minutes
FREEZING: not recommended

*The delicate flavour of this fish is really enhanced by baking it
in a delicious wine and mushroom sauce. This is a lovely dish
to serve with fluffy mash potatoes and broccoli.*

4 fillets of plaice, weighing 225 g–350 g (8 oz–12 oz) each, cleaned
175 g (6 oz) button mushrooms, cleaned and halved
425 ml (15 fl oz) white wine
25 g (1 oz) butter
25 g (1 oz) plain flour
salt and freshly ground black pepper

1 Place the fish fillets, skin side down, in a large ovenproof
  dish. Add the mushrooms and seasoning and pour over the
  wine.
2 Preheat the oven to Gas Mark 4/electric oven 180°C/fan
  oven 160°C. Cover the dish with a lid or foil.
3 Bake for 20–25 minutes until the fish is cooked through.
  To test carefully place a knife into the flesh of the fish, the
  flesh should be white and flaky.
4 Remove from the oven and drain the cooking juices into a
  jug, and keep the fish and mushrooms warm.
5 Melt the butter in a medium saucepan over a gentle heat.
  Stir in the flour and cook for 2 minutes.
6 Gradually stir in 300 ml (½ pint) of the reserved cooking
  liquid stirring continuously to avoid lumps forming and
  then bring to the boil. Stir until thickened. Check the
  seasoning.
7 Place the fish fillets and mushrooms on serving plates and
  pour over the sauce. Serve immediately.

Haddock & Spinach Chowder Tart (right)

SERVES 6
PREPARATION & COOKING TIME: 1 hour
FREEZING: not recommended

Semolina is a wonderful basis for pastry. The pastry case for this tart does not require baking blind and has a crisp, nutty texture. This would make a good 'all-in-one' lunch dish. Reheating dries out the fish, but you could prepare the tart in advance and then bake it just prior to serving.

FOR THE SEMOLINA PASTRY:
80 g (3 oz) semolina
80 g (3 oz) plain flour
80 g (3 oz) butter

FOR THE FILLING:
225 g (8 oz) undyed smoked haddock fillets, skinned
300 ml ($^1/_2$ pint) creamy milk
1 bay leaf
a few parsley stalks
4 black peppercorns
25 g (1 oz) butter
1 small onion, chopped finely
25 g (1 oz) plain flour
2 tablespoons double cream
2 tablespoons chopped fresh parsley
2 large egg yolks, beaten
225 g (8 oz) cooked waxy potatoes, diced
115 g (4 oz) spinach, wilted and well drained
50 g (2 oz) sweetcorn kernels

1 First make the pastry. Mix together the semolina and flour. Rub in the butter and mix to a dough with 1½ tablespoons cold water. Turn out the dough on to a floured work surface and roll it out to line a 23-cm (9-inch) loose-bottomed flan tin. Prick the base well with a fork and chill for 30 minutes, while you prepare the filling.
2 Preheat the oven to Gas Mark 5/electric oven 190°C/fan oven 170°C. Place a baking sheet on the middle shelf.
3 Place the haddock in a medium saucepan with the milk, bay leaf, parsley stalks and peppercorns. Bring to the boil and simmer for 2–3 minutes, until the fish is just cooked. (It will cook further in the oven later, so you don't want to dry it out.) Remove it from the liquid and flake into large pieces (reserve the milk).
4 Melt the butter in a small saucepan and sauté the onion for about 10 minutes, without browning, until it is soft. Stir in the flour and cook for 1 minute. Strain the milk and gradually whisk it in. When the sauce boils, stir in the cream. Remove the pan from the heat, add the parsley and cool slightly. Beat in the egg yolks.
5 Scatter the potatoes over the pastry base. Dot the wilted spinach evenly over the top. Add the sweetcorn and haddock and then pour over the sauce. Bake (on the warmed baking sheet) immediately for about 30 minutes, or until the pastry is golden and the filling is set.

Tuna Pizza Tart with Wilted Rocket & Parmesan Shavings

SERVES 4
PREPARATION & COOKING TIME: 40 minutes + 15 minutes cooling + 30 minutes cooking
FREEZING: not recommended

This tart is simply bursting with both colour and flavour and is easy to make. Olive oil is used in place of butter and lard in the pastry, making a crisp shell, which holds its shape well. This tart is a main course by itself.

FOR THE PASTRY:
175 g (6 oz) plain flour
a pinch of salt
4 tablespoons extra virgin olive oil

FOR THE TOPPING:
1 tablespoon olive oil
350 g (12 oz) plum tomatoes, skinned and chopped roughly
1 garlic clove, peeled
$^1/_4$ teaspoon sea salt
1 teaspoon sherry vinegar
$^1/_2$ teaspoon chopped fresh oregano or $^1/_4$ teaspoon dried oregano
$^1/_2$ teaspoon brown sugar
bay leaf
200 g can of tuna chunks or steaks, drained
2 teaspoons capers
25 g (1 oz) rocket leaves
25 g (1 oz) Parmesan cheese shavings
freshly ground black pepper

1 To make the pastry, combine the flour and salt in a mixing bowl. Add the oil, and enough cold water (about 4 tablespoons) to bind. Bring the mixture together with your hands, and work very gently, using your fingertips, to make a soft dough.
2 Break off small pieces of dough at a time and press them into the bottom, and 2 cm (¾ inch) up the sides, of a 23-cm (9-inch) shallow, loose-bottomed, flan tin. Prick well with a fork and chill while you make the tomato sauce.
3 Heat the oil and add the tomatoes. Using a pestle and mortar pound the garlic and salt to a creamy consistency. Add this to the tomato mixture with the vinegar, oregano, sugar and bay leaf. Season with pepper. Simmer, uncovered, for about 30 minutes, until the mixture is pulpy. You may need to turn up the heat for the last 5 minutes to evaporate the liquid.
4 Preheat the oven to Gas Mark 6/electric oven 200°C/fan oven 180°C. Place a baking sheet on the middle shelf.
5 Cool the tomato sauce for about 15 minutes before spreading it over the pastry base. Scatter the tuna chunks over the top. Bake for about 30 minutes until the pastry is crisp and golden.
6 Remove the tart from the oven, sprinkle with capers and scatter rocket and Parmesan shavings over the surface.

Salmon with Drambuie & Mango Sauce *(below)*

SERVES 4 ★
PREPARATION & COOKING TIME: 20 minutes
FREEZING: not recommended

The combination of Drambuie and mango gives a tangy kick to pan-fried salmon fillets. Serve with boiled potatoes and a selection of green vegetables.

3 tablespoons olive oil
4 boned salmon fillets, approx 175–225 g (6–8 oz) each
425 g (15 oz) canned mango slices, drained or 2 fresh mangos, diced
2 teaspoons sunflower oil
1 garlic clove, crushed
75 ml (5 tablespoons) Drambuie
1 teaspoon soy sauce

1 In a frying pan heat 2 tablespoons of the olive oil, add the salmon and gently fry for 8–10 minutes, turning occasionally, until cooked.
2 Purée the canned or fresh mango with the sunflower oil.
3 In another pan heat the remaining olive oil, gently fry the garlic to release the flavour, then add the mango purée, Drambuie and soy sauce and heat through.
4 Pour the sauce into the frying-pan over the salmon and allow to simmer for 5 minutes.

Turkey & Leek Filo Topped Pie

SERVES 6 ♥
PREPARATION & COOKING TIME: 1 hour
FREEZING: not recommended

Following a healthy eating pattern means avoiding traditional pastry dishes, which are usually very high in fat. However, it's hard to do without completely and this is where filo pastry comes into its own. Instead of brushing it with melted butter, as many recipes instruct, use a small amount of vegetable or olive oil – or even no oil at all, since the pastry still bakes to an attractive golden colour.

2 tablespoons vegetable oil
750 g (1 lb 10oz) turkey breast pieces, cubed
2 leeks, trimmed and sliced into rings
2 celery sticks, sliced
1 onion, sliced
2 small carrots, sliced
2 tablespoons plain flour
150 ml (¼ pint) dry cider
300 ml (½ pint) chicken stock (page 9)
1 tablespoon Dijon mustard
2 tablespoons half fat crème fraîche
6 sheets filo pastry
1 teaspoon sesame seeds
freshly ground black pepper

1 Preheat the oven to Gas Mark 6/electric oven 200°C/fan oven 180°C.
2 Heat 1 tablespoon of the oil in a large pan and fry the turkey cubes in batches until golden brown. Set aside. Add the vegetables to the pan and gently sauté for 4–5 minutes. Sprinkle over the flour and cook for 1 minute.
3 Gradually stir in the cider and stock, followed by the mustard and bring up to the boil, stirring to allow the sauce to thicken. Return the turkey to the pan. Reduce the heat, cover the pan and simmer gently for 15–20 minutes until the vegetables are tender. Stir in the crème fraîche and season with black pepper. Transfer the mixture to a shallow ovenproof dish.
4 Take one sheet of filo pastry at a time, spread it out on a clean work surface and lightly brush with the remaining oil. Crumple each sheet slightly and arrange on top of the turkey mixture to cover it completely. Sprinkle over the sesame seeds.
5 Place the pie in the oven and bake for 15–20 minutes until the pastry is golden brown and crisp. Serve immediately.

Duck Breasts with Plum Sauce

SERVES 4
PREPARATION & COOKING TIME: 45 minutes
FREEZING: not recommended

This tangy plum sauce goes really well with rich duck meat. Victoria plums give the most intense flavour, but other varieties are available throughout the year and enable this simple dish to be prepared any time. Serve with bulgar wheat or couscous.

4 duck breasts
2 tablespoons olive oil
2 shallots, chopped finely
225 g (8 oz) plums, stoned and quartered
150 ml (¼ pint) red wine
zest and juice of 1 orange
2 tablespoons clear honey
3 tablespoons cranberry sauce
15 g (½ oz) unsalted butter

1 Score the duck fat three or four times with a sharp knife. Place the duck breasts in a roasting dish and roast at Gas Mark 6/electric oven 200°C/fan oven 180°C for 20–30 minutes until cooked through.
2 In a pan heat the oil and then gently cook the shallots without colouring.
3 Stir in the plums and cook for 5 minutes.
4 Add the red wine, orange zest and juice and honey. Cook for 8–10 minutes. Allow to cool for 5 minutes.
5 Purée the sauce, then sieve it and pour it back into the pan. Heat to reduce by one-third, stir in the cranberry sauce and butter and heat through. If the sauce is too sharp adjust to taste by adding an extra spoonful of honey
6 Remove the skin from the cooked duck breasts and slice the meat. Serve with the sauce.

Chicken in Dijon Sauce

SERVES 4

PREPARATION & COOKING TIME: 20 minutes + 1 hour
  marinating + 30–40 minutes cooking
FREEZING: recommended

*Chicken breasts are marinated in mustard and wine and then
baked in the oven with courgettes, carrots and mushrooms.
A simple all-in-one meal that can be prepared in advance and
then cooked just before serving. Rice or baked potatoes are
good with this dish.*

4 boneless, skinless chicken breasts
300 ml (½ pint) white wine
4 tablespoons Dijon mustard
3 tablespoons olive oil
2 medium courgettes, topped, tailed and sliced
4 small carrots, diced
115 g (4 oz) button mushrooms
2 tablespoons cornflour
300 ml (½ pint) chicken stock (page 9)

1 Cut each chicken breast into six slices and place the slices
  in a shallow dish.
2 Mix together the white wine and Dijon mustard and pour
  over the chicken. Leave to marinate, covered, in the fridge
  for at least 1 hour.
3 In a frying pan heat the oil and add the chicken strips to
  the pan and brown on all sides. Add the courgettes, carrots
  and mushrooms and cook for 5 minutes.
4 Mix the cornflour with a little of the stock and add to the
  frying pan with the remaining stock and the marinade.
5 Heat gently until the sauce has thickened.
6 Transfer to a casserole dish, cover and cook at Gas Mark 4/
  electric oven 180°C/ fan oven 160°C, for 30–40 minutes
  until the chicken is cooked right through.

Chicken with Smoky Bacon & Cannellini Beans

SERVES 4 ♥ ▼

PREPARATION & COOKING TIME: 50 minutes
FREEZING: recommended

*A quick to prepare recipe suitable for a midweek evening meal
– it only needs to be accompanied by boiled new potatoes and
some lightly steamed broccoli. Although the excess fat should
be removed from the bacon, there should still be sufficient
rendered out in the heat of the pan to cook off the onion and
garlic – so don't be tempted to add any oil.*

1 onion, chopped
4 rashers smoked, reduced salt back bacon, chopped
1 garlic clove, chopped
4 boneless, skinless chicken breasts, cubed
400 g can of chopped tomatoes
1 teaspoon dried thyme
1 teaspoon paprika
410 g can of cannellini beans, rinsed and drained
freshly ground black pepper
chopped fresh parsley, to garnish

1 Gently fry the chopped onion, bacon and garlic in a large
  pan for 5–6 minutes to soften the onion and cook the
  bacon. Add the cubed chicken to the pan and continue to
  cook until the chicken is sealed and lightly golden.
2 Stir in the chopped tomatoes along with the thyme and
  paprika. Bring up to the boil, then cover and reduce the
  heat. Simmer for 20–25 minutes, stirring occasionally.
3 Add the cannellini beans to the pan and stir into the
  mixture. Cook for a further 10 minutes until the beans are
  heated through and the chicken cooked. Season to taste
  with freshly ground black pepper. Serve immediately,
  sprinkled with some chopped parsley as a garnish.

Green Chicken Curry *(below)*

SERVES 4 ★ ▼

PREPARATION & COOKING TIME: 30 minutes

FREEZING: not recommended

This recipe is inspired by classic Thai green curries, but they contain lots more coconut – and lots more calories. Lemon grass gives an authentic flavour; to prepare it for this recipe, top and tail and remove the outer woody layers. If you like your curry mild use one chilli, for a hotter taste use two. Serve with basmati rice.

2 garlic cloves, halved

1 lemon grass stalk, trimmed and cut into 3

1 or 2 fresh green chillies, halved and de-seeded

5 cm (2 inches) fresh ginger, peeled and chopped roughly

25 g (1 oz) fresh coriander, tough stalks removed

1 tablespoon sunflower oil

1 small onion, halved and sliced finely

4 skinless chicken breasts, cut into bite-size pieces

salt

1 chicken stock cube

50 g (2 oz) creamed coconut

1 Put the garlic, lemon grass, chilli, ginger, coriander and 300 ml (½ pint) cold water into the food processor. Process for 2–3 minutes until well mixed.

2 Heat the oil in a non-stick frying pan and add the onion. Fry for 2 minutes then add the chicken. Stir-fry for 3–4 minutes, add the coriander mixture, salt and crumbled stock cube.

3 Bring up to the boil stirring well, turn down the heat, cover, and cook for 10 minutes.

4 Add the coconut, and stir until melted and well mixed. Taste to check the seasoning.

Moussaka

SERVES 4
PREPARATION & COOKING TIME: 30 minutes + 1 hour 20 minutes cooking
FREEZING: not recommended

Moussaka is a little time-consuming but does make a wonderful dish. Make it ahead and then cook for when your friends arrive, and all it needs is a crisp salad of mixed lettuce leaves and cucumber to accompany. The yogurt-based topping is much quicker than a traditional white sauce and low-fat yogurt can be used instead, for even fewer calories.

2 aubergines, weighing about 450 g (1 lb)
450 g (1 lb) cooked waxy potatoes, sliced
2–3 tablespoons olive oil
sea salt and freshly ground black pepper

FOR THE LAMB SAUCE:
450 g (1 lb) minced lamb
1 large onion, chopped finely
1 tablespoon flour
400 g can of chopped tomatoes
1 fat garlic clove, crushed
2 teaspoons tomato purée
1 tablespoon chopped fresh parsley
1 teaspoon ground cinnamon
1/2 teaspoon dried oregano
1 bay leaf

FOR THE TOPPING:
300 ml (1/2 pint) Greek yogurt
2 eggs, beaten
50 g (2 oz) Parmesan cheese, grated finely
grated nutmeg

1 Remove the stalks and cut the aubergines into 1-cm (1/2-inch) slices. Layer in a colander, sprinkling a little salt between each layer. Weigh down and leave for 30 minutes to extract any bitter juices.
2 Meanwhile brown the mince and onion in a non-stick pan over a high heat, breaking up any lumps. Reduce the heat and stir in the flour. Cook for 1 minute. Add the chopped tomatoes, garlic, tomato purée, parsley, cinnamon, oregano and bay leaf. Season, bring to the boil, cover the pan, reduce the heat and simmer for 30 minutes, stirring occasionally.
3 Preheat the grill to high. Preheat the oven to Gas Mark 4/ electric oven180°C/fan oven 160°C.
4 Rinse the salt from the aubergines and pat them dry with a tea towel. Arrange in a single layer on the grill pan and brush with half the olive oil. Grill for about 5 minutes, or until golden. Turn, brush with the remaining oil and grill until golden.
5 Lightly grease a 2.3-litre (4-pint) ovenproof dish. Remove the bay leaf from the mince and adjust the seasoning if necessary. Arrange half the aubergine slices over the base of the dish, and half the sliced potato on top of them. Pour the lamb sauce over the top. Finish with the remaining aubergine and potato slices.
6 In a bowl, whisk together the yogurt, eggs and Parmesan. Season and pour over the potato, covering it completely. Sprinkle a little grated nutmeg over the top and bake for about 40 minutes, until puffy and golden.

Pork & Mushroom Pasta

SERVES 4
PREPARATION & COOKING TIME: 1 hour
FREEZING: not recommended

A variation on the classic Bolognese sauce – a pork, tomato and mushroom sauce is served with pasta shapes and topped with cheese. Serve with a tomato and basil salad, and a glass or two of full-bodied red wine.

2 tablespoons olive oil
1 onion, sliced
2 carrots, sliced thinly
450 g (1 lb) minced pork
225 g (8 oz) button mushrooms, quartered
150 ml (1/4 pint) vegetable or chicken stock (pages 8 and 9)
400 g can of chopped tomatoes
1 tablespoon mixed dried herbs
1 tablespoon Worcestershire sauce
1 tablespoon tomato purée
175 g (6 oz) dried pasta shapes, such as penne or rigatoni
salt and freshly ground black pepper
50 g (2 oz) Cheddar cheese, grated, to serve

1 Heat the oil in a large, deep frying pan and cook the onion and carrots for 5 minutes, until softened. Add the pork and cook over a medium heat until the meat has browned, stirring and breaking up with a wooden spoon, as necessary.
2 Add the mushrooms and cook for 2–3 minutes. Pour in the stock, add the tomatoes, herbs, Worcestershire sauce and tomato purée and bring to the boil.
3 Lower the heat, cover the pan and simmer gently for 30 minutes.
4 While the meat is cooking, cook the pasta in salted, boiling water for 10–12 minutes until just tender. Drain and rinse in cold water to prevent it from sticking.
5 Stir the pasta into the mince mixture and season with salt and pepper. Reheat, stirring, until bubbling. Serve topped with grated cheese.

Pork in Cider with Herby Dumplings

SERVES 4
PREPARATION & COOKING TIME: 1 hour
FREEZING: recommended

This warming casserole is served with light herby dumplings, which are cooked on the top of the dish and absorb lots of the wonderful flavours.

1 tablespoon olive oil
675 g (1½ lb) lean boneless pork, cubed
1 onion, sliced
2 tablespoons plain flour
1 litre (1¾ pints) dry cider
2 carrots, chopped
2 eating apples, cored and sliced
1 bouquet garni
2 tablespoons Dijon mustard
2 tablespoons Worcestershire sauce
salt and freshly ground black pepper

FOR THE HERBY DUMPLINGS:
115 g (4 oz) self-raising flour
50 g (2 oz) shredded beef or vegetable suet
2 tablespoons chopped fresh mixed herbs, such as parsley, sage and
  thyme or 2 teaspoons dried mixed herbs

1 Heat the oil in a large saucepan and fry the pork until browned, then remove with a slotted spoon and set aside. Add the onion to the pan and fry for 5 minutes until lightly browned. Stir in the flour and cook for 1 minute, then gradually stir in the cider until smooth.
2 Return the pork to the pan with the carrots, apples, bouquet garni, Dijon mustard and Worcestershire sauce, season well. Cover and simmer for 30 minutes.
3 Meanwhile, make the herby dumplings: mix the flour, suet, herbs and seasoning together. Add 3–4 tablespoons of water and mix lightly to a soft dough. Shape into eight balls and add to the casserole, slightly apart. Cover and simmer for a further 15–20 minutes until the dumplings are risen and light.

Liver with Vermouth

SERVES 4 ★
PREPARATION & COOKING TIME: 30 minutes
FREEZING: recommended

A tangy one-pan liver dish flavoured with orange, lemon and vermouth. Serve with brown rice or wholemeal noodles for a tasty lunch.

450 g (1 lb) lamb's liver, sliced
1 tablespoon wholemeal flour
2 tablespoons vegetable oil
1 onion, chopped
1 garlic clove, crushed
finely grated zest and juice of 1 orange
finely grated zest and juice of 1 lemon
60 ml (4 tablespoons) sweet vermouth
2 tablespoons chopped fresh parsley
salt and freshly ground black pepper
orange and lemon slices, to garnish

1 Cut the liver into thin strips and coat in the flour.
2 Heat the oil in a flameproof casserole, add the onion and garlic to the casserole and fry gently for 5 minutes until soft but not coloured.
3 Add the liver strips and cook over a high heat until browned on all sides.
4 Add the orange and lemon zest and juices and the vermouth and bring to the boil. Stir constantly with a wooden spoon to scrape up any sediment and juices from the base of the casserole, and continue boiling until the sauce reduces.
5 Lower the heat and cook for 10 minutes or until the liver is cooked. Add half the parsley and season to taste.
6 Garnish the liver with the remaining parsley and the orange and lemon slices. Serve immediately.

Beef in Guinness Cobbler *(right)*

SERVES 4
PREPARATION & COOKING TIME: 2½ hours
FREEZING: recommended

A traditional British stew of chunks of beef cooked in Guinness until tender, with an American twist – the meat is topped with a layer of light scones towards the end of the cooking time. Serve with a selection of green vegetables.

50 g (2 oz) plain flour
½ teaspoon grated nutmeg
675 g (1½ lb) chuck steak, cut into 2.5-cm (1-inch) cubes
3 tablespoons olive oil
25 g (1 oz) butter
2 large onions, sliced finely
2 garlic cloves, crushed
1 teaspoon brown sugar
575 ml (1 pint) Guinness
zest and juice of 1 orange
1 bay leaf
salt and freshly ground black pepper

FOR THE SCONE TOPPING:
225 g (8 oz) self-raising flour
a pinch of salt
50 g (2 oz) butter
7 tablespoons milk

1 Sift the flour into a shallow dish and stir in the nutmeg and plenty of seasoning. Coat the meat in the flour.
2 Heat half the oil and half the butter in a flameproof casserole. Add half the meat and fry for 2–3 minutes until evenly browned. Transfer to a plate, add the remaining oil and butter to the casserole and brown the remaining meat. Transfer to the plate.
3 Put the onions and garlic in the casserole and fry gently for 5 minutes, stirring constantly.
4 Add the sugar to the casserole and cook over a moderate heat for a further minute, stirring constantly, until the sugar caramelises.
5 Return the beef to the casserole and pour the Guinness over the top. Add the orange juice and zest and bay leaf and bring to the boil.
6 Cover and cook at Gas Mark 4/electric oven 180°C/fan oven 160°C for 1–1½ hours, stirring occasionally, adding a little water to the casserole if the liquid becomes too thick.
7 To make the scone topping, sift the flour and salt into a bowl and rub the butter in until the mixture forms fine breadcrumbs. Add enough milk to form a soft dough. Knead on a lightly floured surface and roll out to 1 cm (½ inch) thick and cut out 12 scones using a 5-cm (2-inch) cutter.
8 After 1½ hours cooking time remove the meat from the oven, take off the lid and arrange the scones in an overlapping circle around the edge of the dish.
9 Return the dish, uncovered, to the oven and cook for a further 30 minutes or until the scones are well-risen and golden brown.

Ruby Amber Pie *(right)*

SERVES 6
PREPARATION & COOKING TIME: 40 minutes + 30 minutes
  chilling + 35 minutes cooking
FREEZING: not recommended

*This is a very old recipe – Apple Amber – traditionally made
with just apples. My guess is that its name comes from the
orange colour which the brown sugar turns the apples. This
version includes blackberries, hence I have called it Ruby
Amber Pie.*

FOR THE PASTRY:
shortcrust pastry (page 10) made with 115 g (4 oz) plain flour

FOR THE FILLING:
450 g (1 lb) cooking apples, preferably Bramley's
80 g (3 oz) light muscovado sugar
grated zest and juice of ½ lemon
25 g (1 oz) butter
2 large eggs, separated
175 g (6 oz) blackberries
80 g (3 oz) golden caster sugar

1 Line a 20-cm (8-inch) loose-bottomed, deep flan tin with
  the shortcrust pastry and chill for 30 minutes.
2 Preheat the oven to Gas Mark 6/electric oven 200°C/fan
  oven 180°C. Place a baking sheet on the middle shelf.
3 On the heated baking sheet, bake the pastry case blind for
  15 minutes, remove the foil and beans and cook for a
  further 5–10 minutes. Remove from the oven and reduce
  the heat to Gas Mark 2/electric oven 150°C/fan oven
  130°C.
4 Peel, core and slice the apples. Put them in a pan with the
  muscovado sugar, lemon zest, lemon juice and 1
  tablespoon water. Cover and stew for about 15 minutes,
  until the apples are soft.
5 Allow the apple mixture to cool slightly before beating it
  to a purée. Beat in the butter followed by the egg yolks,
  adding them one at a time. Gently stir in the blackberries.
6 In a clean, dry bowl whisk the egg whites until they are
  stiff. Whisk in a quarter of the golden caster sugar. Add
  another quarter and whisk again. Fold in the remainder,
  reserving 1 teaspoon.
7 Spoon the apple and blackberry mixture into the pastry
  case. Swirl the meringue mixture on top, spreading it to
  the edges of the pastry, making sure to seal the filling in.
  Sprinkle with the remaining sugar and bake in the oven for
  about 35 minutes, until the meringue is risen and golden.
  Serve warm.

Plum & Cardamom Fools

SERVES 6
PREPARATION & COOKING TIME: 1 hour
FREEZING: not recommended

*You can enjoy this dessert throughout the year if you freeze
plums when at their peak. They freeze very well and their
skins peel off easily on thawing. If you don't want to use
any alcohol, simply replace the port with either orange juice
or water.*

750 g (1¾ lb) ripe Victoria plums, stoned
115 g (4 oz) caster sugar
3 cardamom pods, crushed lightly, pods discarded, seeds removed
  and crushed
3 tablespoons port
500 g carton of custard
150 ml (¼ pint) whipping cream, whipped, or half a 200 g tub of
  Greek yogurt
1 ripe plum, stoned and cut into 6 slices, to decorate

1 Put the plums, sugar, cardamom seeds and port in a
  saucepan and bring to the boil. Cover and simmer very
  gently for at least 30 minutes until the plums are cooked
  and soft.
2 Strain into a bowl and allow the fruit to cool while you
  boil the juices for about 3–4 minutes, until they have been
  reduced to 3 tablespoons.
3 Strain the juice into the plums and purée them in a food
  processor or blender. Fold in the custard and spoon or
  pour into six glass dishes. Chill for an hour.
4 Spoon or pipe the cream or yogurt on top and decorate
  with a plum slice.

Plum Strudel Tartlets *(right)*

MAKES 12
PREPARATION & COOKING TIME: 1 hour 15 minutes
FREEZING: recommended

Serve these hot or warm accompanied by crème fraîche.

FOR THE PASTRY:
2 x 48 cm x 26 cm (19 inch x 10 inch) sheets filo pastry
25 g (1 oz) butter, melted

FOR THE FILLING:
350 g (12 oz) small plums, halved and stoned
25 g (1 oz) caster sugar
4 trifle sponges
2 tablespoons amaretto liqueur
25 g (1 oz) ratafia or amaretti biscuits
15 g (½ oz) flaked almonds

1 Preheat the oven to Gas Mark 4/electric oven 180°C/fan oven 160°C.
2 Place the plums in a shallow baking dish with 2 tablespoons cold water and sprinkle over the sugar. Bake them for 35–40 minutes until tender, spoon over the juices half way through the cooking time.
3 For the filo tartlets, lay out the sheets of filo on the work surface, on top of each other with edges matching. Arrange the pastry so that the shortest edge is at the top. Cut it from top to bottom into three equal strips. Now cut across the centre of each strip. You should have six pieces. Stack these on top of each other and cut across them twice to make squares.
4 Take a 12-hole patty tin. Brush each square generously with butter. Lay three squares, at an angle, in each hole so that you have a sort of star effect. Fill all 12 holes in this way.
5 Break up the trifle sponges and place them in the pastry tarts – one sponge per three pastry cases. Sprinkle amaretto over the sponge so that it soaks up the flavour.
6 Remove the plums from the oven and allow them to cool slightly. Increase the temperature to Gas Mark 5/electric oven 190°C/fan oven 170°C. Cut the plums into bite-size pieces. Place three plum pieces in each tart. Spoon 1 teaspoon of plum juice over each.
7 Place the ratafia or amaretti biscuits in a polythene bag and crush them with a rolling pin. Mix the flaked almonds into the crumbs. Scatter this strudel topping over the tartlets.
8 Bake in the centre of the oven for approximately 15 minutes until the pastry and toppings are golden.

Old Fashioned Treacle Tart

SERVES 6
PREPARATION & COOKING TIME: 20 minutes + 30 minutes chilling + 30–35 minutes cooking
FREEZING: not recommended

This recipe needs no introduction. Arguably one of the most potent reminders of school dinners, it remains as popular as ever today.

FOR THE PASTRY:
shortcrust pastry (page 10) made with 175 g (6 oz) flour

FOR THE FILLING:
25 g (1 oz) fresh white breadcrumbs
grated zest of 1 lemon
275 g (9½ oz) golden syrup
milk for brushing

1 Line a 20-cm (8-inch) metal pie plate with the shortcrust pastry, reserving the trimmings for later. Chill for 30 minutes.
2 Preheat the oven to Gas Mark 5/electric oven 190°C/fan oven 170°C. Place a baking sheet in the centre of the oven.
3 Scatter the breadcrumbs and lemon zest over the pastry base.
4 Gently warm the syrup, to make it flow more readily, and pour it over the breadcrumbs.
5 Reroll the pastry trimmings and cut them into 1-cm (½-inch) wide strips. Twist and lay them across the top of the tart in a lattice pattern. Seal the edges with milk and trim.
6 Brush the pastry with milk and bake for 30–35 minutes on the warmed baking sheet. Allow it to rest for about half an hour to give the syrup a chance to set. Serve warm.

Bramley Apple Gingerbread

SERVES 5 ▼
PREPARATION & COOKING TIME: 1 hour + 20 minutes
FREEZING: recommended

Gingerbread is relatively low in fat, so makes an ideal topping for a warming pudding made with our British Bramley apples. Serve with natural low fat yogurt or custard made with skimmed milk.

450 g (1 lb) Bramley apples
1 tablespoon lemon juice
1 tablespoon sugar
65 g (2¹/₂ oz) golden syrup
40 g (1¹/₂ oz) light soft brown sugar
40 g (1¹/₂ oz) sunflower or olive oil spread
110 g (4 oz) plain flour
¹/₂ teaspoon bicarbonate of soda
1 teaspoon ground ginger
1 egg
2¹/₂ tablespoons skimmed milk

1 Peel, core and slice the apples and toss in the lemon juice to prevent them from browning. Add the spoonful of sugar. Spoon into an ovenproof dish.
2 Preheat the oven to Gas Mark 3/electric oven 170°C/fan oven 150°C.
3 Put the syrup, brown sugar and spread into a saucepan and place over a low heat until the spread has melted. Do not allow the mixture to boil. Stir to mix together and leave to cool.
4 Sieve the flour, bicarbonate of soda and ginger into a mixing bowl.
5 Beat the egg and add the milk to it.
6 Make a well in the centre of the dry ingredients and pour in the liquid ingredients. Mix well to form a smooth batter.
7 Spoon the gingerbread over the apples. Place the dish on a baking sheet. Bake in the centre of the oven for about 1 hour, until a skewer inserted in the centre of the cake mix comes out clean. If the top starts to get too brown, cover loosely with a piece of foil.

French Apple Flan (above)

SERVES 6–8
PREPARATION & COOKING TIME: 30 minutes + 1 hour chilling + 30 minutes cooking
FREEZING: not suitable

An old favourite, it really does look stunning with its ever decreasing circles of red-rimmed apples, glistening under an apricot glaze – it never fails to please!

FOR THE PASTRY:
pâte sucrée (page 10) made with 115 g (4 oz) flour

FOR THE FILLING:
675 g (1¹/₂ lb) cooking apples, peeled, cored and sliced thinly
50 g (2 oz) granulated sugar
1 red eating apple
2 tablespoons lemon juice
2 tablespoons apricot jam, sieved and warmed

1 Line a 20-cm (8-inch) loose-bottomed, deep flan tin with the pâte sucrée. Chill for 1 hour.
2 Preheat the oven to Gas Mark 5/electric oven 190°C/fan oven 170°C. Place a baking sheet in the middle of the oven.
3 On the warmed baking sheet, bake the pastry case blind for 15 minutes. Remove the foil or paper and baking beans and cook for a further 5–10 minutes, until the pastry is fully cooked. Allow to cool.
4 In a saucepan, simmer the apples and sugar with 2 tablespoons water for 10–15 minutes until the apples are soft.
5 Pour the apple into a sieve and allow any excess liquid to drain off. Now push the apple mixture through the sieve to make a purée. Allow to cool.
6 Spoon the apple into the pastry case and level the surface.
7 Core and thinly slice the red apple. Arrange the slices in overlapping circles, starting from the edge. Brush the slices with lemon juice and brush over the apricot jam to glaze

Dutch Apple Cake

SERVES 10–12
PREPARATION & COOKING TIME: 30 minutes + 1 hour chilling + 1 hour cooking
FREEZING: recommended

Traditionally this is served warm with mid-morning coffee. The combination of spicy apple and crumbly butter pastry is delicious.

FOR THE PASTRY:
115 g (4 oz) unsalted butter
50 g (2 oz) caster sugar
1 large egg, beaten
175 g (6 oz) self-raising flour

FOR THE FILLING:
80 g (3 oz) sultanas
2 tablespoons Calvados
80 g (3 oz) caster sugar
1 teaspoon mixed spice
900 g (2 lb) cooking apples

1 For the pastry, cream together the butter and sugar. Beat in half the egg, and then gradually work in the flour. Turn it all out on to a lightly floured surface and bring together to form a soft dough. Use two thirds of the dough to line a lightly greased 23-cm (9-inch) loose-bottomed, deep flan tin, pressing the pastry over the base and up the sides. (You may find it quicker to roll the pastry, if possible.) Reserve any leftover pastry. Prick the base well with a fork and chill for at least 1 hour. Wrap any reserved pastry in clingfilm.
2 Preheat the oven to Gas Mark 4/electric oven 180°C/fan oven 160°C.
3 Simmer the sultanas in Calvados until the liquid evaporates. If you prefer, you can plump up the fruit by pouring boiling water over instead and leave to soak for 10 minutes before straining.
4 Mix together the sugar and mixed spice. Peel and thinly slice the apples. Scatter one third over the pastry base. Sprinkle over the spicy sugar and one third of the sultanas. Continue layering in this way, ending with sultanas.
5 Roll out the remaining pastry and cut it into strips, approximately 1.5 cm (½ inch) wide. Brush the rim of the tart with some of the remaining beaten egg. Lay the pastry strips at equal intervals over the top of the tart, arranging them to form a lattice pattern. Finally brush beaten egg over all of the pastry.
6 Bake in the centre of the oven for about 1 hour, until the pastry is golden and the apples are soft.

Date, Raisin & Ginger Stuffed Baked Apples

SERVES 4 ♥
PREPARATION & COOKING TIME: 40 minutes
FREEZING: not recommended

A traditional style dessert, but with a delicious stuffing. Apples with their soluble fibre can help to lower cholesterol and, because of their low glycaemic count, they provide slow release energy, which should prevent us from feeling hungry and snacking. Do ensure that you have removed all the rough core and that there is sufficient space in the centre of the apples to pack in the stuffing. Serve with some custard to pour over.

4 cooking apples, cored
75 g (2¾ oz) dates, chopped
50 g (2 oz) raisins
50 g (2 oz) pecan nuts, chopped finely
2 pieces of stem ginger, chopped finely
1 tablespoon stem ginger syrup
1 tablespoon clear honey

1 Preheat the oven to Gas Mark 4/electric oven 180°C/fan oven 160°C. Line a baking tin with a sheet of non-stick baking parchment.
2 Score the apples lightly around the middle and place in the baking tin.
3 Mix together the dates, raisins, pecans and chopped stem ginger. Pack equal amounts into the centre of the apples, pushing down well.
4 Stir together the stem ginger syrup and the honey and spoon it over the dried fruit filling, allowing it to drizzle down inside the apples and slightly over the surface.
5 Place the apples in the oven and bake for 20 minutes or until the apples feel soft when the sides are pressed gently. Serve warm.

Toffee Apple Baked Alaska

SERVES 6–8 ★
PREPARATION & COOKING TIME: 20 minutes
FREEZING: not recommended

A baked Alaska is an ideal dessert to serve on bonfire night, particularly if you present it at the table with lit sparklers pressed into the meringue. The filling includes toffee ice cream and apple chunks, in keeping with the toffee apples traditionally associated with this night. This is a very speedy dessert to prepare as the only part of it that requires any preparation is the meringue.

25-cm (10-inch) sponge flan case
350 g jar of chunky apple pieces
500 ml tub of toffee (or fudge) ice cream
4 large egg whites
225 g (8 oz) caster sugar
icing sugar and sparklers, to serve

1 Preheat the oven to Gas Mark 8/electric oven 230°C/fan oven 210°C.
2 Place the sponge on an ovenproof serving dish. Spread the apple pieces over the surface, avoiding the raised edges, and then spread the ice cream over the apples. Place in the freezer while you make the meringue.
3 Place the egg whites in a large bowl and whisk on a fast setting until stiff but not dry. Add the sugar, a teaspoon at a time, while continuing to whisk at high speed, until the meringue is thick and glossy.
4 Remove the dish from the freezer and spread the meringue all over the ice cream and sponge, making sure that there are no gaps in the meringue.
5 Place in the oven straight away and bake for 3–4 minutes, until the meringue is golden brown. Dust with icing sugar, place lit sparklers in the meringue and serve immediately.

Cinnamon Brioche Toast with Fried Apples

SERVES 6 ★
PREPARATION & COOKING TIME: 25 minutes
FREEZING: not recommended

Cinnamon toast is usually made with white bread; using brioche makes the dessert richer and sweeter. Clotted cream or some really good-quality vanilla ice cream would be ideal accompaniments.

50 g (2 oz) sultanas
3 tablespoons brandy or apple juice
175 g (6 oz) unsalted butter
2 teaspoons ground cinnamon
6 slices of brioche
50 g (2 oz) light muscovado sugar
6 medium firm dessert apples, such as Cox's, peeled, cored and cut into 6–8 segments

1 Place the sultanas and brandy or apple juice in a bowl and leave to soak for 20 minutes. Preheat the oven to Gas Mark 2/electric oven 150°C/fan oven 130°C.
2 Heat half the butter in a large frying pan over a moderate heat, stir in the cinnamon and fry the bread, a couple of slices at a time, until golden brown and crisp. Place on a baking sheet, cover loosely with foil and keep warm in the oven.
3 Add the remaining butter to the frying pan, together with the sugar, and allow them to bubble together for a minute. Add the apple slices to the pan and increase the heat. Coat the apples in the buttery sugar and fry for a few minutes until the apples are golden brown and tender. Stir in the sultanas and the brandy or apple juice and heat through for a minute.
4 To serve, cut each slice of brioche toast in half diagonally and arrange on each serving plate, preferably warmed. Spoon over the apple slices and pan juices and serve with either clotted cream or ice cream.

Warm Chocolate Tart

SERVES 8
PREPARATION & COOKING TIME: 25 minutes + 1 hour chilling + 45–50 minutes cooking
FREEZING: not recommended

The combination of chocolate and hazelnuts never fails to please, and ground almonds could be substituted if you prefer. This chocolate tart has a lovely, light mousse-like texture and is delicious served with crème fraîche, which has been sweetened and flavoured with Cointreau. If you find the pastry difficult to handle – it can be a little crumbly – press it into the tin, rather than rolling it out.

FOR THE HAZELNUT PASTRY:
115 g (4 oz) plain flour
25 g (1 oz) roasted, chopped hazelnuts, ground
50 g (2 oz) unsalted butter, diced
25 g (1 oz) caster sugar
1 egg, beaten

FOR THE FILLING:
115 g (4 oz) dark chocolate with minimum 70% cocoa solids, broken into pieces
25 g (1 oz) unsalted butter
2 large eggs
50 g (2 oz) golden caster sugar
150 ml (¼ pint), double cream
icing sugar, for dusting

1 Combine the flour and ground hazelnuts in a bowl. Rub in the butter until the mixture resembles breadcrumbs. Stir in the sugar. Add enough egg to make a soft dough. Roll out the dough on a lightly floured surface, and use it to line a greased 20-cm (8-inch) loose-bottomed, deep flan ring. Prick the base with a fork and chill for 1 hour.
2 Preheat the oven to Gas Mark 5/electric oven 190°C/fan oven 170°C. Place a baking sheet in the centre of the oven.
3 On the warmed baking sheet, bake the pastry case blind for 15 minutes. Remove the foil or paper and baking beans and cook for a further 5–10 minutes. Reduce the oven temperature to Gas Mark 4/electric oven 180°C/fan oven 160°C.
4 Melt the chocolate and butter in a bowl over hot (not boiling) water. Stir until smooth and then leave to cool slightly.
5 Whisk the eggs and sugar together, until thick and pale, this will take about 5 minutes. Fold in the chocolate mixture followed by the double cream. Pour this into the flan case and bake for about 20 minutes. The tart should still have a slight tremble in the centre, and will continue to cook when it is removed from the oven.
6 When ready to serve, remove the tart carefully from the flan tin, dust with sifted icing sugar and serve warm.

Pear Tarte Tatin

SERVES 6
PREPARATION & COOKING TIME: 25 minutes + 30 minutes chilling + 40 minutes cooking
FREEZING: not recommended

Apples are traditionally used for this classic French recipe, but pears are equally delicious. If you like, you can add some ground ginger to the pastry to enhance the warm, comforting feel of this tart. A dollop of crème fraîche is all that's required to finish it off. If you need a shortcut, use bought puff pastry.

FOR THE PASTRY:
50 g (2 oz) unsalted butter
115 g (4 oz) plain flour
1 large egg yolk

FOR THE FILLING:
50 g (2 oz) unsalted butter
115 g (4 oz) caster sugar
4 small firm, ripe pears, (approximately 550 g/1¼ lb), peeled, quartered and cored

1 To make the pastry, rub the butter into the flour. Make a well in the mixture and stir in the egg yolk and 1 tablespoon cold water. Bring it all together to form a soft dough. Wrap the dough in clingfilm and chill for at least 30 minutes.
2 Preheat the oven to Gas Mark 6/electric oven 200°C/fan oven 180°C. Place a baking sheet just above the centre of the oven.
3 Melt the butter in a 20-cm (8-inch) saucepan or frying pan. Sprinkle over the sugar and arrange the pear quarters on top – cut side uppermost. Cook over a medium high heat for about 20 minutes, or until the pears are fairly dark golden.
4 If you are not using a frying pan, arrange the pears, cut side uppermost, in a 20-cm (8-inch) round cake tin. Take a little trouble here as this will be the side of the pudding you will see when it is turned out. Pour over the buttery juices from the pears.
5 On a lightly floured surface roll out the pastry to a 22 cm (8½-inch) round. Lay it on top of the pears in the cake tin, or the frying pan, and tuck in the edges.
6 Bake on the heated baking sheet for 20 minutes, or until the pastry is cooked and golden. Leave to stand for 10 minutes before carefully inverting the tart on to a serving dish (the syrup will be very hot). Do not worry if any of the pears are left behind, just remove them carefully and add them into the tart.

NOTE: If using a frying pan, place it on a baking sheet, as the juices do tend to bubble over the edge a bit.

Stuffed Pears with Chocolate Fudge Sauce *(below)*

SERVES 4
PREPARATION & COOKING TIME: 40 minutes
FREEZING: not recommended

Pears with chocolate sauce is a classic French dessert. Stuffing the base of the pears with a crunchy nut filling adds an interesting taste and texture to the dish. Large ripe pears, such as Comice or William, are ideal for this elegant dinner party dessert.

2 tablespoons lemon juice
50 g (2 oz) caster sugar
300 ml (10 fl oz) water
1 cinnamon stick
4 ripe pears

FOR THE FILLING:
25 g (1 oz) chopped roasted hazelnuts
1 tablespoon light muscovado sugar
15 g (½ oz) butter, melted

FOR THE SAUCE:
50 g (2 oz) butter
115 g (4 oz) light muscovado sugar
1 tablespoon golden syrup
225 ml (8 fl oz) double cream
115 g (4 oz) plain chocolate, broken into pieces

1 Place the lemon juice, caster sugar, water and cinnamon stick in a saucepan and heat gently to dissolve the sugar.
2 In the meantime, peel the pears carefully, leaving the stalk intact. Scoop out the cores from the base and create a hole for the filling. Place the pears in the syrup, turning them over to coat them. Bring to the boil, cover and simmer for 15–20 minutes or until they are tender. Remove the pears from the poaching liquid and allow to cool.
3 To make the filling, simply combine the ingredients together. When the pears have cooled, fill the cavities with the nut mixture and place each pear on a serving plate.
4 To make the sauce, place the butter, muscovado sugar and syrup in a saucepan and melt over a low heat. Add the cream and chocolate and bring to the boil, whisking continuously. Simmer for a minute over a low heat, cool a little and then pour the sauce over the top of the pears.

Blackberry Mousses

SERVES 6 ★ ▼
PREPARATION TIME: 20 minutes
FREEZING: not recommended

It's hard to believe that this deliciously creamy dessert is so healthy – low in fat and calories, high in vitamin C!

350 g (12 oz) fresh or frozen blackberries
80 g (3 oz) caster sugar
11.7 g sachet of gelatine
250 g tub of ricotta cheese
200 g tub of light cream cheese
2 large egg whites, whisked to stiff peaks
fresh mint leaves, to decorate

1 Place the blackberries (reserving a few to decorate), caster sugar and 2 tablespoons of water in a saucepan and bring to the boil over a moderate heat. Lower the heat straight away and simmer very gently for 3–4 minutes.
2 Sieve the blackberries and their liquid into a bowl to remove the pips and then sprinkle the gelatine over the purée. Whisk with a hand whisk or stir with a spoon until the gelatine has dissolved. Allow to cool.
3 Beat the ricotta and cream cheeses together in a bowl and stir in the blackberry mixture. Fold in a tablespoon of the egg whites with a metal spoon to loosen the mixture and then fold in the remaining whites until there is no white visible.
4 Spoon into wine glasses or glass dessert dishes and decorate with the reserved blackberries and mint leaves.

NOTE: Replace gelatine with Vegegel, if you are vegetarian.

Autumn Fruit Salad

SERVES 4 ♥ ★ ▼
PREPARATION TIME: 20 MINUTES
FREEZING: not recommended

This is a very pretty and simple fruit salad using fruits available in the autumn. The pomegranate is sweet and pink, and adds an unusual flavour.

2 William, Comice or Conference pears
2 russet apples
juice of ½ orange
a little clear honey (optional)
1 pomegranate

1 Peel the pears and cut into quarters. Remove the core and slice into a serving dish. Leave the apples unpeeled. Cut them into quarters, remove the core and slice into the dish.
2 Pour over the orange juice and honey, if used, and turn to mix. This prevents the fruit from going brown.
3 Cut the pomegranate in half over a large dinner plate (to save all the juices). With a teaspoon handle or a fork, ease out the pink seeds, making sure to remove all the membranes as these can be bitter.
4 Add the pomegranate seeds and all their juices to the other fruit. Stir to mix and serve alone or with little biscuits.

Apricot, Orange & Almond Gâteau

SERVES 6–8
PREPARATION TIME: 30 minutes + 1 hour chilling
FREEZING: recommended

This dessert is not baked and can be prepared hours in advance. It freezes extremely well and it is worth keeping one in the freezer for when you have unexpected visitors.

80 g (3 oz) unsalted butter
80 g (3 oz) caster sugar
1 large egg yolk
115 g (4 oz) ground almonds
grated zest and juice of 2 oranges
80 ml (3 fl oz) single cream
50 g (2 oz) dried apricots, chopped finely
3 tablespoons Cointreau or any other orange liqueur
about 24 sponge fingers
300 ml (½ pint) whipping cream, whipped

TO DECORATE:
extra dried apricots, chopped, and/or fresh orange slices
toasted flaked almonds

1 Grease a 450 g (1 lb) loaf tin and line the base and narrow sides with a strip of baking parchment or greaseproof paper.
2 Cream the butter and sugar together until light and fluffy. Add the egg yolk, almonds, orange zest and single cream and beat until smooth. Fold in the apricots.
3 Combine the orange juice and Cointreau. Dip a third of the sponge fingers, one at a time, into the orange-juice mixture and arrange in a row in the base of the tin. Spread half the almond mixture on top. Repeat the layers once more and then finish with the sponge fingers (you may need some extra orange juice). Chill in the fridge to set.
4 Turn out on to a serving dish. Spread two-thirds of the cream all over the gâteau. Pipe the remaining cream on top and decorate with the apricots/orange slices and flaked almonds.

Plum & Marzipan Tarts

MAKES 12
PREPARATION & COOKING TIME: 50 minutes
FREEZING: recommended

Plums have been used for this recipe but many other fruits, such as apricots, pears, apples and greengages, would work equally well. If you don't have the time to make almond paste, white marzipan can be rolled out and used instead. Do try making the paste if you can though – it really is very quick and easy and the amaretto gives it a lovely flavour.

FOR THE PASTRY:
350 g (12 oz) ready-made puff pastry
1 egg, beaten

FOR THE ALMOND PASTE:
115 g (4 oz) ground almonds
50 g (2 oz) caster sugar
50 g (2 oz) icing sugar
3–4 tablespoons amaretto liqueur

FOR THE PLUM TOPPING:
900 g (2 lb) small plums, stoned and quartered
2 tablespoons redcurrant jelly, warmed, to glaze

1 Preheat the oven to Gas Mark 6/electric oven 200°C/fan oven 180°C.
2 Roll out the pastry on a lightly floured surface to make a rectangle 40 x 30 cm (16 x 12 in). Cut it into 12 squares, each measuring 10 cm (4 in). Place the squares on two baking sheets. Using a sharp knife, score a line 1 cm (½ inch) in from the edge around each one and prick the centres with a fork. Brush each square with beaten egg.
3 Combine the almond paste ingredients in a bowl, adding enough amaretto to give a gritty sand-like texture. Spoon a tablespoon of paste on the centre of each pastry.
4 Arrange six pieces of plum, skin side up and overlapping, on each square within the scored border. Brush with redcurrant jelly.
5 Bake, one sheet at a time, towards the top of the oven for 25 minutes, or until the pastries are puffy and golden. Remove them from the oven and brush once more with redcurrant jelly glaze.

Almond Plum Crumble *(right)*

SERVES 4–6
PREPARATION & COOKING TIME: 1 hour
FREEZING: recommended

There is something about cooked plums – it probably lies in the consistency of the liquid which their natural juices make when combined with sugar – that results in a fabulous base for crumbles. The ratio of fruit to crumble topping is purposefully generous here, to reduce the fat and sugar content while upping the proportion of fruit.

Rhubarb, with some powdered ginger rubbed into the crumble topping, would make a delicious alternative. Crumble just wouldn't be the same without its traditional companion, custard. If you want to reduce the calories, make it with skimmed or semi-skimmed milk.

675 g (1½ lb) plums, washed, halved and stoned
50 g (2 oz) golden granulated sugar

FOR THE CRUMBLE:
115 g (4 oz) plain flour
50 g (2 oz) golden granulated sugar
50 g (2 oz) butter
50 g (2 oz) ground almonds
25 g (1 oz) flaked almonds

1 Preheat the oven to Gas Mark 4/electric oven 180°C/fan oven 160°C. Grease a 1.75-litre (3-pint) shallow ovenproof dish.
2 Arrange the plums in a single layer in the prepared dish. Sprinkle enough sugar to sweeten over the top.
3 Place the flour and sugar in a bowl. Rub in the butter until the mixture resembles fine breadcrumbs. Stir in the ground almonds and half the flaked almonds.
4 Scatter the crumble mixture over the plums and press down lightly. Sprinkle the reserved flaked almonds over the top.
5 Bake in the centre of the oven for 40–45 minutes, until the crumble is golden and the plums are cooked. Serve hot or warm.

Harvest Fruit Crumble

SERVES 6 ♥
PREPARATION & COOKING TIME: 1 hour
FREEZING: recommended

Fruit crumbles are one of the most popular desserts ever but if butter is used the topping can be high in saturated fat. Substituting a polyunsaturated margarine, as well as using oats and walnuts in the crumble, is a much healthier option. Serve with some low fat custard to pour over.

2 Bramley apples, peeled, cored and sliced
2 pears, peeled, cored and sliced
3 plums, stoned and sliced
75 g (2¼ oz) soft light brown sugar
½ teaspoon ground cinnamon

FOR THE CRUMBLE:
150 g (5 oz) plain flour
75 g (2¼ oz) rolled oats
100 g (3½ oz) sunflower margarine
50 g (2 oz) walnuts, chopped roughly
½ teaspoon ground cinnamon
75 g (2¼ oz) demerara sugar

1 Preheat the oven to Gas Mark 4/electric oven 180°C/fan oven 160°C.
2 Place the prepared fruit, the light brown sugar and the cinnamon in an ovenproof dish. Stir lightly to combine and ensure the sugar coats the fruit.
3 Put the plain flour and oats in a mixing bowl and rub in the margarine. Stir in the walnuts, cinnamon and demerara sugar and mix well. Spoon the crumble topping evenly over the fruit.
4 Bake the crumble in the oven for 30–35 minutes until the fruit is tender and the topping crisp and lightly golden.

Spiced Caramelised Bananas with Orange & Oatmeal Crust

SERVES 6
PREPARATION & COOKING TIME: 20 minutes + 30 minutes chilling + 25 minutes cooking
FREEZING: not recommended

This crunchy pastry is almost good enough to make into biscuits! A wonderfully fragrant autumn or winter tart for when there is little other fruit around. Ginger gives a subtle warming undertone to the distinctive cardamom flavour. Serve this comforting pudding with a dollop of crème fraîche or vanilla ice cream.

FOR THE ORANGE & OATMEAL PASTRY:
80 g (3 oz) plain flour
25 g (1 oz) medium oatmeal
50 g (2 oz) caster sugar
grated zest of 1 orange
80 g (3 oz) unsalted butter, diced
1 tablespoon freshly squeezed orange juice

FOR THE TOPPING:
25 g (1 oz) unsalted butter
50 g (2 oz) caster sugar
7 medium bananas
¼ teaspoon ground ginger
seeds of 10 cardamom pods, crushed (about ¼ teaspoon)

1 To make the pastry, mix together the flour, oatmeal, sugar and orange zest. Rub in the butter and bind it all to a dough with the orange juice. Bring it together to form a ball and wrap it in a polythene bag. Chill for at least 30 minutes.
2 Preheat the oven to Gas Mark 6/electric oven 200°C/fan oven 180°C. Place a baking sheet on the middle shelf of the oven.
3 Prepare the topping by warming a 23-cm (9-inch) frying pan over a medium heat. Melt the butter and then sprinkle caster sugar evenly over the surface. Cook for 1–2 minutes, until you see it just beginning to caramelise. Remove the pan from the heat. Take care with this as the mixture will continue to cook and darken further, even when it is removed from the heat.
4 Peel the bananas and cut them into five batons. Arrange them to cover the base of the frying pan, packing them closely together.
5 Sprinkle ground ginger and cardamom over the bananas.
6 On a lightly floured surface roll out the pastry to a 24-cm (9½-inch) round. Using the rolling pin to help you, place the pastry over the bananas, and tuck in any spare down the edges.
7 On the warmed baking sheet, bake at once for about 25 minutes, or until the pastry is crisp and golden. Remove from the oven and allow it to stand for about 10 minutes before inverting it on to a serving plate. This tart is best eaten warm.

NOTE: If you don't own a frying pan suitable for putting in the oven, use a heavy-based saucepan for step 3, and then pour the caramel into a 23-cm (9-inch) shallow, round cake tin. Arrange the bananas on top.

Pecan Pie *(below)*

SERVES 6
PREPARATION & COOKING TIME: 20 minutes
+ 30 minutes chilling + about 1 hour cooking
FREEZING: not recommended

*This looks good, tastes great, and is as easy as pie to make.
Serve it with whipped cream – and enjoy!*

FOR THE PASTRY:
shortcrust pastry (page 10) made with 115 g (4 oz) plain flour

FOR THE FILLING:
2 large eggs, beaten
115 g (4 oz) light muscovado sugar
115 g (4 oz) golden syrup
1 teaspoon vanilla essence
25 g (1 oz) unsalted butter, melted
25 g (1 oz) plain flour
175 g (6 oz) pecan nuts
1 tablespoon apricot jam, warmed and sieved

1 Line a deep 20-cm (8-inch) flan tin with the shortcrust pastry. Chill for 30 minutes.
2 Preheat the oven to Gas Mark 6/electric oven 200°C/fan oven 180°C. Put a baking sheet on the middle shelf of the oven.
3 On the heated baking sheet, bake the pastry case blind for 15 minutes, remove the foil or paper and beans and cook for a further 5–10 minutes, until the pastry is cooked.
4 To make the filling, combine the eggs, sugar, syrup and vanilla in a bowl. Stir in the butter and flour.
5 Chop 115 g (4 oz) of the pecan nuts and add these to the bowl.
6 Reduce the oven temperature to Gas Mark 4/electric oven 180°C/fan oven 160°C. Pour the filling into the pastry case and arrange the remaining whole pecan nuts on the top. Bake for 30–35 minutes until the filling is set and browned.
7 Brush with apricot jam and serve warm.

Desserts

Italian Mocha Fools

PREPARATION TIME: 15 minutes + 30 minutes chilling
FREEZING: only recommended if made in freezerproof dishes

This is simplicity itself to prepare and is an ideal finale to an Italian meal. Mascarpone and ricotta cheeses both work well in this recipe but mascarpone has far more calories.

2 tablespoons strong espresso coffee
2 tablespoons coffee liqueur, such as Tia Maria or Kahlua
250 g tub of mascarpone or ricotta cheese
200 g tub of Greek yogurt
25 g (1 oz) demerara sugar
115 g (4 oz) amaretti biscuits, roughly crushed
amaretti biscuits, grated plain chocolate or chocolate-covered coffee beans, to decorate

1 Combine the coffee and alcohol. Place the chosen cheese, yogurt and sugar in a bowl, mix well and fold in the coffee mixture.
2 Divide half the biscuits between stemmed glasses. Spoon half the mocha cream over the biscuits. Sprinkle the remaining biscuits on top, followed by the rest of the cream mixture.
3 Chill for about 30 minutes or until ready to serve.
4 Decorate with either amaretti biscuits (whole or finely crushed), grated chocolate or chocolate-covered coffee beans.

Chocolate Crème Brûlée

SERVES 6
PREPARATION TIME: 25 minutes + 2 hours chilling
FREEZING: not recommended

This version of this universally popular dessert has the advantage of not requiring any baking. If you don't possess a blowtorch, place the ramekins in a roasting tin with enough cold water to come two-thirds up the sides of the dishes – this prevents the chocolate custards from getting hot and cooking while under the grill.

50 g (2 oz) caster sugar
4 egg yolks
1 heaped teaspoon cornflour
1 tablespoon cocoa powder
300 ml (½ pint) double cream
300 ml (½ pint) milk
100 g bar of plain chocolate, broken into squares
6 teaspoons icing sugar, sifted

1 Put the caster sugar, egg yolks, cornflour and cocoa powder in a bowl and mix well.
2 Place the cream and milk in a medium saucepan and gently bring to the boil. Pour this on to the egg mixture, whisking continuously. Return the mixture to the pan and heat gently, stirring, until it has thickened.
3 Remove the pan from the heat and stir in the chocolate pieces until they have melted. Pour the mixture into six ramekin dishes and allow to cool before placing in the fridge to chill for a couple of hours.
4 Sprinkle the surfaces evenly with the icing sugar and caramelise the top either by using a blowtorch or placing under a hot preheated grill. Chill for at least 2 hours, or until ready to serve.

Sachertorte

SERVES 8
PREPARATION & COOKING TIME: 1½ hours
FREEZING: recommended

This famous Austrian chocolate gâteau was created by Franz Sacher in 1832. It is very rich, so small slices are advisable.

FOR THE CAKE:
225 g (8 oz) plain chocolate, broken into pieces
175 g (6 oz) unsalted butter, softened
150 g (5 oz) caster sugar
1 teaspoon vanilla essence
5 eggs, separated
80 g (3 oz) ground almonds
50 g (2 oz) plain flour

FOR THE FILLING AND ICING:
8 tablespoons apricot jam
1 tablespoon lemon juice
2 tablespoons whisky
175 g (6 oz) plain chocolate, broken into pieces
80 g (3 oz) butter, cut into small dice
80 g (3 oz) double cream
50 g (2 oz) milk chocolate, broken into pieces

1 Preheat the oven to Gas Mark 4/electric oven 180°C/fan oven 160°C. Grease and line the base of a 20-cm (8-inch) cake tin with baking parchment.
2 Melt the chocolate by placing it in a bowl and set it over a pan of barely simmering hot water. Stir and allow to cool. Meanwhile, whisk the butter and sugar in another bowl until the mixture is light and creamy. Beat in the vanilla essence followed by the egg yolks, one at a time. Add the ground almonds and flour and mix in thoroughly. Whisk the egg whites until they are stiff in a large spotlessly clean bowl. Add a large spoonful to the chocolate mixture and beat in to loosen the mixture. Add the remaining whites and fold them in gently using a figure-of-eight action.
3 Spoon the mixture into the prepared tin, level the surface and bake for 45–50 minutes until the cake has risen and is firm to the touch. Allow to cool for a few minutes in the tin, and then turn out and cool completely on a wire rack.
4 Heat the apricot jam with the lemon juice and sieve it. Cut the cake in half horizontally. Sprinkle the whisky over the cut surfaces. Place the bottom half on a plate and spread the cut surface with a third of the jam mixture. Place the other cake half on top. Spread the remaining jam all over the top and sides of the cake and then leave it to set
5 Melt the plain chocolate as in Step 2. Remove the bowl from the heat and stir in the butter until it has melted. Stir in the cream and leave the sauce to thicken a little so that it will spread easily. Pour the chocolate icing on to the cake and spread it evenly all over. Leave it to set.
6 Melt the milk chocolate as in Step 2. Spoon it into a small disposable piping bag or plastic food bag and snip off a small corner. Pipe the name 'Sacher' across the top and, once again, leave to set.

'Jaffa Cake' Tart

SERVES 6
PREPARATION AND COOKING TIME: 1 hour
FREEZING: recommended

This is a fun yet sophisticated chocolate tart based on the same layers you find in Jaffa Cakes. The base is a shortbread one rather than the pastry normally associated with tarts.

80 g (3 oz) plain flour
40 g (1½ oz) caster sugar
50 g (2 oz) butter, softened
115 g (4 oz) plain chocolate (at least 70% cocoa solids)
1 tablespoon butter, softened
2 tablespoons Cointreau
300 ml (½ pint) double cream, whipped
3 heaped tablespoons thin-cut orange marmalade
cocoa powder, to decorate

1 Preheat the oven to Gas Mark 6/electric oven 200°C/fan oven 180°C.
2 Place the flour and sugar in a bowl and mix. Add the butter and rub into the flour mix. Bring the mixture together to form a ball, wrap in clingfilm and chill for 15 minutes.
3 Press the shortbread dough into the base of a 20 cm (8-inch) loose-bottomed flan tin, using a potato masher. Prick it lightly with a fork and bake in the oven for 10 minutes until golden brown. Allow to cool.
4 In the meantime, melt the chocolate with 2 tablespoons of water in a bowl set over a pan of barely simmering water. Remove from the heat and mix thoroughly. Stir in the tablespoon of butter followed by the Cointreau. Allow to cool for a few minutes and then fold in the whipped cream.
5 Spread the marmalade evenly over the shortbread base and then spoon over the chocolate mixture. Chill for at least 15 minutes to set, preferably overnight.
6 Sift some cocoa powder over the tart to decorate before serving.

Apricot, Pineapple & Nut Cake

MAKES 12–16 slices
PREPARATION & COOKING TIME: 1–1½ hours

Using the flavoured ale gives this fruit cake a new twist. The ale can usually be found on the alcohol shelves in the supermarket.

225 g (8 oz) butter, softened
350 g (12 oz) soft dark brown sugar
3 tablespoons set honey
2 eggs
450 g (1 lb) plain flour, sieved
115 g (4 oz) ready-to-eat dried apricots, diced
115 g (4 oz) crystallised pineapple, diced
175 g (6 oz) chopped mixed nuts
2 teaspoons bicarbonate of soda
2 teaspoons ground cinnamon
about 250 ml (9 fl oz) cherry-flavoured ale

1 Cream together the butter, sugar and the honey until light and fluffy. Beat in the eggs.
2 Fold in the flour, then the fruit, nuts, bicarbonate of soda and the cinnamon.
3 Add enough ale to produce a soft dropping mixture.
4 Spoon the mixture into a greased and lined 23-cm (9-inch) round cake tin; smooth the top.
5 Bake at Gas Mark 4/electric oven l80°C/fan oven 160°C for 1–1¼ hours until a skewer inserted into the centre of the cake comes out clean.
6 Leave the cake in the tin until it is completely cold.

Tropical Fruit Cake

MAKES 16–20 slices
PREPARATION & COOKING TIME: 1–1½ hours

The mix of tropical fruits, marzipan and orange produces a handsome, modern cake.

175 g (6 oz) butter, softened
175 g (6 oz) caster sugar
3 eggs
50 g (2 oz) ready-to-eat dried mango, chopped
50 g (2 oz) ready-to-eat dried papaya, chopped
50 g (2 oz) glacé cherries, halved
50 g (2 oz) glacé pineapple, chopped
225 g (8 oz) sultanas
115 g (4 oz) walnut pieces, roughly chopped
115 g (4 oz) marzipan, cut into 12 pieces
grated zest and juice of 2 unwaxed oranges
sieve together: 115 g (4 oz) plain flour and 115 g (4 oz) plain wholemeal flour and 1 teaspoon baking powder and 2 teaspoons ground cinnamon
25 g (1oz) flaked almonds (optional)

1 Cream the butter and sugar together until light in colour and fluffy. Gradually beat in the eggs.
2 Stir in the prepared fruits, walnuts and marzipan.
3 Fold in the zest and juice of the oranges, the flours, baking powder and cinnamon.
4 Spoon the mixture into a greased and lined 20-cm (8-inch) round cake tin, level the top and sprinkle over the flaked almonds if required.
5 Bake at Gas Mark 2/electric oven 150°C/fan oven 130°F for 1½–2 hours until the cake is firm, dark golden and a skewer inserted in the centre of the cake comes out clean.
6 Leave the cake to cool in the tin for 15 minutes before turning it out on to a wire rack to cool completely.

Apple, Orange & Pecan Cake

MAKES 10–12 slices
PREPARATION & COOKING TIME: 1¼–1½ hours

For a good flavour use Bramley apples. Prepare apples last to avoid browning.

175 g (6 oz) butter, softened
175 g (6 oz) molasses sugar
2 eggs
sieve together: 150 g (5 oz) wholemeal self-raising flour and 115 g (4 oz) self-raising flour
350 g (12 oz) cooking apples, peeled, cored and diced
80 g (3 oz) pecan nuts, roughly chopped
juice of 1 orange

1 Cream the butter and the sugar together until light in colour and fluffy.
2 Beat in each egg, then fold in the flours, stir in the prepared apples and the pecans, together with the orange juice.
3 Spoon the mixture into a greased and lined 900 g (2 lb) loaf tin; smooth its top.
4 Bake at Gas Mark 4/electric oven 180°C/fan oven 160°C for 50–70 minutes, until the cake is well risen and firm to the touch.
5 Allow the cake to cool in the tin for 15 minutes before placing it on a wire rack to cool completely.

Honey & Cherry Cake

MAKES 10–12 slices
PREPARATION & COOKING TIME: 1¼-1½ hours

Try different flavoured honeys according to taste.

175 g (6 oz) butter, softened
80 g (3 oz) caster sugar
80 g (3 oz) set honey
2 eggs
sieve together: 115 g (4 oz) plain flour and 115 g (4 oz) wholemeal flour and 2 teaspoons baking powder
50 g (2 oz) ground almonds
115 g (4 oz) glacé cherries, quartered
2–3 tablespoons milk

1 Cream the butter, sugar and the honey together until light in colour and fluffy; however, be careful not to over beat.
2 Beat in the eggs. Then fold in the flours, baking powder, ground almonds and the cherries.
3 Stir in enough milk to give a soft mixture.
4 Spoon the mixture into a greased and lined 900 g (2 lb) loaf tin.
5 Bake at Gas Mark 3/electric oven 160°C/fan oven 140°C for 60–75 minutes until the cake is well risen, firm to the touch, and dark golden in colour.
6 Leave the cake in the tin for 10 minutes before placing it on a wire rack to cool completely.

Wensleydale Apple Cake

MAKES 12–16 slices
PREPARATION & COOKING TIME: 1 hour

The apples and cheese produce an unusual cake, ideal for teatime or for supper. Cox's apples are ideal, but any crisp dessert apple will produce good results.

225 g (8 oz) self-raising flour, sieved
115 g (4 oz) caster sugar
115 g (4 oz) butter, chilled
1 egg
4 tablespoons milk
3 medium-sized apples, peeled, cored and sliced
150 g (5 oz) Wensleydale cheese, grated coarsely

FOR THE TOPPING:
25 g (1 oz) caster sugar
1 teaspoon ground cinnamon
50 g (2 oz) butter, chilled

1 Place the flour in a bowl, add the sugar and rub in the butter until the mixture resembles fine breadcrumbs.
2 Add the egg and milk, and mix to a soft dough.
3 Spread half the mixture into a well-greased and lined 20-cm (8-inch) round cake tin. Arrange half the apple slices on top.
4 Spread the remaining mixture over the layer of apple; smooth the top.
5 Arrange the remaining apple slices on top, and sprinkle over the cheese.
6 For the topping, sprinkle with sugar and cinnamon, and dot with butter.
7 Bake at Gas Mark 5/electric oven 190°C/fan oven 170°C for 35–45 minutes until the top of the cake is dark golden and firm to the touch
8 Leave the cake in the tin to cool for 20 minutes before turning it out on to a wire rack to cool completely.

Jewel Cake

MAKES 12–16 slices
PREPARATION & COOKING TIME: 1½–1¾ hours

The glacé cherries, dried fruit and nuts give this cake a jewelled appearance. It has a moist texture and fruity flavour.

175 g (6 oz) glacé cherries, halved
175 g (6 oz) sultanas
175 g (6 oz) raisins
25 g (1 oz) blanched almonds, chopped
25 g (1 oz) walnut pieces, chopped
115 g (4 oz) ready-to-eat dates, chopped
sieve together: 175 g (6 oz) plain flour, and a pinch of salt and 1
   teaspoon ground mixed spice
50 g (2 oz) ground almonds
115 g (4 oz) butter, softened
115 g (4 oz) soft dark brown sugar
3 eggs
1 tablespoon sweet sherry

1 In a bowl, mix together the glacé cherries, sultanas, raisins, chopped nuts and dates.
2 Sift together the sieved flour mixture with the ground almonds.
3 In a large mixing bowl, cream the butter and the sugar until light in colour and fluffy. Beat in each egg.
4 Fold in the flour and almond mixture, and then stir in the fruit and the sherry.
5 Spoon the mixture into a greased and lined 18-cm (7-inch) round cake tin.
6 Bake at Gas Mark 3/electric oven 170°C/fan oven 150°C for 1¼–1½ hours until dark golden in colour, and a skewer inserted in the centre comes out clean.
7 Leave to cool in the tin for 15 minutes before turning out on to a wire rack to cool completely.

Date, Apple & Madeira Cake (right)

MAKES 12–16 slices
PREPARATION & COOKING TIME: 15 minutes + overnight
   soaking + 20 minutes + 50–60 minutes

This moist apple cake has a delicious date filling sandwiched between the cake and almond topping.

FOR THE FILLING:
350 g (12 oz) ready-to-eat dates, chopped
80 g (3 oz) caster sugar
150 ml (¼ pint) water
80 ml (3 fl oz) sweet Madeira

FOR THE ALMOND TOPPING:
80 g (3 oz) self-raising flour, sieved
25 g (1oz) butter, chilled
80 g (3 oz) demerara sugar
50 g (2 oz) flaked almonds

FOR THE CAKE:
sieve together: 80 g (3 oz) self-raising flour and ½ teaspoon baking
   powder
50 g (2 oz) butter, chilled
25 g (1 oz) ground almonds
50 g (2 oz) caster sugar
1 large egg
2 tablespoons milk
1 small eating apple, cored and diced

1 To prepare the filling, place the chopped dates, sugar and water in a small saucepan and simmer gently for 15 minutes. Stir in the Madeira and leave until cold or, if possible, overnight.
2 To make the topping, place the flour in a bowl, rub in the butter until a breadcrumb-like mixture is achieved, stir in the sugar and flaked almonds. Next stir in 2 tablespoons of water to form a coarse, lumpy mixture; leave to one side.
3 To make the cake, place the flour and baking powder in a large bowl, add the remaining ingredients and beat until smooth.
4 Spoon the cake mixture into a greased and lined 20-cm (8-inch) round cake tin.
5 Spread the date mixture over the cake mixture, then sprinkle the almond topping evenly over the top.
6 Bake at Gas Mark 4/electric oven 180°C/fan oven 160°C for 50–60 minutes until the cake is firm and golden in colour. Leave it in the tin to cool completely.

Tropical Loaf with Papaya, Mango & Pineapple

MAKES a 450 g (1 lb) loaf
PREPARATION & COOKING TIME: 10–15 minutes + rising +
  20–25 minutes
FREEZING: recommended

*A delicious soft bread with chunks of exotic dried fruit
throughout.*

225 g (8 oz) strong white flour
1 teaspoon easy-blend yeast
1/2 teaspoon salt
25 g (1 oz) margarine
50 g (2 oz) ready-to-eat dried papaya, chopped
50 g (2 oz) ready-to-eat dried mango, chopped
50 g (2 oz) ready-to-eat dried pineapple, chopped
25 g (1 oz) caster sugar
1 egg, beaten
125 ml (4 1/2 fl oz) hand-hot milk

1 In a large bowl, sift together the flour, yeast and salt. Rub
  in the margarine. Stir in the chopped fruits and sugar. Stir
  in the egg and enough milk to give a soft dough.
2 Turn on to a floured surface and knead for 8–10 minutes,
  until the dough is smooth, elastic and no longer sticky.
3 Oil or grease a 450 g (1 lb) loaf tin. Press the dough out
  and shape to fit the tin. Cover the tin with an oiled
  polythene bag and leave to rise in a warm place for about
  1 hour until doubled in size.
4 Preheat the oven to Gas Mark 7/electric oven 220°C/fan
  oven 200°C.
5 Bake for 20–25 minutes, until the loaf is golden and the
  base sounds hollow when tapped.
6 Transfer to a wire rack to cool.

Banana Pecan Teabread

PREPARATION & COOKING TIME: 1 hour + 20 minutes
FREEZING: recommended

*Cakes made using the rubbing-in method generally have the
advantage of being much lower in fat and sugar than creamed
cake mixtures.*

*You can eat this teabread as a pudding – warm from the
oven. Be sure to use ripe bananas, as these have the best
flavour. As a variation, omit the nuts and stir in some dried
fruit, such as chopped dates or sultanas, with the sugar.*

275 g (10 oz) self-raising flour
1 teaspoon bicarbonate of soda
1 1/2 teaspoons ground cinnamon
115 g (4 oz) butter or margarine
115 g (4 oz) light muscovado sugar
450 g (1 lb) ripe bananas (about 3 medium bananas), mashed
2 large eggs, beaten
2 tablespoons milk
80 g (3 oz) pecan nuts
warmed, sieved apricot jam, or clear honey, to glaze

1 Preheat the oven to Gas Mark 4/electric oven 180°C/fan
  oven 160°C. Grease and line a 900 g (2 lb) loaf tin with
  foil.
2 Sift the flour, bicarbonate of soda and cinnamon into a
  bowl.
3 Rub in the butter or margarine, until the mixture
  resembles fine breadcrumbs. Stir in the sugar.
4 Add the bananas, eggs and milk. Stir to combine and pour
  into the prepared tin. Smooth to level the surface. Scatter
  the pecans evenly over the top.
5 Bake in the centre of the oven for about 1 hour (depending
  on the shape of your tin) or until a skewer inserted in the
  middle, comes out clean. Check the top after about 45
  minutes. If it is browning too much (the nuts are
  susceptible to burning), cover with a piece of foil.
6 Remove the cake from oven and cool on a wire rack.
  Brush with the jam or honey glaze, to give a shiny finish,
  and serve warm or cold.

Bara Brith *(below)*

MAKES 10–12 slices
PREPARATION & COOKING TIME: 1½ hours

This is a cake made with a mixture of dried fruits, and is especially good for afternoon tea. It can be served plain or buttered.

80 g (3 oz) currants
80 g (3 oz) sultanas
80 g (3 oz) butter, chilled
50 g (2 oz) candied peel
2 eggs, beaten
½ teaspoon ground mixed spice, sieved
80 g (3 oz) soft light brown sugar
350 g (12 oz) self-raising flour, sieved

TO GLAZE:
2 tablespoons honey, warmed

1 Place the currants and the sultanas in a saucepan, add 100 ml (3½ fl oz) water, simmer on a gentle heat for 15 minutes, drain well, and allow to cool for 15 minutes.
2 Put the cooled fruit into a bowl, mix in the butter and the peel. Beat in the eggs, spice and sugar. Fold in the flour and mix well.
3 Spoon the mixture into a greased and lined 900 g (2 lb) loaf tin. Smooth the top.
4 Bake at Gas Mark 2/electric oven 150°C/fan oven 130°F for 50–70 minutes, until the cake is dark golden in colour, and a skewer inserted in the centre comes out clean.
5 Allow the cake to cool in the tin for 15 minutes. Place it on a wire rack to cool completely.
6 Glaze with warmed honey.

Chocolate & Cinnamon Mousse Cake

MAKES 12–16 slices
PREPARATION & COOKING TIME: 1 hour

You must not worry if this moist mousse-like cake sinks. It is delicious eaten warm with ice cream. For the most intense chocolate flavour, use a plain chocolate with at least 70% chocolate solids.

300 g (11 oz) plain chocolate
150 g (5 oz) unsalted butter
6 eggs, separated
50 g (2 oz) caster sugar
2 teaspoons ground cinnamon

1 In a bowl over a pan of simmering water, melt the chocolate and the butter together.
2 Beat the egg yolks and 25 g (1 oz) sugar for about 1 minute, and then beat in the cinnamon.
3 With the chocolate and butter mixture still over the pan of water, stir in the egg yolk mixture and mix together thoroughly. Then remove the bowl from the heat.
4 In a clean, grease-free bowl, whisk the egg whites until they are very stiff. Beat the remaining sugar into the egg whites.
5 Gradually fold the egg whites into the chocolate mixture.
6 Spoon the mixture into a greased and lined 20-cm (8-inch) round cake tin.
7 Bake at Gas Mark 4/electric oven 180°C/fan oven 160°C for 30–40 minutes until the cake is dark golden in colour, well risen and springy to the touch.
8 Having removed the cake tin from the oven, place a sheet of foil over the top and allow to cool. This ensures that the steam from the cake produces a soft crust. Don't worry when the cake sinks, this is normal. Leave it in the tin to cool for 10 minutes before transferring it on to a wire rack to cool completely, unless you decide to eat it warm, which is also delicious.

Chocolate, Walnut & Banana Loaf *(right)*

MAKES 10–12 slices
PREPARATION & COOKING TIME: 1½–2 hours

The chocolate, banana and walnuts used in this cake give it a tasty, moist and crunchy texture.

115 g (4 oz) butter
175 g (6 oz) caster sugar
2 large bananas, peeled and mashed
2 eggs
sieve together: 80 g (3 oz) plain flour and 80 g (3 oz) plain
   wholemeal flour and 1 teaspoon bicarbonate of soda and
   1 teaspoon ground cinnamon
5 tablespoons boiling water
115 g (4 oz) walnut pieces, chopped
175 g (6 oz) milk chocolate chips

1 In a large bowl, beat the butter and sugar together until light and creamy. Beat in the bananas and then the eggs; don't worry if the mixture looks curdled.
2 Fold in the flours, bicarbonate of soda and cinnamon. Stir in the boiling water, this will produce a soft mixture.
3 Gently fold in the walnuts and the chocolate chips.
4 Spoon the mixture into a greased and lined 900 g (2 lb) loaf tin and smooth the top.
5 Bake at Gas Mark 4/electric oven 180°C/fan oven 160°C for 1–1½ hours until dark golden in colour and well risen.
6 Leave the cake in the tin for 10 minutes before placing it on a wire rack to cool completely.

Honey, Nut & Polenta Cake

MAKES 10–12 slices
PREPARATION & COOKING TIME: 1¼ hours

This very light-textured cake is ideal for lunch boxes.

140 g (4½ oz) butter, softened
150 g (5 oz) icing sugar, sieved
2 eggs
sieve together: 140 g (4½ oz) plain flour and 1 teaspoon baking
   powder and a large pinch bicarbonate of soda
100 ml (3½ fl oz) full-fat milk
50 g (2 oz) brazil nuts, chopped finely
3 tablespoons clear honey
65 g (2½ oz) polenta

1 Cream the butter and icing sugar together until light in
   colour and fluffy. Beat in the eggs.
2 Fold in the flour, baking powder and bicarbonate of soda.
   Stir in the milk. Stir in the nuts, honey and polenta, mixing
   well.
3 Spoon the mixture into a lightly greased and floured 20-cm
   (8-inch) tube tin.
4 Bake at Gas Mark 5/electric oven 190°C/fan oven 170°C
   for 40–50 minutes until pale golden in colour, firm to the
   touch and a skewer inserted in the centre of the cake
   comes out clean.
5 Leave the cake in the tin for 15 minutes before turning it
   on to a wire rack to cool completely.
6 Wrap tightly in foil and leave for 2 days before serving.

Pecan Oat Biscuits

MAKES approximately 16 ★
PREPARATION & COOKING TIME: 25 minutes

These crunchy oat biscuits are ideal with a cup of coffee.

115 g (4 oz) butter, softened
80 g (3 oz) soft dark brown sugar
1 egg
50 g (2 oz) porridge oats
50 g (2 oz) pecan nuts, finely chopped
sieve together: 80 g (3 oz) plain flour and ½ teaspoon baking
   powder

1 Cream the butter and sugar together until light in colour
   and fluffy.
2 Beat in the egg and then stir in the oats, nuts, flour and
   baking powder. Mix well to a soft dough.
3 Drop large teaspoonfuls of the mixture on to greased
   baking sheets, being sure to give them room to spread a
   little.
4 Bake at Gas Mark 4/electric oven 180°C/fan oven 160°C
   for 10–20 minutes until they are pale golden in colour. Put
   them to cool on a wire rack.
5 Stored in an airtight container, they will remain crisp for
   about a week.

Gingerbread

MAKES 20–25 squares
PREPARATION & COOKING TIME: 1½–2 hours

*This moist cake, containing ginger and black treacle, is very
popular. It develops a deliciously sticky top if it is stored for a
couple of days before being eaten. It is usually served cut into
squares.*

225 g (8 oz) butter, chilled
225 g (8 oz) dark brown soft sugar
16 tablespoons black treacle
2 eggs
sieve together: 350 g (12 oz) plain flour and 1 tablespoon ground
   ginger and 2 teaspoons ground cinnamon
1 teaspoon bicarbonate of soda
300 ml (½ pint) milk, warmed

1 In a large saucepan place the butter, sugar and black
   treacle and melt over a gentle heat until melted together.
   Allow to stand for 5 minutes.
2 Stir in the eggs and then mix in the flour and spices,
   ensuring everything is thoroughly mixed.
3 Dissolve the bicarbonate of soda in the milk; then
   gradually stir this into the melted mixture until well
   blended. The mixture will be very liquid.
4 Pour the mixture into a greased and lined 25-cm (10-inch)
   square cake tin.
5 Bake at Gas Mark 1/electric oven 140°C/fan oven 120°C
   for 1–1½ hours until dark golden in colour, set and firm to
   the touch.
6 Remove the cake from the oven and leave it in the tin to
   cool for 15 minutes before placing it on a wire rack to
   cool completely.
7 This cake is best stored for 2–3 days, well wrapped in foil,
   before being eaten.

Fruit Cookies *(above)*

MAKES 24
PREPARATION & COOKING TIME: 40 minutes

The bitter-sweet flavour of the cardamom and the hot sweetish flavour of the ginger produce a delicious lightly flavoured cookie.

80 g (3 oz) butter, softened
80 g (3 oz) soft light brown sugar
1 egg
175 g (6 oz) self-raising flour, sieved
1 teaspoon almond essence
8 cardamom pods, seeds removed from husks and crushed
50 g (2 oz) glacé cherries, finely chopped
50 g (2 oz) ready-to-eat dried apricots, finely chopped
50 g (2 oz) glacé ginger, finely chopped

1 Cream the butter and sugar until light in colour and fluffy. Beat in the egg.
2 Stir in the remaining ingredients to form a stiff dough.
3 Using two teaspoons, make small rounds. Place on lightly greased baking sheets, and flatten slightly.
4 Bake at Gas Mark 4/electric oven 180°C/fan oven 160°C for 20–25 minutes until pale golden in colour.
5 When cooked, place on a wire rack to cool completely.

Rye Ring

MAKES an 18-cm (7-inch) ring ♥
PREPARATION TIME: 25–30 minutes + rising + 20–30 minutes cooking
FREEZING: recommended

Rye tends to produce a heavier bread, but mixing it with another flour gives this ring a lighter texture.

25 g (1 oz) margarine
200 ml (7 fl oz) hand-hot water
150 g (5 oz) rye flour
175 g (6 oz) strong wholemeal flour
1 teaspoon salt
½ sachet easy-blend yeast
1 tablespoon chopped fresh herbs
1 teaspoon poppy seeds

1 Melt the margarine in the water.
2 In a large bowl, sift the flours and salt together and then mix in the yeast and herbs.
3 Carefully pour in the liquid and mix to form a soft dough.
4 Turn out on to a floured surface and knead well for 10 minutes until smooth and elastic.
5 Place in a clean greased bowl, cover and leave in a warm place to double in size.
6 Knock back and knead again. Shape into a long sausage shape. Place on a greased baking sheet, joining the ends to form a ring. Cover and leave to prove in a warm place, until doubled in size.
7 Preheat the oven to Gas Mark 6/electric oven 200°C/fan oven 180°C.
8 Make slits around the ring, brush the top with water and sprinkle with poppy seeds. Bake for 20–30 minutes, until well risen and golden in colour.
9 Transfer to a wire rack to cool.

Oatcakes *(below)*

MAKES 15 bars ★
PREPARATION & COOKING TIME: 30 minutes

These are an unleavened form of bread usually found in the north of England and Scotland They are traditionally eaten with cheese. Oatcakes can be round, triangular or bar shaped.

175 g (6 oz) medium oatmeal
115 g (4 oz) self-raising flour, sieved
½ teaspoon salt
25 g (1 oz) caster sugar
175 g (6 oz) butter
2 tablespoons water

1 In a large bowl, place the oatmeal, flour, salt and sugar. Mix well together.
2 Melt the butter and water together, stir into the dry ingredients and mix to a firm dough.
3 Knead the dough gently. Then press into a lightly greased 33 x 23 cm (13 x 9 inch) Swiss roll tin.
4 Bake at Gas Mark 4/electric oven 180°C/fan oven 160°C for 20–25 minutes until pale golden in colour and firm to the touch.
5 Remove the tin from the oven and leave to cool for 5 minutes. Then mark and cut into 15 bars. Place the bars on a wire rack to cool completely.

Pumpkin Marmalade *(above, left)*

MAKES about 2.5 kg (5½ lb)
PREPARATION & COOKING TIME: 2½ hours

Pumpkin makes a lovely marmalade, with a beautiful colour.

1.5 kg (3 lb 5 oz) pumpkin, peeled, all seeds and fibre removed, and
   then flesh sliced
1 litre (1¾ pints) water
675 g (1½ lb) oranges, halved and sliced thinly
675 g (1½ lb) lemons, halved and sliced thinly
80 g (3 oz) fresh root ginger, shredded finely
1.3 kg (3 lb) granulated sugar

1 Place the pumpkin in a large pan, with the water, oranges, lemons and ginger. Bring to the boil and then simmer for 45 minutes–1 hour until the citrus peel is very soft.
2 Add the sugar, stirring until it has dissolved. Return to the boil and then cook over a medium heat until the mixture is thick enough for a wooden spoon to be drawn through the centre to leave a clear channel.
3 Pour the marmalade into cooled, sterilised jars and seal with waxed discs or twist top lids (see page 13). Label and store.

Bramble & Apple Curd *(opposite, middle)*

MAKES about 1.1–1.3 kg (2–3 lb)

PREPARATION & COOKING TIME: 20 minutes and about 20 minutes cooking in a microwave or 40 minutes in bowl over water

This is quick and easy to make, a gorgeous colour and delicious to eat. Use it in the same way as lemon curd, for fillings, folded through yogurt or just spooned on to wholemeal toast or muffins – you don't need butter. Fruit curds cook very well in the microwave. If you prefer your curds to have a smooth consistency, sieve the fruit pulp to remove the bramble seeds and again at the end, if necessary, to remove any cooked egg bits. If you prefer a chunkier result, simply mash the fruit down with a fork or potato masher.

450 g (1 lb) brambles (blackberries)

450 g (1 lb) prepared weight peeled, cored and chopped cooking apples

grated zest and juice of 2 lemons

450 g (1 lb) caster sugar

4 eggs, beaten

115 g (4 oz) butter, preferably unsalted

1 Cook the fruit with the lemon zest and 2 tablespoons of water in a pan (or in the microwave) until pulpy. Purée the fruit by passing it through a sieve.
2 Transfer to a bowl if necessary, add the lemon juice and sugar and stir until the sugar is dissolved. Beat the eggs and strain on to the fruit pulp.
3 Cook over a saucepan of water on a low heat or in the microwave, stirring occasionally, until a thick and creamy consistency is obtained. Strain the curd, to remove the bramble seeds and any bits of cooked egg.
4 Pour into cooled sterilised jars and cover with a waxed disc and cellophane cover (see page 13). Label and store in the fridge for up to 6 weeks.

Autumn Marmalade *(opposite, right)*

MAKES 4.5 kg (10 lb)

PREPARATION & COOKING TIME: 3–3½ hours

This has a lovely flavour and the apples give the marmalade a more unusual texture. Make sure that you cook the citrus fruit well before adding the sugar and apples.

450 g (1 lb) lemons, chopped roughly after removing pips, pips reserved

450 g (1 lb) limes, as for lemons

1 litre (13/4 pints) water

675 g (1½ lb) cooking apples, peeled, cored and chopped

2.7 kg (6 lb) sugar

1 Place the lemons and limes in a large pan, with the water. Place the pips in a muslin bag and add to the pan. Bring to the boil and simmer for about 2 hours, until the fruit is soft and the contents of the pan are reduced in volume by about half.
2 Squeeze the bag of pips to extract the pectin and set aside. Liquidise the fruit, using some of the liquid, until it is completely smooth. Return the purée to the pan and stir into the remaining cooking liquid.
4 Meanwhile, cook the apples over a very low heat until soft – you could use the microwave for this. Add to the citrus mixture, with the sugar.
5 Stir until the sugar is dissolved and then bring to the boil. Boil rapidly until setting point is reached (see page 12). Remove any scum (see page 12).
6 Pour into cooled, sterilised jars and seal. Label and store.

West Country Curd

MAKES: about 675–900 g (1½–2 lb)
PREPARATION & COOKING TIME: 1 hour

Yet another way of capturing the last of the sunshine and a delicious alternative to the more traditional lemon curd. This can also be cooked in a double saucepan or in a bowl over a pan of simmering water.

350 g (12 oz) cooking apples, cored and sliced, no need to peel
350 g (12 oz) pears, cored and sliced, no need to peel
grated zest and juice of 1 lemon
150 ml (¼ pint) cider
350 g (12 oz) granulated sugar
115 g (4 oz) butter, preferably unsalted
4 eggs, beaten

1 Place the fruit and cider in a large bowl and cover with pierced clingfilm. Microwave on full power for 10–15 minutes or until the fruit is soft and pulpy.
2 Rub the fruit through a sieve and return to the bowl. Add the sugar and butter. Microwave on full power for 2 minutes and then stir well, making sure that the butter is melted and the sugar is dissolved.
3 Add the eggs and stir thoroughly. Continue cooking in the microwave until thick and the mixture coats the back of a spoon. Stir frequently. This can be done on full power or reduce the cooking power to medium and cook for a longer time.
4 Strain again into a jug. Pour the curd into cooled, sterilised jars, seal with a waxed disc and cover with cellophane (page 13). Store in the fridge for up to 6 weeks. Once opened, eat within 2 weeks.

Hedgerow Jam

MAKES: about 2.2 kg (5 lb)
PREPARATION & COOKING TIME: about 2½ hours

This recipe was supplied by Thea Hogg, who lives on the edge of the Lincolnshire Wolds.

225 g (8 oz) rose hips
225 g (8 oz) haws
225 g (8 oz) rowan berries
225 g (8 oz) sloes
450 g (1 lb) crab apples
450 g (1 lb) blackberries
450 g (1 lb) elderberries
115 g (4 oz) hazelnuts, chopped
900 g (2 lb) sugar, plus equivalent to weight of fruit pulp (see step 3)

1 Wash and clean all the fruit well. Put the rose hips, haws, rowan berries, sloes and crab apples in a large preserving pan and add water to cover. Cook until all the fruit is tender – about 1 hour.
2 Sieve the fruits and weigh the resulting pulp. Put the pulp back into the washed preserving pan and add the blackberries, elderberries and chopped nuts. Simmer for about 15 minutes.

3 Add the 900 g (2 lb) of sugar plus as much extra sugar as the weight of the pulp. Cook over a low heat to dissolve the sugar and then boil rapidly until setting point is reached (see page 12). Remove any scum (see page 12).
4 Pour into cooled, sterilised jars, seal and label (pages 12–13).

Plum & Mulled Wine Jam

MAKES 2.7 KG (6 LB)
PREPARATION & COOKING TIME: 50 minutes

This recipe was devised by former WI Country Markets Director, Judi Binns, once of Hertfordshire and now living in Yorkshire.

1.8 kg (4 lb) red plums, halved and stoned
½ bottle of red wine (whatever is cheap or on offer)
mulled wine spices, e.g., cinnamon, nutmeg, cloves or your own choice
piece of orange zest without pith
1.8 kg (4 lb) sugar

1 Put the plums and wine into a preserving pan.
2 Place the spices and zest in a spice ball or muslin bag and add to the pan. Cook gently for 15–20 minutes or until the skins are soft.
3 Remove the spice ball or bag and add the sugar, stirring until dissolved. Bring to the boil and boil rapidly for about 10 minutes or until setting point is reached (see page 12). Remove any scum (see page 12).
4 Pot into cooled, sterilised jars, seal and label (pages 12–13).

Spiced Plum Chutney

MAKES: about 1.8 kg (4 lb)
PREPARATION & COOKING TIME: about 1½ hours

A recipe from Gill Worrell, for which you can use any type of plum. Gill says red plums produce a lovely colour and it is delicious served with smoked mackerel. It is cheap to produce when plums and apples are in plentiful supply. The cooking time can be reduced by cooking the plums, apples and onions in the microwave first.

675 g (1½ lb) plums, stoned and quartered
450 g (1 lb) onions, chopped
225 g (8 oz) cooking apples, peeled, cored and chopped
300 ml (½ pint) pickling malt vinegar
115 g (4 oz) sultanas
175 g (6 oz) soft brown sugar
1 cinnamon stick

1 Place all the ingredients in a large preserving pan. Bring to the boil and simmer, uncovered, for about 45 minutes, or until the chutney is thick and pulpy.
2 Spoon into cooled, sterilised jars and seal with a vinegar-proof cover. Label and store for at least 4–6 weeks before use.

High Dumpsy Dearie Jam

MAKES: 3.2–3.6 kg (7–8 lb)
PREPARATION & COOKING TIME: 1½ hours

No one seems to know where this delightful name comes from but it is thought to originate in Worcestershire. It was always a great conversation piece at the Royal Show at Stoneleigh in Warwickshire, where WI Markets had a selling stand in the WI Pavilion. The passage behind the selling area was affectionately known as 'the jam run' as the walls were lined with shelves bearing every imaginable variety of jam, jelly, marmalade, chutney and pickle! They were all in alphabetical order so that a particular variety for a discerning customer could be found quickly. Other stand-holders used to bring their boxes to stock up with jars for the storecupboard to keep them going through the year. The jam is a delicious variety to use in traditional puddings, such as jam roly-poly and steamed sponge.

900 g (2 lb) cooking apples, peeled, cored and sliced
900 g (2 lb) pears, peeled, cored and sliced
900 g (2 lb) plums, halved and stoned
50 g (2 oz) fresh root ginger, bruised and tied in a muslin bag
2 kg (4½ lb) sugar
zest and juice of 1 lemon

1 Place all the fruit and ginger in a large pan and add just enough water to cover the base of the pan. Simmer until the fruit is tender – about 45 minutes.
2 Remove from the heat and add the sugar, stirring until dissolved. Add the lemon zest and juice.
3 Bring to the boil and cook rapidly until the setting point of the jam is reached – test after 15 minutes (see page 12). Remove any scum (see page 12).
4 Pour into cooled, sterilised jars (see page 12), discarding the ginger, and seal. Label and store.

Orchard Cottage Chutney

MAKES 2.7 kg (6 lb)
PREPARATION & COOKING TIME: about 2 hours and 45 minutes

Even if you haven't got a garden in which to grow and harvest, friends, family or someone in the neighbourhood may be happy to off-load the odd pound or two of produce, especially if there is a glut or a particularly good crop. If not, visit one of the growing number of farm shops or pick-your-own places or call in to your nearest WI, Farmers' or local market for some of the best and freshest produce around. There are also lots of roadside/outside the garden gate stalls around at this time of year, offering really excellent produce at unbeatable prices.

900 g (2 lb) plums, washed, halved and stoned
900 g (2 lb) ripe tomatoes, skinned and sliced
850 ml (1½ pints) malt vinegar
6 garlic cloves
450 g (1 lb) onions
225 g (8 oz) raisins
1.1 kg (2¼ lb) cooking apples, peeled and cored
450 g (1 lb) demerara sugar
25 g (1 oz) salt
50 g (2 oz) whole pickling spices, e.g. peppercorns, allspice berries, ginger, celery seeds and dried chillies, tied in a muslin bag

1 Put the plums, tomatoes and vinegar into a large preserving pan. Bring to the boil and then simmer gently until very soft.
2 Mince together the garlic, onions, raisins and apples, or use a food processor to chop them finely. Add to the plum mixture, with the sugar, salt and bag of spices.
3 Heat gently until the sugar is dissolved. Bring to the boil and then simmer uncovered for about 2 hours, or until the chutney is well reduced and very thick. Stir from time to time, to prevent sticking.
4 Spoon into cooled, sterilised jars and seal with a vinegar-proof lid (see pages 12–13). Label and store for 2–3 weeks before use.

Apricot & Marrow Chutney

MAKES: about 2.2 kg (5 lb)
PREPARATION & COOKING TIME: about 30 minutes +
   overnight or several hours soaking + 1½ hours cooking

This is a variation suggested in the recipe which appeared in
A Taste of WI Markets, *a cookbook produced for the Markets'*
75th Anniversary in 1994. This chutney is particularly good
in a cheese sandwich but goes equally well with cold meats
or as an alternative to apple sauce as an accompaniment for
roast pork.

450 g (1 lb) dried apricots, chopped
450 g (1 lb) prepared marrow, diced
450 g (1 lb) cooking apples, peeled and quartered
350 g (12 oz) onions, chopped
2 teaspoons each whole cloves, cardamom seeds and peppercorns
80 g (3 oz) fresh root ginger, bruised
575 ml (1 pint) white malt vinegar
450 g (1 lb) granulated sugar

1 Cover the apricots with water and soak for several hours
   or overnight. If you have 'no-need-to-soak' apricots, you
   can omit this step.
2 Pour into a large preserving pan. Add the marrow, apple
   and onion. Tie the whole spices and ginger in a piece of
   muslin and add to the mixture. Cook until the apples are
   pulpy, adding more water if necessary to prevent sticking;
   stir occasionally. This will take about 20 minutes.
3 Add the vinegar and sugar and simmer, uncovered, until all
   the liquid has been absorbed.
4 Pot into cooled sterilised jars, seal with a vinegar-proof lid
   and label (see pages 12–13). Store for 6–8 weeks before
   using.

APRICOT, MARROW & WALNUT CHUTNEY: Add 115 g (4 oz) of
chopped walnuts towards the end of the cooking time.

Beetroot & Ginger Chutney

MAKES about 2.2–2.7 kg (5–6 lb)
PREPARATION & COOKING TIME: about 2 hours 40 minutes

1.3 kg (3 lb) beetroot, cooked
450 g (1 lb) onions, chopped
1.1 litres (2 pints) vinegar
450 g (1 lb) cooking apples, peeled and chopped
450 g (1 lb) seedless raisins or dates, chopped
3 tablespoons ground ginger
1 teaspoon salt
900 g (2 lb) granulated sugar

1 Peel and cut the beetroot into cubes or mash well if a
   smoother chutney is preferred.
2 Place the onion in a large preserving pan, with a little of
   the vinegar, and cook for a few minutes, to soften the
   onion. Add the apples, raisins or dates and continue
   cooking until pulpy.
3 Add the beetroot, ginger, salt and half the remaining
   vinegar. Simmer gently until thick.
4 Stir in the sugar and remaining vinegar and continue
   cooking until thick again.
5 Pot into cooled, sterilised jars, seal with a vinegar-proof lid
   and label (see pages 12–13). Store for 6–8 weeks before
   using.

Diana's Uncooked Chutney

MAKES about 2.2 kg (5 lb)
PREPARATION TIME: soaking overnight + 20 minutes

We are not allowed to sell uncooked chutneys and relishes in
WI Markets because of possible fermentation, but they can be
very good. This recipe was a popular choice for a Denman
College swap-shop on the 'Preserves' course one year and was
brought along by Diana Cuthbert of Surrey WI Federation.

225 g (8 oz) dried apricots
900 g (2 lb) Bramley cooking apples
225 g (8 oz) sultanas
225 g (8 oz) dates, stoned
450 g (1 lb) onions
2 garlic cloves
350 g (12 oz) light soft brown sugar
425 ml (¾ pint) malt vinegar
1 teaspoon ground ginger

1 Place the apricots in a bowl and cover with water. Leave to
   soak overnight and then drain. If you use 'no-need-to-
   soak' dried apricots, you can omit this step.
2 Mince all the fruits and onion and garlic together or finely
   chop in a food processor. Add the sugar, vinegar and
   ginger.
3 Stir well and spoon into cooled, sterilised jars, seal with
   vinegar-proof covers and label (see pages 12–13). Store in
   a cool, dark place for at least 3 months before using.

Aunt Mary's Green Tomato Chutney

MAKES: about 2.7 kg (6 lb)
PREPARATION & COOKING TIME: 30 minutes + standing overnight + about 2 hours cooking

There must be so many green tomatoes around come autumn because there seems to be a never-ending supply of recipes for green tomato chutney. This one is from Betty Grant, who worked on Market Rasen WI Market for several years and was very popular for her croissants and cream horns. She remembers having this at her Aunt Mary's when she was at college. Betty uses sultanas but you could use raisins or dates.

1.3 kg (3 lb) green tomatoes
675 g (1½ lb) cooking apples
675 g (1½ lb) onions
2 tablespoons salt
350 g (12 oz) sugar
2 teaspoons ground mixed spice
225 g (8 oz) sultanas
575 ml (1 pint) malt vinegar

1 Mince the tomatoes, apples and onions. Place in a large bowl and sprinkle over the salt. Cover and leave overnight.
2 Next day, pour off the liquid that has been drawn out by the salt and discard it. Transfer everything to a large preserving pan. Bring to the boil, with the vinegar, and then add the sugar, spice and fruit.
3 Bring to the boil and then simmer until soft and pulpy, about 1½ hours.
4 Spoon into cooled, sterilised jars, seal with a vinegar-proof lid and label. Store for 6–8 weeks, to mature, before using.

Pumpkin Chutney

MAKES about 2.7 kg (6 lb)
PREPARATION & COOKING TIME: 2½–3 hours

This recipe is from an old WI Home and Country *magazine. Pumpkin makes a beautiful chutney, and, as with any chutney, the contents can be varied to suit your taste. The texture can be varied by cutting the fruits into larger pieces and, if you want a hotter chutney, add 3–4 fresh red chillies and 2–3 tablespoons of mustard seed.*

675 g (1½ lb) prepared pumpkin, peeled, de-seeded and cut into 2.5cm (1-inch) chunks
450 g (1 lb) cooking apples, peeled, cored and chopped coarsely
350 g (12 oz) onions, chopped
175 g (6 oz) sultanas or raisins
2 tablespoons salt
2 teaspoons ground ginger or 50 g (2 oz) fresh root ginger, shredded finely
½ teaspoon ground black pepper
2 teaspoons ground allspice
4–6 garlic cloves, crushed
575 ml (1 pint) malt or cider vinegar
450 g (1 lb) granulated or soft brown sugar
50 g (2 oz) stem ginger preserved in syrup, chopped finely (optional)

1 Put all the ingredients, except the sugar and stem ginger, in a large preserving pan and mix well.
2 Bring to the boil and then reduce the heat and simmer for about 45 minutes, stirring occasionally, until the contents are very soft.
3 Stir in the sugar until dissolved and then continue to simmer, uncovered, for about 1–1½ hours or until the chutney is very thick and there is no liquid left on the surface.
4 Add the stem ginger, if using. Spoon into cooled, sterilised jars and seal with a vinegar-proof lid (see pages 12–13). Label and store for 6–8 weeks before use.

NOTE: Some cooks prefer to tie whole spices into a muslin bag, which is removed before potting the chutney; others prefer to use the ground spices, although this tends to give a cloudier result.

Cinnamon Grape Pickle
(opposite, top)

MAKES enough to fill a 425 ml (15 fl oz) jar ★
PREPARATION & COOKING TIME: 20 minutes

This is an unusual and quite delicious pickle from Terry Clarke, which is particularly good with smoked meats and with pork loin, duck and chicken. Terry says that the balsamic vinegar and the cinnamon give the pickle a warm mellowness but that it is the 'little zippy splat' each time you bite into a grape that makes it really addictive. Terry also serves these along with the olives and other nibbles with drinks.

275 g (10 oz) white sugar
225 ml (8 fl oz) white wine vinegar
1 tablespoon balsamic vinegar
1/2 tablespoon cracked peppercorns
1 cinnamon stick
350 g (12 oz) white or black seedless grapes

1 Put the sugar and vinegars into a small saucepan and stir over a low heat until the sugar is dissolved. Raise the heat and add the peppercorns and cinnamon stick and boil for 5–6 minutes.
2 While the syrup is boiling, de-stalk enough grapes to fill your chosen jar. Remove and wash them under cold water, drain thoroughly and dry with kitchen paper. Return to the cooled, sterilised jar (see page 12), ensuring that they are firmly positioned but being careful not to bruise the fruit.
3 Remove the cinnamon stick from the pan and insert it in the jar. Pour over the boiling syrup, filling right to the top. Cover tightly with a vinegar-proof lid and store in a cool place for 3–4 weeks before use. It will keep for up to a year. If using white grapes, remember to store them out of the light to prevent them from discolouring.

Spiced Apple Jelly *(opposite, below)*

MAKES about 900 g (2 lb)
PREPARATION TIME: 15 minutes + minimum 2 hours standing
COOKING TIME: 1 hour

Another delicious recipe from Terry Clarke, who recommends this to serve with roast pork or lamb as well as for delicious sandwiches.

900 g (2 lb) cooking apples, chopped, no need to peel or core
2 lemons, sliced
25 g (1 oz) fresh root ginger, chopped
1 cinnamon stick
1/2 teaspoon cloves
sugar (see step 3)

1 Place the apples and 1.7 litres (3 pints) of water in a preserving pan, with the lemons, ginger and spices. Bring to the boil and simmer for 45 minutes to an hour, or until the apples are very soft.
2 Pour into a jelly bag and leave to strain for at least 2 hours.
3 Measure the juice and add 450 g (1 lb) sugar for each 575 ml (1 pint) of juice.
4 Dissolve over a gentle heat and then bring to a boil until setting point is reached, then remove any scum (see page 12).
5 Pour into cooled, sterilised jars and seal (see pages 12–13). Label and store.

Piccalilli *(right)*

MAKES about 2.7 kg (6 lb)
PREPARATION & COOKING TIME: 1¼ hours

This is Terry Clarke's recipe, which, she admits, seems to break all the rules about brining vegetables, which is the usual procedure for this type of pickle. Terry says it works beautifully and keeps well if you can persuade the family to leave it for at least two weeks. Terry has kept it for up to nine months when, if anything, the flavour has improved!

1 large cauliflower, broken into florets
450 g (1 lb) pickling onions, chopped
1.4 litres (2½ pints) white malt vinegar
900 g (2 lb) mixed vegetables,
diced or cut into 2.5-cm (1-inch) lengths; choose from: French or
    runner beans, cucumber, marrow or green tomatoes
2 fat cloves of garlic, crushed
450 g (1 lb) caster sugar
50 g (2 oz) dry mustard
115 g (4 oz) plain flour, sieved
25 g (1 oz) ground turmeric
1 teaspoon ground coriander
2 teaspoons salt

1 In a large preserving pan, simmer the cauliflower and onions in 1.1 litres (2 pints) of the vinegar for 10 minutes.
2 Add the other vegetables, garlic and sugar and cook for a further 10 minutes.
3 Mix the mustard, flour, spices and salt with the remaining vinegar and add to the cooked vegetables, stirring all the time to prevent lumps from forming.
4 Stir well and simmer for a further 10 minutes.
5 Spoon into cooled, sterilised jars and cover with a vinegar-proof top (see pages 12–13). Label and store for 2 weeks before using.

Spiced Pears in Raspberry Vinegar

MAKES: about three 450 g (1 lb) jars
PREPARATION & COOKING TIME: 45 minutes

Try this lovely recipe using raspberry or red-wine vinegar. The pears are delicious served as an unusual accompaniment to cold turkey or a game pie at Christmas. This recipe was given to a group of WI members from the East Midlands area at Brackenhurst College in Nottinghamshire, by Susan Jervis of Shropshire.

900 g (2 lb) firm eating pears, peeled, cored and quartered
450 g (1 lb) granulated sugar
450 ml (16 fl oz) raspberry vinegar
1 cinnamon stick
1 teaspoon whole cloves
1 teaspoon allspice berries

1 Place the pears in a pan and cover with boiling water. Simmer for 5 minutes.
2 Drain in a colander, saving 300 ml (½ pint) of the cooking water.
3 Mix the sugar, the reserved water and the vinegar in the pan. Heat and stir until the sugar dissolves. Add the spices and pears and simmer gently until the pears are translucent – about 20 minutes.
4 Drain the pears, reserving the cooking liquid, and place in cooled, sterilised jars (see page 12). Remove any scum from the liquid (see page 12). Pour the liquid, including the spices, over the pears to cover. Cover with vinegar-proof lids, label and store.

Mostarda di Frutta

MAKES about three 350 g (12 oz) jars
PREPARATION & COOKING TIME: 30 minutes + 1 hour
  standing

*Terry Clarke describes this as a tongue-tingling combination
of sweet and hot rather than sweet and sour; it makes a
classic accompaniment to ham and poultry, particularly at
Christmas time.*

115 g (4 oz) English mustard powder
115 g (4 oz) light soft brown sugar
300 ml (½ pint) white-wine vinegar
115 g (4 oz) each dried apricots, figs, raisins and glacé cherries,
  chopped coarsely
50 g (2 oz) dried apple rings, chopped
6 pieces of stem ginger preserved in syrup, chopped or sliced
1 teaspoon sea salt

1 In a bowl, put 300 ml (½ pint) of water and stir in the
   mustard. Cover and leave for at least 1 hour.
2 Place the sugar and vinegar in a saucepan and heat gently,
   stirring until the sugar is dissolved. Raise the heat and boil
   until the mixture starts to thicken.
3 Stir in the fruits, ginger, mustard and salt and return to the
   boil, stirring. Simmer until the mixture thickens.
4 Spoon into small jars or bottles, ensuring that there are no
   air bubbles, and seal with a vinegar-proof cover (see page
   13). Label and store in a cool, dark and dry place for 6–8
   weeks before use.

Plum Pot *(following page, top, left)*

MAKES: about four 450 g (1 lb) jars
PREPARATION & COOKING TIME: 20 minutes + standing
  overnight + 45 minutes cooking

*Helen Snee, of Willingham-by Stow WI, submitted this recipe
for our WI Federation's* Millennium Cookbook. *Helen says she
got the original idea from a magazine years ago and this is the
version she brings out every time she has a good plum crop.
Helen uses sultanas with Victoria or greengage plums and
raisins and a dark brown sugar with dark plums. The recipe
has also been made using fresh apricots.*

1.3 kg (3 lb) plums, washed, stoned and chopped into large pieces
450 g (1 lb) raisins or sultanas
2 large oranges (175–225 g/6–8 oz each), sliced and chopped into
  small pieces
1.3 kg (3 lb) sugar

1 Put all the fruit and the sugar into a large non-metallic
   bowl. Cover and leave overnight.
2 Next day, transfer the mixture to a large preserving pan
   and heat slowly until the sugar is dissolved, stirring all the
   time.
3 Bring to the boil and then simmer until the mixture is
   fairly thick – about 30 minutes. A knob of butter can be
   added during cooking, to reduce any scum.
4 Pour into cooled, sterilised jars and seal (see pages 12–13).
   Label and store.

Plum, Grape & Cardamom Jelly *(opposite, top right)*

MAKES about 675 g (1½ lb)
PREPARATION & COOKING TIME: 10 minutes + minimum 2
  hours standing + 1 hour

*Another delicious jelly from Terry Clarke, which Terry
recommends to serve with roast beef as well as in the usual
way as a spread.*

1.8 kg (4 lb) plums, any variety, stoned and chopped roughly
225 g (8 oz) white grapes
225 g (8 oz) purple grapes
1 tablespoon crushed cardamom pods
sugar (see step 2)

1 Place the fruit and cardamoms with 575 ml (1 pint) water
  in a preserving pan and bring slowly to the boil. Simmer
  until all the ingredients are cooked, mashing down the
  fruit to release all the flavours – about 30–45 minutes.
2 Pour into a jelly bag and leave to drip – a minimum of 2
  hours. Measure the juice and take a pectin test, adding
  citric acid if necessary. To each 575 ml (1 pint) of juice,
  add 450 g (1 lb) granulated sugar.
3 Dissolve over a low heat. Bring to the boil and boil rapidly
  until setting point is reached (see page 12). Remove any
  scum (see page 12).
4 Pour into cooled, sterilised jars and seal (see pages 12–13).
  Label and store.

Red Tomato & Celery Chutney *(opposite, bottom left)*

MAKES about 2.7 kg (6 lb)
PREPARATION & COOKING TIME: 2¾–3¼ hours

*This is a lovely chutney found in the WI magazine Home and
Country a few years back. It uses celery, which is not often to
be found in chutneys but here it marries very well with the
tomatoes, making it an ideal accompaniment to cheeses.*

450 g (1 lb) onions, chopped finely or processed
1 large or 2 small heads of celery, trimmed and chopped finely or
  processed
900 ml (1½ pints) malt vinegar
50 g (2 oz) whole pickling spices, e.g., peppercorns, allspice berries,
  ginger, celery seeds and dried chillies, tied in muslin
1 kg (2¼ lb) ripe tomatoes, skinned and chopped
450 g (1 lb) cooking apples, peeled, cored and finely chopped or
  processed
2 teaspoons salt
a good pinch of cayenne pepper
350 g (12 oz) light soft brown sugar
225 g (8 oz) sultanas or raisins, chopped roughly

1 Place the onions and celery, with half the vinegar and the
  bag of spices, in a large preserving pan. Bring to the boil
  and then simmer for about 30 minutes, until almost tender.
2 Add the tomatoes and apples, the remaining vinegar and
  the other ingredients. Bring slowly to the boil, stirring
  frequently, and continue to cook slowly, uncovered for
  1½–2 hours, or until the chutney is thick and there is no
  liquid left on the surface. Stir from time to time, to prevent
  sticking.
3 Remove the muslin bag and then spoon the chutney into
  cooled, sterilised jars and seal with a vinegar-proof top (see
  pages 12–13). Label and store for 2–3 weeks before use.

Orange & Beetroot Jam *(opposite, bottom right)*

MAKES 1.1–1.3 kg (2¼ –3 lb)
PREPARATION & COOKING TIME: 1 hour 20 minutes

*This is a delicious combination that is a rather nice change
from the usual. It is very good with cheese and cold meats or
with hot roast meats. The recipe comes from Market Rasen
WI's cookbook, compiled to celebrate its Golden Jubilee back
in 1973; it was contributed by Shirley Sanderson. It also makes
an excellent accompaniment to a vegetarian nut roast. If you
can't find the fresh beetroot to cook yourself, use the vacuum-
packed, ready-cooked variety – saves a job.*

900 g (2 lb) cooked beetroot, skinned and cut into strips
2 teaspoons grated zest of orange
150 ml (¼ pint) orange juice
150 ml (¼ pint) lemon juice
½ teaspoon ground cinnamon
3 oranges, peeled and cut into segments, reserve peel and pith and
  any pips
900 g (2 lb) sugar

1 Place the beetroot, orange zest, juices and cinnamon in a
  large preserving pan with 300 ml (½ pint) of water. Place
  the reserved peel, pith and pips in a muslin bag and add to
  the pan.
2 Bring to the boil and then simmer for 30 minutes.
3 Remove the bag and squeeze the bag to extract all the
  juice. Add the sugar and stir until completely dissolved.
  Add the orange segments.
4 Boil rapidly until setting point is reached, then remove any
  scum (see page 12). Leave to stand for 5–10 minutes and
  then pour into cooled, sterilised jars (see page 12) and seal
  and label.

In terms of fresh produce, winter isn't the culinary desert you might expect, particularly in terms of fresh vegetables. Even in **January**, kale, kohlrabi, swede and the ever-versatile leek are still fresh in the ground. Kale thrives in winter and is a source of greens right through to March. Kohlrabi, related to turnips and swedes, can be eaten raw (grated in salads), braised, roasted and added to soups or stews. It's at its best when it's the size of a tennis ball.

Carrots that have been lifted and stored before the winter frosts are plentiful and add welcome colour to the plate. Swedes, hardier than turnips, have a lovely sweet flavour. Try mashing them with potatoes or carrots or roasting them – the high sugar content makes the swede caramelise beautifully.

Leeks, with their subtle flavour, are incredibly versatile and have a long season, right through to **March**. They are best steamed or braised – use the tough green leaves for flavouring stocks.

In February, Savoy cabbage with its attractive texture and nutty flavour is still going strong. Just steam it and toss in butter and black pepper – **it's a gourmet treat**. Another delicious vegetable is purple sprouting broccoli, tender and sweet.

The first fruit of the year is forced rhubarb in **February**. It was originally grown to fill a gap in the dessert fruit calendar but now, with the arrival of imported tropical fruits, it's less popular, but still available at a price.

Winter

Cream of Celery, Apple & Stilton Soup

SERVES 4 **V**
PREPARATION & COOKING TIME: 40 minutes
FREEZING: recommended before adding cheese and croûtons

The sharpness of the apple counteracts the richness of the cheese in this unusual soup.

25 g (1 oz) butter
1 onion, chopped
3 celery sticks, chopped
1 tablespoon plain flour
575 ml (1 pint) vegetable stock (page 8)
150 ml (¹⁄₄ pint) white wine
300 ml (¹⁄₂ pint) milk
1 bay leaf
¹⁄₂ teaspoon dried mixed herbs
1 cooking apple, peeled and chopped
80 g (3 oz) Stilton cheese, finely diced
salt and freshly ground black pepper
croûtons (page 23), to serve

1 Heat the butter in a large saucepan and sauté the onion and celery for 2–3 minutes, until softened but not browned.
2 Stir in the flour and cook for a further minute. Gradually add the stock and wine. Bring to the boil, stirring, until thickened.
3 Add the milk, bay leaf, herbs and apple. Bring back to the boil, cover and simmer for 20 minutes.
4 Meanwhile, make the croûtons and keep them warm.
5 Remove the bay leaf from the soup, allow to cool slightly, and then liquidise.
6 Return to the pan, add the cheese and heat gently until melted.
7 Season to taste and serve each bowlful with a few croûtons on top.

Celery & Cashew Nut Soup

SERVES 4 **V** ★
PREPARATION & COOKING TIME: 25 minutes
FREEZING: recommended

25 g (1 oz) butter
1 onion, chopped finely
1 potato, diced
¹⁄₂ head of celery, chopped, leaves reserved to garnish
80 g (3 oz) cashew nuts, chopped roughly
700 ml (1¹⁄₄ pints) vegetable stock (page 8)
15 g (¹⁄₂ oz) plain flour
450 ml (16 fl oz) milk
salt and freshly ground black pepper

1 Gently melt the butter in a large saucepan.
2 Add the onion and potato and cook for 5 minutes.
3 Stir in the celery and nuts and cook for a further 5 minutes.
4 Stir in the stock, bring to the boil and then reduce the heat and simmer for 15 minutes.
5 Blend the flour with a little of the milk, stir in the remainder of the milk and pour into the soup, stirring until the soup has thickened. Gently reheat but do not allow to boil.
6 Adjust the seasoning and serve garnished with celery leaves.

Brazil Nut & Lemon Soup

SERVES 6 **V** ★
PREPARATION & COOKING TIME: 30 minutes
FREEZING: recommended

This is a good way to use up any leftover Christmas nuts. The soup is light and fresh in flavour, and not at all filling.

25 g (1 oz) butter
1 onion, sliced
1.1 litres (2 pints) chicken stock (page 9)
115 g (4 oz) shelled brazil nuts, chopped roughly
grated zest of 1 lemon
90 ml (6 tablespoons) single cream
salt and freshly ground black pepper

1 In a large pan, melt the butter and sweat the onion, covered, for about 15 minutes. Shake the pan often.
2 Add the stock, nuts and lemon zest. Season lightly, cover and simmer for about 20 minutes.
3 Remove from the heat, allow to cool slightly and purée the mixture. It's preferable to use a hand-blender or a food processor rather than a liquidiser for this, in order to leave some of the texture of the nuts.
4 Reheat the soup, stir in the cream and check the seasoning before serving hot.

Green Pea, Ham & Leek Soup *(right)*

SERVES 4
PREPARATION & COOKING TIME: 40 minutes
FREEZING: recommended after step 3

This is a substantial, satisfying soup with a very good flavour and is ideal for lunch on a cold day. For extra taste, use a thick slice of the best quality ham you can get.

1 tablespoon oil
3 leeks, sliced
175 g (6 oz) frozen peas
850 ml (1½ pints) chicken stock (page 9)
175 g (6 oz) ham, cut into chunks
2 tablespoons chopped fresh mint
150 ml carton of double cream, to serve

1 Heat the oil in a large saucepan and sauté the leeks for 8 minutes, stirring occasionally. Add the peas and stock and bring to the boil.
2 Cover and simmer for 15 minutes.
3 Cool slightly and then purée until coarsely blended.
4 Return to the pan, stir in the ham and chopped mint and heat through.
5 Serve in individual bowls, with a swirl of cream.

Hearty Winter Soup

SERVES 4 V
PREPARATION & COOKING TIME: 1 hour
FREEZING: recommended

This is a substantial soup that is simple to make but very tasty.

575 ml (1 pint) vegetable or chicken stock (page 8 or 9)
1 potato, diced
1 onion, diced
1 large carrot, diced
1 tomato, skinned (page 82) and chopped roughly
1 turnip or half a swede, diced
1 small parsnip, diced
1 tablespoon tomato purée
2 tablespoons chopped fresh parsley
salt and freshly ground black pepper

1 Put the stock into a large saucepan and bring to the boil.
2 Add the vegetables as they are prepared, together with the tomato purée.
3 When it is just at the boil, reduce the heat, cover and simmer gently for about 30 minutes or until the vegetables are tender.
4 Stir in most of the parsley and then check and adjust the seasoning.
5 Serve this soup as it is or let it cool slightly and purée until smooth.
6 Serve sprinkled with the rest of the parsley.

Bean & Tomato Soup

SERVES 4 V ♥ ★
PREPARATION & COOKING TIME: 15 minutes
FREEZING: recommended

This is a simple, satisfying, tasty soup and was one of the recipes devised when WI members in Wales took part in a health initiative to reduce fat, sugar and salt and increase fibre in their diets.

2 celery sticks, chopped finely
1 small onion, chopped finely
fresh thyme sprig
575 ml (1 pint) vegetable stock (page 8)
400 g can of tomatoes
200 g can of baked beans in tomato sauce
Worcestershire sauce
salt and freshly ground black pepper
chopped fresh parsley, to garnish

1 Cook the celery, onion and thyme in a small amount of stock until tender.
2 Meanwhile, purée the tomatoes and baked beans until smooth.
3 Mix the tomato mixture with the celery and onion; add the remaining stock, a few drops of Worcestershire sauce and seasoning to taste.
4 Remove the sprig of thyme. Bring the soup to the boil and then reduce the heat and leave to simmer for 5 minutes before serving.

Chick Pea & Tomato Soup

SERVES 4 **V**
PREPARATION & COOKING TIME: 40 minutes
FREEZING: recommended

We have all said at one time or another, 'What on earth is there to eat?' This soup is a good answer, as it can be made mostly from ingredients in the storecupboard but is nevertheless tasty and satisfying.

2 tablespoons sunflower oil
1 red onion, chopped
2 garlic cloves, crushed
2 teaspoons cumin seeds
1 teaspoon mild curry powder
2 x 400 g cans of chopped tomatoes
175 g (6 oz) carrots, diced
50 g (2 oz) red lentils
finely grated zest and juice of 1 orange
425 g can of chick-peas, drained
salt and freshly ground black pepper
croûtons, to serve (page 23)

1 Heat the oil in a large pan and cook the onion, garlic, cumin seeds and curry powder for 5 minutes.
2 Add the tomatoes, carrots, lentils and orange zest to the pan. Then make up the orange juice to 575 ml (1 pint) with water and stir into the soup. Bring to the boil, cover and simmer for 30 minutes, until the carrots are tender.
3 Meanwhile, make the croûtons and keep them warm.
4 Allow the soup to cool briefly. Purée the soup or use a potato masher to give a fairly coarse texture. Then toss in the chick peas and season to taste.
5 Reheat the soup and serve with the croûtons.

Spicy Bean Soup with Guacamole Salsa *(left)*

SERVES 6 **V**
PREPARATION & COOKING TIME: 40 minutes
FREEZING: recommended for the soup, not the salsa

Sîan Cook submitted this recipe. She says: 'It is a hot, spicy soup and the salsa is a cooling complement. The colour is vibrant and the younger generation love it.'

FOR THE SOUP:
2 tablespoons oil
2 onions, chopped
4 fat garlic cloves, crushed
2 teaspoons ground cumin
a pinch of cayenne pepper
1 tablespoon paprika
1 tablespoon tomato purée
2 tablespoons ground coriander
400 g can of chopped tomatoes
400 g can of red kidney beans, drained
1 litre (1³/₄ pints) vegetable stock (page 8)
salt and freshly ground black pepper

FOR THE SALSA:
2 avocados, chopped
1 red onion, chopped finely
1 green chilli, de-seeded and chopped finely
1 tablespoon chopped
fresh coriander
juice of 1 lime

1 Heat the oil in a large saucepan and cook the onion and garlic until softened.
2 Add all the remaining ingredients for the soup, bring to the boil, season and cook over a low heat for 20 minutes.
3 Meanwhile, mix the salsa ingredients together.
4 Leave the soup to cool briefly. Then purée the soup and return to the pan. Adjust the seasoning and reheat gently.
5 Serve a little salsa in the middle of each bowl of soup.

Winter Lentil & Mint Soup

SERVES 4–6 **V**
PREPARATION & COOKING TIME: 3–4 hours soaking
  + 10 minutes + 30 minutes cooking
FREEZING: recommended, after step 4

*This is a lovely soup for a cold wintery day, served piping
hot with a nice bread roll. Dried mint loses its flavour quickly
once the jar is opened, so if you don't have any fresh, use mint
sauce instead.*

115 g (4 oz) brown lentils
1 tablespoon oil
a knob of butter
1 onion, sliced finely
1 small garlic clove, sliced
2 tablespoons tomato purée
1.1 litres (2 pints) vegetable or chicken stock (page 8 or 9)
40 g (1½ oz) bulgar wheat
2 teaspoons lemon juice
2 heaped teaspoons mint sauce or 2 tablespoons chopped fresh mint
salt and freshly ground black pepper

1 Put the lentils in a bowl, cover with cold water and leave
  to soak for 3–4 hours.
2 In a roomy pan, melt the oil and butter together. Add the
  onion and garlic and cook gently until the onion starts to
  soften.
3 Drain and rinse the lentils. Stir the tomato purée and
  drained lentils into the pan and stir so that all is well
  mixed. Add the stock and bring to the boil.
4 Reduce the heat and leave to simmer for about 30 minutes,
  or until the lentils are soft.
5 Leave to cool briefly and then spoon out 2 tablepoonfuls
  of the lentils and set them aside. Purée the soup.
6 Return to the pan and stir in the bulgar wheat, lemon juice
  and mint sauce or chopped mint. Adjust the seasoning,
  adding more mint if you wish.
7 Simmer for another 2 minutes. Return the whole lentils to
  the soup and serve piping hot.

Chestnut & Cranberry Soup

SERVES 6 **V** ★ ▼
PREPARATION & COOKING TIME: 25 minutes
FREEZING: recommended, after step 4

*This is a recipe Dilwen Phillips developed to use up Christmas
leftovers. It is easy to make and takes very little cooking. The
sweet chestnuts and the sharp cranberries combine to give a
delicious flavour and a delicate mushroom-coloured, satisfying,
yet low-calorie soup. It can be made at any time during the
year, using frozen cranberries and canned or vaccuum-packed
chestnuts or unsweetened chestnut purée. If you decide to use
fresh chestnuts, skinning them is time-consuming! Puncture
each chestnut with a fork, put in a pan of boiling water and
keep at simmering point. Remove a few chestnuts at a time and
plunge into cold water. Skin with the help of a vegetable knife.*

6 shallots, chopped
3 celery sticks, chopped
1 litre (1¾ pints) vegetable stock (page 8)
a sprig of thyme
450 g (1 lb) peeled, cooked chestnuts
115 g (4 oz) cranberries
4 tablespoons port
2 tablespoons lemon juice
salt and freshly ground black pepper
celery leaves, to garnish

1 Soften the shallots and celery in 2 tablespoons of stock
  over a low heat until transparent.
2 Add the remaining stock and thyme. Bring to the boil.
  Reduce the heat and leave to simmer for 10 minutes.
3 Add the chestnuts and cranberries. Bring to the boil and
  simmer for a further 5 minutes.
4 Remove the thyme and a few cranberries for the garnish.
  Allow the soup to cool slightly and then liquidise.
5 Stir in the port and lemon juice to taste. Adjust the
  seasoning.
6 Reheat gently and serve garnished with cranberries and
  celery leaves.

Leek, Onion & Potato Soup

SERVES 6
PREPARATION & COOKING TIME: 50 minutes
FREEZING: recommended, without the cream

*This is an ever-popular soup. The easiest way to wash leeks is to
discard the outer tough layer and then slit the leek from top to
root and to the centre and wash under a running tap, holding
the root end nearest to the tap, so any grit washes towards the
open end.*

50 g (2 oz) butter
1 onion, chopped
350 g (12 oz) potatoes, chopped
4 large leeks, sliced
1 litre (1¾ pints) vegetable or chicken stock (page 8 or 9)
300 ml (½ pint) milk
salt and freshly ground black pepper
6 tablespoons cream, to serve

1 In a large pan, melt the butter and add the onion, potato
  and leek. Cover the pan with a lid and sweat the
  vegetables over a low heat for 15 minutes, shaking the pan
  from time to time.
2 Add the stock, bring to the boil and then reduce the heat
  and leave to simmer for 15 minutes, until the vegetables
  are cooked.
3 Add the milk and purée the soup. Return to the pan.
4 Adjust the seasoning and then reheat the soup gently,
  without boiling.
5 Serve with a swirl of cream in each bowlful.

Vegetable Chowder

SERVES 4 V
PREPARATION & COOKING TIME: 50 minutes
FREEZING: recommended

1 tablespoon oil
1 large onion, chopped
225 g (8 oz) potatoes, chopped
225 g (8 oz) carrots, diced
3 celery sticks, diced
400 g can of chopped tomatoes
115 g (4 oz) macaroni
425 ml (³/₄ pint) vegetable stock (page 8)
1 bay leaf
2 teaspoons dried oregano
300 ml (¹/₂ pint) milk
salt and freshly ground black pepper
chopped fresh parsley, to garnish

1 Heat the oil in a large saucepan. Add the onion, potatoes, carrots and celery and sauté for 5 minutes, stirring occasionally.
2 Add the tomatoes, pasta, stock and herbs. Bring to the boil, reduce the heat, cover and simmer for 15 minutes.
3 Stir in the milk and season to taste. Bring back to the boil and then discard the bay leaf.
4 Serve sprinkled with chopped parsley.

Broccoli & Stilton Soup

SERVES 6 V
PREPARATION & COOKING TIME: 50 minutes
FREEZING: not recommended

1 tablespoon oil
1 onion, chopped
2 large potatoes, chopped
1.1 litres (2 pints) vegetable or chicken stock (page 8 or 9)
350 g (12 oz) broccoli, chopped roughly
80 g (3 oz) Stilton cheese, crumbled
150 ml (¹/₄ pint) milk
salt and freshly ground black pepper
juice of ¹/₂ lemon
6 tablespoons cream, to serve

1 Heat the oil in a fairly large pan and soften the onion for a few minutes. Add the potatoes and stock and bring to the boil. Simmer for 10 minutes.
2 Add the broccoli and cook for further 10 minutes. Purée the soup or just mash the vegetables roughly, if you prefer a chunkier texture.
3 Add the Stilton and milk and season to taste with salt, pepper and lemon juice. Heat through, without boiling.
4 Serve with a swirl of cream in each bowl.

Sweet Potato & Red Pepper Soup with Coconut

SERVES 4 V
PREPARATION & COOKING TIME: 1 hour
FREEZING: recommended

The pinkish colour of the sweet potato and deep red of the pepper give this soup a delightful colour and the coconut milk adds a tropical flavour.

25 g (1 oz) butter
1 onion, chopped
1 garlic clove, crushed
1 tablespoon ground coriander
450 g (1 lb) sweet potato, grated
2 red peppers, chopped
700 ml (1¹/₄ pints) vegetable stock (page 8)
400 g can of coconut milk

1 Melt the butter in a large pan. Add the onion and garlic and cook over a low heat until soft.
2 Stir in the ground coriander and cook for 2 minutes.
3 Add the sweet potato and red pepper to the pan and cook for 5 minutes.
4 Pour the vegetable stock over and bring to the boil; cover and simmer for 20 minutes.
5 Allow to cool a little and then purée.
6 Return to the rinsed-out pan and add the coconut milk. Heat gently until piping hot and then serve at once.

NOTE: If coconut milk isn't available, use 100 g (3¹/₂ oz) of creamed coconut, chopped, and increase the amount of stock by about 150 ml (¹/₄ pint).

Cabbage & Bacon Soup

SERVES 4 ★
PREPARATION & COOKING TIME: 20 minutes
FREEZING: recommended

This is a modern version of boiled bacon and cabbage, a perennial favourite. It is quick and easy to make, looks good and tastes even better!

25 g (1 oz) butter
2 onions, chopped finely
6 rashers of rindless bacon, chopped
1 litre (1³/₄ pints) vegetable stock (page 8)
450 g (1 lb) savoy cabbage, sliced thinly
salt and freshly ground black pepper

1 Melt the butter in a large pan and soften the onion over a low heat, without browning.
2 Add the bacon and increase the heat. Stirring continuously, cook until the onions and bacon begin to brown.
3 Add the stock and bring to the boil.
4 Add the cabbage. Cook until the cabbage is tender but still firm, approximately 5 minutes.
5 Adjust the seasoning before serving.

Watercress, Orange & Almond Soup

SERVES 5–6
PREPARATION & COOKING TIME: 20 minutes + 2 hours
  chilling
FREEZING: recommended, before adding the milk and cream

2 bunches of fresh, perky watercress, thoroughly washed and
  patted dry
1 tablespoon oil
1 small onion, chopped finely
850 ml (1½ pints) vegetable or chicken stock (page 8 or 9)
2 tablespoons ground almonds
juice of 1 sweet orange
1 teaspoon grated orange zest
300 ml (½ pint) mixed milk and single cream
salt and freshly ground black pepper
6 whole almonds, skinned, chopped and toasted, to garnish

1 Pick over the watercress, removing any yellow leaves.
  Reserve a few small leaves to garnish.
2 Heat the oil in a roomy pan and cook the onion, without
  browning. When the onion is soft, add the stock, ground
  almonds and watercress. Season to taste. Simmer for just a
  few minutes.
3 Stir the orange juice and zest into the soup. Simmer for
  another 3–4 minutes only.
4 Allow to cool and then reduce the soup to a smooth purée.
  Stir in the milk and cream mixture.
5 Allow the soup to cool and then refrigerate it for 2 hours.
6 Check the seasoning. Serve in small bowls – it should be
  chilled but not icy. Sprinkle a few chopped toasted
  almonds on top of each bowl of soup, along with the
  reserved watercress leaves.

Turkey Noodle Soup

SERVES 6 ★
PREPARATION & COOKING TIME: 30 minutes
FREEZING: recommended

*The juices left in the roasting tin after cooking the turkey set to
form a jelly. Remove the fat once it has set and use the jelly as
a delicious stock, making up the quantity with chicken stock.*

1 onion, chopped finely
1.1 litres (2 pints) turkey stock
50 g (2 oz) noodles
225 g (8 oz) cooked turkey, chopped finely
salt and freshly ground black pepper

1 In a large pan, cook the onion in a little of the stock until
  tender, about 5 minutes.
2 Add the remaining stock and the noodles. Cook following
  the instructions on the noodle packet.
3 Add the chopped turkey and heat through. Adjust the
  seasoning.
4 Spoon the noodles into warmed soup bowls, using a slotted
  spoon. Ladle the soup over the noodles and serve at once.

Beef Soup with Dumplings *(above)*

SERVES 4
PREPARATION & COOKING TIME: 1 hour 15 minutes
FREEZING: recommended, without dumplings

*This is a traditional recipe and a great favourite. It is a
complete meal, tasty and very satisfying.*

40 g (1½ oz) butter
400 g (12 oz) stewing beef, trimmed of fat and cubed
1 onion, chopped finely
1 litre (1¾ pints) beef stock (page 9)
450 g (1 lb) mixed root vegetables, e.g. carrots, swede, parsnips,
  turnips, chopped
1 leek, sliced thinly
2 tablespoons chopped fresh parsley
salt and freshly ground black pepper

FOR THE DUMPLINGS:
50 g (2 oz) self-raising flour
15 g (½ oz) suet
1 teaspoon chopped fresh parsley
fresh thyme leaves
salt and freshly ground black pepper
2 teaspoons milk

1 Melt half the butter in a pan and quickly fry the beef to
  seal and brown. Remove the beef with a slotted spoon.
2 Melt the remainder of the butter and fry the onion until
  golden.
3 Add the stock and beef. Bring to the boil and then reduce
  the heat and leave to simmer.
4 Meanwhile, prepare the vegetables and then add to the
  beef. Bring back to the boil and then leave to simmer until
  the beef and vegetables are tender, about 45–60 minutes.
5 Add the leek and parsley and simmer the soup for a
  further 5 minutes.
6 Meanwhile, make the dumplings. Mix the flour, suet, herbs
  and seasoning together in a bowl. Blend together with milk
  until you have a soft but not sticky dough. Shape into
  walnut-sized balls by rolling in floury hands.
7 Add the dumplings to the soup and cook for 5 minutes.
  Turn after 5 minutes and cook for about 5 minutes more.
  The dumplings will be light and fluffy when cooked.
8 Check and adjust the seasoning of the soup and serve
  straight away, piping hot.

Roasted Garlic & Chive Dip

MAKES: 300 ml (¹/₂ pint)
PREPARATION & COOKING TIME: 10 minutes + 30 minutes
  cooking + chilling
FREEZING: not recommended

Garlic, when roasted, undergoes some kind of metamorphosis, resulting in a divinely pungent, creamy taste. Garlic itself has long been used in herbal medicine for its health benefits – particularly in protecting the immune system by encouraging the body to release anti-infection cells. So this makes an ideal choice for wintertime. Dips are notoriously high in fat so this low-fat alternative makes a welcome change. Serve with a rainbow of mixed vegetable crudités or wedges (page 220).

1 head of garlic
olive oil, for brushing
¹/₂ x 250 g tub of ricotta cheese
150 ml (¹/₄ pint) low-fat natural 'bio' yogurt
1 tablespoon very finely chopped fresh chives
freshly ground black pepper

1 Preheat the oven to Gas Mark 6/electric oven 200°C/fan oven 180°C.
2 Place the whole head of garlic in a roasting dish and brush with a little oil, to prevent it from burning. Cook towards the top of the oven for about 30 minutes. Test that the flesh is ready by inserting a sharp knife into the cloves, the pulp should be soft. Leave to cool.
3 Separate the garlic into individual cloves and, holding the pointed end, squeeze the soft, creamy flesh out of the skin. Pound to a paste with a pestle and mortar.
4 Beat together the ricotta and yogurt. Stir in the puréed garlic and chives. Season to taste with pepper and chill prior to serving.

Iceberg Salad with Stilton Dressing

SERVES 4–6 **V**
PREPARATION & COOKING TIME: 30 minutes
FREEZING: not recommended

The creamy cheese dressing gives this salad a refreshing tangy flavour. Replace the bulgar wheat with couscous if preferred.

115 g (4 oz) bulgar wheat
1 small Iceberg lettuce, shredded
2 small courgettes, sliced thinly
1 small onion or 3–4 spring onions, chopped finely
4 tablespoons finely chopped fresh parsley

FOR THE DRESSING:
50 g (2 oz) blue Stilton, crumbled
3 tablespoons olive oil
6 tablespoons natural yogurt
salt and freshly ground black pepper

1 In a medium saucepan cover the bulgar wheat with cold water, bring to the boil and simmer for 15 minutes. Drain well and leave to cool.
2 Place the lettuce in a large salad bowl.
3 Add the courgettes, onion or spring onions, parsley and cooled bulgar wheat to the bowl.
4 To make the dressing mix the Stilton and oil together to form a smooth paste, gradually stir in the yogurt until well blended. Season to taste.
5 Pour the dressing over the salad and toss thoroughly to coat.

Garlic Mushroom & Taleggio Tart

SERVES 6
PREPARATION & COOKING TIME: 45 minutes
FREEZING: recommended

This is a favourite tart because it's so easy and quick to prepare – and so delicious. You could even make mini ones to serve with drinks – ideal for Christmas time when you have 101 other things to do!

FOR THE PASTRY:
375 g packet of ready rolled-puff pastry

FOR THE FILLING:
70 g (2¹/₂ oz) butter
450 g (1 lb) mushrooms, sliced (dark gilled ones are best)
2 garlic cloves, sliced thinly
4 tablespoons chopped fresh parsley
1 egg, beaten lightly
200 g packet of Taleggio cheese, cut into 12 slices
salt and freshly ground black pepper

1 Preheat the oven to Gas Mark 6/electric oven 200°C/fan oven 180°C.
2 Melt the butter in a large frying pan and add the sliced mushrooms with the garlic. Fry gently for about 5 minutes, or until all the liquid has evaporated.
3 Season and add 3 tablespoons of the chopped parsley to the pan.
4 Divide the pastry into six rectangles, measuring approximately 14 x 11 cm (5¹/₂ inches x 4¹/₄ inches). Score a line, about 1 cm (¹/₂ inch) in from the edge of each rectangle. Place the pastries on a baking sheet, pricking each one all over with a fork. Brush them with beaten egg.
5 Divide the mushroom topping between the pastry bases within the scored border. Place a couple of slices of Taleggio on top of each and bake for 20–25 minutes, until the cheese has melted and the pastries are golden. Serve with a scattering of chopped parsley over each.

Garlicky Stuffed Mushrooms (below)

SERVES 4 V ▼
PREPARATION & COOKING TIME: 50 minutes
FREEZING: not recommended

1 tablespoon extra virgin olive oil, plus extra for greasing
4 large field or portobello mushrooms
1 egg, lightly beaten
2 garlic cloves, chopped finely
1 small tomato, de-seeded and chopped finely
75 g (2³/₄ oz) fresh wholemeal breadcrumbs
125 g ball light mozzarella cheese, cubed finely
1 tablespoon snipped fresh chives
1 tablespoon chopped fresh flat leaf parsley
freshly ground black pepper
2 tablespoons freshly grated Parmesan cheese

This is a favourite way of serving large field or portobello mushrooms. It makes an excellent starter for four people with a light salad garnish or makes an equally tasty 'veggie' main course for two. Use wholemeal breadcrumbs for preference since they add a lovely depth of flavour.

1 Preheat the oven to Gas Mark 6/electric oven 200°C/fan oven 180°C.
2 Lightly oil a shallow ovenproof dish large enough to contain the four mushrooms in a single layer.
3 Detach the stalks from the mushrooms and chop these stalks finely.
4 Place the beaten egg in a medium bowl and add the chopped mushroom stalks, garlic and tomato, 50 g (1³/₄ oz) breadcrumbs, the cubed mozzarella, chives and parsley. Season with a grinding of black pepper.
5 Mix everything well together to form a stuffing and use it to fill the mushroom caps. Place the filled mushrooms in the baking dish.
6 Sprinkle the mushrooms with the remaining breadcrumbs.
7 Bake in the oven for 20–25 minutes until the breadcrumb topping is crisp and golden brown and the mushrooms are tender. Serve immediately with Parmesan cheese.

Chicory & Orange Salad

SERVES 4 ♥ v ▼
PREPARATION TIME: 1 hour soaking + 15 minutes
FREEZING: not recommended

Chicory is sometimes bitter, but soaking it in cold water makes it less strong. This makes a very refreshing salad which is particularly good with cold chicken.

4 heads of chicory
2 oranges
salt and freshly ground black pepper

1 Trim the base of the chicory with a stainless steel knife, and cut into slices crossways. Put in a bowl, cover with cold water and leave to soak for at least an hour.
2 With a sharp knife (a serrated one is best) peel the oranges over a serving bowl to reserve the juice, removing all the white pith with the peel.
3 Cut the oranges into slices or segments, removing any pips, and place in the bowl with the juice. Drain the chicory well and add to the oranges with a little salt and lots of black pepper.

Butter Bean Dip with Crudités

SERVES 4 ♥ v ▼
PREPARATION TIME: 35 minutes
FREEZING: not recommended

A great snack or starter, which can also be served as 'nibbles' with drinks. Other vegetable suggestions for the crudités include: radishes, yellow/orange peppers, baby sweetcorn, courgettes, French beans, cherry tomatoes or fennel.

FOR THE DIP:
200 g can of butter beans, rinsed and drained
1 or 2 garlic cloves, halved
4 tablespoons olive oil
juice of $1/2$ lemon
salt and freshly ground black pepper

FOR THE CRUDITÉS:
2 carrots
3 celery sticks
1 green pepper, halved, de-seeded and white pith removed
1 red pepper, halved, de-seeded and white pith removed
3 spring onions, trimmed and halved
$1/2$ cucumber, quartered lengthways and seeds removed

1 Put all the dip ingredients in a food processor, and whizz until smooth. If too thick add a little water. Taste to check the seasoning, and spoon into a deep bowl.
2 To prepare the crudités, use a sharp knife to cut the vegetables into neat evenly sized sticks. Arrange around the bowl of dip.

Golden Vegetable Pâté

SERVES: 4 ♥ v ▼
PREPARATION & COOKING TIME: 30 minutes + 1 hour chilling
FREEZING: not recommended

Serve this lovely coloured pâté with thinly sliced toast or use as a dip with crudités. Half-fat cream cheese can be used instead of the yogurt; it will give a richer pâté but triple the fat content.

1 onion, sliced
1–2 garlic cloves
125 g ($4^1/2$ oz) carrot, chopped
125 g ($4^1/2$ oz) swede, chopped
1–2 teaspoons grated orange zest
$1^1/2$ tablespoons light Greek yogurt
$1/2$ teaspoon ground coriander
freshly grated nutmeg
freshly ground black pepper

1 Place the onion in a small, heavy-based saucepan and cover with the lid. Heat over a gentle heat for 10 minutes, shaking the pan occasionally until the onion starts to soften but not brown.
2 Add the garlic, carrots and swede to the pan, with enough boiling water to cook them. Simmer until the vegetables are tender. If possible evaporate off any remaining water; if too much is left to do this, pour it off and retain it to use as stock. Cool the vegetables.
3 Add the orange zest, yogurt and the coriander to the vegetables; process in a small blender or liquidise until smooth. Season to taste with nutmeg and pepper. Chill for at least an hour before serving.

Tuna & Chick Peas

SERVES 4
PREPARATION & COOKING TIME: overnight soaking + 1
    hour + 15 minutes cooling
FREEZING: not recommended

This dish is loosely based on the classic Italian dish tonno e fagioli *(tuna and beans). The tuna and chick peas partner each other really well. It makes a great snack dish, and will keep in the fridge for 2–3 days. In fact, it is almost more tasty the next day.*

175g (6oz) dried chick peas, soaked in cold water overnight
$^{1}/_{2}$ red onion, finely sliced
grated zest and juice of 1 lemon
4 tablespoons good quality olive oil
185 g can of tuna in brine, well drained
salt and freshly ground black pepper
2 tablespoons chopped fresh parsley

1 Put the drained chick peas in a saucepan, cover with water and simmer for about 45–50 minutes until they are soft but still retain some bite.
2 Meanwhile, put the onion, lemon zest, juice and olive oil in a wide shallow dish. Drain the chick peas and put straight into the dish while still hot. Stir to mix.
3 Season well with salt and pepper, add the tuna and mix together to break up the tuna chunks. Cover and leave to cool. Taste to check the seasoning and sprinkle with chopped parsley.

Spicy Sausage Rice Salad

SERVES 4–6
PREPARATION & COOKING TIME: 40 minutes
FREEZING: not recommended

A wide variety of ready-to-eat spicy sausages are available from most major supermarkets – try Spanish chorizo, Polish kabanos or Italian pepperoni to add a kick to this simple salad. It is ideal to serve as an accompaniment to a main course or as part of a buffet when you are entertaining.

175 g (6 oz) long grain brown rice
50 g (2 oz) wild rice
1 yellow pepper, de-seeded and diced coarsely
115 g (4 oz) raisins
50 g (2 oz) walnuts, chopped
50 g (2 oz) green olives, pitted
1 orange, cut into segments
225 g (8 oz) spicy sausage, chopped
salt and freshly ground black pepper

1 Place the rice in a pan, cover with cold water and bring to the boil. Reduce the heat to a simmer, cover and cook for 20–25 minutes until tender. Drain well, rinse in cold water and allow to cool completely.
2 Place the cooled rice in a large serving bowl. Stir in the remaining ingredients and mix thoroughly.
3 Serve as part of a main course or on a buffet table.

Classic Caesar Salad with Croûtons

SERVES 4 ▼
PREPARATION & COOKING TIME: 35 minutes
FREEZING: not recommended

No salt is needed because the anchovy essence is very salty. Any extra croûtons will keep well in a tin, so cook more than you need and use to garnish soups. If you use a Microplane Grater for the Parmesan, the cheese will be very fine, and will go a long way.

2 slices thick wholemeal or granary bread, crusts removed
$^{1}/_{2}$ x 200 g pot of low fat crème fraîche
1 garlic clove, crushed
a squeeze of lemon juice
1 dessertspoon anchovy essence
freshly ground black pepper
1 Cos lettuce or 2 Little Gem lettuces
50 g (2 oz) half fat Parmesan cheese, freshly grated

1 Preheat the oven to Gas Mark 4/electric oven 180°C/fan oven 160°C.
2 To make the croûtons, cut the bread into small squares, put on a flat baking sheet and bake for about 20 minutes until completely dry and crispy.
3 Put the crème fraîche in a small bowl and mix in the garlic, lemon juice, anchovy essence and pepper. Taste to check the seasoning.
4 Chop the lettuce roughly and put in a deep bowl. When you are ready to serve, pour over the crème fraîche dressing, mix well and sprinkle over the croûtons and Parmesan.

Warm Chilli Beef Salad

SERVES 4 ▼ ★
PREPARATION & COOKING TIME: 30 minutes
FREEZING: not recommended

Somewhat of a paradox of a title for this Thai-style main-course salad, packed with plenty of vegetables! It makes a wonderful informal supper party recipe, as all the preparation can be done in advance and, because it is equally good warm or cold, an exact serving schedule is not necessary.

Chicken could equally well be used instead of beef, if you prefer. In the absence of pak choi, spinach is an excellent substitute, but stir this in at step 5 rather than 4.

FOR THE DRESSING:
2 tablespoons reduced-salt soy sauce
2 teaspoons sesame oil
2 teaspoons sweet chilli sauce
juice of $^1/_2$ lime
freshly ground black pepper

FOR THE SALAD:
115 g (4 oz) stir-fry rice noodles
1 tablespoon sunflower or vegetable oil
$^1/_2$ red pepper, de-seeded and sliced thinly
1 red chilli, de-seeded and chopped finely
1 garlic clove, crushed
1 teaspoon grated fresh root ginger
200 g (7 oz) sirloin steak, fat trimmed, cut into very thin strips
1 head of pak choi, quartered and rinsed
115 g (4 oz) baby button mushrooms, wiped and halved
1 carrot, scrubbed and cut into matchstick-size batons
1 bunch of spring onions, sliced thinly
2 rounded tablespoons chopped fresh coriander

1 Whisk together all the dressing ingredients, and set on one side.
2 Bring a pan of water to the boil. Break the rice noodles into three sections. Add to the water, making sure that they are fully immersed. Cover the pan, turn off the heat, and leave for 4 minutes. Drain and toss the noodles in the dressing.
3 In a wok, heat the oil until hot. Stir in the pepper, chilli, garlic and ginger. Stir-fry for 1 minute, moving the ingredients around the pan the whole time.
4 Add the steak and pak choi and cook for a further 2–3 minutes.
5 Remove the pan from the heat and stir in the mushrooms, carrot, spring onions, coriander and noodles. Mix well and serve warm.

Cranberry, Blue Cheese, Pear & Walnut Salad (right)

SERVES: 4–6 ▼ ★ ∨
PREPARATION TIME: 10 minutes
FREEZING: not recommended

Cranberries, native to North America, are now more widely available over here (if all other avenues fail, try a health food shop for dried ones) and a good source of fibre and vitamin C. This is a winter salad – the dark green salad leaves and red, berry-like cranberries are reminiscent of holly. Delicious with ham and Stilton at Christmas time.

FOR THE DRESSING:
$^1/_4$ teaspoon English mustard powder
$^1/_4$ teaspoon soft brown sugar
$1^1/_2$ teaspoons balsamic vinegar
$1^1/_2$ teaspoons white wine vinegar
1 tablespoon extra virgin olive oil
1 tablespoon sunflower or vegetable oil
sea salt and freshly ground black pepper

FOR THE SALAD:
120 g bag of salad leaves, including red chard or red beet
115 g (4 oz) Saint Agur, dolcelatte or Stilton
40 g ($1^1/_2$ oz) walnut pieces
40 g ($1^1/_2$ oz) dried cranberries
1 large, ripe Comice pear

1 Place the mustard, sugar, salt, pepper and vinegars in a bowl. Mix together. Gradually whisk in the oils.
2 Put the salad leaves in a serving bowl. Cube or crumble the cheese into bite-sized pieces and add to the salad, with the walnut pieces and cranberries.
3 Wash the pear and, leaving its skin on, core and thinly slice. Stir into the dressing to coat it thoroughly.
4 Just before serving, add the pear and dressing to the salad and toss well.

Bean & Vegetable Hotpot

SERVES 6 **V** ▼
PREPARATION & COOKING TIME: 2 hours
FREEZING: recommended

Easy to make, this colourful dish is good with herby dumplings, naan breads, rice or a jacket potato. If you wish, add 4 tablespoons of port with the sweetcorn. The flavour is even better if stored in the refrigerator for a day or two before eating.

1 small aubergine, sliced and larger slices halved
1 tablespoon lemon juice
2 garlic cloves, chopped finely
1 large onion, chopped
1 red pepper, de-seeded and chopped into 5–10 mm
   ($^{1}/_{4}$ –$^{1}/_{2}$-inch) pieces
1 yellow pepper, de-seeded and chopped into 5–10 mm
   ($^{1}/_{4}$ –$^{1}/_{2}$-inch) pieces
1 green pepper, de-seeded and chopped into 5–10 mm
   ($^{1}/_{4}$ –$^{1}/_{2}$-inch) pieces
400 g can of red kidney beans in water, drained well, rinsed
   and drained again
2 x 400 g cans of chopped tomatoes with herbs
2 tablespoons fresh or 2 teaspoons dried basil or similar herb
   (increase this if you can't get tomatoes with herbs)
2 courgettes, sliced
225 g (8 oz) frozen sweetcorn kernels
freshly ground black pepper

1 Brush the aubergine slices with the lemon juice to prevent browning.
2 Put the garlic, onion, peppers, beans, tomatoes and herbs into a large pan.
3 Cover, bring to the boil and simmer for 30 minutes, until the vegetables are beginning to soften.
4 Add the courgettes and aubergine, bring back to the boil and simmer for a further 45–60 minutes.
5 Add the sweetcorn, bring back to the boil and simmer for 5 minutes. Season to taste with black pepper.

Lentil & Vegetable Curry

SERVES 4 ♥ **V**
PREPARATION & COOKING TIME: 1 hour 20 minutes
FREEZING: recommended

The classic Indian fragrant spice cardamom is combined with ready-blended curry powder and ground cinnamon to make this really simple and healthy vegetarian curry. Serve it as a vegetarian main course for four with garlic and coriander naan bread or as an accompanying vegetable dish for eight.

2 tablespoons vegetable oil
1 onion, chopped finely
2 garlic cloves, crushed
2 tablespoons curry powder
6 cardamom pods, crushed
$^{1}/_{2}$ teaspoon ground cinnamon
2 bay leaves

115 g (4 oz) red lentils, rinsed well
175 g (6 oz) okra
1 aubergine, topped, tailed and cubed
2 carrots, sliced
1 cauliflower, divided into small florets
fresh bay leaves, to garnish

1 Heat the oil in a large pan, fry the onion and garlic until soft. Add the spices and bay leaves and cook for 1 minute.
2 Add the lentils and vegetables to the pan, cook for 5 minutes.
3 Pour in 850 ml (1$^{1}/_{2}$ pints) water and bring to the boil. Reduce to a gentle simmer and cover and cook gently for 1 hour.
4 Garnish with the bay leaves before serving.

Chestnut Casserole

SERVES 4 **V** ★ ▼
PREPARATION & COOKING TIME: 30 minutes
FREEZING: recommended

Though they are traditionally a Christmas ingredient, use chestnuts to make this sweet-flavoured casserole all through the wintertime.

1 teaspoon oil
$^{1}/_{2}$ level teaspoon ground ginger
$^{1}/_{2}$ teaspoon grated nutmeg
a pinch of ground cloves
2 leeks, sliced
1 green pepper, de-seeded and sliced
1 red pepper, de-seeded and sliced
2 celery sticks, sliced
1 bay leaf
425 ml ($^{3}/_{4}$ pint) vegetable stock (page 8)
2 x 200 g packs cooked, whole peeled chestnuts
15 g ($^{1}/_{2}$ oz) flour
3 tablespoons skimmed milk
freshly ground black pepper

1 Heat the oil in a large saucepan over a medium heat and fry the spices for 1 minute.
2 Add the vegetables and the bay leaf. Stir-fry for 1 minute, to mix the spices in well.
3 Pour the stock over the vegetables and bring to the boil. Simmer, covered, for 5 minutes.
4 If the chestnuts are packed closely, separate them. Add to the vegetables and simmer for a further 10 minutes.
5 Blend the flour to a smooth paste with the milk. Pour into the chestnut casserole, stirring briskly. Simmer for 1 minute. Season to taste with the pepper.

Smoked Haddock Stew (below)

SERVES 4 ▼
PREPARATION & COOKING TIME: 40 minutes
FREEZING: not recommended

*This is a lovely recipe, half way between a stew and a soup.
It's very nourishing and filling.*

300 ml (½ pint) boiling water
225 g (8 oz) smoked haddock fillet
1 tablespoon sunflower oil
1 onion, sliced finely
2 celery sticks, chopped finely
1 carrot, sliced finely
1 potato, peeled and diced finely
½ teaspoon turmeric powder
1 sprig fresh thyme
2 fresh bay leaves
salt and freshly ground black pepper
300 ml (½ pint) semi skimmed milk
75 g (2¾ oz) frozen peas
freshly ground nutmeg

1 Pour the boiling water over the haddock. Leave for 5
  minutes, drain and reserve the liquid.
2 Heat the oil in a saucepan and gently fry the onion for 2
  minutes. Add the celery, carrot and potato and continue to
  fry for 2 more minutes. Add half the reserved fish stock,
  the turmeric, thyme, bay leaves and salt and pepper.
3 Bring to the boil and simmer very gently with the lid on,
  until the vegetables are soft, about 15 minutes. Add the
  rest of the stock, the milk and peas.
4 Cook for a further 3 minutes. Gently flake in the fish,
  remove the bay leaves and thyme, and grate in a little
  nutmeg. Taste to check the seasoning before serving.

Oat Crushed Salmon

SERVES 4 ★▼
PREPARATION & COOKING TIME: 15 minutes
FREEZING: not recommended

*Using low fat cooking spray oil (available in the supermarket)
and a non-stick pan makes this fish lovely and crusty on the
outside while only using very little oil.*

600 g (1 lb 5oz) salmon fillet, skinned (ask the fishmonger to do this
  for you)
2 tablespoons porridge oats
2 teaspoons sesame seeds
salt and freshly ground black pepper
sunflower oil cooking spray
1 large lemon, cut into 4, to serve

1 Cut the salmon into four evenly sized pieces. On a plate
  mix together the oats, sesame seeds, salt and pepper.
2 Dip each salmon portion into the oat mixture, and press in
  to coat all over. The dampness of the fish will make the
  mixture stick.
3 Heat a non-stick frying pan, spray in the oil and put in the
  salmon. Cook over a medium heat for about 3 minutes on
  each side, covering with a lid. The fish will be brown and
  crispy on the outside, and the lid will provide steam to
  help it cook through. Serve with the lemon wedges.

Winter

Smoked Haddock Lasagne

SERVES 5 ▼
PREPARATION & COOKING TIME: 1 hour 20 minutes
FREEZING: recommended

FOR THE SAUCE:
600 ml (1 pint) skimmed milk
1 onion, halved
2 cloves (optional)
1 bay leaf
6 level tablespoons cornflour
300 ml (½ pint) fish stock (from cooking the fish)
15 g (½ oz) low fat spread
freshly grated nutmeg
freshly ground black pepper

FOR THE FILLING:
400 g (14 oz) undyed smoked haddock fillet, skinned
200 g (7 oz) mushrooms, wiped and chopped
3 tablespoons ricotta cheese
2 tablespoons chopped fresh chives
6 sheets no-egg dried lasagne

1 Measure 90 ml (3 fl oz) of the milk into a basin. Pour the remaining milk into a saucepan, add the onion halves, cloves and bay leaf and bring to the boil. When the milk is at boiling point, remove it from the heat, cover with a lid and leave the flavourings to infuse.

2 Place the haddock in a wide, shallow pan, cover with cold water and bring to the boil. As soon as boiling point is reached, discard the water; this will remove some of the salt. Cover again with cold water and bring to the boil.

3 Once boiling point is reached again, remove from the heat and cover with a lid. Leave for 5 minutes, then test to see if the fish is cooked. If it is, drain off the fish stock and reserve (otherwise reheat the water and leave for another minute or two). It is important for the flavour and texture that the fish is only just cooked.

4 Allow the fish to cool, then flake. Mix with the mushrooms, ricotta cheese and chives. Season with pepper.

5 Measure the reserved stock. If necessary make it up to the required 300 ml (½ pint) with water.

6 Blend the cornflour with the reserved milk until smooth.

7 Remove the flavouring ingredients from the infused milk and add the fish stock to it. Heat to boiling point. Pour the boiling liquid over the cornflour paste, stirring constantly to mix well.

8 Return the sauce to the pan, add the low fat spread and bring to the boil. Simmer gently for 1 minute, stirring all the time. Season with the nutmeg and pepper. The sauce will be thin because the lasagne sheets need to absorb some of the liquid.

9 Preheat the oven to Gas Mark 4/electric oven180°C/fan oven 160°C.

10 Pour one-third of the sauce into the base of a shallow ovenproof dish. Place half the lasagne sheets over this, not allowing them to overlap. Spoon over half the fish mixture. Repeat the layers, finishing with the sauce.

11 Place the dish on a baking sheet in the oven and bake for 30 minutes, until the lasagne is hot and bubbling.

Spicy Chicken on a Bed of Couscous

SERVES 4
PREPARATION & COOKING TIME: 15 minutes + 2 hours marinating + 35 minutes cooking
FREEZING: not recommended

This dish is based on the wonderfully warming North African harissa paste. If you have never used it before, the quantity in this recipe will give a medium spiciness. Once you have gauged its strength you can adjust to suit your own preference. Jars of harissa paste are found in most of the large supermarkets.

4 skinless, boneless chicken breasts
150 ml ($^1/_4$ pint) low fat plain yogurt
juice of 1 lemon
2 teaspoons harissa paste
$^1/_2$ teaspoon ground cumin
$^1/_2$ teaspoon ground coriander
fresh coriander leaves, to garnish (optional)

FOR THE COUSCOUS:
300 g (10$^1/_2$ oz) couscous
500 ml (18 fl oz) hot chicken stock (page 9)
1 tablespoon olive oil
1 red onion, chopped
1 fresh red chilli, de-seeded and chopped finely
1 garlic clove, crushed
1 red pepper, de-seeded and diced
3 tablespoons finely chopped fresh coriander
freshly ground black pepper

1 Make three slashes in the top surface of each chicken breast and place them in a shallow dish.
2 Mix together the yogurt, 1 tablespoon of lemon juice, the harissa paste, cumin and coriander and pour over the chicken pieces, coating them completely. Cover and place in the fridge to marinate for 2 hours, turning them once.
3 Preheat the oven to Gas Mark 6/electric oven 200°C/fan oven 180°C.
4 Lift the chicken pieces out of the marinade and place them in a small roasting tin. Bake in the oven for 30–35 minutes until the chicken is thoroughly cooked and lightly browned on top.
5 Meanwhile, place the couscous in a large bowl and pour over the hot stock, stirring once or twice to prevent any dry pockets of grains. Leave aside for 10 minutes to allow the couscous to swell and absorb the stock.
6 Heat the olive oil in a frying pan and gently fry the onion for 5–6 minutes until softened. Stir in the chilli, garlic and red pepper and continue to cook for a further 5 minutes. Stir this into the hot couscous along with the chopped fresh coriander and a grinding of black pepper.
7 Divide the couscous mixture equally between four serving plates. Remove the chicken from the oven and place each portion on a bed of couscous. Garnish with some whole coriander leaves if desired and serve immediately.

Chicken Korma

SERVES 4
PREPARATION & COOKING TIME: 20 minutes + overnight marinating + 30 minutes
FREEZING: not recommended

For the very best flavour the chicken is best left to marinate overnight. The mild and creamy sauce is flavoured with a combination of fragrant spices such as coriander seeds, ginger and cinnamon, that are fried together to release their wonderful aroma. Serve with plain naan bread or steamed rice.

4 boneless, skinless chicken breasts
150 ml ($^1/_4$ pint) natural yogurt
2 garlic cloves, crushed
2 teaspoons turmeric
40 g (1$^1/_2$ oz) unsalted butter
1 large onion, sliced
5-cm (2-inch) piece of fresh root ginger, peeled and diced finely
1 teaspoon chilli powder
1 teaspoon coriander seeds, crushed
10 whole cloves
1 teaspoon salt
5-cm (2-inch) piece of cinnamon stick
1 tablespoon cornflour
150 ml ($^1/_4$ pint) single cream
25 g (1 oz) unsalted cashew nuts, to serve

1 Score each chicken breast with a sharp knife.
2 In a large bowl mix together the yogurt, garlic and turmeric, add the chicken and coat well. Cover and marinate overnight in the fridge.
3 In a large frying pan melt the butter, add the onion and cook until soft and browned, stir in the ginger, chilli powder, coriander seeds, cloves, salt and cinnamon stick and cook for 2–3 minutes.
4 Add the chicken and its marinade and cook on a gentle heat for 20–25 minutes until the chicken is completely cooked.
5 Blend the cornflour and cream together and stir into the chicken, reheat very gently to prevent the cream from curdling.
6 Sprinkle over the cashew nuts to serve.

Turkey Stir-fry with Orange & Redcurrant Sauce (below)

SERVES 2 ▼
PREPARATION & COOKING TIME: 35 minutes
FREEZING: not recommended

The vegetables in this stir-fry remain very crisp; if you prefer them softer add them to the wok at the same time or just after the turkey. Cranberries can be used in place of the redcurrants; these would not need sieving and some could be reserved to add whole to the stir-fry at the same time as the sauce.

FOR THE SAUCE:
150 g (5¹/₂ oz) fresh or frozen redcurrants
1 teaspoon grated orange zest
juice of 1 orange
about 1 tablespoon light soft brown sugar
lemon juice, to taste (optional)

FOR THE STIR-FRY:
¹/₂ sweet potato, peeled
1 courgette, trimmed
200 g (7 oz) turkey stir-fry pieces
¹/₂ teaspoon oil

1 Make the sauce first. Put the redcurrants, orange zest and juice in a pan and bring to the boil. Simmer for 7–8 minutes or until the currants are tender. Stir in the sugar and stir until it has dissolved.
2 Press the sauce through a sieve to remove the seeds. It should be slightly syrupy. If it is not, boil again for 1 or 2 minutes to reduce it. Taste for sweetness. If necessary, adjust with more sugar or a little lemon juice.
3 Cut the sweet potato into four lengthways and then cut each piece into thin slivers. Cut the courgette into four lengthways and then cut each piece into 3-mm (¹/₈-inch) slices. Cut the stir-fry turkey into evenly sized pieces.
4 Heat the oil in a wok or large frying pan. Add the turkey and stir-fry for 4–5 minutes, until it is just cooked and the juices run clear when pierced and pressed. Add the vegetables and stir-fry for 2 minutes.
6 Spoon in the sauce and stir-fry for 1 minute to heat through. Serve immediately.

Turkey & Sweet Pepper Wraps with Potato Wedges

SERVES 4
PREPARATION & COOKING TIME: 45 minutes
FREEZING: not recommended

Traditional Mexican fajitas are very tasty but, with the guacamole, soured cream and grated cheese, can also be very high in fat. This healthier version of fajitas is brilliant served with a crisp green salad and some low fat home made potato wedges.

FOR THE POTATO WEDGES:
3 medium to large baking potatoes
1 teaspoon paprika
¹/₂ tablespoon olive oil
freshly ground black pepper

FOR THE WRAPS:
1 tablespoon olive oil
500 g (1 lb 2 oz) thinly sliced turkey breast, cut into strips
1 red onion, sliced
2 garlic cloves, crushed
1 red pepper, de-seeded and sliced
1 green pepper, de-seeded and sliced
1 teaspoon paprika
¹/₄ teaspoon chilli powder
200 g can of chopped tomatoes
4 flour tortilla wraps
150 g pot fat free Greek yogurt
1¹/₂ tablespoons reduced fat green pesto sauce

1 To make the wedges, preheat the oven to Gas Mark 5/ electric oven 190°C/fan oven 170°C.
2 Wash and dry the potatoes but do not peel them. Cut each one in half lengthways, then cut each half into four wedges. Place in a large mixing bowl and sprinkle over the paprika, olive oil and black pepper. Stir well to coat the wedges evenly. Tip them on to a baking sheet, spread out and then bake for about 35 minutes until they are golden and tender.
3 To make the wraps, heat the oil in a large frying pan and cook the strips of turkey breast over a moderate heat until browned and cooked through. Transfer to a plate and set aside.
4 Add the onion, garlic and peppers to the pan and cook for 5–6 minutes until just tender. Stir in the paprika, chilli powder and chopped tomatoes. Mix well and bring up to simmering point. Return the turkey to the pan and simmer for about 10 minutes, stirring occasionally.
5 Meanwhile, wrap the tortillas in foil and place in the oven to warm through for 8–10 minutes.
6 Mix together the Greek yogurt and the pesto. Divide the mixture evenly between the warmed tortillas and spread almost to the edge. Place equal quantities of the turkey and pepper mixture down the centre of each tortilla. Roll up and serve immediately, accompanied by the potato wedges.

Lamb in Mushroom Sauce

SERVES 4
PREPARATION & COOKING TIME: 1¹/₂–1³/₄ hours
FREEZING: recommended

Lamb chops in a fruity mushroom sauce are baked in the oven until tender. Serve with boiled brown rice and stir-fried courgettes and peppers.

40 g (1¹/₂ oz) butter
8 best end of neck lamb chops, trimmed
225 g (8 oz) button mushrooms
1 tablespoon plain flour
300 ml (¹/₂ pint) lamb stock
4 tablespoons redcurrant jelly
2 tablespoons Worcestershire sauce
2 tablespoons freshly squeezed lemon juice
a pinch of nutmeg
salt and freshly ground black pepper

1 In a frying-pan melt the butter and quickly brown the chops on all sides. Place the chops in a deep casserole dish with the mushrooms.
2 Stir the flour into the remaining fat in the frying pan, blend in the stock and add the redcurrant jelly, Worcestershire sauce, lemon juice and nutmeg. Season and heat until boiling, stirring continuously.
3 Pour the sauce over the lamb in the casserole dish, cover and cook at Gas Mark 3/electric oven 170°C/fan oven 150°C for 1¼–1½ hours or until the chops are tender.

Sausage Casserole with Red Wine & Puy Lentils *(below)*

SERVES 4 ♥
PREPARATION & COOKING TIME: 1 hour 15 minutes
FREEZING: recommended

A superior sausage casserole which is flavoursome enough to serve at an informal dinner party. Using a good quality low fat sausage and the soluble fibre from the lentils makes this a much healthier option to the traditional sausage casserole. Serve with mashed potatoes and lightly steamed Savoy cabbage.

1 tablespoon olive oil
454 g pack of good quality reduced fat sausages
1 onion, sliced
2 garlic cloves, crushed
1 teaspoon ground allspice
¹/₂ teaspoon ground nutmeg
2 x 400 g cans of chopped tomatoes
2 sprigs of rosemary
2 bay leaves
200 ml (7 fl oz) red wine
100 g (3¹/₂ oz) Puy lentils

1 Heat the oil in a large flameproof casserole and cook the sausages for 5–8 minutes until nicely browned all over. Remove and set aside.
2 Add the onion and garlic to the pan and cook gently until the onion is softened. Stir in the allspice and the nutmeg and mix well.
3 Pour in the tomatoes and bring to the boil. Simmer for 4–5 minutes to thicken slightly then add the rosemary, bay leaves, red wine and Puy lentils. Stir in 200 ml (7 fl oz) cold water. Return the sausages to the pan and bring back up to the boil.
4 Cover the pan and reduce the heat. Simmer for 35–40 minutes until the lentils are tender. Stir several times during the cooking to prevent the lentils sticking to the base of the pan, and add a little more water if the sauce is becoming too thick. Remove the rosemary sprigs and the bay leaves before serving.

Pork Chops with a Creamy Dijonnaise Sauce

SERVES 4
PREPARATION & COOKING TIME: 35 minutes
FREEZING: not recommended

This is based on a wonderful French recipe which normally uses lashings of butter and cream. This much healthier version tastes equally delicious but contains about half the fat. Don't be tempted to use English mustard instead of the Dijon, because it is far too fiery and would completely spoil the sauce. However, a good quality dry cider could be used instead of the white wine, to give the recipe a hint of flavours from Normandy. Serve the chops accompanied by some boiled new potatoes and a selection of lightly steamed vegetables.

1 tablespoon sunflower oil
4 large pork loin chops, all visible fat removed
freshly ground black pepper
100 ml (3¹/₂ fl oz) dry white wine
1 teaspoon dried thyme
150 ml (¹/₄ pint) half fat crème fraîche
1 teaspoon tomato purée
1 tablespoon Dijon mustard
1 tomato, peeled, de-seeded and diced
1 tablespoon chopped fresh parsley

1 Heat the oil in a large frying pan. Season the pork chops with freshly ground black pepper and add to the pan. Seal quickly on both sides then reduce the heat. Cook the chops for a further 3 minutes each side then remove from the pan to a plate. Pour off all the excess fat and wipe out the pan with kitchen paper.
2 Return the pan to the heat and pour in the wine and thyme. Bubble vigorously for 2–3 minutes until the wine is reduced to about one third of its original volume. Stir in the crème fraîche and tomato purée then return the pork chops to the pan. Cook the chops for 5–6 minutes over a medium heat until tender, being careful not to overcook.
3 Stir in the Dijon mustard, diced tomato and chopped parsley. Continue to cook for a further 2–3 minutes until heated through. Serve the chops immediately, with the sauce.

Steak, Kidney & Whisky Pie

SERVES 4
PREPARATION & COOKING TIME: 3¹/₄ hours
FREEZING: recommended

A favourite comfort food but with a modern twist – steak, kidney and onions flavoured with whisky and simmered until tender then topped with puff pastry and baked until golden brown. Serve with mashed potatoes, carrots and swede for a warming winter meal.

2 tablespoons plain flour
675 g (1¹/₂ lb) braising steak, diced
225 g (8 oz) lamb's kidneys, cleaned and chopped
2 tablespoons vegetable oil
1 large onion, sliced thinly
4 tablespoons whisky
425 ml (³/₄ pint) beef stock (page 9)
350 g (12 oz) puff pastry
beaten egg, to glaze
salt and freshly ground black pepper

1 Mix together the flour and seasoning on a plate. Coat the diced steak and kidneys evenly in the seasoned flour.
2 Heat the oil in a large saucepan; fry the meat for 5–6 minutes until browned all over. Transfer to a plate.
3 Add the onion to the pan and fry until soft. Stir in the whisky and simmer until all the liquid has evaporated.
4 Return the meat and juices to the pan and gradually stir in the stock. Season.
5 Cover and simmer gently for 2 hours or until the beef is tender. Leave to cool.
6 Spoon the cooled mixture into a 1-litre (1¾-pint) pie dish.
7 Roll out the pastry 2.5 cm (1 inch) wider than the dish. Cut out a wide strip of pastry to fit the edge of the dish and stick it to the rim with water.
8 Place the pastry lid on to the dish and trim if necessary. Crimp the edges. Cut out leaf shapes from any remaining pastry and stick in place with water. Brush with beaten egg. Make a slit in the top.
9 Bake at Gas Mark 6/electric oven 200°C/ fan oven 180°C for 30–40 minutes until risen and golden.

Lasagne

SERVES 4–6

PREPARATION & COOKING TIME: 15 minutes + 30 minutes
for salting the aubergine + 1¼ hours

FREEZING: recommended

*Layers of pasta sheets, meat sauce and cheese sauce make up
this traditional Italian main course. Aubergine is included in
the meat sauce in this version for an added flavour. Serve
with rocket leaves drizzled with balsamic vinegar and a little
extra virgin olive oil.*

1 medium aubergine

25 g (1 oz) butter

1 garlic clove, crushed

350 g (12 oz) minced beef

1 teaspoon plain flour

350 g (12 oz) tomatoes, skinned and chopped

2 tablespoons tomato purée

300 ml (½ pint) dry white wine

2 teaspoons dried mixed herbs

225 g (8 oz) no pre-cook dried lasagne

salt and freshly ground black pepper

FOR THE CHEESE SAUCE:

25 g (1 oz) butter

25 g (1 oz) plain flour

300 ml (½ pint) milk

115 g (4 oz) Cheddar cheese, grated

1 Slice the aubergine and sprinkle with salt, leave for 30
minutes, pat dry.

2 Heat the butter in a large frying-pan and fry the aubergine
slices and garlic together until soft.

3 Add the minced beef and fry until brown. Stir in the flour
and cook for 2 minutes.

4 Add the tomatoes, tomato purée, wine and herbs, season
and bring to the boil, simmer for 30 minutes.

5 Make the cheese sauce, melt the butter in a medium pan.
Stir in the flour and cook for 1 minute, remove from the
heat and gradually mix in the milk. Return to the heat and
bring to the boil stirring continuously. Remove from the
heat and stir in half the cheese.

6 Grease a large shallow ovenproof dish.

7 Arrange a layer of lasagne on the base of the dish, top with
half the meat sauce, then half the cheese sauce. Repeat the
layers and sprinkle with the remaining grated cheese.

8 Bake at Gas Mark 5/electric oven 190°C/fan oven 170°C
for 30–40 minutes until golden brown.

Beef Olives

SERVES 4
PREPARATION & COOKING TIME: 2½ hours
FREEZING: recommended

A time-honoured dish of slices of beef rolled around a simple vegetable stuffing. They look really impressive, but are quick and easy to prepare.

450 g (1 lb) topside of beef
2 medium carrots, diced finely
1 large onion, diced finely
1 teaspoon dried mixed herbs
2 tablespoons tomato purée
1 tablespoon Worcestershire sauce
2 teaspoons cornflour blended with a little cold water
300 ml (½ pint) beef stock (page ??)
salt and freshly ground black pepper
1 tablespoon finely chopped fresh parsley, to garnish

1 Slice the topside into four thick slices. Place each slice between greaseproof paper and flatten it by bashing it with a rolling pin.
2 Sprinkle the slices with salt and pepper.
3 In a bowl mix together the carrots, onion, herbs, tomato purée, Worcestershire sauce, blended cornflour and 4 tablespoons of the stock.
4 Divide the stuffing mixture between the flattened slices and roll each up into a neat parcel. Tie each parcel securely with string.
5 Place the olives in a shallow roasting dish and pour in the remaining stock. Cover the dish tightly with foil and cook at Gas Mark 4/electric oven 180°C/fan oven 160°C for 1½–2 hours or until the meat is really tender.
6 To serve, remove the string from each beef olive and garnish with parsley.

Oriental Beef

SERVES 4 ★ ▼
PREPARATION & COOKING TIME: 25 minutes
FREEZING: not recommended

This is a delicious, different and easy way to cook fillet steak. It's very good served with noodles and a green salad.

1 small fresh green chilli, halved and de-seeded (optional)
1 lemon grass stalk, bruised
1 chicken stock cube
4 thin slices of fresh ginger
1 garlic clove, crushed
2 x 175 g (6 oz) fillet steaks, trimmed of all fat
2 tablespoons sesame oil
cooked Chinese noodles, to serve

1 Put the chilli, lemon grass, stock cube, ginger, garlic and 300 ml (½ pint) water in a frying pan. Bring to the boil, stirring well to melt the stock cube.
2 Pop in the steaks, making sure they are completely covered with the stock. Poach in barely simmering stock for 4 minutes (for medium rare).

3 Remove the steaks and keep warm, resting on kitchen paper. Boil the stock to reduce to about 4 tablespoons. With a slotted spoon remove the flavourings and stir in the oil.
3 Thinly slice the steaks, arrange on top of the noodles and pour the sauce over.

Venison & Chestnut Casserole

SERVES 4–6
PREPARATION & COOKING TIME: 2–2½ hours
FREEZING: recommended

This rich and tasty dish is lovely made with fresh chestnuts, but can also be made with dried or canned – simply add them to the casserole in step 4. Serve the casserole with mashed potato and a selection of vegetables.

18 fresh chestnuts
3 tablespoons olive oil
3 shallots, chopped finely
4 rashers unsmoked streaky bacon, chopped
3 celery sticks, chopped
25 g (1 oz) plain flour
675 g (1½ lb) venison, diced
425 ml (¾ pint) beef stock (page 9)
150 ml (¼ pint) red wine
8 juniper berries, crushed lightly
3 tablespoons Grand Marnier
salt and freshly ground black pepper

1 To prepare the fresh chestnuts, make a slit in each one, place in a pan of boiling water and simmer for 10 minutes. Remove a couple at a time and carefully remove the outer and inner skin. If the inner skin remains, place the chestnuts in fresh boiling water and boil for a further 3 minutes, the skin will then rub off easily.
2 Heat the oil in a large frying-pan or deep pan and fry the shallots gently until cooked.
3 Stir in the bacon and celery and cook for 3–4 minutes.
4 Mix together the flour and seasoning and coat the venison in the seasoned flour. Add to the pan and fry until browned on all surfaces.
5 Stir in the stock and wine and bring to the boil, add the chestnuts, juniper berries and Grand Marnier.
6 Place in a casserole dish, cover and cook at Gas Mark 3/electric oven 170°C/fan oven 150°C for 1½–1¾ hours or until the meat is tender.

Spicy Beef Stir-fry *(below)*

SERVES 4 ▼
PREPARATION & COOKING TIME: 35 minutes
FREEZING: not recommended

350 g (12 oz) lean rump steak, sliced finely
1½ teaspoons Chinese five spice powder
2 teaspoons cornflour
1 tablespoon vegetable oil
1 onion, sliced
1 garlic clove, chopped finely
1 fresh red chilli, de-seeded and chopped finely
4-cm (1½-inch) piece of fresh root ginger, peeled and chopped finely
1 red pepper, de-seeded and sliced
1 green pepper, de-seeded and sliced
125 g (4½ oz) baby sweetcorn, sliced on the diagonal
150 ml (¼ pint) beef stock (page 9)
3 tablespoons oyster sauce
3 spring onions, sliced finely
freshly ground black pepper

Stir-frying is an excellent cooking method for retaining the maximum amount of nutrients in the food. Although cooked at high temperatures, the whole process takes no more than a few minutes so vegetables stay crunchy and valuable vitamins and minerals are not lost. Always prepare the ingredients before starting to cook to ensure that cooking flows as rapidly as possible. Serve with cooked noodles or rice.

1 Toss the sliced rump steak with the five spice powder and cornflour to coat the meat. Set aside.
2 Heat the oil in a wok or large frying pan and stir-fry the onion slices for 2 minutes. Add the garlic, chilli and root ginger and fry for a further minute. Finally, add the sliced peppers and baby sweetcorn and stir-fry until the vegetables are just tender – no more than 3–4 minutes. Transfer the vegetables to a plate and keep warm.
3 Add the sliced beef to the wok and stir-fry to brown the beef completely. Pour in the stock and the oyster sauce and cook for about 2 minutes until the stock thickens slightly. Season with freshly ground black pepper.
4 Return the vegetables to the wok and stir-fry for a further 2 minutes until everything is heated through. Take care not to overcook. Serve the stir-fry immediately, sprinkled with the sliced spring onions.

Baked Custard Tart
with Caramel Oranges *(right)*

(right)

SERVES 6–8
PREPARATION & COOKING TIME: 25 minutes + 1 hour
  chilling + 70–75 minutes baking
FREEZING: not recommended

*This is a large version of the individual custard tarts. The filling
should still tremble slightly when you gently shake the pastry
case; the soft, creamy texture is what really makes this pudding.
The caramel oranges offset the delicate flavour of this tart with
their bittersweet taste.*

FOR THE PASTRY:
pâte sucrée made using 115g (4 oz) plain flour (page 10)

FOR THE FILLING:
300 ml (1/2 pint) single cream
150 ml (1/4 pint) full cream milk
1/2 cinnamon stick, crushed slightly
1/4 teaspoon ground mace
2 large eggs, plus 2 large egg yolks, beaten
50 g (2 oz) caster sugar
freshly grated nutmeg

FOR THE CARAMEL ORANGES:
175 g (6 oz) granulated sugar
3 oranges

1 Line a deep 20-cm (8-inch) loose-bottomed, flan tin with
   the pâte sucrée and chill for 1 hour.
2 Preheat the oven to Gas Mark 5/electric oven 190°C/fan
   oven 170°C. Place a baking sheet in the centre of the oven.
3 On the warmed baking sheet, bake the pastry case blind
   for 15 minutes. Remove the foil or paper and beans and
   continue cooking for a further 5–10 minutes, until the
   pastry is golden.
4 Meanwhile, pour the cream and milk into a medium
   saucepan. Put in the piece of cinnamon stick and the mace
   and bring slowly to the boil.
5 Whisk together the eggs and yolks with the sugar until it is
   all combined. Strain the hot cream and gradually pour it
   on to the egg mixture, whisking all the time. Strain this
   again into a jug.
6 Reduce the oven temperature to Gas Mark 2/electric oven
   150°C/fan oven 130°C. Half slide the pastry case into the
   oven. Carefully pour in the custard and sprinkle it with
   nutmeg. Slide the shelf back and cook for about 35
   minutes, or until the filling is just set.
7 Meanwhile make the caramel oranges. In a heavy-based
   saucepan, dissolve the sugar over a low heat with 150 ml
   (1/4 pint) water. Increase the heat and bubble hard for
   about 15 minutes until you have a golden caramel. You
   will need to keep an eye on it towards the end as it colours
   very quickly.
8 Rest the pan in a bowl of cold water, to prevent the
   caramel cooking further, and with your free hand
   (wrapped in a tea towel for protection) carefully pour in
   another 150 ml (1/4 pint) warm water, swilling the pan
   around to mix it in. Leave to cool.

9 Peel the oranges, removing the pith as well as the skin,
   and slice them. Place the slices in a glass serving bowl and
   pour over the cooled caramel.
10 Serve the tart warm with the caramel oranges.

Little Fig & Orange
Couscous Puddings

SERVES 4
PREPARARTION & COOKING TIME: 1 1/4 hours
FREEZING: not recommended

*These light little puddings are an ideal end to a winter meal.
Vary the flavours to suit your tastes: apricot and orange or
date and apple juice are both good. Fresh orange juice gives
a better flavour than the concentrated variety.*

110 g (4 oz) ready-to-eat dried figs, chopped
475 ml (17 fl oz) fresh orange juice
100 g (3 1/2 oz) couscous
1/2 teaspoon ground dried coriander
low fat natural yogurt or low fat Greek yogurt, to serve

1 Prepare a steamer so that it is hot when the puddings are
   ready.
2 Put the figs and orange juice into a pan, bring to the boil
   and then cover and simmer for 3 minutes.
3 Meanwhile, grease four individual heatproof moulds, cups
   or ramekins.
4 Remove half the fruit with a slotted spoon and divide this
   between the moulds.
5 Add the couscous and coriander to the remaining fruit and
   juice. Bring back to the boil, turn off the heat and cover.
   Leave to stand for 10 minutes.
6 Divide the couscous mixture between the moulds and
   cover tightly with foil.
7 Steam for 30 minutes. Tip from the moulds on to
   individual plates and serve with low fat natural yogurt or
   low fat Greek yogurt.

Clementines in Orange Jelly with a Port Syllabub *(above)*

SERVES 6
PREPARATION TIME: 20 minutes + 30 minutes chilling
FREEZING: not recommended

This pretty dessert includes festive ingredients but in a much lighter style than many traditional Christmas desserts. The syllabub complements the clementine jelly beautifully.

4 clementines, peeled
1 packet of orange jelly
150 ml (¹/₄ pint) freshly squeezed orange juice

FOR THE PORT SYLLABUB:
150 ml (¹/₄ pint) ruby port
juice of 1 lemon
65 g (2¹/₂ oz) caster sugar
225 ml (8 fl oz) double cream

1 Segment the clementines and cut each segment in half. Divide the clementines between six glass sundae dishes or wine glasses.
2 Make up the jelly with 300 ml (¹/₂ pint) of boiling water and, once it has dissolved, add the orange juice. Pour the jelly over the clementines and chill for 30 minutes or longer, until the jelly has set.
3 Place the port, lemon juice and sugar in a large bowl and stir until the sugar has dissolved. Stir in the cream and whisk until the cream is just beginning to hold its shape. Pour over the jellies and refrigerate until ready to serve.

Chocolate & Clementine Cheesecake

SERVES 8–10
PREPARATION & COOKING TIME: 2–2¹/₂ hours
FREEZING: not recommended

This is a wonderful dessert to offer chocolate lovers at Christmas time. The clementines add a seasonal flavour and are natural partners for chocolate. It is very rich so serve in fairly small wedges.

225 g (8 oz) clementines, unpeeled
25 g (1 oz) caster sugar
175 g (6 oz) chocolate digestive biscuits, crushed
50 g (2 oz) butter, melted
675 g (1¹/₂ lb) curd cheese
3 large eggs
80 g (3 oz) soft brown sugar
225 g (8 oz) plain chocolate, broken into squares
150 ml (¹/₄ pint) single cream

TO DECORATE:
whipped cream
1 peeled clementine
cocoa powder

1 Wash the clementines and place them in a saucepan. Cover them with water and bring to the boil. Simmer for 25 minutes until the fruit is tender. Drain the clementines and purée them with the caster sugar. Set aside.
2 Preheat the oven to Gas Mark 2/electric oven 150°C/fan oven 130°C. Combine the biscuit crumbs and butter and spoon this into a greased 20-cm (8-inch) spring form tin. Press down (a potato masher does this well) and place the tin in the fridge to chill.
3 Beat the curd cheese, eggs and soft brown sugar together.
4 Melt the chocolate and cream together in a bowl over a pan of gently simmering water. Allow the chocolate mixture to cool and then fold it into the curd cheese mixture.
5 Spoon the cheesecake mixture over the biscuit base. Put dollops of the clementine purée on top of the cheesecake and swirl with a skewer or pointed knife.
6 Bake in the oven for 1¹/₄–1¹/₂ hours until it is set. Allow the cheesecake to cool in the switched-off oven. Chill in the fridge for at least 2 hours. To decorate, spread whipped cream over the surface, arrange some clementine segments on top and dust with sifted cocoa powder.

Apricot Rice Fool

SERVES 4–6 ♥ ★
PREPARATION TIME: 25 minutes
FREEZING: not recommended

*This is basically a dessert made using storecupboard
ingredients. It also is a very healthy one, with the exception of
the cream, which could be replaced with yoghurt.*

115 g (4 oz) ready-to-eat dried apricots
150 ml ($^1/_4$ pint) orange juice
575 ml (1 pint) fresh milk
25 g (1 oz) caster sugar
50 g (2 oz) ground rice
300 ml ($^1/_2$ pint) whipping cream, lightly whipped
toasted, flaked almonds, to decorate (optional)

1 Place the apricots and orange juice in a saucepan, bring to
   the boil, cover and simmer gently for 5 minutes. Allow to
   cool and then liquidise.
2 Place the milk and sugar in a saucepan and gradually stir
   in the ground rice. Bring to the boil gradually, stirring all
   the time and then simmer very gently for 6 minutes (or
   according to the pack instructions), stirring from time to
   time. Remove from the heat and allow to cool. Fold in a
   tablespoon of the apricot purée.
3 Fold the whipped cream into the rice mixture – if the rice
   seems quite thick, it would be an idea to fold in a
   tablespoon of the cream first, to loosen the mixture.
   Divide the remaining apricot purée between glass dessert
   dishes or wine glasses and then spoon the rice mixture on
   top. Chill until ready to serve. Decorate with toasted,
   flaked almonds, if wished.

Thai Rice Pudding Brûlées

SERVES 6
PREPARATION & COOKING TIME: 40 minutes
FREEZING: not recommended

*This version of rice pudding uses rice flakes to give a creamier
texture and lime, coconut and cardamom to give a subtle Thai
flavour. The brûlée topping gives it an up-to-date dimension.*

50 g (2 oz) flaked pudding rice
50 g (2 oz) caster sugar
1 lime
3 cardamom pods, crushed open
300 ml ($^1/_2$ pint) semi-skimmed milk
300 ml ($^1/_2$ pint) coconut milk
300 ml ($^1/_2$ pint) double cream, whipped to soft peaks
demerara sugar

1 Place the rice in a saucepan with the sugar, a few pieces of
   the lime zest, cardamoms and both milks. Bring to the boil
   over a moderate heat, stirring from time to time. Simmer
   over a low heat for about 15–20 minutes, stirring every
   now and then to prevent it from sticking, until the rice is
   cooked and the milk has been absorbed.

2 Allow to cool and then remove the lime zest and the
   cardamoms.
3 Fold in the cream, followed by the juice of the lime, and
   spoon into six ramekin dishes. Sprinkle demerara sugar
   generously over the surfaces of the puddings and place
   under a hot grill until the sugar has caramelised.
4 Chill for at least an hour or until ready to serve.

Linzertorte *(right)*

SERVES 8
PREPARATION & COOKING TIME: 20 minutes + at least 1
    hour chilling + 30 minutes baking
FREEZING: recommended

*This Austrian tart takes its name from the town of Linz. Tortes
can be defined as somewhere between a biscuit and a tart. This
one may be likened to an extremely up-market lattice jam tart,
subtly flavoured with cinnamon and lemon zest. Traditionally it
is served with whipped cream not just as a dessert, but often
with coffee or tea. The dough is very soft and therefore quite
tricky to handle, so you could always make it up the night
before, refrigerate, and then bake in the morning to serve it
warm with coffee – wonderful on a cold winter's day.*

115 g (4 oz) unsalted butter, softened
80 g (3 oz) caster sugar
grated zest of $^1/_2$ lemon
80 g (3 oz) plain flour
$^1/_2$ teaspoon ground cinnamon
80 g (3 oz) ground almonds or ground hazelnuts
2 large egg yolks
a few drops almond or vanilla essence
225 g (8 oz) red jam or jelly (raspberry, cranberry or redcurrant)
icing sugar, for dusting

1 Cream the butter, sugar and lemon zest until the mixture is
   pale and fluffy.
2 Mix together the flour, cinnamon and ground nuts.
   Gradually work them into the creamed mixture,
   alternating with the egg yolks. Add the almond or vanilla
   essence. Wrap in clingfilm and chill for at least 1 hour.
3 Preheat the oven to Gas Mark 5/electric oven 190°C/fan
   oven 170°C. Place a baking sheet on the middle shelf for
   the tart.
4 Press three-quarters of the dough into the base and 2.5 cm
   (1 inch) up the sides of a 20-cm (8-inch) loose-bottomed,
   shallow flan tin. Spread jam or jelly over the base. Add a
   little more flour to the remaining dough, to make it more
   manageable, and roll it out fairly thinly. Cut it into strips
   and lay the strips across the tart to make a lattice effect.
   Trim the ends and seal the edges, by pressing a fork all the
   way around the edge.
5 On the warmed baking sheet, bake for about 30 minutes,
   until golden. Dust with sifted icing sugar and serve warm.

Apple, Apricot & Amaretti Layer Dessert

SERVES 4
PREPARATION & COOKING TIME: 30 minutes + 1 hour chilling
FREEZING: not recommended

Plenty of soluble fibre is found in this dessert, but don't over process the fruit into a too smooth purée because it is nice to have some texture from the apricots. This dessert layers up very attractively in glass tumblers.

500 g (1lb 2 oz) apples, peeled, cored and sliced
225 g (8 oz) ready-soaked apricots, chopped roughly
2 tablespoons amaretto liqueur
125 g (4½ oz) amaretti biscuits, crushed
250 g (9 oz) fromage frais

1 Place the apples and apricots in a pan and add 100 ml (3½ fl oz) water. Cook gently until the apples are pulpy and the apricots have softened. Allow to cool and then place in a food processor and process to a rough purée. Stir in the amaretto liqueur.
2 Put a layer of crushed amaretti biscuits in the base of each of four glasses. Using half of the fruit purée, put an equal layer in each glass.
3 Reserve 4 dessertspoons of the fromage frais, then divide the rest equally between the glasses.
4 Reserve 1 tablespoon of the crushed biscuits and layer the rest equally over the fromage frais. Divide the fruit purée between the glasses to create the last layer.
5 Place a dessertspoon of the reserved fromage frais in the centre of each and sprinkle with the last of the crushed biscuits. Chill the dessert for an hour before serving.

Date & Apple Streusel Pie

SERVES 10–12
PREPARATION & COOKING TIME: 30 minutes + 30 minutes chilling + 35–40 minutes cooking
FREEZING: recommended

Oats, breadcrumbs and toasted hazelnuts make a delectable light and crunchy topping for this tart. It cuts very well so makes an ideal choice for a buffet, being equally delicious hot or cold. Serve with a generous spoonful of West Country clotted cream.

FOR THE PASTRY:
shortcrust pastry made using 115 g (4 oz) flour (page 10)

FOR THE FILLING:
115 g (4 oz) stoned dates, chopped roughly
juice of 1 orange
40 g (1½ oz) caster sugar
1 tablespoon cornflour
550 g (1 lb 4 oz) eating apples

FOR THE STREUSEL TOPPING:
50 g (2 oz) fresh wholemeal breadcrumbs
50 g (2 oz) rolled oats
50 g (2 oz) light muscovado sugar
25 g (1 oz) chopped roasted hazelnuts
50 g (2 oz) unsalted butter, melted

1 Line a 23-cm (9-inch) loose-bottomed, deep flan tin with the shortcrust pastry and chill for 30 minutes.
2 Preheat the oven to Gas Mark 6/electric oven 200°C/fan oven 180°C. Place a baking sheet on the middle shelf of the oven.
3 Put the dates and orange juice in a small saucepan and simmer for about 5 minutes, until the juice has evaporated and the dates are soft. Allow to cool.
4 Combine the sugar and cornflour. Peel, core and thinly slice the apples. Stir the cornflour mixture into the sliced apples. Arrange a layer of apple over the pastry base. Now dot the date mixture on top and then cover with the remaining apple slices.
5 To make the streusel topping, stir the breadcrumbs, oats, sugar and hazelnuts into the butter. Scatter this over the apples.
6 Bake on the warmed baking sheet for 35–45 minutes, until the crumble is golden and the pastry is cooked – check the topping after 20–25 minutes, and cover with foil if it is sufficiently browned.

Apple, Date & Walnut Pudding

SERVES 6
PREPARATION & COOKING TIME: 1 hour
FREEZING: recommended

This would be a perfect dessert to serve after a Sunday lunch – it could be put in the oven as you sit down to eat your roast. You could substitute pears or plums for the apples and vary the nuts accordingly.

125 g (4¹/₂ oz) self-raising flour
1 teaspoon ground cinnamon
1 teaspoon baking powder
100 g (3¹/₂ oz) caster sugar
3 tablespoons vegetable oil
3 tablespoons milk
3 medium eggs, separated
625 g (1 lb 6 oz) Bramley apples, peeled, cored and cut into chunks
50 g (2 oz) dates, cut into small pieces
25 g (1 oz) walnut pieces

1 Preheat the oven to Gas Mark 5/electric oven 190°C/fan oven 170°C.
2 Sift the flour, cinnamon and baking powder into a bowl and stir in the caster sugar. Whisk the oil, milk and egg yolks together and pour over the flour mixture. Beat until smooth.
3 Whisk the egg whites until they are stiff.
4 Fold a spoonful into the mixture to loosen it and then gently fold in the remainder, followed by the apples, dates and walnuts.
5 Spoon into a greased 23-cm (9-inch) flan or gratin dish, level the surface and bake in the oven for about 40 minutes, until golden brown and firm to the touch (you may need to cover the top loosely with foil if it browns too quickly).
6 Serve warm, with custard or cream.

Creamy Date & Walnut Bombe

SERVES 6–8
PREPARATION TIME: 25–30 minutes + 2 hours chilling
FREEZING: recommended

This pudding improves on keeping and freezes very well.

225 g (8 oz) ricotta cheese
80 g (3 oz) caster sugar
80 g (3 oz) unsalted butter, melted
175 g (6 oz) dried dates, cut into small pieces
50 g (2 oz) walnuts, chopped
grated zest and juice of 3 oranges
11.7 g sachet of gelatine
8 trifle sponges, each cut horizontally into 3 slices

TO DECORATE:
150 ml (¹/₄ pint) whipping cream, whipped
selection of seasonal fruit, prepared as necessary

1 Combine the ricotta, sugar and butter and mix well. Fold in the dates, walnuts and orange zest. Dissolve the gelatine in 2 tablespoons of water over a pan of hot water or by heating in the microwave for 20 seconds. Allow to cool and then add to the citrus juices in a jug.
2 Place 3–4 sponge slices in the base of a 1.1-litre (2-pint) pudding basin and spread a thinnish layer of the cheese mixture on top. Continue to layer, finishing with sponge to fit neatly on top. Strain the orange mixture and then pour very carefully over the pudding, making sure that the juices reach the bottom – this can be done by pulling back the sides with a knife. Chill for 2 hours, until set.
3 To serve, dip the basin in hot water and invert on to the serving plate. Spread the cream evenly all over the surface. Extra cream could be piped around the base. Decorate with fruit.

Coffee & Walnut Marshmallow Mousse with a Mocha Sauce

SERVES 4–6
PREPARATION TIME: 20 minutes + 45 minutes chilling
FREEZING: not recommended

Marshmallows contain gelatine and so they act as a setting agent as well as a sweetener for this dessert. Pour over some mocha sauce once it has set.

150 g (5 oz) marshmallows, halved
100 ml (3¹/₂ fl oz) hot strong black coffee
200 g tub of soft cheese
150 ml (¹/₂ pint) double cream, whipped to soft peaks
25 g (1 oz) walnuts, chopped

FOR THE SAUCE:
2 heaped tablespoons granulated sugar
1¹/₂ tablespoons cocoa powder
1¹/₂ tablespoons strong black coffee

1 Place the marshmallows and coffee in a large bowl over a pan of hot water and leave until the marshmallows have dissolved, stirring from time to time. Allow to cool a little and then sit the bowl in iced water until on the point of setting.
2 Fold in the soft cheese, the cream and walnuts. Spoon into dessert or wine glasses and chill for 45 minutes.
3 To make the sauce, place the sugar and 100 ml (3¹/₂ fl oz) of water in a saucepan, bring to the boil and simmer for a minute. Add the cocoa and whisk until it has been incorporated and the sauce is smooth. Remove from the heat, whisk in the coffee and allow to cool. Spread the sauce to cover the surface of the mousses completely and serve.

Chocolate Sauce

SERVES 4
PREPARATION & COOKING TIME: 10 minutes
FREEZING: not recommended

3 tablespoons cornflour
1¹/₂ tablespoons cocoa powder
1¹/₂ tablespoons sugar, or to taste
425 ml (³/₄ pint) skimmed or semi-skimmed milk

1 Mix the cornflour, cocoa and sugar with a little of the measured milk to form a smooth paste.
2 Heat the remaining milk in a saucepan to just below boiling point.
3 Pour the hot milk on to the blended mixture, stirring well. Ensure the liquid is well mixed.
4 Return the mixture to the saucepan and bring to the boil, stirring constantly.
5 Reduce the heat and allow the sauce to simmer for 20–30 seconds, still stirring. Check for sweetness, adding more sugar if necessary.
6 Pour into a serving jug or dish and serve immediately.

Steamed Chocolate & Pear Puddings *(above)*

SERVES 4
PREPARATION & COOKING TIME: 1 hour + 15 minutes
FREEZING: recommended

Serve this warming winter pudding with Chocolate Sauce.

1 pear, weighing about 175 g (6 oz)
1 teaspoon lemon juice
55 g (2 oz) low fat spread
55 g (2 oz) light soft brown sugar
1 egg, beaten
100 g (3¹/₂ oz) self-raising flour
¹/₂ teaspoon baking powder
25 g (1 oz) cocoa powder
55 g (2 oz) golden syrup, warmed

1 Peel, core and dice the pear and toss in the lemon juice to prevent it from browning.
2 Cream together the low fat spread and sugar and then beat in the egg.
3 Sieve together the flour, baking powder and cocoa. Fold these into the creamed mixture.
4 Fold in the golden syrup and the diced pear.
5 Spoon the mixture into a greased 600-ml (1-pint) pudding basin or four individual basins and cover either with a greased lid or with a double thickness of greaseproof paper, well secured.
6 Place in a steamer and steam for 45 minutes for the individual puddings, 1 hour for the large pudding, or until a skewer inserted into the centre comes out clean.

Pear & Walnut Tart

SERVES 8–10
PREPARATION & COOKING TIME: 25 minutes + 1 hour chilling + 40–45 minutes cooking
FREEZING: not recommended

This is one of those tarts that you'd see in the window of a pâtisserie or coffee house to tempt you inside. Pear fans, artistically arranged over a walnut batter, glisten with an apricot glaze. Ground almonds can be substituted for the walnuts and apples, and apricots or plums work equally as well as pears. Serve it warm with a generous dollop of crème fraîche.

FOR THE PASTRY:
pâte sucrée made using 175 g (6 oz) flour (page 10)

FOR THE FILLING:
80 g (3 oz) unsalted butter
80 g (3 oz) caster sugar
$^1/_2$ teaspoon vanilla essence
2 large eggs, lightly beaten
80 g (3 oz) walnuts, ground in a liquidizer
3–4 ripe pears, Comice are ideal

FOR THE GLAZE:
2 tablespoons apricot jam, sieved
1 tablespoon lemon juice

1 Line a 23-cm (9-inch) loose-bottomed, deep flan tin with the pâte sucrée. Chill for 1 hour.
2 Preheat the oven to Gas Mark 5/electric oven 190°C/fan oven 170°C. Put a baking sheet on the middle shelf for the tart.
3 To make the filling, cream the butter and sugar with the vanilla essence until the mixture is pale. Fold in the beaten eggs along with the ground walnuts, a little at a time (this helps prevent the mixture from curdling).
4 Spread the walnut paste over the base of the pastry case. Peel, halve and core the pears. Cut them thinly into 8–10 slices, leaving 1 cm ($^1/_2$ inch) uncut at the top so that the sections are held together. Gently ease out the pear halves into fans, and arrange them on top of the filling.
5 Bake the tart on the heated baking sheet for 15 minutes. Reduce the oven temperature to Gas Mark 4/electric oven 180°C/fan oven 160°C and cook for a further 25–30 minutes.
6 Blend together the apricot jam and lemon juice. Remove the tart from the oven and, while still hot, brush over the glaze – this prevents the pears from discolouring.

Pear & Cranberry Crackers

SERVES 6
PREPARATION & COOKING TIME: 1 hour
FREEZING: not recommended

These filo pastry crackers make a novel alternative to Christmas pudding. They can be made in advance and then simply popped into the oven to warm through. Serve them with a brandy custard – just add a good splash of brandy to custard and stir in.

It is worth noting that you should keep the remaining filo pastry sheets covered while you are making the crackers, otherwise they will dry out.

18 small sheets filo pastry (such as Cypressa's, from Waitrose)
80 g (3 oz) butter, melted
caster sugar

FOR THE FILLING:
grated zest and juice of 1 lemon
50 g (2 oz) caster sugar, plus extra for sprinkling
2 tablespoons ground almonds
1 teaspoon ground cinnamon
4 large pears, peeled, cored and diced
115 g (4 oz) fresh cranberries
50 g (2 oz) chopped walnuts

1 Preheat the oven to Gas Mark 5/electric oven 190°C/fan oven 170°C.
2 Combine the filling ingredients in a large bowl and mix thoroughly.
3 Lay one sheet of pastry on the work surface, brush with the melted butter and repeat with two more sheets. Spoon a sixth of the pear and cranberry mixture on to the long side nearest to you, leaving a gap at either end.
4 Roll up the pastry to enclose the filling – you should end up with the seam underneath. Pinch each end to create a cracker. Brush with the melted butter and lay on a baking sheet. Repeat to make six crackers.
5 Sprinkle each cracker with caster sugar and bake in the oven for about half an hour. Check them after 10–15 minutes; you will probably need to cover the 'ends' with pieces of foil to prevent them from burning before the centres of the crackers are cooked.
6 Serve hot or warm, with brandy custard.

Apricot & Brandy Trifle

SERVES 6–8
PREPARATION TIME: 40 minutes + 2 hours chilling
FREEZING: not recommended

Until recently, trifles had a dated image and were not served at dinner parties. Thankfully, they have regained their popularity. This recipe uses ready-made custard – this is generally so good nowadays that point in making your own.

24 ready-to-eat dried apricots
150 ml (¹/₂ pint) fresh orange juice
75 ml (5 tablespoons) brandy
1 packet of trifle sponges
apricot conserve
500 g carton of custard
300 ml (¹/₂ pint) whipping cream, whipped
toasted flaked almonds and dried apricots, to decorate

1 Place the apricots and orange juice in a small saucepan, bring to the boil and simmer very gently, covered, for 15–20 minutes, until very tender. Add the brandy and allow to cool.
2 Split the sponges in half, horizontally, and spread generously with the apricot conserve. Sandwich together again and cut into cubes. Put in the base of a glass trifle bowl and spoon the apricots and all the orange and brandy juices on top. Pour the custard on top and level the surface.
3 Spread two-thirds of the cream over the custard and spoon the remainder into a piping bag fitted with a star nozzle. Sprinkle the surface with the flaked almonds. Pipe cream rosettes around the edges and decorate them with dried apricot pieces. Chill for a couple of hours.

Exotic Fruit Trifle

SERVES 6–8
PREPARATION TIME: 30 minutes + 2 hours chilling
FREEZING: not recommended

This variation on the traditional trifle will have your guests trying to guess the ingredients in the 'cream' topping. Including natural yogurt in the topping makes it a lot lighter.

1 packet of trifle sponges
apricot jam
75 ml (5 tablespoons) rum or sweet sherry
2 passion fruit, halved and the pulp removed
250 g (9 oz) prepared papaya (pawpaw), cut into pieces
1 kiwi fruit, peeled and cut into wedges
155 g bar of white chocolate (Lindt is recommended), broken into pieces
300 ml (¹/₂ pint) whipping cream, whipped to soft peaks
500 g (1 lb 2 oz) natural yogurt
1 large ripe mango, peeled and the flesh puréed

TO DECORATE:
slices of fresh mango and kiwi fruit
grated plain chocolate

1 Cut the trifle sponges in half horizontally, spread with jam, sandwich together and cut into cubes. Place in the base of a glass bowl and sprinkle the rum or sherry over the sponges.
2 Scatter the passion fruit pulp over the sponges, followed by the papaya and kiwi fruit.
3 Melt the chocolate in a bowl over a pan of barely simmering water. Allow to cool. Combine half the cream with the yogurt and the mango purée. Fold in the melted white chocolate.
4 Spoon the white chocolate cream over the trifle base. Spread or pipe the remaining cream on top and decorate with the mango, kiwi fruit and grated plain chocolate. Chill for at least 2 hours or until ready to serve.

Chocolate Log

SERVES 8–10
PREPARATION & COOKING TIME: 30 minutes + chilling overnight
FREEZING: recommended

This log will look very impressive served after a Christmas meal and the fact that it freezes so well means that you can prepare it well in advance. It is quite rich so it is best to serve in small slices with some brandy sauce or a fruit compote.

115 g (4 oz) dried berries and cherries (or dried cranberries)
3 tablespoons brandy or kirsch
200 g (7 oz) cream cheese
175 g (6 oz) plain chocolate (at least 70% cocoa solids), melted
300 ml (¹/₂ pint) double cream, whipped
16 digestive biscuits
icing sugar and Christmas decorations, to decorate

1 Place the dried berries and cherries and brandy or kirsch in a food processor and blend until the fruit is finely chopped. Add the cream cheese and blend again. Transfer to a bowl and stir in the chocolate. Fold in the cream thoroughly.
2 Use about half this mixture to sandwich the biscuits together – it is easier if you do so in three stacks – and then press them together to create a log on a tray covered with baking parchment.
3 Use the remaining mixture to cover the log completely, making sure that no biscuits are visible. To finish the log-effect, use a fork to make a pattern that resembles tree bark. Chill overnight.
4 Just before serving, dust with icing sugar and arrange Christmas decorations on top.

Christmas Star Trifle *(below)*

SERVES: 6–8
PREPARATION TIME: 20 minutes + chilling
FREEZING: not recommended

This is quick to prepare using good quality convenience products – the inclusion of chocolate in the custard really complements the orange in the poached cranberries.

3 chocolate muffins, standard size
4 tablespoons cranberry sauce
115 g (4 oz) fresh cranberries
45 ml (3 tablespoons) fresh orange juice
190 g (6¹/₂ oz) caster sugar
500 g carton of custard
115 g (4 oz) Green and Black's Maya Gold chocolate, broken into pieces
150 ml (¹/₄ pint) ruby port
juice of 1 lemon
225 ml (8 fl oz) double cream
cocoa powder, to decorate

1 Cut each muffin into three and spread each slice with cranberry sauce. Arrange in the base of a glass trifle bowl.
2 Place the cranberries, orange juice, 3 tablespoons water and 115 g (4 oz) of the caster sugar in a saucepan; bring to the boil and simmer gently until the cranberries are cooked. Strain the cranberries, reserving the liquid, and spoon them over the muffins. Sprinkle 3 tablespoons of the reserved liquid over the cranberries and muffins.
3 Empty the custard into a saucepan and heat very gently until it is on the point of boiling. Remove from the heat, add the chocolate pieces and stir until the chocolate has melted. Allow to cool and then pour this mixture over the cranberries and chill while you prepare the syllabub.
4 Place the port, lemon juice and remaining sugar in a large bowl and stir until the sugar has dissolved. Add the cream and whisk, starting on a low speed, until the mixture has begun to thicken. Pour this over the trifle.
5 To decorate, cut out about seven stars from card and arrange lightly on the syllabub. Sift cocoa powder all over the surface and carefully lift the pieces of card from the top. Alternatively, you could simply dust the surface with sifted cocoa powder

Festive Pavlova

SERVES 6–8
PREPARATION & COOKING TIME: 30 minutes + 1 hour
  cooking + 1 hour cooling
FREEZING: recommended

Another alternative to Christmas pudding.

FOR THE MERINGUE:
225 g (8 oz) icing sugar
1 tablespoon cocoa powder
2 teaspoons cornflour
4 large egg whites
a pinch of salt
1 teaspoon white wine vinegar

FOR THE TOPPING:
115 g (4 oz) plain chocolate (at least 70% cocoa solids)
250 g can of sweetened chestnut purée
2 tablespoons dark rum or brandy
250 ml (9 fl oz) double cream, whipped to soft peaks

1 Preheat the oven to Gas Mark 1/electric oven 130°C/fan
  oven 110°C. Place a piece of baking parchment on a
  baking sheet and mark a 20-cm (8-inch) circle on it.
2 Sift 3 tablespoons of icing sugar with the cocoa and
  cornflour. Whisk the egg whites in a large bowl until they
  are frothy. Add the salt and continue to whisk until they
  are stiff. Continue to whisk, adding a teaspoon of icing
  sugar at a time, making sure each teaspoon has been
  incorporated before adding the next. Fold in the sugar and
  cocoa mixture and then quickly fold in the vinegar.
3 Spoon or pipe the meringue on to the parchment circle and
  make the sides higher than the centre. Bake in the oven for
  an hour until it is set.
4 Turn off the oven and leave the pavlova in the oven until it
  has cooled – at least an hour. At this stage the pavlova will
  crack – don't worry about this.
5 Melt 80 g (3 oz) of the chocolate in a bowl set over a pan
  of hot water (or you could melt it in the microwave). Put
  the chestnut purée in a bowl together with the rum or
  brandy and beat until it is smooth. Add the melted
  chocolate and mix thoroughly. Fold in half the cream and
  spoon on to the pavlova. Spoon the remaining cream on
  top and grate the remaining chocolate on top of the cream.
  Serve with single cream.

Mince Pies with Citrus Pastry

MAKES 12
PREPARATION & COOKING TIME: 20 minutes + 30 minutes
  chilling + 15 minutes cooking
FREEZING: recommended

*There must have been countless variations of mince pies
concocted over the years – and here is another! Open-topped
tarts look attractive, especially when they feature rich,
glistening mincemeat decorated with a star or holly leaf. If you
are not a fan of marzipan, there will be enough pastry
trimmings left over to stamp out shapes. Serve these warm with
brandy butter or lightly whipped double cream, flavoured with
Cointreau.*

FOR THE PASTRY:
115 g (4 oz) plain flour
grated zest of $^1/_2$ orange + $^1/_2$ lemon
50 g (2 oz) unsalted butter
25 g (1 oz) caster sugar
1 large egg yolk

FOR THE FILLING:
350 g (12 oz) luxury mincemeat
80 g (3 oz) white marzipan

1 Combine the flour and citrus zests in a bowl. Rub in the
  butter and then stir in the sugar. Bind it all to a dough
  with the egg yolk and 1 tablespoon cold water.
2 Roll out the dough on a lightly floured surface. Stamp out
  12 rounds using an 8-cm (3¼-inch) round pastry cutter, re-
  rolling pastry if necessary. Place the rounds in a patty tin.
  Chill for at least 30 minutes.
3 Preheat the oven to Gas Mark 5/electric oven 190°C/fan
  oven 170°C.
4 Spoon a heaped teaspoon of mincemeat into each pastry
  case. Roll out the marzipan on a sugared surface and cut
  out star or holly shapes. Place a shape in the centre of each
  tart.
5 Bake the mince pies in the middle of the oven for about 15
  minutes, or until the pastry is golden.

Black Forest Gâteau (*below*)

SERVES 8–10
PREPARATION & COOKING TIME: 1¼ hours
FREEZING: recommended

A really good Black Forest Gâteau is something special. It is a little time-consuming to make but well worth the effort. It freezes well, but is best decorated with the reserved cherries after it is defrosted.

FOR THE SPONGE:
4 eggs
115 g(4oz) caster sugar
95 g (3½ oz) plain flour, sifted
15 g (½ oz) cocoa powder, sifted
40 g (1½ oz) butter, melted

FOR THE FILLING AND DECORATION:
2 x 425 g tins of black cherries in syrup, drained, reserving 225 ml
    (8 fl oz) syrup
2 tablespoons kirsch
1 tablespoon arrowroot
250 g tub of Quark
300 ml (½ pint) double cream
2 tablespoons icing sugar
150 ml (¼ pint) cream, for piping rosettes
115 g (4 oz) chocolate, to make scrolls

1 Preheat the oven to Gas Mark 4/electric oven 180°C/fan oven 160°C. Grease a 20-cm (8-inch) loose-bottomed tin and line the base with baking parchment.
2 Make the sponge by whisking the eggs and sugar together in a large bowl set over a pan of hot water for about 10 minutes, until the mixture is thick and creamy. Remove the bowl from the heat and continue to whisk for 1 minute. Sift together the flour and cocoa over the surface of the mixture and fold it in gently, using a figure-of-eight action. When it is nearly all incorporated, add the melted butter and mix it in. Pour the mixture into the prepared tin. Bake for 25–30 minutes, until the cake starts coming away from the sides and is fairly firm to the touch.
3 Allow the cake to cool in the tin for 5 minutes and then turn it out on to a cooling rack and allow to cool completely. Cut it twice horizontally to create three equal layers. Place the top layer on a serving plate, cut side up.
4 Mix 2 tablespoons of the reserved cherry syrup with the kirsch and sprinkle this over the three layers. Mix a further 2 tablespoons of the reserved syrup with the arrowroot. In a small saucepan, bring the remaining syrup to boiling point, and then stir in the arrowroot mixture. Heat gently until the syrup thickens. Remove the pan from the heat. Reserve 12 cherries and cut the rest in half. Add the halved cherries to the thickened syrup and allow the mixture to get cold.
5 Place the Quark in a mixing bowl and beat it to loosen it slightly. Whip the cream to soft peaks. Fold a quarter of the cream into the Quark. Spread this evenly on the sponge on the plate and the middle sponge layer. Divide the cherry mixture between these two sponge layers, but don't spread it right to the edges. Place the middle sponge on top of the bottom layer and then top with the remaining sponge layer.
6 Spoon the remaining cream on top and spread it over the entire gâteau, making sure there is no sponge visible. Use the cream to pipe rosettes around the gâteau and decorate with the reserved cherries and chocolate scrolls.

Italian Ricotta Tart

SERVES 8
PREPARATION & COOKING TIME: 25 minutes + 1 hour
    chilling + 1¼ hours cooking
FREEZING: not recommended

This traditional Italian cheesecake is evocative of Christmas with its candied and dried fruit steeped in Galliano. Pine nut kernels are strongly flavoured, and can easily be omitted if not to your taste – just use 25 g (1 oz) more fruit. The cocoa pastry, while not authentic, contrasts well with the filling, but you can use the traditional sweet rich shortcrust base if you prefer. A compote of fresh apricots, poached in sugar syrup and flavoured with the zest of lemon, a cinnamon stick and a halved vanilla pod, would make a perfect accompaniment.

FOR THE COCOA PASTRY:
sweet rich shortcrust pastry made with 115 g (4 oz) flour
2 teaspoons cocoa powder sifted with the flour and icing sugar

FOR THE FILLING:
50 g (2 oz) candied and dried fruits (sultanas, raisins, currants,
    candied peel, dried apricots) soaked overnight in 2 tablespoons
    Galliano liqueur
25 g (1 oz) pine nut kernels
350 g (12 oz) ricotta
3 large egg yolks
80 g (3 oz) caster sugar
grated zest of 1 lemon
25 g (1 oz) plain flour
150 ml (¼ pint) double cream, whipped lightly

1 Use the cocoa pastry to line a deep 20-cm (8-inch) flan tin. Chill for 1 hour.
2 Preheat the oven to Gas Mark 5/electric oven 190°C/fan oven 170°C. Place a baking sheet on the middle shelf.
3 On the warmed baking sheet, bake the pastry case blind for 15 minutes. Remove the foil or paper and beans and return to the oven for a further 5 minutes.
4 Toast the pine kernels in the oven for 4–5 minutes until golden, watch them carefully as they burn easily! Reduce the temperature to Gas Mark 3/electric oven 160°C/fan oven 140°C.
5 Beat the ricotta until smooth. Whisk together the egg yolks, sugar and lemon zest until you have a thick and light mixture. Add the ricotta to the mixture and fold in the flour, followed by the whipped cream, fruit and nuts with any unabsorbed Galliano.
6 Spoon the filling into the cooked case and bake for 50 minutes, or until the filling is just set (it will carry on cooking for a little while after it comes out of the oven). This tart is best served chilled.

Banoffee Brandy Snap Tartlets

MAKES 6
PREPARATION & COOKING TIME: 15 minutes + cooling
FREEZING: not recommended

Ready-made brandy snap baskets make ideal substitutes for the traditional ginger biscuit crumb base of Banoffee Pie and they look so pretty too. These tartlets need to be assembled shortly before eating, otherwise the baskets will soften – but all the preparation can be done in advance.

80 g (3 oz) unsalted butter
80 g (3 oz) golden caster sugar
218 g can of condensed milk
100 g packet of 6 brandy snap baskets
2 small bananas, sliced and tossed in a little lemon juice
150 ml (¼ pint) double cream, whipped lightly
15 g (½ oz) milk chocolate, grated

1 Melt the butter in a medium saucepan. Stir in the sugar and condensed milk. Bring this to the boil, stirring constantly. Cook over a medium heat for 5 minutes, stirring occasionally, until the sauce thickens slightly and becomes pale golden. Do not be tempted to cook for longer otherwise the mixture will separate.
2 Remove the pan from the heat and cover the surface of the banoffee mixture with a piece of wetted clingfilm. Leave to cool completely.
3 Spoon 1 tablespoon of banoffee mixture into each brandy snap case – you may have a spoonful left over.
4 Divide the banana between the baskets and spoon a dollop of cream on top.
5 Sprinkle with grated chocolate and serve immediately.

Mocha Pie with Baileys

SERVES 8
PREPARATION & COOKING TIME: 25 minutes + 30 minutes
   chilling + 15 minutes cooking
FREEZING: not recommended

This pie is really rich and has a lovely fudgy texture. A combination of layers – a biscuit base, a coffee centre flavoured with Baileys and a smooth chocolate cream top – ensures a mix of wonderful flavours and textures. It is equally delicious warm or cold.

FOR THE BASE:
200 g (7 oz) digestive biscuits, crushed
80 g (3 oz) unsalted butter, melted

FOR THE FILLING:
80 g (3 oz) unsalted butter, softened
80 g (3 oz) light muscovado sugar
2 large eggs
2 tablespoons self-raising flour
2 tablespoons instant coffee dissolved in 1 tablespoon boiling water
1 tablespoon Baileys liqueur

FOR THE TOPPING:
80 g (3 oz) milk chocolate
3 tablespoons double cream

1 Preheat the oven to Gas Mark 5/electric oven 190°C/fan oven 170°C.
2 Combine the crushed biscuits and melted butter. Press the crumb mixture into the base, and up the sides of a 20-cm (8-inch) loose-bottomed, shallow flan tin. Chill for at least 30 minutes.
3 Cream together the butter and sugar until pale. Separate one of the eggs. Gradually beat in the whole egg and a yolk. Fold in the flour, followed by the coffee and Baileys. Whisk the egg white until stiff and fold it in (don't worry if the mixture curdles). Pour this into the crumb case and bake in the oven for 15 minutes, or until the filling is just set.
4 Melt the chocolate and cream in a bowl over a pan of hot, not boiling, water. Stir until smooth and pour this over the tart while it is still warm. Spread it evenly over the surface.

Tiramisù Roulade (*left*)

SERVES 6–8
PREPARATION & COOKING TIME: 30 minutes + 20 minutes
   cooking + 2 hours standing
Freezing: recommended

There's no need to be daunted at the prospect making a roulade – it isn't as difficult as you might imagine. Covering the cooked mixture with a damp tea towel for at least a couple of hours before rolling it up really helps.

175 g (6 oz) plain chocolate, broken into pieces
5 eggs, separated
175 g (6 oz) caster sugar
icing sugar, for dusting
250 g tub of mascarpone
150 ml ($^1/_4$ pint) whipping cream, whipped to soft peaks
50 g (2 oz) chocolate-covered coffee beans

1 Preheat the oven to Gas Mark 4/electric oven 180°C/fan oven 160°C. Grease and line a 35 x 25 cm (14 x 10 inch) Swiss roll tin with baking parchment.
2 Melt the chocolate by placing it in a bowl set over a pan of barely simmering water. Remove from the heat.
3 Meanwhile, place the egg yolks and sugar in another bowl and whisk until pale and creamy. Wash the whisks thoroughly and whisk the egg whites in another bowl until they are stiff.
4 Whisk or beat the melted chocolate into the egg yolk mixture. Spoon a little of the egg whites into the chocolate mixture and beat in to loosen it. Using a large metal spoon, fold in the remaining whites carefully using a figure-of-eight action until there are no whites visible.
5 Pour the mixture into the prepared tin and gently spread it to the corners. Bake for 15–20 minutes, until the roulade has risen and is firm to the touch. Place a cooling rack to balance on the edges of the tin and then place a damp tea towel on top to cover the whole roulade (the wire rack should not touch the roulade). Leave for at least 2 hours.
6 Cut a piece of greaseproof paper larger than the roulade and dust liberally with sifted icing sugar. Turn out the roulade on to the paper. Empty the mascarpone cheese into a mixing bowl and beat to soften it. Fold in the whipped cream and spread the mixture all over the surface of the roulade but not right up to the edges. Scatter the chocolate coffee beans over the cream.
7 Position the roulade so that a short side is facing you. Hold the edge of the paper and use it to roll up the roulade. Slide it on to a serving plate with the seam underneath and dust with a little more icing sugar

Croissants

MAKES 8–10
PREPARARTION & COOKING TIME: 45–50 minutes + 25–30
   minutes baking
FREEZING: recommended

*Croissant means 'crescent' in French, hence the name of these
traditional French buttery breakfast rolls.*

FOR THE YEAST BATTER:
15 g (¹/₂ oz) fresh yeast
1 teaspoon caster sugar
115 ml (4 fl oz) hand-hot water

FOR THE DOUGH:
275 g (10 oz) strong white flour
¹/₂ teaspoon salt
15 g (¹/₂ oz) unsalted butter, melted
115 ml (4 fl oz) hand-hot water
150 g (5 oz) unsalted butter
beaten egg, to glaze

1 Dissolve the yeast and sugar in the warm water and leave
   to stand until frothy.
2 Sift the flour and salt into a bowl. Add the yeast mixture,
   melted butter and enough of the water to make a soft
   dough.
3 Turn on to a floured surface and knead until smooth.
   Cover and leave to rise until doubled in size.
4 Roll the dough into a rectangle 30 x 15 cm (12 x 6
   inches). Place half the butter in small pieces over the
   bottom two-thirds of the dough. Fold the top third over
   the centre third and the bottom third up over that. Place in
   the fridge for 15 minutes.
5 Repeat step 4 with the second half of the butter.
6 Roll the dough out thinly and cut into triangles.
7 Starting at a long edge, roll towards the opposite point.
   Form into a crescent shape and place on a greased baking
   sheet.
8 Leave to prove for about 40 minutes or until doubled in
   size.
9 Preheat the oven to Gas Mark 7/electric oven 220°C/fan
   oven 200°C. Brush with beaten egg and bake for 25–30
   minutes, until golden brown. Place on a wire rack to cool.

CHOCOLATE CROISSANTS Before starting to roll at step 7,
add a square of chocolate in the centre.

SAVOURY CROISSANTS Roll a slice of cooked ham and a little
grated Cheddar cheese inside in the same way.

Chelsea Buns

MAKES 9 buns
PREPARARTION TIME: 30–35 minutes + rising
   + 25–30 minutes baking
FREEZING: recommended

*A traditional recipe for this sweet bun. A real old English
favourite.*

FOR THE YEAST BATTER:
2 teaspoons dried yeast or 15 g (¹/₂ oz) fresh yeast
¹/₂ teaspoon caster sugar
5 tablespoons hand-hot milk
50 g (2 oz) strong white flour

FOR THE DOUGH:
175 g (6 oz) strong white flour
¹/₂ teaspoon salt
25 g (1 oz) caster sugar
25 g (1 oz) margarine
1 egg, beaten

FOR THE FILLING:
25 g (1 oz) butter, melted
115 g (4 oz) mixed dried fruit
50 g (2 oz) dark brown sugar
¹/₂ teaspoon ground cinnamon

1 To make the yeast batter using dried yeast, place the yeast
   and sugar in a small jug. Stir in the milk and leave for 5
   minutes.
2 Stir in the flour and leave in a warm place until frothy
   (about 15–20 minutes).
3 Alternatively, to make the yeast batter using fresh yeast,
   place the yeast, sugar and milk in a small jug. Stir in the
   flour and leave in a warm place until frothy (about 15–20
   minutes).
4 In a large bowl, sift together the flour and salt and mix in
   the sugar. Rub in the margarine. Stir in the egg and the
   yeast batter and mix to give a soft dough.
5 Turn on to a floured surface and knead for 8–10 minutes,
   until the dough is smooth, elastic and no longer sticky.
   Place the dough in a clean, greased bowl, cover and leave
   to rise until doubled in size.
6 Transfer the risen dough to a lightly floured surface.
   Knock back and knead. Roll the dough into a rectangle 30
   x 23 cm (12 x 9 inches). Brush the surface with the melted
   butter. Sprinkle with the fruit, sugar and cinnamon.
7 Roll up the dough like a Swiss roll, starting at the longest
   side.
8 Cut into nine equal pieces and place on a greased baking
   sheet, cut-side down, to form a square, about 1 cm (¹/₂
   inch) apart. Cover and leave to prove for about 30 minutes
   until well risen.
9 Preheat the oven to Gas Mark 7/electric oven 220°C/fan
   oven 200°C. Bake for 25–30 minutes, until golden brown.
   Place on a wire rack to cool

Battenberg Cake (*left*)

MAKES 8–10 slices
PREPARATION & COOKING TIME: 1½ hours

This famous sponge cake, traditionally made with pink and yellow squares and covered with marzipan, is sometimes called Window Cake or Tennis Cake, the last name because the squares resemble the layout of a tennis court. For a change, here is a version made with chocolate squares.

FOR THE CAKE:
175 g (6 oz) butter, softened
175 g (6 oz) caster sugar
3 eggs
225 g (8 oz) self-raising flour, sieved
1 teaspoon vanilla essence
115 g (4 oz) milk chocolate, melted
2 tablespoons warmed raspberry jam, sieved

FOR THE COVERING:
115 g (4 oz) ground almonds
115 g (4 oz) icing sugar, sieved
1 egg, beaten lightly
1 teaspoon lemon juice
½ teaspoon almond essence

1 Cream together the butter and the sugar until light and fluffy.
2 Beat in the eggs. Fold in the flour.
3 Divide the mixture into two bowls. Into one, stir the vanilla essence; into the other, stir the melted chocolate. Mix thoroughly.
4 Grease and line an 18-cm (7-inch) square cake tin. Divide the tin in half with folded greaseproof paper.
5 Place each of the mixtures in one half of the prepared tin; smooth the tops.
6 Bake at Gas Mark 4/electric oven 180°C/fan oven 160°C for 40–50 minutes until golden in colour and springy to the touch.
7 Remove the cake from the tin, carefully remove the paper from between the two halves and separate into the two halves. Place them on a wire rack to cool completely.
8 Divide each cake in half, down the length.
9 To cover the cake, first spread each of the length's sides evenly with the warm jam, which should hold the four pieces together, and assemble into a square with alternate colours on each side.
10 Make the covering by mixing the covering ingredients together; knead gently.
11 Roll out the covering on a surface lightly dusted with icing sugar.
12 Cut a strip long enough to fit the top, bottom and two sides. Then cut 2 squares to fit the remaining 2 sides. Remember to smooth the edges to give a neat finish. Dust with icing sugar.

Orange & Cinnamon Muffins

MAKES 12 small muffins ★
PREPARATION & COOKING TIME: 20–30 minutes
FREEZING: recommended

Muffins are an American tradition which make a change from toast for breakfast, served with a mug of hot chocolate. This is a particularly wonderful combination of flavours.

175 g (6 oz) plain flour
½ teaspoon ground cinnamon
1½ teaspoons baking powder
50 g (2 oz) caster sugar
grated zest of 1 orange
1 egg, beaten
125 ml (4½ fl oz) milk
50 g (2 oz) butter, melted

1 Preheat the oven to Gas Mark 5/electric oven 190°C/fan oven 170°C. Place 12 small muffin cases into muffin tins.
2 Sift the flour, cinnamon and baking powder into a mixing bowl. Stir in the sugar, orange zest, egg, milk and melted butter, until just mixed.
3 Divide the mixture between the paper cases.
4 Bake for 10–15 minutes. Press the top of one muffin lightly with your fingertip; if it feels springy, the muffins are cooked. Transfer to a wire rack to cool.

Cherry & Apricot Scones

MAKES about 15 scones ⭐
PREPARATION & COOKING TIME: 25 minutes
FREEZING: recommended

A colourful sweet scone to serve with coffee or tea. Delicious eaten warm or cool.

450 g (1 lb) plain flour
2 teaspoons cream of tartar
1 teaspoon bicarbonate of soda
115 g (4 oz) block margarine
50 g (2 oz) caster sugar
80 g (3 oz) glacé cherries, chopped
80 g (3 oz) ready-to-eat dried apricots, chopped
225 ml (8 fl oz) milk

1 Preheat the oven to Gas Mark 7/electric oven 220°C/fan oven 200°C.
2 Sift the flour, cream of tartar and bicarbonate of soda into a mixing bowl. Rub in the margarine until the mixture resembles fine breadcrumbs. Stir in the sugar, chopped cherries and apricots.
3 Make a well in the centre and stir in enough milk to give a fairly soft dough.
4 Turn the dough on to a floured surface and knead lightly to remove any cracks.
5 Roll out to about 2 cm (³/₄ inch) thick and cut out 6-cm (2¹/₂-inch) rounds with a cutter. Knead the remaining dough and re-roll and cut.
6 Place the scones on a greased baking sheet. Bake until well risen and golden brown, about 10–15 minutes. Transfer to a wire rack to cool.

Irish Brack

MAKES a 20-cm (8-inch) cake
PREPARATION TIME: 10 minutes + soaking overnight
  1¹/₂–2 hours baking
FREEZING: recommended

500 ml (18 fl oz) strong tea, made using 3 teabags
225 g (8 oz) dark muscovado sugar
500 g (1 lb 2 oz) mixed dried fruit
2 eggs
500 g (1 lb 2 oz) self-raising flour

1 Mix the tea and sugar together in a large mixing bowl and stir to dissolve the sugar. Add the fruit and leave to soak overnight.
2 Beat the eggs into the fruit mixture, and then carefully fold in the sifted flour.
3 Transfer the mixture into a 20-cm (8-inch) greased and lined deep cake tin.
4 Bake for 1¹/₂–2 hours until well risen and a skewer inserted into the centre comes out clean. Leave in the tin for 10 minutes before turning on to a wire rack to cool.

Chairman's Cake

MAKES 20–24 slices
PREPARATION & COOKING TIME: 2–4 hours marinating +
  30 minutes + 2–2¹/₂ hours baking

This cake was designed for Mrs Eileen Meadmore in celebration of her term of office as NFWI National Chairman.

115 g (4 oz) glacé cherries, halved
175 g (6 oz) ready-to-eat dried apricots, chopped
115 g (4 oz) ready-to-eat dried pineapple, chopped
115 g (4 oz) raisins
115 ml (4 fl oz) Drambuie
100 g (3¹/₂ oz) brazil nuts, chopped roughly
100 g (3¹/₂ oz) walnut pieces, chopped roughly
150 g (5 oz) butter, softened
150 g (5 oz) dark muscovado sugar
225 g (8 oz) set honey
4 eggs
175 g (6 oz) plain flour, sieved
115 g (4 oz) ground almonds
200 g (7 oz) dark plain chocolate, cut into chunks

1 Place the prepared cherries, apricots, pineapple and raisins in a bowl, add the Drambuie, cover and leave to stand for 2–4 hours.
2 At the end of the marinating time, add the nuts to the fruit mixture.
3 Cream the butter and sugar together in a large bowl until light and fluffy. Stir in the honey; then beat in each egg separately.
4 Fold in the flour and ground almonds, mixing well.
5 Carefully stir in the fruit, nuts and chocolate.
6 Spoon the mixture into a greased and lined 23-cm (9-inch) round cake tin.
7 Bake at Gas Mark 2/electric oven 150°C/fan oven 130°C for 2–2¹/₂ hours or until a skewer inserted in the centre comes out clean. Remove from the oven and leave in the tin until cool.
8 This cake is best stored for 5–7 days, well wrapped in foil, before being eaten.

Whisky Spice Cake *(left)*

MAKES 12–16 slices
PREPARATION & COOKING TIME: 1 hour including the
   soaking of the fruit + 50–70 minutes baking

*Soaking the raisins in the whisky syrup produces a moist, light-
textured cake.*

225 g (8 oz) raisins
5 tablespoons whisky
5 tablespoons water
115 g (4 oz) butter, softened
115 g (4 oz) soft light brown sugar
2 eggs
sieve together: 225 g (8 oz) plain flour and 1 teaspoon bicarbonate
   of soda and 1 teaspoon ground mixed spice
115 g (4 oz) walnut pieces, roughly chopped

FOR THE BUTTERCREAM FILLING:
115 g (4 oz) butter, softened
225 g (8 oz) icing sugar, sieved
2 tablespoons whisky
25 g (1 oz) walnut pieces, roughly chopped

1 Place the raisins, whisky and water in a small saucepan
   and heat until steaming; then remove from the heat and
   leave to stand for 30 minutes.
2 Cream the butter and sugar together until light in colour
   and fluffy. Beat in the eggs.
3 Fold in the flour, bicarbonate of soda and the spice. Stir in
   the raisins and any remaining liquid; add the walnuts and
   mix thoroughly.
4 Place the mixture in a greased and lined 20-cm (8-inch)
   round cake tin; smooth the top.
5 Bake at Gas Mark 3/electric oven 160°C/fan oven 140°C
   for 50–70 minutes until golden and firm to the touch.
6 Remove the cake from the oven and leave it in the tin for
   10 minutes before placing it on a wire rack to cool
   completely.
7 To make the buttercream, beat together the butter and the
   icing sugar until creamy. Stir in the whisky and the
   walnuts.
8 Cut the cake in half through the middle and then sandwich
   the two halves together with the buttercream. Spread the
   remainder over the top and the sides.
9 Stored in an airtight container, the cake will keep for 2–3
   days.

Cinnamon & Raisin Swirl

*A delicious American bread that is lovely toasted and served
for breakfast with maple syrup drizzled over it.*

MAKES a 450 g (1 lb) loaf
PREPARATION TIME: 30–35 minutes + rising + 25–30
   minutes baking
FREEZING: recommended

225 g (8 oz) strong white flour
¹/₂ teaspoon salt
25 g (1 oz) caster sugar
25 g (1 oz) margarine
¹/₂ sachet easy-blend yeast
1 egg, beaten
5 tablespoons hand-hot milk
grated zest and juice of ¹/₂ orange
1 tablespoon ground cinnamon
25 g (1 oz) dark brown sugar

1 In a large bowl, sift together the flour and salt and then
   mix in the sugar. Rub in the margarine and add the yeast.
   Stir in the egg and milk to give a soft dough.
2 Turn on to a floured surface and knead for 8–10 minutes,
   until the dough is smooth, elastic and no longer sticky.
3 Place the dough in a clean, greased bowl, cover and leave
   to rise until doubled in size
4 Transfer the risen dough to a lightly floured surface.
   Knock back and knead in the orange, cinnamon and sugar
   until evenly distributed.
5 Roll the dough into a rectangle 33 x 15 cm (13 x 6
   inches). Roll up tightly and place in a greased 450 g (1 lb)
   loaf tin. Cover and prove until doubled in size.
6 Preheat the oven to Gas Mark 6/electric oven 200°C/fan
   oven 180°C.
7 Bake for 25–30 minutes, until golden brown. Place on a
   wire rack to cool.

Dundee Cake

MAKES 12–16 slices
PREPARATION & COOKING TIME: 2–2³/₄ hours

This fairly rich Scottish fruit cake, which is topped with almonds, is a time-honoured favourite.

115 g (4 oz) raisins
115 g (4 oz) sultanas
115 g (4 oz) currants
50 g (2 oz) mixed peel, chopped
grated zest of 1 unwaxed lemon
175 g (6 oz) butter, softened
175 g (6 oz) caster sugar
3 eggs
sieve together: 225 g (8 oz) plain flour, a pinch of salt and ¹/₂
    teaspoon baking powder and ¹/₂ teaspoon ground mixed spice
1 tablespoon sweet sherry
50 g (2 oz) whole blanched almonds

1 Mix together the raisins, sultanas, currants, mixed peel and lemon zest.
2 In a mixing bowl, cream together the butter and sugar until light in colour and fluffy. Beat in the eggs.
3 Fold in the flour, salt, baking powder and spice; mix well. Add the dried fruit and sherry and mix thoroughly.
4 Transfer the mixture to a greased and lined 18-cm (7-inch) round cake tin. Smooth the top and arrange the almonds in a circle around the top of the cake.
5 Bake at Gas Mark 3/electric oven 160°C/fan oven 140°C for 1³/₄–2¹/₂ hours or until a skewer inserted in the centre comes out clean.
6 Leave the cake in the tin for 15 minutes, then place on a wire rack to cool completely. To follow the Scottish tradition, present the cake with a tartan ribbon tied round its middle.

Chocolate Potato Cake *(below, left)*

MAKES 8–12 slices
PREPARATION & COOKING TIME: 1 hour

The potato in this cake gives it a moist texture; you will find that everyone will be amazed that this contains potato. You can get the chocolate-coated coffee beans in most good confectioners or delicatessens.

80 g (3 oz) butter, softened
200 g (7 oz) caster sugar
115 g (4 oz) mashed potato, warm
2 tablespoons double cream
1 tablespoon cocoa powder
3 eggs, separated
sieve together: 80 g (3 oz) self-raising flour and 1 teaspoon baking
    powder
2 tablespoons milk, if required

FOR THE ICING:
225 g (8 oz) icing sugar, sieved
2 tablespoons cocoa powder, sieved
50 g (2 oz) butter, softened
2 tablespoons coffee concentrate
2 tablespoons rum
chocolate-coated coffee beans

1 Cream the butter and sugar together until well blended.
2 Mash the potato with the double cream and cocoa powder; then stir this into the creamed mixture. Beat in the egg yolks, and stir in the flour and baking powder. If the mixture is rather stiff, add enough milk to give a dropping consistency.
3 In a clean grease-free bowl, whisk the egg whites until stiff; then gently fold them into the mixture.
4 Divide the mixture between two greased and lined 18-cm (7-inch) sandwich tins and smooth the top.
5 Bake at Gas Mark 5/electric oven 190°C/fan oven 170°C for 25–35 minutes until springy and set.
6 Cool the cakes in the tins for 10 minutes before turning them out on to a wire rack to cool completely.
7 To make the icing, place the icing sugar and cocoa in a bowl, beat in the butter, then stir in the coffee and rum.
8 Use the icing to sandwich the two halves of the cake together, and then spread the remainder over the top and sides. Decorate the top with chocolate-covered coffee beans.

Chocolate Muffins *(right)*

MAKES 16 muffins ★
PREPARATION & COOKING TIME: 30 minutes
FREEZING: recommended

*These can be eaten by themselves or try serving them with
some chocolate ice cream.*

250 g (9 oz) plain wholemeal flour
4 teaspoons baking powder
100 g (3¹/₂ oz) muscovado sugar
100 g (3¹/₂ oz) shredded coconut
175 ml (6 fl oz) milk
125 g (4¹/₂ oz) low fat spread, melted
3 eggs, beaten
175 g (6 oz) chocolate chips

1 Preheat the oven to Gas Mark 5/electric oven 190°C/fan
   oven 170°C. Place 16 large muffin cases into muffin tins.
2 Sift the flour and baking powder into a mixing bowl. Stir
   in the sugar and the bran left in the sieve. Stir in the
   coconut, milk, low fat spread, eggs and chocolate chips
   until just mixed.
3 Divide between the paper cases.
4 Bake for 20 minutes. Press the top of one muffin lightly
   with your fingertip; if it feels springy the muffins are
   cooked. Transfer to a wire rack to cool.

NOTE: If you use smaller muffin cases, this recipe will make
30 muffins. For this size, cook for 12–15 minutes.

Chocolate Hazelnut Brownies

MAKES 9 squares
PREPARATION & COOKING TIME: 1 hour
FREEZING: recommended

*Brownies are a rich traditional American chocolate-based cake,
eaten as a snack or for dessert. They were called brownies
due to their colour and they have been eaten in the USA for
about 100 years. You can store these in an airtight container
for 2–3 days.*

150 g (5 oz) plain chocolate
90 g (3¹/₂ oz) plain flour
150 g (5 oz) icing sugar, plus extra for dusting
20 g (3³/₄ oz) cocoa powder
90 g (3¹/₂ oz) unsalted butter, melted
2 tablespoons golden syrup
2 eggs, beaten
1¹/₂ teaspoons vanilla essence
40 g (1¹/₂ oz) hazelnuts, roasted, skinned and chopped

1 Preheat the oven to Gas Mark 4/electric oven 180°C/fan
   oven 160°C. Grease and line the base of a 25-cm (10-inch)
   square baking tin.
2 Melt the chocolate in a bowl over a pan of simmering
   water.
3 Meanwhile, sift the plain flour, icing sugar and cocoa
   powder into a bowl.

4 Add the butter and syrup to the chocolate and stir until
   smooth. Allow to cool slightly.
5 Stir in the eggs and vanilla essence to the chocolate
   mixture.
6 Fold the dry ingredients into the chocolate mixture and stir
   quickly until smooth. Add the nuts.
7 Pour into the baking tin and bake for 35–45 minutes, until
   the top and edges are crusty and the inside is still gooey
   but not runny.
8 Leave to cool slightly in the tin. Dust with more sifted
   icing sugar and cut into nine squares. Serve warm with
   cream as a dessert or leave to cool completely, as you
   prefer.

VARIATION: Substitute 40 g (1¹/₂ oz) ground almonds and
1 teaspoon of almond essence for the hazelnuts and vanilla
essence.

Spicy Brandy Cookies

MAKES 18–20
PREPARATION & COOKING TIME: 45 minutes

The moist raisins give these spicy cookies a soft texture.

50 g (2 oz) raisins, chopped
2 tablespoons brandy
175 g (6 oz) butter, softened
115 g (4 oz) granulated sugar
50 g (2 oz) soft dark brown sugar
4 tablespoons milk
sieve together: 225 g (8 oz) plain flour, ¹/₂ teaspoon bicarbonate of
    soda, 1 teaspoon ground cinnamon and 1 teaspoon finely ground
    nutmeg
finely grated zest of 1 unwaxed orange

1 Soak the raisins in the brandy for 15 minutes, until almost
  all the liquid has been absorbed.
2 Cream the butter and sugars together until light in colour
  and fluffy. Stir in the milk, raisins, then the flour,
  bicarbonate of soda and the spices. Add the grated orange
  zest. Mix everything together well.
3 Using a teaspoon, place small mounds of the mixture on
  greased baking sheets, leaving room for them to spread.
4 Bake at Gas Mark 4/electric oven 180°C/fan oven 160°C
  for 10–15 minutes until the cookies are pale golden.
5 Allow the cookies to stand on the sheets for 5 minutes
  before placing them on wire racks to cool completely.
6 Stored in an airtight container, these will keep for up to
  one week.

Shortbread

MAKES approximately 20 slices
PREPARATION & COOKING TIME: 1 hour

225 g (8 oz) butter, softened
115 g (4 oz) icing sugar
sieve together: 225 g (8 oz) plain flour and 115 g (4 oz) cornflour
caster sugar, to dredge

This is a truly melt-in-the-mouth recipe.

1 Beat together the butter and sugar until creamy and pale in
  colour.
2 Blend in the flour and cornflour until thoroughly mixed.
3 Place the mixture into a well-greased 33 x 23 cm (13 x 9
  inch) Swiss roll tin. Using floured hands, press down so the
  mixture is evenly spread in the tin. Prick with a fork.
4 Bake at Gas Mark 2/electric oven 150°C/fan oven 130°F
  for 40–50 minutes until pale golden in colour.
5 Remove the shortbread from the oven, dredge generously
  with caster sugar, and then cut into fingers.
6 Leave the shortbread to stand for 10 minutes before
  placing the fingers on a wire rack to cool completely.
7 Stored in an airtight container, they will stay crisp for up
  to 2 weeks.

Prune & Maple Syrup Flapjacks

MAKES 16 flapjacks
PREPARATION & COOKING TIME: 45 minutes
FREEZING: not recommended

*A variation on the traditional flapjack with a layer of moist
fruit in the centre, this is ideal for picnics, lunch boxes or
afternoon tea and is a real energy-booster for the young.*

225 g (8 oz) ready-to-eat stoned prunes, chopped
200 g (7 oz) unsalted butter
4 tablespoons golden syrup
2 tablespoons maple syrup
80 g (3 oz) light muscovado sugar
350 g (12 oz) rolled oats

1 Preheat the oven to Gas Mark 5/electric oven 190°C/fan
  oven 170°C.
2 Make the filling by heating 3 tablespoons water in a
  saucepan, adding the prunes and leaving to soak for 15
  minutes.
3 Purée the prune mixture.
4 Heat the butter, golden and maple syrups and sugar in a
  saucepan, until the butter is melted.
5 Add the rolled oats and mix well.
6 Press half the mixture into a greased 18 x 30 (7-inch x 12-
  inch) tin. Spread the prune purée on top and cover with
  the remaining flapjack mixture.
7 Bake for 20–25 minutes, until golden.
8 Mark into bars and leave to cool before removing from the
  tin. Store in an airtight container for up to a week.

Stilton & Bacon Scones

(opposite, left)

MAKES 8 scones ★
PREPARATION & COOKING TIME: 25 minutes
FREEZING: recommended

The flavour of these scones can be varied by using smoked or unsmoked bacon or pancetta.

200 g (7 oz) self-raising flour
a pinch of salt
$^1/_2$ teaspoon dry mustard powder
50 g (2 oz) unsalted butter
50 g (2 oz) blue Stilton cheese, crumbled
50 g (2 oz) white Stilton cheese, crumbled
2 bacon rashers, cooked and chopped
100 ml ($3^1/_2$ fl oz) milk
beaten egg, to glaze

1 Preheat the oven to Gas Mark 6/electric oven 200°C/fan oven 180°C.
2 Sift the flour, salt and mustard powder into a mixing bowl and rub in the butter.
3 Stir in the crumbled cheeses and the chopped bacon.
4 Make a well in the centre and add enough milk to make a soft dough.
5 Turn on to a floured surface and knead lightly. Roll to 2 cm (¾-inch) thick and cut into 6-cm (2½-inch) rounds with a scone cutter.
6 Place on a greased baking sheet and brush with beaten egg.
7 Bake for 10–15 minutes, until well risen and golden. Transfer to a wire rack to cool.

Cheese & Onion Loaf

MAKES 1 ring
PREPARATION & COOKING TIME: 15–20 minutes + rising + 25–30 minutes
FREEZING: recommended

A well flavoured bread that is delicious with cheese and salad.

15 g ($^1/_2$ oz) fresh yeast or 1 sachet of easy-blend yeast
1 teaspoon caster sugar
15 g ($^1/_2$ oz) ascorbic acid (if using fresh yeast)
200–250 ml (7–9 fl oz) hand-hot water
2 tablespoons sunflower oil
1 small onion, chopped
375 g (13 oz) strong white flour
1 teaspoon salt
1 teaspoon mustard powder
50 g (2 oz) Cheddar cheese, grated
beaten egg, for brushing
poppy seeds, to decorate

1 For fresh yeast, blend the yeast, sugar, ascorbic acid and half the water together. Leave until frothy. Add the remaining water and a tablespoon of the oil.

2 Meanwhile, heat the remaining oil in a small pan and cook the onion until soft but not browned.
3 Sift the flour into a bowl. Add the salt, mustard powder, cheese and onion. If using easy-blend yeast, mix it and the sugar with the flour now.
4 Add the yeast liquid if using fresh yeast, or just the water and oil and mix to form a soft dough.
5 Turn on to a lightly floured surface and knead until smooth.
6 Divide the mixture in half. Roll one half into a circle and place on a greased, loose-bottomed tin.
7 Divide the remaining dough into six and form into rolls. Place the rolls on top of the circle. Cover and leave to rise until doubled in size.
8 Preheat the oven to Gas Mark 7/electric oven 220°C/fan oven 200°C.
9 Brush with egg and sprinkle with poppy seeds. Bake in the preheated oven for 25–30 minutes until golden and hollow-sounding when the base is tapped. Remove from the tin and transfer to a wire rack to cool.

Garlic & Herb Muffins

MAKES 6 muffins ★
PREPARATION & COOKING TIME: 25 minutes
FREEZING: recommended

Using course-ground cornmeal (polenta) gives these muffins a lovely crunchy texture.

65 g ($2^1/_2$ oz) plain flour
$^1/_4$ teaspoon salt
$1^1/_2$ teaspoons baking powder
55 g ($2^1/_4$ oz) coarse cornmeal
1 garlic clove, crushed
1 teaspoon dried mixed herbs
100 ml ($3^1/_2$ fl oz) milk
1 small egg
1 tablespoon corn oil

1 Preheat the oven to Gas Mark 6/electric oven 200°C/fan oven 180°C and place six paper cases into muffin tins.
2 Sift the flour, salt and baking powder into a mixing bowl. Stir in the cornmeal, garlic and herbs.
3 Combine the milk, egg and oil and stir into the dry ingredients until just mixed.
4 Divide the muffin mixture between the paper cases. Bake for 10–15 minutes. Press the top of one muffin lightly with your fingertip; if it feels springy the muffins are cooked. Transfer to a wire rack to cool.

Preserves

Traditional Seville Orange Marmalade

MAKES about 4.5 kg (10 lb)
PREPARATION TIME: 2½–3 hours

1.3 kg (3 lb) seville oranges
2 lemons
2.8 litres (5 pints) water
2.7 kg (6 lb) sugar

This is the time-honoured traditional way of making marmalade with seville oranges. January into February is the time to make it, as this is the very short season for fresh sevilles, which are bitter oranges with a rough skin and a deep colour. The recipe is followed by several variations.

The preparation time will vary according to how you choose to prepare the peel but traditionalists will say that, if the peel is minced or processed, it is not, strictly speaking, marmalade! It is essential to allow enough cooking time for the peel to be really soft before adding the sugar, otherwise you will have a very tough and chewy marmalade.

1 Wash and scrub the oranges and lemons. Cut the fruit in half and squeeze out the juice. Remove the pips and membrane and tie in a muslin bag.
2 Cut the peel into thin shreds (or coarse ones, if preferred) and then place in a large preserving pan, with the juice, the bag of pips and the water.
3 Bring to the boil and then simmer gently, uncovered, for about 2 hours, until the contents of the pan are reduced by about a half and the peel is really soft and tender.
4 Remove the muslin bag and squeeze the bag hard and carefully, to remove all the gooey liquid; this contains the pectin which is so important for a good set.
5 Add the sugar and stir until completely dissolved. Bring to the boil and boil rapidly until setting point is reached (see page 12).
6 Remove any scum from the surface (see page 12). Cool for 5–10 minutes.
7 Stir well to distribute the peel. Pour into cooled, sterilised jars and seal. Label and store.

CORIANDER MARMALADE: Add 1 tablespoon of crushed coriander seeds to the peel or pop them into the muslin bag when cooking, to enhance the orange flavour.

BLACK TREACLE MARMALADE: Add 2 tablespoons or more of black treacle with the sugar, for a different flavour and a rich colour.

NUTTY MARMALADE: Stir in few lightly toasted flaked almonds or chopped walnuts just before potting into jars.

BOOZY MARMALADE: Stir in 2–4 tablespoons of whisky or other spirit or liqueur per 2.7 kg (6 lb) quantity just before potting. To achieve a variety of boozy flavours from one batch, put 2 teaspoons of a different spirit or liqueur in each jar before pouring in the hot marmalade.

EXTRA-FRUITY MARMALADE: For an extra fruity flavour, add a couple of peeled, cored and chopped cooking apples about 10 minutes before the end of the simmering time, when cooking the fruit peel.

GINGER MARMALADE: Add 115 g (4 oz) of finely chopped, crystallised ginger, or stem ginger preserved in syrup, at the same time as the sugar.

Claire Macdonald's Citrus Fruit Marmalade

MAKES 5–5.4 kg (11–12 lb)
PREPARATION & COOKING TIME: 2½–3½ hours

This is Claire's recipe from her book Seasonal Cooking.

675 g (1½ lb) seville oranges
675 g (1½ lb) other citrus fruit, e.g. a grapefruit, a sweet orange and the balance of the weight made up with tangerines or clementines, but not satsumas
2.2 litres (4 pints) water
2.7 kg (6 lb) granulated or preserving sugar

1 Place the fruit in a large saucepan or preserving pan with the water and simmer gently for 2–3 hours, or until the peel is very soft.
2 Remove the fruit from the pan, leaving the cooking liquid, and, when cool enough to handle, cut each orange, grapefruit or tangerine in half. Scoop out all the pips into a small saucepan.
3 Cover with another 300 ml (½ pint) of water and simmer for 10 minutes. Leave to cool, and then strain this liquid into the pan, with the liquid that the fruit was cooked in. (Make sure that you press out all of the liquid from the solids in the sieve.)
4 While the pips are simmering, cut up the fruit or use a food processor. Put the cut-up fruit back in the pan. Add the sugar and cook on a low heat, stirring occasionally, until the sugar has completely dissolved. Remove any scum (see page 12).
5 Now boil furiously; after 10 minutes, pull the pan off the heat to test the marmalade for a set (see page 12). If not ready, boil again for 5 minutes and test again.
6 When a set is achieved, pour into cooled, sterilised jars and seal. Label and store.

Ruby Red Grapefruit Marmalade *(below)*

MAKES 2.2–2.7 kg (5–6 lb)
PREPARATION & COOKING TIME: 3½ hours

This seems to be a very popular variety, going by the number of recipes around. The added colour of the fruit gives a lovely blush to the finished marmalade, so try to find the ruby red variety rather than just a pink one. You could also use the ingredients for Claire Macdonald's Citrus Fruit Marmalade, cooking the fruit whole and boiling the pips and peel separately.

900 g (2 lb) ruby red grapefruit, washed and quartered
1 lemon, washed and quartered
1.1 litres (2 pints) water
1.8 kg (4 lb) granulated sugar

1 Remove the pulp from the peel of the grapefruit and lemon. Remove the pips and tie them in a muslin bag. If the peel is really thick, remove most of the pith and put it in the bag also.
2 Cut all the peel finely and place in a large preserving pan, with the chopped pulp, bag of pips and water. Bring to the boil and then simmer until the peel is soft, 1–2 hours.
3 Remove the muslin bag. Add the sugar and stir until dissolved. Bring to the boil and boil rapidly until setting point is reached – about 20–30 minutes (see page 12). Remove any scum (see page 12).
4 Pour into cooled, sterilised jars and seal. Label and store.

GINGER & GRAPEFRUIT MARMALADE: Add 2 teaspoons of ground ginger and 115 g (4 oz) of chopped crystallised ginger or stem ginger preserved in syrup at the initial cooking stage.

TIPSY GRAPEFRUIT MARMALADE: Add 4 tablespoons of any spirit or liqueur (try whisky, brandy, rum or how about Campari or a liqueur?) just before potting.

Banana Chutney *(above, left)*

MAKES about 3.6 kg (9 lb)
PREPARATION & COOKING TIME: 1½–2 hours

This chutney was the result of a 'happy accident' – so says Sue Prickett of Hutton Roof in Lancashire and a producer for Kirkby Lonsdale WI Market. Someone gave Sue some very cheap bananas which were 'past their best'. Sue says that 'very ripe' bananas give a far better flavour than under-ripe ones anyway. Sue buys peppers when they are cheaper, chops them and freezes them in the quantities she needs for her recipes, which helps save time and cuts the cost too. A very similar recipe suggested by Liz Dawson-Margrave does without the peppers and raisins and includes a fresh green chilli, sliced finely.

1.8 kg (4 lb) bananas, chopped
4 peppers, chopped
4 onions, chopped
450 g (1 lb) raisins
1.1 litres (2 pints) malt vinegar
4 garlic cloves, crushed
2 teaspoons salt
½ teaspoon pepper
4 teaspoons curry powder
2 teaspoons ground turmeric
a pinch of ground cloves
900 g (2 lb) sugar
cornflour, if necessary (see step 2)

1 Cook everything, except the sugar and cornflour, together until soft and pulpy – about 1 hour.
2 Add the sugar and cook until the vinegar is reduced. Thicken with a little cornflour, slaked in a small amount of cold water, if necessary.
3 Spoon into cooled, sterilised jars, seal and label. Store for 6–8 weeks before using.

Pink Grapefruit & Cranberry Marmalade *(opposite above, right)*

MAKES about 4.5 kg (10 lb)
PREPARATION TIME: 30 minutes
COOKING TIME: 2 hours

This recipe was devised by Glenys Gibson, following a visit to a friend in Florida who has a huge pink grapefruit tree in her front garden. Put that together with the Americans' love for cranberries and you have a wonderful and colourful marmalade. Glenys first brought dried cranberries back from America but they are now readily available in most supermarkets and other outlets, on the dried vine-fruit shelf.

1.5 kg (3 lb 5 oz) pink grapefruit, sliced, pips removed
150 g (5 oz) dried cranberries
2 litres (3¹/₂ pints) water
juice of 1 lemon or 2 teaspoons citric acid
3 kg (6¹/₂ lb) sugar

1 Place the sliced grapefruit and the cranberries, with the water and the lemon juice or citric acid, in a large saucepan and simmer, covered, until the peel is very tender. This can also be done in a large casserole in the oven. It is also very successful done in a slow-cooker overnight but reduce the amount of water used, remembering to add the remainder when you transfer to a preserving pan.
2 Transfer the fruit and liquid to a large preserving pan and add the sugar, stirring until dissolved. Bring to a full rolling boil and test for a set after 5 minutes. It does set quite quickly – usually within 10 minutes (see page 12). Remove any scum (see page 12).
3 Pour into cooled, sterilised jars, seal and label.

Rum & Raisin Marmalade

MAKES about 4.5 kg (10 lb)
PREPARATION & COOKING TIME: about 3 hours

This delicious recipe comes from Sara Getley at Denman College.

675 g (1¹/₂ lb) sweet oranges, sliced thinly
675 g (1¹/₂ lb) lemons, sliced thinly
1.7 litres (3 pints) water
175 g (6 oz) raisins
2.7 kg (6 lb) granulated sugar
rum (see step 3)

1 Place the citrus fruits in a preserving pan, with the water and the raisins, and bring to the boil.
2 Simmer slowly for 2 hours, until the peel is very tender.
3 Add the sugar and boil to setting point (see page 12). Remove any scum (see page 12).
4 Put 2 teaspoons of rum per 450 g (1 lb) into the cooled, sterilised jars. Pour the marmalade into the jars containing the measured rum.

Claire Macdonald's Mincement

MAKES about 2.2 kg (5 lb)
PREPARATION TIME: about 45 minutes + 1 week standing

This recipe is from Claire Macdonald's book Sweet Things *and combines all the usual mincemeat ingredients but without the addition of treacle and other items that can mask the fruity flavours. Claire comments what a world of difference there is between a home-made mincemeat and a commercial sort. There are endless variations to mincemeat, so feel free to put your own mark on the recipe. Try adding apricots or red and green glacé cherries for a more festive look. You could also add cranberriess in place of some of the apple. There are several puddings in which mincemeat features and a home-made variety makes them all the more sumptuous.*

350 g (12 oz) raisins
225 g (8 oz) sultanas
225 g (8 oz) currants
115 g (4 oz) chopped mixed peel
115 g (4 oz) chopped blanched almonds
225 g (8 oz) shredded suet (beef or vegetarian)
450 g (1 lb) dark muscovado sugar
350 g (12 oz) apples, cored and chopped (Claire uses Cox's apples)
grated zest of 2 lemons
juice of 1 lemon
grated zest of 2 oranges
juice of 1 orange
115 ml (4 fl oz) brandy
1 teaspoon ground cinnamon
1 rounded teaspoon grated nutmeg
1 rounded teaspoon ground allspice

1 Mix all the ingredients together in a large, non-metallic bowl. Cover with clingfilm and leave for a week, giving the occasional stir.
2 After a week, pot into cooled, sterilised jars and cover. Keep for a further 2 weeks before using.

Home-made Gentlemen's Relish

MAKES 225 g (8 oz) ★
PREPARATION TIME: 15 minutes

This is Sue Jones' Dad's favourite and she always makes him some for his Christmas tree present.

3 x 50 g cans of anchovy fillets
6 tablespoons milk
150 g (5 oz) unsalted butter
freshly ground black and cayenne pepper

1 Drain the anchovy fillets and soak in the milk for 10 minutes.
2 Drain off the milk and put the anchovies in a food processor, with the butter and seasoning.
3 Purée to a smooth paste. Pot into small cooled, sterilised jars, seal and store in the fridge for up to 3 weeks.

Apricot & Orange Marmalade (top)

MAKES about 2.7 kg (6 lb)
PREPARATION & COOKING TIME: 3 hours

This is easily my favourite marmalade and used to be that of my bed-and-breakfast guests, once they'd been persuaded to try something other than – plain Seville orange.

450 g (1 lb) dried apricots (use the ready-soaked ones), sliced, chopped or scissor-snipped
675 g (1¹/₂ lb) Seville oranges, washed, halved, squeezed of juice and sliced thinly, pips reserved
2 litres (3¹/₂ pints) water
2.2 kg (5 lb) sugar

1 Put the prepared fruit and the water in a large pan. Tie the pips and any membrane in a muslin bag and add to the pan. Bring to the boil and then simmer until the fruit is very soft and the contents are reduced by about half – about 2 hours.
2 Remove the muslin bag and squeeze the bag to extract all the juice. Add the sugar and stir until dissolved. Bring to a rolling boil and boil until setting point is reached – about 15–20 minutes (see page 12). Remove any scum (see page 12).
3 Pour into cooled, sterilised jars and seal. Label and store.

NOTE: If using ordinary dried apricots, add an extra 300 ml (¹/₂ pint) of water and leave to stand for at least 6 hours, or overnight.

Exotic Fruits Jam (centre)

MAKES 1.3–1.8 kg (3–4 lb)
PREPARATION & COOKING TIME: 1 hour

A real taste of summer sunshine to brighten winter days! This lovely combination needs no pre-cooking before adding the sugar.

900 g (2 lb) ripe pineapples, skin and core removed, cut into 1-cm (¹/₂-inch) pieces
450 g (1 lb) mangoes, peeled and flesh cut into 1-cm (¹/₂-inch) pieces
grated zest and juice of 1 lemon, pips and pith reserved and tied in a muslin bag
1.3 kg (3 lb) sugar

1 Place the fruit and its juices, lemon zest and 4 tablespoons of juice (any remaining juice won't be needed), the muslin bag and the sugar in a large preserving pan. Heat gently and stir until all the sugar is dissolved.
2 Bring to the boil, and then reduce the heat and simmer for 30–40 minutes, or until setting point is reached (see page 12). Remove any scum (see page 12).
3 Pot into cooled, sterilised jars and seal. Label and store.

Cranberry Curd (bottom)

MAKES: about 900 g (2 lb)
PREPARATION & COOKING TIME: 45 minutes

This makes a curd with a fabulous colour and would look great on the Christmas breakfast table or in a pretty pot for someone's Christmas present. A selection of Christmas preserves is even better and can be presented in an attractive basket or container for later use.

450 g (1 lb) cranberries
115 g (4 oz) unsalted butter
450 g (1 lb) caster sugar
4 large eggs, beaten and sieved

1 Put the cranberries and 150 ml (¹/₄ pint) of water in a saucepan and cook on a low heat until tender and popped – or you could cook them in the microwave.
2 Process them or pass through a sieve, if you prefer a smoother curd. Put back in the saucepan, with the butter and sugar, and heat until the butter is melted and the sugar is dissolved.
3 Add the eggs and stir the curd continuously over a low heat until thickened. If you are nervous of this, use a bowl over a pan of simmering water or the microwave.
4 Pour into small cooled, sterilised jars and cover with a waxed disc and a cellophane cover. Store in the fridge for up to 6 weeks. Once opened, eat within 2 weeks.

Storecupboard Chutney

MAKES about 2.2 kg (5 lb)
PREPARATION & COOKING TIME: 1¹/₂ hour

The ingredients for this recipe can vary, depending on the type of dried fruit you have in your cupboard at the time of making. This is another of Terry Clarke's recipes – Terry is a stalwart cook for Southwell WI Market.

675 g (1¹/₂ lb) mixed dried fruit, e.g., apricots, dates, figs, peaches, prunes, sultanas, etc.
1.3 kg (3 lb) cooking apples, peeled and chopped
450 g (1 lb) onions, chopped
675 g (1¹/₂ lb) soft brown sugar
6 garlic cloves, crushed or chopped
50 g (2 oz) fresh root ginger, finely chopped
2–4 dried chillies, crushed
850 ml (1¹/₂ pints) cider vinegar

1 Cut the dried fruit into even-sized pieces.
2 Mix everything together in a large preserving pan and bring to the boil, stirring well.
3 Simmer the mixture over a medium heat until very thick, stirring regularly – about 45 minutes.
4 Spoon into cooled, sterilised jars and seal with vinegar-proof tops. Label and store for 6–8 weeks before using.